THE
FOREIGN POLICY
OF THE
SOVIET UNION

THE FOREIGN POLICY OF THE SOVIET UNION

Edited, with introductions and notes,

BY

ALVIN Z. RUBINSTEIN

University of Pennsylvania

SECOND EDITION

RANDOM HOUSE NEW YORK

To Frankie

Preface to the Second Edition

The purpose of this volume is to fulfill more nearly the objectives which were set forth in the first edition. The essays dealing with ideology, the Khrushchev and post-Khrushchev period, disarmament, the role of developing areas in Soviet thought, Soviet policy in Africa, Asia, the Middle East, and Latin America, and the problems and prospects facing Soviet leaders have been revised and expanded. A number of changes have been made in the readings, with a view toward illumining various aspects of Soviet policy since 1955. Thus, selections are included from Soviet speeches and analyses which deal with the Sino-Soviet dispute, India, Latin America, disarmament problems, etc.

I would like to acknowledge here my appreciation to the editors of the Princeton University Press, *Current History*, and *Orbis*— the journal of the Foreign Policy Research Institute of the University of Pennsylvania—for their permission to use passages of my writings which appeared in their publications. I would also like to thank Miss Jeannine Ciliotta for her assistance with this edition.

ALVIN Z. RUBINSTEIN

Philadelphia, Pa.
October 1, 1965

Preface

Science has brought the dream of a more abundant world within the realm of the possible. It has also given rise to fears of incomprehensible disaster. In seeking to master nature, man is in danger of bringing about his own self-destruction. The ultimate test for mankind will be the ability of statesmen, scientists, and citizens of contending political systems to master themselves. Specifically, the crucial question facing us today is: Can the Soviet and Western worlds peacefully coexist given their incompatible goals? Can the irreconcilable be reconciled? Can there, in fact, be an acceptable and continuing accommodation between them?

The purpose of this study is to provide an analytical and historical examination of Soviet foreign policy since 1917—its origins and evolution, its character and objectives—thus increasing the student's understanding of the nature of the contemporary Soviet challenge. Careful attention has been devoted to the historical, ideological, and political determinants influencing Kremlin policy. Each chapter treats a particular aspect or period of Soviet foreign policy. Essays on the key developments affecting Soviet behavior and the changing and varied character of Soviet objectives are followed by excerpts from important writings and official pronouncements, designed to familiarize the student with the Soviet rationale for its own actions, as well as with Soviet views on the motivations and behavior of its antagonists. The interrelationship between Soviet policy in Europe and in Asia is discussed and an attempt is made to trace the threads of continuity between Czarist and Soviet foreign policy objectives. It is hoped that this introduction to the subject will stimulate the student to further exploration. An extensive bibliography is included for the benefit of those who desire to pursue various phases of Soviet foreign policy in greater detail.

It is a pleasure to express my appreciation to my colleagues and friends who have given so generously of their time and knowledge. I am grateful for their encouragement and patience. This study has benefited from their criticisms and suggestions.

Dr. Garold W. Thumm, of the University of Pennsylvania, read the entire manuscript and I am indebted to him for his penetrating comments. Professors David J. Dallin, Philip E. Jacob, and Norman D. Palmer, of the University of Pennsylvania, and Dr. Gene D. Overstreet, of Swarthmore College, contributed greatly of their specialized knowledge. My thanks to the Editors of *Current History* for their permission to use parts of my articles which appeared in the February 1957 and January 1959 issues (Copyright, 1957, 1959, by Events Publishing Co., Inc.). Grateful acknowledgment is also made to all the publishers and organizations whose permission to reprint specific material is indicated in the footnote at the beginning of each reading.

I wish also to thank the editors, artists, and staff of Random House for their cooperation and counsel in the making of this book. I wish particularly to express my appreciation to Leonore C. Hauck for patiently and skillfully editing the manuscript.

ALVIN Z. RUBINSTEIN

Contents

CHAPTER IV THE SEARCH FOR SECURITY, 1934-1941

CHAPTER VI SOVIET POLICY AND THE ROOTS OF THE COLD WAR

CHAPTER VII STALINIZATION AND EMPIRE, 1948–1953

Introduction **240**

§ READINGS

CHAPTER VIII THE KHRUSHCHEV ERA AND AFTER

CHAPTER IX SOVIET POLICY AND THE DILEMMA OF DISARMAMENT

THE
FOREIGN POLICY
OF THE
SOVIET UNION

CHAPTER I

THE IDEOLOGICAL BASES OF SOVIET FOREIGN POLICY

Sir Winston Churchill once described Soviet foreign policy as "a riddle wrapped in a mystery inside an enigma."[1] This appraisal is both a challenge and a warning. It is particularly pertinent at this time, for during the coming decade Soviet foreign policy may be expected to remain the most crucial problem confronting the United States. An understanding of the nature of Soviet policy, its assumptions, objectives, and operating procedures, is therefore essential. To prepare for the future we must seek to know the past.

The expansion of the Soviet Union since 1945 into the heart of Europe has been the outstanding determinant of the pervasive and irreconcilable antagonism between East and West. The resulting insecurity has been further heightened by a fundamental ideological hostility. Other factors have been involved as well: the challenging economic-military-political strength of the Soviet Union; the decreased international power of the Western European countries; the rise of Communist China as the leading power on the mainland of Asia; the continued division of Germany; and the difficulties and uncertainties occasioned by the postwar emergence of the politically significant developing areas. These factors have all served to exacerbate international tension and give to the Cold War its all-inclusive quality.

In a world dominated by expanding economic appetites and burgeoning populations but limited by resources and technological backwardness, the revolution in expectations among the developing countries has become enmeshed in the global hostility of the Soviet and Western worlds. Increasingly, the Soviet Union has sought to undermine traditional Western influence in these areas. Its confident posture toward the non-Soviet world has stemmed largely from its postwar imperial expansion and has been strengthened by a firm belief in the eventual communization of the world. The Soviet Union regards the future with assurance. It is encouraged in this attitude by ideological assumptions that, in turn, receive support from the significantly improved power-political position of the Soviet Union in the post-World War II period.

The foreign policy of the Soviet Union, like that of any great power, is an amalgam of discrete elements. It is the result of an often unfathomable ordering of history, of fundamental generally understandable historical forces, and, finally, of the influence of dynamic personalities endowed with a thirst for power and empire. Thus Soviet foreign policy can be seen as the end product of a complex interaction of many determinants, which, though always changing, are ever present. Throughout Russia's history, from the ninth century on, the physical attributes—geography, climate, population, and resources—have played important roles. They have influenced the unique features of Russia's economic, social, and political growth; its religion and culture; its reaction to external events; and the key figures in its history.

With this myriad of determinants it is apparent that many interpretations of present-day Soviet policy are possible. Each has some validity; each can be supported by impressive bodies of evidence. None can claim exclusiveness. In general, though, we may distinguish three approaches.

The first interpretation views present Soviet policy as a mere continuation of traditional Czarist objectives. Its supporters realize that recent Soviet aggrandizement has been aided by an impressive economic and technological growth, by the new balance of international power, and by the availability for manipulation of disciplined, Moscow-controlled, foreign Communist Parties. But they believe that the increments of strength have served only to promote the attainment of traditional strategic objectives. Foremost among these is the urge to the sea—the age-old Russian desire for ports on the Baltic, the Mediterranean, and the Yellow Seas—one of the most basic trends in Russian history, one that will endure regardless of modifications of doctrine, method, or governmental structure. A corollary to this drive is the persisting desire for more secure frontiers, for additional natural resources, and for greater international influence. Finally, this approach stresses the importance of the Eastern motif in Soviet policy—the expansion of Russia into Asia as well as into the center of Europe. When thwarted in one direction, Russia has moved in the other. This long-term orientation of expansion is considered a constant of Soviet policy.

A second school of thought sees in Soviet foreign policy a blueprint for world domination, for the establishment of world communism. Its adherents point to the revolutionary character of Bolshevik declarations and to an ideology committed to unremitting hostility toward the non-Communist world. Just as Hitler set forth, in amazing clarity, his plan for world conquest, so too have contemporary Soviet leaders made clear their global pretensions. The writings of the Soviet deities have never been repudiated. Marxist-Leninist ideology conditions its followers to view non-Communist nations as hostile, separated by a unbridgeable gulf from the Communist world. The spread of communism as a social system is inevitable. Add to such an ideology the conspiratorial background of the original Bolsheviks and a tradition of elite rule inherited from the past and refined by totalitarian techniques, and one can, according to some interpreters, expect the Communists to use all the methods of deceit and diplomacy to reach the desired end.

A third interpretation lies somewhere between these two broad schools of thought—the traditionalist and the ideological. It holds that any meaningful approach must weigh this dualism with care and sophistication. For whatever policy the Soviet rulers adopt can be explained in terms of a combination of ideological and nonideological determinants. (Whether such policies are justified by subsequent events is another matter. For example, Stalin's attitude toward Hitler and Nazi Germany in 1933, and again in 1939–1940, as well as the Soviet estimate of the course of revolution in China, reveal the fallibility of Soviet efforts at prognosis.) Mindful of the fact that history, in the words of Max Beloff, "above all is the study of the imperfect, the contingent and the unique,"[2] let the interpreter remain alert to all the more important constants of Soviet policy formulation: the geographic position of the Soviet Union; traditional Russian expansionism in quest of strategically secure frontiers; the impact of the changing international scene; and the influence of a Marxian world outlook whose historical antecedent consisted of deep-rooted Russian messianism.

The ideological ingredient tends to compound and confuse the already hazardous task of interpreting Soviet foreign policy. Just as no explanation of Soviet policy can afford to ignore ideology, so would it be the height of naivete to accept all ideological pronouncements at face value. But in view of Lenin's oft-repeated dictum that "without revolutionary theory there can be no revolutionary movement," it is essential that students of Soviet affairs study carefully the ideological treatises of Marx, Lenin, Stalin, Khrushchev, and their disciples. These writings attempt to present and justify theory and practice as an integrated whole. Action is always explained in terms of ideology; ideology is used to justify action. It is not possible to tell to what extent such ideological justifications influence the formulation of policy or serve merely to cloak in an aura of infallibility and inevitability the tactical maneuvers of the moment. But it would be folly to assume that because the relationship between ideology and behavior is neither readily apparent nor easily determined, it is therefore nonexistent; and that ideology and the perceptions and assumptions that derive from it do not affect the ultimate choice of policy alternatives. It is important that the fundamental tenets be understood, for not only do they underlie the Soviet view of the non-Communist world, but they also provide us with an indispensable key to interpreting the explanations that are given for adopted courses of policy.

In general, Soviet ideology may be regarded as a systematic body of goals, ideas, and assumptions shared by the elite and affecting their attitudes and behavior. It helps to shape the mode of their response to social, economic, and political phenomena; conditions their perception of reality; and provides the terminology and the methodological tools for an allegedly "scientific" interpretation of history, as well as the categories for dialectically viewing, assessing, and rationalizing events. "Facts"—that is, propositions of known, accepted, or verifiable character—are selected and ordered according to the leadership's evaluation of any particular situation, and developments are related to one another within a rationalistic system. Soviet practitioners have never pretended that ideology could mark each path, crossroad, or detour on the international landscape, but the general direction of history is purportedly revealed through the Marxist-Leninist time-telescope which enables one to "look into the future and see the outlines of impending historical changes." Ideology provides the key to "the unshakable laws of social development." Thus, though Soviet foreign policy is rooted in Russian history, it is conditioned by a dynamic world outlook.

Karl Marx provided many of the fundamental principles of

Soviet ideology, but it was Lenin who adapted Marx's approach to the international arena and gave it contemporary validity. Lenin was above all a revolutionary strategist. His theoretical writings resulted usually from an effort to explain specific developments in terms of Marxist thought. A case in point is *Imperialism: The Highest Stage of Capitalism*, one of Lenin's important works (reading 1). Published in Switzerland in 1916 during Lenin's exile, it is primarily an attempt to extend the Marxian concept of the class struggle to the international arena, and to show thereby that World War I stemmed from the avarice of monopoly capital and the big financial interests. The importance of Lenin's work can scarcely be overestimated, for it has conditioned the Soviet view of the capitalist world. It purports to explain the "inevitability" of capitalism's demise. In addition, it links the inevitability of war to capitalism as a social system. Its appeal is strengthened by the converse proposition: that only through socialism can permanent and universal peace be assured. Though written more than fifty years ago, Lenin's interpretation of imperialism remains an integral part of Communist ideology and helps account for the continuing and complete hostility of the Soviet Union toward the capitalist world.

For his new analysis of capitalist society, Lenin relied heavily upon two earlier works, *Imperialism* (1902), by the English economist J. A. Hobson, and *Das Finanzkapital* (1910), by the Austrian Marxist Rudolf Hilferding. Previously, Marx had explained the coming doom of capitalism in terms of the social forces it itself created—the simultaneous trends toward monopoly and ever greater concentration of economic (and hence, political) power, on the one hand, and a growing proletarianization and impoverishment of society, on the other. The resultant insoluble contradictions and conflicts, accompanied by a heightened class consciousness on the part of the proletariat, precipitate the downfall of capitalism. But events did not follow Marx's prognosis. By 1914 it had become apparent that his concept of capitalism did not approximate the reality existing in Western Europe. The proletariat had not come to power, nor had revolution occurred in the most highly developed countries. Indeed, world capitalism was strong, seemingly stable, and expanding. Why, then, had Marx's predictions about the collapse of capitalism not proved true? Lenin gave his answer.

According to Lenin, there is a fundamental disequilibrium between production and consumption in a maturing capitalist economy which makes profitable employment of capital increasingly difficult. To overcome the declining rate of profit, the capitalists compel their compliant, controlled governments to seek relief for them abroad in the form of colonies and spheres of influence. These acquisitions are exploited by the capitalists as sources of cheap labor and raw materials, as well as markets for excess capital and for surpluses of manufactured goods. The quest for colonies was the outstanding characteristic of the period from 1870 to 1914. Through this expansion capitalism was able temporarily to postpone revolution and disaster. It should be emphasized that this expansion of capitalism is what Lenin meant by imperialism. To Lenin, imperialism was not a "policy," since that would imply an element of choice, but rather a matter of compulsion (i.e., inevitability).[3]

However, once the available underdeveloped areas of the world have been absorbed, the persistent pressure for profit, an essential of capitalism, drives the capitalist states into competition over the redistribution of the spoils. Their conflicts can be settled only by war, the ultimate "contradiction of capitalism." According to Lenin, World War I represented the initial convulsions of a moribund world capitalism. Subsequently, this imperialist war would be transformed into a global war, out of which would come the final triumph of socialism.

Marx analyzed capitalist society within a national framework and, specifically, in terms of Western European industrial development. Lenin, on the other hand, considered capitalism as a global phenomenon. The more capitalism develops, "the stronger the need for raw materials is felt, the more bitter competition and the hunt for raw materials become throughout the world, the more desperate the struggle for the acquisition of colonies becomes." This competition is a struggle between nations and national oligarchies, and not between individual capitalists. For Lenin, the imperialist nation assumes the role previously held in Marx's analysis by the individual capitalist. This struggle between the capitalist nations stems from the uneven development of capitalism—the fact that some nations develop later than others and that these newcomer imperialists are left with barren pickings, others having pre-empted the choice colonies. But the newcomers, more aggressive, ambitious, and dissatisfied with the existing distribution of colonies, strive to redress this inequality by empire by *force*. "There can be *no other* conceivable basis, under capitalism, for partition of spheres of influence, of interests, of colonies, etc.," said Lenin. And the clash arising out of these basic inequalities cannot long be avoided. In modifying Marxist theory, Lenin held that, even though competition *within a nation* may be controlled, the struggle *between sovereign capitalist nations* cannot be similarly regulated. Imperialist wars are merely the clash of capitalists transplanted to the international arena. They will shake the foundations of capitalism and usher in an era of revolutionary change, in which world capitalism will break, as does a chain, at its weakest link. Lenin and his successors explained the unexpected success of the Bolshevik revolution in backward Russia in these terms. The previously held Marxist expectation that revolution would occur first in a highly developed country was dropped from the Soviets' doctrinal baggage. No longer is it considered "un-Marxist" for Communists to seize power in a backward country. "Where will the chain break in the near future? Again, where it is weakest," said Stalin. Thus does "creative" Marxism tailor theory to reality.

Marxist thought holds that the historical process is governed by objective laws, functioning as inexorably as the laws of nature. These laws contain and allow for the "subjective factor," i.e., the conscious, human element, "not merely as the obedient servant and executor of the law, but as the medium through whose actions and thoughts alone the historical laws become laws."[4] In the dialectical process the interaction of these two factors, of the objective and subjective forces, determines the course of history. Though human will cannot materially change the unalterable design of these historical forces, man must understand their character and direction, for he can facilitate and promote the realization of this design. Soviet ideologists insist that an understanding of the laws of historical development is possible through the conceptual tools provided by Marx's philosophical system, "dialectical materialism." "It is, in effect, revolution writ large into the cosmos; its basic postulates are so many reasons why 'the bourgeoisie' are on the way down and 'the proletariat' on the way up, why 'capitalism' must inevitably give way to 'socialism' everywhere, and why this must occur by violent revolution."[5]

Very briefly, dialectical materialism is believed to afford a "scientific" basis for determining historical development. Nature is regarded as a single, interrelated whole, which is in a constant state of change. This change derives from contradictions "inherent in things and phenomena" and from the struggle of opposites stemming from these contradictions. Thus, the proletariat, though produced by the capitalist system, is at the same time antagonistic toward it and is the vehicle for its eventual downfall. Each social system gives rise to mutually antagonistic social classes. Through the ensuing class struggle, an inherent feature of all societies, a higher form of society evolves, with communism considered as the highest stage of human development. As mentioned previously, the imperialist stage of capitalism actually denotes the transference of the class struggle from a particular society to the world at large. The basic incompatibility and hostility between

capitalism and socialism are *inevitabilities* of historical development, the result of operative "objective forces." Coexistence for
long is unthinkable; inevitably, socialism must supplant capitalism. This helps account for the continuing policy assumption,
by the Soviet leaders, of unmitigated hostility between the two
systems. Ideologically, it serves to rationalize the "necessity" for
the cold war. As the "objective" contradictions between capitalism
and socialism intensify, a period of revolutionary crises develops.
These crises differ in intensity and come in rhythmic cycles of
ebb and flow. In a speech in 1925, Stalin held that whereas
World War I constituted a crest in this unfolding drama of revolution, the subsequent period was one of decline, in which a
"partial and temporary stabilization of capitalism" had set in.[6]

The "subjective" forces refer to the influences which personality
and organization may consciously exert on the historical process.
This brings us to a consideration of strategy and tactics, i.e., of
long-term objectives and of the short-term means used to effect
them. In April 1924, shortly after the death of Lenin, Stalin
delivered a series of lectures at Sverdlov University, Moscow, in
which he enunciated the essential guides to Soviet political behavior (reading 2). According to Stalin, the "strategy and tactics
of Leninism constitute the science of leadership in the revolutionary struggle of the proletariat." *Strategy* deals with the main
forces of the revolution; it determines the general direction "along
which the revolutionary movement of the proletariat should be
directed with a view to achieving the biggest results with the . . .
developing correlation of forces." The Soviet Union, as the base
from which world revolution is to be organized, is linked with
the international proletariat in a single movement seeking liberation from imperialism. In the meantime, its defense and preservation must remain the principal concern of all foreign Communist Parties. *Tactics* "are a part of strategy, subordinate to
it and serving it." They are the methods used to achieve the
directives of strategy. As such, they demand a constant appraisal
of existing political potentialities, both within the capitalist and
socialist camps, and must be adjusted according to flow and
ebb, that is, the rise and decline of revolutionary forces. It is
the responsibility of the most politically advanced element (the
Communist Party) to gauge the direction and intensity of the
tide and then to devise tactics best able to promote the over-all
objectives of Soviet strategy. Thus, calls for "coexistence" and
"peaceful competition" can be reconciled with the basic strategy
of world revolution if we view the former merely as expedient
tactics.

It is never really possible to say where tactics leave off and strategy begins, but the distinction does exist between day-to-day operations and broad policy directives.[7] In any event, even a tactic of "retreat" may, and usually does, involve effort focused on further weakening the capitalist camp in the economic, political, or military areas. To paraphrase the theoretician of war, Karl von Clausewitz, this signifies a continuation of the struggle by other means. Regardless of the shifting political positions of Soviet spokesmen, nothing fundamental changes in their attitude toward the capitalist world.

In his report to the Eighth Congress of the Communist Party, on March 18, 1919, Lenin had stated:

> We are living not merely in a state but in a system of states, and the existence of the Soviet Republic side by side with imperialist states for a long time is unthinkable. One or the other must triumph in the end. And before this end supervenes, a series of frightful collisions between the Soviet Republic and the bourgeois states will be inevitable.[8]

This classic statement of the irreconcilability of capitalism and socialism and the inevitability of their clash has never been officially repudiated or superseded. It remained central, though varying in prominence, to Stalin's pronouncements on the subject until the Nineteenth Party Congress of October 1952, at which time he formulated a rather interesting modification.

After 1917, and especially before World War II, the Soviet Government stressed the theory of "capitalist encirclement," partially out of a genuine sense of insecurity, but primarily to justify the suffering and sacrifice demanded of its people by Stalin's decisions to embark on a program of rapid industrialization and collectivization of agriculture. This theory reflected the pervasive fear of an "imperialist" attack against the Soviet Union, and implied a type of war quite distinct from Lenin's "inevitable" *inter-capitalist* wars stemming from the nature and contradictions of twentieth-century capitalism. No systematic attempt was ever made, however, to link Lenin's theory of "inevitable" inter-capitalist wars with the subsequent Stalinist corollary of the "inevitable" capitalist war against the Soviet Union. Thus there were, in fact, two distinct Communist doctrines on war, though the impression that they were one and the same was encouraged:[9] first, the Leninist theory of imperialism, with its focus on inter-capitalist wars and rivalries; second, the theory of "capitalist encirclement," with its focus on the inevitability of war between socialist and capitalist camps. Although both doctrines were retained in the Soviet ideological arsenal, after World War II the emphasis was on the first one.

Shortly before the Nineteenth Party Congress (October 1952),

Stalin published his *Economic Problems of Socialism in the USSR* (reading 3). In this final appraisal of the world scene and effort to ensure his prominence as an architect of Communist theory, Stalin held that, as an aftermath of the war, capitalism had suffered grievous wounds and no longer embraced a global market. Economically, the world had split into two parallel trading systems. Politically, capitalism had lost much of its former awesome power and therefore was not likely to attack the Soviet Union, although the contradictions and antagonisms between the two systems continued to exist. A capitalist attack on the Soviet Union was unlikely because "war with the USSR . . . is more dangerous to capitalism than war between capitalist countries; for whereas war between capitalist countries puts in question only the supremacy of certain capitalist countries over others, war with the USSR must certainly put in question the existence of capitalism itself." On the other hand, Stalin maintained that wars between capitalist countries would inevitably result from the intensified competition for shrinking world markets which attended the division of the world into two camps and the end of capitalism's era of expansion. Finally, though implying that *armed* conflict between the socialist and capitalist systems was not probable, Stalin did stress their continued and fundamental hostility.

This orthodox Leninist position was reaffirmed by Nikita S. Khrushchev at the Twentieth Party Congress of February 1956. But he also reinforced the prevailing political strategy of the post-Stalinist period—the theme of "peaceful coexistence"—by introducing an important modification of Marxist-Leninist doctrine (reading 4): the noninevitability of war. Khrushchev's contention that "war is not fatalistically inevitable" marks a retreat, if not a categorical shift, from the deterministic notion that war between the two systems is inevitable and, as such, constitutes a significant change in ideology. He suggested, in effect, that the altered balance of world power makes it possible for the "camp of peace" (socialist camp) to offer the hope of permanent peace to all peoples. Wars, whether between capitalism and socialism or within the capitalist world itself, may be not only forestalled but prevented—provided that the "progressive social and political forces" within the capitalist world actively check "the schemes of the war-makers." Khrushchev called for popular pressure against those parliamentary governments who are opposed to Soviet policy. If "progressive" groups can capture a stable parliamentary majority or force their governments to accede to Soviet wishes, war can be avoided. Thus the formula for peace is based upon Soviet-determined ingredients. Nonetheless, Khrushchev's thesis that (nuclear) war is not inevitable is of crucial importance, for it connotes the recognition by Soviet leaders of the mutually catastrophic character of an all-out nuclear war. Having struggled and suffered to develop an advanced, stable, and gradually prospering society, they are not likely to jeopardize all this by provoking a nuclear showdown with the United States. The technological revolution in military weaponry has induced a significant change in Soviet ideology and strategic thinking.

In addition, the concept of "capitalist encirclement" was largely abandoned during the Khrushchev period for a number of reasons—*inter alia*, the emergence in the mid-1950s of the USSR as a superpower, the unpalatability of total war as a solution to *political* problems in view of the development of thermonuclear weapons, and the emergence of the "system of socialist states" existing side by side with the "system of capitalist states." Further, "capitalist encirclement" was a self-isolating concept; by implication it regarded the entire non-Communist world as hostile to the USSR and contradicted post-1955 Soviet efforts to encourage neutralism and nonalignment in the "zone of peace" —the areas of Afro-Asia and Latin America not committed militarily or politically to either of the two major power blocs. By 1958, the Soviet leadership explained that the danger of "capitalist encirclement" in a geographical sense had been ended by the emergence of Communist political systems in Eastern Europe and China. They also asserted that since the balance of international forces was shifting to the socialist camp, it was now "capitalism" that was being encircled by "socialism." Nevertheless, Soviet writers continue to talk of "capitalist encirclement" as a political threat and to emphasize the need for vigilance and strength because of the ever-present danger of "aggression" from the capitalist world, particularly the United States which is increasingly disturbed over its progressively eroding power and political influence.

The ideological innovations of the Khrushchev period (1954–1964) do not mean that Soviet leaders have relinquished any of their principal political objectives. What they do signify is the recognition, in this period of nuclear stalemate, of the need to attain these objectives by essentially nonmilitary means. Soviet leaders are as convinced today as ever of communism's eventual victory. As long as they believe that their interests can benefit most through a "policy of peace," not only as a positive propaganda device but also as a useful additive to Soviet power, they will retain such an approach.

Most specialists on Soviet affairs today agree that important,

far-reaching changes have been made since 1955 in those elements of Soviet ideology that have particular relevance for the
formulation of foreign policy. There is also agreement on what
these doctrinal changes have been: e.g., abandonment of the
Zhdanov "two-camp thesis" (see Chapter VI); virtual abandonment of the concept of "capitalist encirclement" which was
enunciated by Stalin in the late 1930s; introduction of Khrushchev's thesis that war is no longer "fatalistically inevitable";
and the promulgation at the Twentieth Party Congress of the
"zone of peace" concept relative to developing areas (see Chapter
XI). There is widespread disagreement, however, over the significance of these changes.

Certain Western analysts offer the comforting notion that for
Soviet leaders, ideology is less and less a determinant of foreign
policy. This study, it may be noted, reflects the view that Soviet
ideology plays an important role in conditioning the Soviet
"image" of the outside world and, consequently, in influencing
the range and choice of policy alternatives.

Soviet leaders may indeed no longer believe in impending
world revolution or in the necessity of using force to bring about
the downfall of capitalism (though they justify its relevance in
"just wars" of national liberation), but it is reasonable to assume
that they continue to believe in the inevitable triumph of communism, in the growing ascendancy of Soviet power and influence, and in the validity of their analyses of developments in the
non-Communist world. Their meteoric rise to world power can
only make them more confident that the balance of power is
shifting in their favor, and this confidence may be presumed
to reinforce the belief of the Soviet elite in the essential validity
of their Marxist-Leninist evaluation of international developments.

Soviet foreign policy accepts change as a permanent feature
of the historical process. It affirms the ideological conviction that
through the dialectical method future trends can be anticipated.
If ideology is in fact one of the important influences shaping the
outlook and choice of alternatives of Soviet decision-makers, we
can agree that "the belief system which the Soviet leadership has
inherited has served to condition, if not to determine, its every
move."[10] Thus, for example, the Soviet attitude toward the Western Powers derives in important measure from Soviet *perceptions*
of their motivations, policies, and objectives. These perceptions,
which are significantly fashioned by the ideology, lead the Soviets
to see Western actions and motivations in the worst possible light.

Soviet writers postulate the inevitable continued "ideological
struggle" of the camp of communism and the camp of capitalism

until communism triumphs. There is no recognition in Soviet analyses of the fact that the resolution of political tensions is seriously complicated by the intensification of ideological conflict, that the Soviets' perception of current military and political problems is distorted by their *a priori* views and assumptions. On the one hand, Soviet writers contend that international tensions can be resolved without discarding the ideological struggle because Cold War tensions are not a matter of ideology; on the other hand, *all* Soviet analyses of Western policies are presented in Marxist-Leninist terms and rest, as far as can be determined, on assumptions that stem from the ideology.

Ideology conditions the Soviet leaders to view the outside world with hostility and mistrust. [The analysis contained in the new Program of the Communist Party of the Soviet Union (CPSU), adopted in October 1961 at the Twenty-second Party Congress, may be regarded as typical (reading 5).] Accordingly, they take actions to safeguard their security. Paradoxically, these actions arouse responses in the West which confirm in the minds of Soviet leaders their initial and ingrained prejudices about the innate hostility of the outside world. Once the circle is completed, and self-interest becomes the exclusive and overriding concern, it is futile to argue whether a particular development is a cause or an effect.

From what we know of political infighting in Soviet decision-making circles, it is clear that the engineers of the Soviet state are not rigid determinists. Their sharing of a Marxist-Leninist heritage does not signify unanimity on all major policy questions. Though they may agree at a given time in their evaluation of the "objective" conditions controlling in the ever-shifting pattern of international forces, they may disagree on which of several policy alternatives to adopt. A common perception of reality does not necessarily produce uniform answers to specific policy problems. Debate and discord in the inner circles of the Party are probably as intensive as that found in the decision-making circles of any government, though they are not aired publicly. The range of possible alternatives is limited by ideology, but we do not know how stringently or how loosely any faction adheres to accepted doctrine to formulate its position, or to what degree naked power considerations and personality factors affect these calculations.

NOTES

1. Winston S. Churchill, *The Gathering Storm* (Boston: Houghton Mifflin Company, 1948), p. 449.
2. Max Beloff, *The Foreign Policy of Soviet Russia, 1936–1941* (New York: Oxford University Press, 1949), Vol. II, p. 395.

3. Alfred G. Meyer, *Leninism* (Cambridge, Mass.: Harvard University Press, 1957), p. 241.
4. From an essay by Herbert Marcuse, "Dialectic and Logic Since the War," in *Continuity and Change in Russian and Soviet Thought* (New York: Columbia University Press, 1955), p. 353, an anthology compiled under the editorship of Ernest J. Simmons.
5. Historicus, "Stalin on Revolution," *Foreign Affairs*, Vol. xxvii (1949), p. 181.
6. *Ibid.*, p. 195.
7. From Marshall D. Shulman, "Can Soviet Objectives Change?" Address delivered at the University of Virginia (February 25, 1956).
8. V. I. Lenin, *Selected Works* (New York: International Publishers Co., 1943), Vol. viii, p. 33.
9. U. S. Department of State, Intelligence Report No. 7284, "The 20th CPSU Congress and the Doctrine of the 'Inevitability of War'" (June 22, 1956), pp. 9–10.
10. John S. Reshetar, Jr., *Problems of Analyzing and Predicting Soviet Behavior* (New York: Random House, 1955), p. 13.

1. IMPERIALISM: THE HIGHEST STAGE OF CAPITALISM*

V . I . L E N I N

While capitalism remains capitalism, surplus capital will not be used for raising the standard of living of the masses in a given country, for this would mean a decrease in profits for the capitalists; rather, it will be exported abroad to backward countries in order to increase profits. In these backward countries profits are usually high, for capital is scarce, the price of land is comparatively cheap, wages are low, and raw materials are cheap. The possibility of exporting capital is created by the fact that a number of backward countries are drawn into the system of world capitalism; main railway lines either have been built or are being built there, the basic conditions for the development of industry have been assured, etc. The need to export capital arises from the fact that in a few countries capitalism has become "overripe," and capital cannot find (due to the backward state of agriculture and the impoverishment of the masses) field for "profitable" investment . . .

---

* V. I. Lenin, *Sochinenia*, 2nd ed. (Moscow: State Publishing House, 1929), Vol. xix, pp. 120–175, *excerpts*. Editor's translation.

The Division of the World Among the Capitalist Combines

The monopolistic corporations of the capitalists—cartels, syndicates, trusts—divide among themselves first of all the internal market, seizing control more or less completely of the production of a given country. But the internal market, under capitalism, is inevitably linked with the foreign market. Capitalism long ago created a world market. As the export of capital increased, and as foreign and colonial relations and "spheres of influence" spread in every possible way by the biggest monopolistic corporations, affairs "naturally" tended toward a global agreement among them, toward the establishment of international cartels . . .

The capitalists do not divide the world out of personal malice, but because the degree of concentration which has been reached impels them to adopt this course in order to obtain profits; they divide the world according to "capital," and according to "strength," for there can be no other method of division under the system of commodity production and capitalism. Power varies with the degree of economic and political development; in order to understand what is taking place, it is necessary to know what questions are solved by such changes in power; whether these changes are "purely" economic or *non*economic (e.g., military) is a question of secondary importance which cannot in the least affect the basic views on the latest epoch of capitalism. To substitute for the question of the *content* of the struggle and agreement among capitalist combines, the question of the form of the struggle and agreement (today peaceful, tomorrow not peaceful, the day after tomorrow again not peaceful) is a peaceful way to descend to the role of the sophist.

The epoch of modern capitalism shows us that certain relations are established among combines of capitalists *based* on the economic division of the world; parallel with these relations, and in connection with them, certain relations are established among political alliances, among states, on the basis of the territorial division of the world, of the struggle for colonies, and of "the struggle for economic territory." . . .

The Division of the World Among the Great Powers

Colonial policy and imperialism existed before the latest stage of capitalism, and even before capitalism. Rome, founded on slavery, conducted a colonial policy and carried out imperialism. But "general" arguments about imperialism, which ignore or put into the background the fundamental difference of socio-economic systems, inevitably degenerate into empty banalities or bragging, such as the comparison of "greater Rome with greater Britain." Even the capitalistic colonial policy of the *previous* stages of capitalism is essentially different from the colonial policy of finance capital.

The basic feature of contemporary capitalism is the domination of monopolist combines by the biggest entrepreneurs. These monopolies are most durable when *all* the sources of raw materials are controlled by one group, and we have seen with what zeal the international capitalist combines exert their effort to make it impossible for their rivals to compete with them; for example, by buying up mineral rights, oil fields, etc. Only possession of colonies provides a complete guarantee of success to the monopolies against all competitors, including the possibility that the competitors will defend themselves by means of a law establishing a state monopoly. The more capitalism develops, the stronger the need for raw materials is felt, the more bitter competition and the hunt for raw materials become throughout the world, the more desperate the struggle for the acquisition of colonies becomes. . . .

Imperialism, as a Particular Stage of Capitalism

Imperialism emerged as a development and direct continuation of the basic characteristics of capitalism in general. But capitalism became capitalist imperialism only at a definite, very high stage of its development, when certain of the basic characteristics of capitalism began to change into their opposites, when the features of a period of transition from capitalism to a higher socio-economic system began to take shape and reveal themselves in all spheres. Economically, the replacement of capitalist free competition by capitalist monopolies is of key importance. Free competition is the fundamental characteristic of capitalism, and of commodity production generally; monopoly is exactly the opposite of free competition, but we have seen the latter being transformed into monopoly before our eyes, creating large-scale industry, squeezing out small-scale industry, replacing large-scale industry by still larger-scale industry, and finally bringing about such a concentration of industry and capital that monopoly has become and is the result. . . . At the same time, the monopolies growing out of free competition do not eliminate it, but exist over it and alongside of it, thereby giving rise to a number of particularly acute and intense antagonisms, frictions, and conflicts. Monopoly is the transition from capitalism to a higher order.

If it were necessary to give the briefest possible definition of imperialism, we should have to say that imperialism is the monopoly stage of capitalism. Such a definition would include, on the one hand, that finance capital is bank capital of the few biggest monopolist banks, merged with the capital of the monopolist combines of industrialists; and on the other hand, that the division of the world is the transition from a colonial policy which has spread without opposition to territories unoccupied by any capitalist power, to a colonial policy of monopolistic possession of the territories of the world.

But too brief definitions, although convenient, since they summarize the main points, are nevertheless inadequate. . . . Therefore, without forgetting the conditional and relative value of all definitions in general, which can never include all facets of a phenomenon in its complete development, we must give a definition of imperialism that will include the following five essential features: (1) The concentration of industry and capital, pushed to such a high stage of development that it has created monopolies which play a decisive role in economic life; (2) The merging of bank capital with industrial capital and the creation, on the basis of this "finance capital," of a financial oligarchy; (3) The export of capital, as distinguished from the export of commodities, acquires particular importance; (4) International monopoly combines of capitalists are formed which divide up the world; (5) The territorial division of the world by the largest capitalist powers is completed.

Imperialism is capitalism in that stage of development in which the domination of monopolies and finance capital has been established, in which the export of capital has acquired outstanding importance, in which the division of the world by the international trusts has started, and in which the partition of all the territory of the earth by the largest capitalist countries has been completed. . . .

The Parasitism and Decay of Capitalism

We now have to examine another very important aspect of imperialism. . . . We refer to parasitism, which is inherent in imperialism. . . . Imperialism is the immense accumulation of money capital in a few countries. Hence, the extraordinary growth of a class, or rather of a stratum, of *rentiers*, i.e., people who live by "clipping coupons," who do not engage at all in production, whose profession is idleness. The export of capital, one of the most essential economic bases of imperialism, isolates this rentier group still further from production and sets the seal of parasitism on the entire country. . . .

The Critique of Capitalism

The question of whether it is possible to change the bases of imperialism by reforms, whether to proceed to a further aggravation and deepening of the contradictions which it engenders, or backward toward allaying them, is a fundamental question in the critique of imperialism . . . Let us take India, Indochina, and China. It is well-known that these three colonial and semi-colonial countries, inhabited by six-seven hundred million souls, are subjected to the exploitation of the finance capital of several imperialist powers: England, France, Japan, the United States, etc. Let us assume that these imperialist countries form alliances against one another in order to protect or expand their possessions, interests, and "spheres of influence" in these Asiatic countries. These will be "inter-imperialist" or "ultra-imperialist" alliances. Let us assume that *all* the imperialist powers conclude an alliance for the "peaceful" partition of these Asiatic countries; this alliance would be "internationally united finance capital." There have been actual examples of such an alliance in the twentieth century, for example, in the relations of the powers with China. We ask, is it "conceivable," assuming the preservation of capitalism . . . that such alliances would not be short-lived, that they would preclude frictions, conflicts, and struggles in any and every possible form?

It is enough to state this question clearly in order to make any reply other than a negative one impossible. For, under capitalism, there can be *no* other conceivable basis for partition of spheres of influence, of interests, of colonies, etc., than a calculation of the *strength* of the participants, their general economic, financial, military, and other strength. But the relative strength of these participants is not changing uniformly, for under capitalism there cannot be an *equal* development of different enterprises, trusts, branches of industry, or countries. Half a century ago, Germany was a pitiful nonentity if its strength was compared with that of England; the same was true with Japan as compared with Russia. Is it "conceivable" that in ten or twenty years the relative strength of the imperialist powers will have remained *un*changed? Absolutely inconceivable.

Therefore, "inter-imperialist" or "ultra-imperialist" alliances, given the realities of capitalism . . . no matter what form the alliances take, whether of one imperialist coalition against another or of a general alliance embracing *all* the imperialist powers, are *inevitably* only "breathing spells" between wars. Peaceful alliances prepare the ground for wars, and in their turn grow out of wars; one is the condition of the other, giving rise to alternating forms of peaceful and nonpeaceful struggle on *one and the same basis*, namely, that of imperialist connections and relationships between world economics and world politics.

2. STRATEGY AND TACTICS IN COMMUNIST THOUGHT*

JOSEPH STALIN

1. Strategy and Tactics as the Science of Leadership in the Class Struggle of the Proletariat

The mortal sin of the Second International was not that it pursued the tactics of utilizing the parliamentary forms of struggle, but that it overestimated the importance of these forms; that it considered them virtually the only forms; and that when the period of open revolutionary battles set in and the question of extraparliamentary forms of struggle came to the fore, the parties of the Second International turned their back on these new tasks, refused to shoulder them.

Only in the subsequent period, the period of direct action by the proletariat, the period of proletarian revolution, when the question of overthrowing the bourgeoisie became a question of immediate action; when the question of the reserves of the proletariat (strategy) became one of the most burning questions; when all forms of struggle and of organization, parliamentary and extraparliamentary (tactics) had fully manifested themselves and became well-defined—only in this period could an integral strategy and elaborated tactics for the struggle of the proletariat be drawn up. It was precisely in that period that Lenin brought out into the light of day the brilliant ideas of Marx and Engels on tactics and strategy that had been immured by the opportunists of the Second International. . . . The strategy and tactics of Leninism constitute the science of leadership in the revolutionary struggle of the proletariat.

* Joseph Stalin, *Problems of Leninism* (Moscow: Foreign Languages Publishing House, 1953), pp. 80–95, *excerpts*.

2.   Stages of the Revolution, and Strategy

Strategy is the determination of the direction of the main blow of the proletariat at a given stage of the revolution, the elaboration of a corresponding plan for the disposition of the revolutionary forces (main and secondary reserves), the fight to carry out this plan throughout the given stage of the revolution.

Our revolution has already passed through two stages, and after the October Revolution it entered a third one. Our strategy changed accordingly.

First Stage.   1903 to February 1917. Objective: to overthrow tsarism and completely wipe out the survivals of medievalism. The main force of the revolution: the proletariat. Immediate reserves: the peasantry. Direction of the main blow: isolation of the liberal-monarchist bourgeoisie, which was striving to win over the peasantry and liquidate the revolution by *compromising* with tsarism. Plan for the disposition of forces: alliance of the working class with the peasantry.

Second Stage.   March 1917 to October 1917. Objective: to overthrow imperialism in Russia and to withdraw from the imperialist war. The main force of the revolution: the proletariat. Immediate reserves: the poor peasantry. The proletariat of neighboring countries as probable reserves. The protracted war and the crisis of imperialism as the favorable factor. Direction of the main blow: isolation of the petty-bourgeois democrats (Mensheviks and Socialist-Revolutionaries) who were striving to win over the toiling masses of the peasantry and to put an end to the revolution by *compromising* with imperialism. Plan for the disposition of forces: alliance of the proletariat with the poor peasantry.

Third Stage.   Commenced after the October Revolution. Objective: to consolidate the dictatorship of the proletariat in one country, using it as a base for the defeat of imperialism in all countries. The revolution is spreading beyond the confines of one country; the epoch of world revolution has commenced. The main forces of the revolution: the dictatorship of the proletariat in one country, the revolutionary movement of the proletariat in all countries. Main reserves: the semi-proletarian and small-peasant masses in the developed countries, the liberation movement in the colonies and dependent countries. Direction of the main blow: isolation of the petty-bourgeois democrats, isolation of the parties of the Second International, which constitute the main support of the policy of *compromise* with imperialism. Plan for the disposition of forces: alliance of the proletarian revolution with the liberation movement in the colonies and the dependent countries.

Strategy deals with the main forces of the revolution and their reserves. It changes with the passing of the revolution from one stage to another, but remains essentially unchanged throughout a given stage.

3. The Flow and Ebb of the Movement and Tactics

Tactics are the determination of the line of conduct of the proletariat in the comparatively short period of the flow or ebb of the movement, of the rise or decline of the revolution, the fight to carry out this line by means of replacing old forms of struggle and organization by new ones, old slogans by new ones, by combining these forms, etc. While the object of strategy is to win the war against tsarism, let us say, or against the bourgeoisie, to carry out the struggle against tsarism or against the bourgeoisie to its end, tactics pursue less important objects, for the object of tactics is not the winning of the war as a whole, but the winning of some particular engagement or some particular battles, the carrying through successfully of some particular campaigns or actions corresponding to the concrete circumstances in the given period of rise or decline of the revolution. Tactics are a part of strategy, subordinate to it and serving it.

Tactics change according to flow and ebb. While the strategic plan remained unchanged during the first stage of the revolution (1903 to February 1917), tactics changed several times during that period. In the period from 1903 to 1905 the Party pursued offensive tactics, for the tide of the revolution was rising, the movement was on the upgrade, and the tactics had to proceed from this fact. Accordingly, the forms of struggle were revolutionary, corresponding to the requirements of the rising tide of the revolution. Local political strikes, political demonstrations, the general political strike, boycott of the Duma, insurrection, revolutionary fighting slogans—such were the successive forms of the struggle during that period. . . .

In the period from 1907 to 1912 the Party was compelled to resort to tactics of retreat; for we then experienced a decline in the revolutionary movement, the ebb of the revolution, and tactics necessarily had to take this fact into consideration. The forms of struggle, as well as the forms of organization, changed accordingly: instead of the boycott of the Duma there was participation in the Duma; instead of open, direct revolutionary action outside the Duma, there were parliamentary speeches and work in the

Duma; instead of general political strikes, there were partial economic strikes, or simply a lull in activities. Of course, the Party
had to go underground during that period, while the revolutionary
mass organizations were superseded by cultural, educational,
cooperative, insurance and other legal organizations.

The same must be said of the second and third stages of the
revolution, during which tactics changed dozens of times, whereas
the strategical plans remained unchanged.

Tactics deal with the forms of struggle and the forms of
organization of the proletariat, with their changes and combinations. During a given stage of the revolution tactics may change
several times, depending on the flow or ebb, the rise or decline,
of the revolution.

4. Strategic Leadership

The reserves of the revolution can be:

Direct: (a) the peasantry and in general the intermediate strata
of the population within the country; (b) the proletariat of the
neighboring countries; (c) the revolutionary movement of the
colonies and dependent countries; (d) the conquests and gains
of the dictatorship of the proletariat—part of which the proletariat may give up temporarily, while retaining superiority of
forces, in order to buy off a powerful enemy and gain a respite;
and

Indirect: (a) the contradictions and conflicts among the non-
proletarian classes within the country, which can be utilized by
the proletariat to weaken the enemy and to strengthen its own
reserves; (b) contradictions, conflicts and wars (the imperialist
war, for instance) among the bourgeois states hostile to the
proletarian state, which can be utilized by the proletariat in its
offensive or in maneuvering in the event of a forced retreat. . . .

The task of strategic leadership is to make proper use of all
these reserves for the achievement of the main object of the
revolution at the given stage of its development.

What does making proper use of reserves mean?

It means fulfilling certain necessary conditions, of which the
following must be regarded as the principal ones.

First. The concentration of the main forces of the revolution
at the enemy's most vulnerable spot at the decisive moment, when
the revolution has already become ripe, when the offensive is
going full-steam ahead, when insurrection is knowingly knocking
at the door, and when bringing up the reserves to the vanguard is
the decisive condition of success. The Party's strategy during the

period from April to October 1917 well illustrates this manner of utilizing reserves. Undoubtedly, the enemy's most vulnerable spot at that time was the war. Undoubtedly, it was on this question, as the fundamental one, that the Party rallied the broadest masses of the population around the proletarian vanguard. . . .

Second. The selection of the moment for the decisive blow, of the moment for starting the insurrection, so timed as to coincide with the moment when the crisis has reached its climax, when it is fully apparent that the vanguard is prepared to fight to the end, the reserves are prepared to support the vanguard, and maximum consternation reigns in the ranks of the enemy. The decisive battle, says Lenin, may be deemed to have fully matured when

(1) all the class forces hostile to us have become sufficiently entangled, are sufficiently at loggerheads with each other, have sufficiently weakened themselves in a struggle which is beyond their strength; (2) all the vacillating, wavering, unstable, intermediate elements—the petty bourgeoisie, the petty-bourgeois democrats as distinct from the bourgeoisie—have sufficiently exposed themselves in the eyes of the people, have sufficiently disgraced themselves through their practical bankruptcy; (3) among the proletariat a mass sentiment in favor of supporting the most determined, supremely bold, revolutionary action against the bourgeoisie has arisen and begun vigorously to grow. Then revolution is indeed ripe; then, indeed, if we have correctly gauged all the conditions indicated . . . above, and if we have chosen the moment rightly, our victory is assured.

The manner in which the October insurrection was carried out may be taken as a model of such strategy.

Nonobservance of this condition leads to a dangerous error called "loss of tempo," when the Party lags behind the movement or runs far ahead of it, courting the danger of failure.

Third. Undeviating pursuit of the course adopted, no matter what difficulties and complications are encountered on the road towards the goal; this is necessary in order that the vanguard may not lose sight of the main goal of the struggle and that the masses may not stray from the road while marching towards that goal and striving to rally around the vanguard. Failure to observe this condition leads to a grave error, well known to sailors as "losing the course."

Fourth. Maneuvering the reserves with a view to effecting a proper retreat when the enemy is strong, when retreat is inevitable, when to accept battle forced upon us by the enemy is obviously disadvantageous, when, with the given alignment of forces, retreat becomes the only way to ward off a blow against the vanguard and to keep the reserves intact. . . .

The object of this strategy is to gain time, to demoralize the enemy, and to accumulate forces in order later to assume the offensive.

The signing of the Brest-Litovsk Peace may be taken as a model of this strategy, for it enabled the Party to gain time, to take advantage of the conflicts in the camp of the imperialists, to demoralize the forces of the enemy, to retain the support of the peasantry, and to accumulate forces in preparation for the offensive against Kolchak and Denikin. "In concluding the separate peace," said Lenin at that time, "we free ourselves as much *as is possible at the present moment* from both hostile imperialist groups, we take advantage of their mutual enmity and warfare, which hamper concerted action on their part against us, and for a certain period have our hands free to advance and to consolidate the socialist revolution." "Now even the biggest fool," said Lenin, three years after the Brest-Litovsk Peace, "can see that the 'Brest Peace' was a concession that strengthened us and broke up the forces of international imperialism."

Such are the principal conditions which ensure correct strategic leadership.

5. *Tactical Leadership*

Tactical leadership is a part of strategic leadership, subordinated to the tasks and the requirements of the latter. The task of tactical leadership is to master all forms of struggle and organization of the proletariat and to ensure that they are used properly so as to achieve, with the given relation of forces, the maximum results necessary to prepare for strategic success.

What is meant by making proper use of the forms of struggle and organization of the proletariat?

It means fulfilling certain necessary conditions, of which the following must be regarded as the principal ones:

First. To put in the forefront precisely those forms of struggle and organization which are best suited to the conditions prevailing during the flow or ebb of the movement at a given moment, and which therefore can facilitate and ensure the bringing of the masses to the revolutionary positions, the bringing of millions to the revolutionary front, and their disposition at the revolutionary front. . . .

Second. To locate at any given moment the particular link in the chain of processes which, if grasped, will enable us to hold the whole chain and to prepare the conditions for achieving strategic success.

The point here is to single out from all the problems confronting the Party, the particular immediate problem, the answer to which constitutes the central point, and the solution of which will ensure the successful solution of the other immediate problems.

6. Reformism and Revolutionism

What is the difference between revolutionary tactics and reformist tactics?

Some think that Leninism is opposed to reforms, opposed to compromises and to agreements in general. This is absolutely wrong. Bolsheviks know as well as anybody else that in a certain sense "every little helps," that under certain conditions reforms in general, and compromises and agreements in particular are necessary and useful. . . . Obviously, therefore, it is not a matter of reforms or of compromises and agreements, but of the use people make of reforms and compromises.

To a reformist, reforms are everything, while revolutionary work is something incidental, something just to talk about, mere eyewash. That is why, with reformist tactics under the bourgeois regime, reforms are inevitably transformed into an instrument for strengthening that regime, an instrument for disintegrating the revolution.

To a revolutionary, on the contrary, the main thing is revolutionary work and not reforms; to him reforms are by-products of the revolution. That is why, with revolutionary tactics under the bourgeois regime, reforms are naturally transformed into instruments for disintegrating this regime, into instruments for strengthening the revolution, into a base for the further development of the revolutionary movement.

The revolutionary will accept a reform in order to use it as an aid in combining legal work with illegal work, to intensify, under its cover, the illegal work for the revolutionary preparation of the masses for the overthrow of the bourgeoisie.

That is what making revolutionary use of reforms and agreements under the conditions of imperialism means.

3. THE POSTWAR VIEW OF THE CRISIS
OF CAPITALISM*

JOSEPH STALIN

The distintegration of the single, all-embracing world market must be regarded as the most important economic sequel of the Second World War and of its economic consequences. It has had the effect of further deepening the general crisis of the world capitalist system.

The Second World War was itself a product of this crisis. Each of the two capitalist coalitions which locked horns in the war calculated on defeating its adversary and gaining world supremacy. It was in this that they sought a way out of the crisis. The United States of America hoped to put its most dangerous competitors, Germany and Japan, out of action, seize foreign markets and the world's raw material resources, and establish its world supremacy.

But the war did not justify these hopes. It is true that Germany and Japan were put out of action as competitors of the three major capitalist countries: the USA, Great Britain, and France. But at the same time China and European People's Democracies broke away from the capitalist system and, together with the Soviet Union, formed a united and powerful socialist camp confronting the camp of capitalism. The economic consequence of the existence of two opposite camps was that the single all-embracing world market disintegrated, so that now we have two parallel world markets, also confronting one another.

It should be observed that the USA and Great Britain and France, themselves contributed—without themselves desiring it, of course—to the formation and consolidation of the new, parallel world market. They imposed an economic blockade on the USSR, China, and the European People's Democracies, which did not join the "Marshall Plan" system, thinking thereby to strangle them. The effect, however, was not to strangle, but to strengthen the new world market.

But the fundamental thing, of course, is not the economic

* Joseph Stalin, *Economic Problems of Socialism in the USSR* (Moscow: Foreign Languages Publishing House, 1952), *excerpts*.

blockade, but the fact that since the war these countries have joined together economically and established economic cooperation and mutual assistance. The experience of this cooperation shows that not a single capitalist country could have rendered such effective and technically competent assistance to the People's Democracies as the Soviet Union is rendering them. The point is not only that this assistance is the cheapest possible and technically superb. The chief point is that at the bottom of this cooperation lies a sincere desire to help one another and to promote the economic progress of all. The result is a fast pace of industrial development in these countries. It may be confidently said that, with this pace of industrial development, it will soon come to pass that these countries will not only be in no need of imports from capitalist countries, but will themselves feel the necessity of finding an outside market for their surplus products.

But it follows from this that the sphere of exploitation of the world's resources by the major capitalist countries (USA, Britain, France) will not expand, but contract; that their opportunities for sale in the world market will deteriorate, and that their industries will be operating more and more below capacity. That, in fact, is what is meant by the deepening of the general crisis of the world capitalist system in connection with the disintegration of the world market.

This is felt by the capitalists themselves, for it would be difficult for them not to feel the loss of such markets as the USSR and China. They are trying to offset these difficulties with the "Marshall Plan," the war in Korea, frantic rearmament, and industrial militarization. But that is very much like a drowning man clutching at a straw.

This state of affairs has confronted the economists with two questions:

(a) Can it be affirmed that the thesis expounded by Stalin before the Second World War regarding the relative stability of markets in the period of the general crisis of capitalism is still valid?

(b) Can it be affirmed that the thesis expounded by Lenin in the spring of 1916—namely, that, in spite of the decay of capitalism, "on the whole, capitalism is growing far more rapidly than before"—is still valid?

I think that it cannot. In view of the new conditions to which the Second World War has given rise, both of these theses must be regarded as having lost their validity.

Inevitability of Wars Between Capitalist Countries

Some Comrades hold that, owing to the development of new international conditions since the Second World War, wars between capitalist countries have ceased to be inevitable. They consider that the contradictions between the socialist camp and the capitalist camp are more acute than the contradictions among the capitalist countries; that the USA has brought the other capitalist countries sufficiently under its sway to be able to prevent them going to war among themselves and weakening one another; that the foremost capitalist minds have been sufficiently taught by the two world wars and the severe damage they caused to the whole capitalist world, not to venture to involve the capitalist countries in war with one another again—and that, because of all this, wars between capitalist countries are no longer inevitable.

These Comrades are mistaken. They see the outward phenomena that come and go on the surface, but they do not see those profound forces which, although they are so far operating imperceptibly, will nevertheless determine the course of developments.

Outwardly, everything would seem to be "going well": the USA has put Western Europe, Japan, and other capitalist countries on rations; Germany (Western), Britain, France, Italy, and Japan have fallen into the clutches of the USA and are meekly obeying its commands. But it would be mistaken to think that things can continue to "go well" for "all eternity," that these countries will tolerate the domination and oppression of the United States endlessly, that they will not endeavor to tear loose from American bondage and take the path of independent development.

Take, first of all, Britain and France. Undoubtedly, they are imperialist countries. Undoubtedly, cheap raw materials and secure markets are of paramount importance to them. Can it be assumed that they will endlessly tolerate the present situation, in which, under the guise of "Marshall Plan aid," Americans are penetrating into the economies of Britain and France and trying to convert them into adjuncts of the United States economy, and American capital is seizing raw materials and markets in the British and French colonies and thereby plotting disaster for the high profits of the British and French capitalists? Would it not be truer to say that capitalist Britain, and, after her, capitalist France, will be compelled in the end to break from the embrace of the USA and enter into conflict with it in order to secure an independent position and, of course, high profits?

Let us pass to the major vanquished countries, Germany

(Western) and Japan. These countries are now languishing in misery under the jackboot of American imperialism. Their industry and agriculture, their trade, their foreign and home policies, and their whole life are fettered by the American occupation "regime." Yet only yesterday these countries were great imperialist powers and were shaking the foundations of the domination of Britain, the USA, and France in Europe and Asia. To think that these countries will not try to get on their feet again, will not try to smash U. S. domination and force their way to independent development, is to believe in miracles.

It is said that the contradictions between capitalism and socialism are stronger than the contradictions among the capitalist countries. Theoretically, of course, that is true. It is not only true now, today; it was true before the Second World War. And it was more or less realized by the leaders of the capitalist countries. Yet the Second World War began not as a war with the USSR, but as a war between capitalist countries. Why? Firstly, because war with the USSR, as a socialist land, is more dangerous to capitalism than war between capitalist countries; for whereas war between capitalist countries puts in question only the supremacy of certain capitalist countries over others, war with the USSR must certainly put in question the existence of capitalism itself. Secondly, because the capitalists, although they clamor, for "propaganda" purposes, about the aggressiveness of the Soviet Union, do not themselves believe that it is aggressive, because they are aware of the Soviet Union's peaceful policy and know that it will not itself attack capitalist countries.

After the First World War it was similarly believed that Germany had been definitely put out of action, just as certain Comrades now believe that Japan and Germany have been definitely put out of action. Then, too, it was said and clamored in the press that the United States had put Europe on rations; that Germany would never rise to her feet again, and that there would be no more wars between capitalist countries. In spite of this, Germany rose to her feet again as a great power within the space of some fifteen or twenty years after her defeat, having broken out of bondage and taken the path of independent development. And it is significant that it was none other than Britain and the United States that helped Germany to recover economically and to enhance her economic war potential. Of course, when the United States and Britain assisted Germany's economic recovery, they did so with a view to setting a recovered Germany against the Soviet Union, to utilizing her against the land of socialism. But Germany directed her forces in the first place against the Anglo-French-American bloc. And when Hitler Germany declared war on the Soviet Union, the Anglo-French-American bloc, far from joining with Hitler Germany, was compelled to enter into a coalition with the USSR against Hitler Germany.

Consequently, the struggle of the capitalist countries for markets and their desire to crush their competitors proved in practice to be stronger than the contradictions between the capitalist camp and the socialist camp.

What guarantee is there, then, that Germany and Japan will not rise to their feet again, will not attempt to break out of American bondage and live their own independent lives? I think there is no such guarantee.

But it follows from this that the inevitability of wars between capitalist countries remains in force.

It is said that Lenin's thesis that imperialism inevitably generates war must now be regarded as obsolete, since powerful popular forces have come forward today in defense of peace and against another world war. That is not true.

The object of the present-day peace movement is to rouse the masses of the people to fight for the preservation of peace and for the prevention of another world war. Consequently, the aim of this movement is not to overthrow capitalism and establish socialism—it confines itself to the democratic aim of preserving peace. In this respect, the present-day peace movement differs from the movement of the time of the First World War for the conversion of the imperialist war into civil war, since the latter movement went further and pursued socialist aims.

It is possible that in a definite conjuncture of circumstances, the fight for peace will develop here or there into a fight for socialism. But then it will no longer be the present-day peace movement; it will be a movement for the overthrow of capitalism.

What is most likely, is that the present-day peace movement, as a movement for the preservation of peace, will, if it succeeds, result in preventing a *particular* war, in its temporary postponement, in the temporary preservation of a *particular* peace, in the resignation of a bellicose government and its supersession by another that is prepared temporarily to keep the peace. That, of course, will be good. Even very good. But, all the same, it will not be enough to eliminate the inevitability of wars between capitalist countries generally. It will not be enough, because, for all the successes of the peace movement, imperialism will remain, continue in force—and, consequently, the inevitability of wars will also continue in force.

To eliminate the inevitability of war, it is necessary to abolish imperialism.

4. SOME FUNDAMENTAL QUESTIONS OF PRESENT-DAY INTERNATIONAL DEVELOP-MENT—REPORT OF THE CENTRAL COMMITTEE OF THE CPSU TO THE TWENTIETH PARTY CONGRESS*

February 1956

N . S . K H R U S H C H E V

Comrades, I should like to dwell on some fundamental questions concerning present-day international development, which determine not only the present course of events, but also the prospects for the future.

These questions are the peaceful coexistence of the two systems, the possibility of preventing wars in the present era, and the forms of transition to socialism in different countries.

Let us examine these questions in brief.

The Peaceful Coexistence of the Two Systems

The Leninist principle of peaceful coexistence of states with different social systems has always been and remains the general line of our country's foreign policy.

It has been alleged that the Soviet Union advances the principle of peaceful coexistence merely out of tactical considerations, considerations of expediency. Yet it is common knowledge that we have always, from the very first years of Soviet power, stood with equal firmness for peaceful coexistence. Hence, it is not a tactical move, but a fundamental principle of Soviet foreign policy.

This means that if there is indeed a threat to the peaceful coexistence of countries with differing social and political systems, it by no means comes from the Soviet Union or the rest of

* Moscow: Foreign Languages Publishing House, 1956, pp. 38–47, *excerpts*.

the socialist camp. Is there a single reason why a socialist state should want to unleash aggressive war? Do we have classes and groups that are interested in war as a means of enrichment? We do not. We abolished them long ago. Or, perhaps, we do not have enough territory or natural wealth, perhaps we lack sources of raw materials or markets for our goods? No, we have sufficient of all those and to spare. Why then should we want war? We do not want it; as a matter of principle we renounce any policy that might lead to millions of people being plunged into war for the sake of the selfish interests of a handful of multi-millionaires. Do those who shout about the "aggressive intentions" of the USSR know all this? Of course they do. Why then do they keep up the old monotonous refrain about some imaginary "communist aggression"? Only to stir up mud, to conceal their plans for world domination, a "crusade" against peace, democracy, and socialism.

To this day the enemies of peace allege that the Soviet Union is out to overthrow capitalism in other countries by "exporting" revolution. It goes without saying that among us Communists there are no supporters of capitalism. But this does not mean that we have interfered or plan to interfere in the internal affairs of countries where capitalism still exists. Romain Rolland was right when he said that "freedom is not brought in from abroad in baggage trains like Bourbons." (*Animation*) It is ridiculous to think that revolutions are made to order. We often hear representatives of bourgeois countries reasoning thus: "The Soviet leaders claim that they are for peaceful coexistence between the two systems. At the same time they declare that they are fighting for communism, and say that communism is bound to win in all countries. Now if the Soviet Union is fighting for communism, how can there be any peaceful coexistence with it?" This view is the result of bourgeois propaganda. The ideologists of the bourgeoisie distort the facts and deliberately confuse questions of ideological struggle with questions of relations between states in order to make the Communists of the Soviet Union look like advocates of aggression.

When we say that the socialist system will win in the competition between the two systems—the capitalist and the socialist—this by no means signifies that its victory will be achieved through armed interference by the socialist countries in the internal affairs of the capitalist countries. Our certainty of the victory of communism is based on the fact that the socialist mode of production possesses decisive advantages over the capitalist mode of production. Precisely because of this, the ideas of Marxism-Leninism are more and more capturing the minds of the broad masses of the working people in the capitalist countries, just as they have captured the minds of millions of men and women in our country and the People's Democracies. (*Prolonged applause*) We believe that all working men in the world, once they have become convinced of the advantages communism brings, will sooner or later take the road of struggle for the construction of socialist society. (*Prolonged applause*) Building communism in our country, we are resolutely against war. We have always held and continue to hold that the establishment of a new social system in one or another country is the internal affair of the peoples of the countries concerned. . . . Indeed, there are only two ways: either peaceful coexistence or the most destructive war in history. There is no third way. . . .

The Possibility of Preventing War in the Present Era

Millions of people all over the world are asking whether another war is really inevitable, whether mankind which has already experienced two devastating world wars must still go through a third one? Marxists must answer this question taking into consideration the epoch-making changes of the last decades.

There is, of course, a Marxist-Leninist precept that wars are inevitable as long as imperialism exists. This precept was evolved at a time when (1) imperialism was an all-embracing world system, and (2) the social and political forces which did not want war were weak, poorly organized, and hence unable to compel the imperialists to renounce war.

People usually take only one aspect of the question and examine only the economic basis of wars under imperialism. This is not enough. War is not only an economic phenomenon. Whether there is to be a war or not depends in large measure on the correlation of class, political forces, the degree of organization and the awareness and resolve of the people. Moreover, in certain conditions the struggle waged by progressive social and political forces may play a decisive role. Hitherto the state of affairs was such that the forces that did not want war and opposed it were poorly organized and lacked the means to check the schemes of the warmakers. Thus it was before the First World War, when the main force opposed to the threat of war— the world proletariat—was disorganized by the treachery of the leaders of the Second International. Thus it was on the eve of the Second World War, when the Soviet Union was the only country that pursued an active peace policy, when the other Great Powers to all intents and purposes encouraged the aggressors, and the right-wing Social-Democratic leaders had split the labor movement in the capitalist countries.

In that period this precept was absolutely correct. At the present time, however, the situation has changed radically. Now there is a world camp of socialism, which has become a mighty force. In this camp the peace forces find not only the moral, but also the material means to prevent aggression. Moreover, there is a large group of other countries with a population running into many hundreds of millions which are actively working to avert war. The labor movement in the capitalist countries has today become a tremendous force. The movement of peace supporters has sprung up and developed into a powerful factor.

In these circumstances certainly the Leninist precept that so long as imperialism exists, the economic basis giving rise to wars will also be preserved remains in force. That is why we must display the greatest vigilance. As long as capitalism survives in the world, the reactionary forces representing the interests of the capitalist monopolies will continue their drive towards military gambles and aggression, and may try to unleash war. But war is not fatalistically inevitable. Today there are mighty social and political forces possessing formidable means to prevent the imperialists from unleashing war, and if they actually try to start it, to give a smashing rebuff to the aggressors and frustrate their adventurist plans. To be able to do this all anti-war forces must be vigilant and prepared, they must act as a united front and never relax their efforts in the battle for peace. The more actively the peoples defend peace, the greater the guarantees that there will be no new war. (*Stormy, prolonged applause*)

Forms of Transition to Socialism in Different Countries

In connection with the radical changes in the world arena new prospects are also opening up in respect to the transition of countries and nations to socialism.

As far back as the eve of the Great October Socialist Revolution Lenin wrote: "All nations will arrive at socialism—this is inevitable, but not all will do so in exactly the same way, each will contribute something of its own in one or another form of democracy, one or another variety of the dictatorship of the proletariat, one or another rate at which socialist transformations will be effected in the various aspects of social life. There is nothing more primitive from the viewpoint of theory or more ridiculous from that of practice than to paint, 'in the name of historical materialism,' this aspect of the future in a monotonous grey. The result will be nothing more than Suzdal daubing." (*Works*, Vol. 23, p. 58)

Historical experience has fully confirmed Lenin's brilliant precept. Alongside the Soviet form of reconstructing society on socialist lines, we now have the form of People's Democracy. . . .

It is probable that more forms of transition to socialism will appear. Moreover, the implementation of these forms need not be associated with civil war under all circumstances. Our enemies like to depict us Leninists as advocates of violence always and everywhere. True, we recognize the need for the revolutionary transformation of capitalist society into socialist society. It is this that distinguishes the revolutionary Marxists from the reformists, the opportunists. There is no doubt that in a number of capitalist countries the violent overthrow of the dictatorship of the bourgeoisie and the sharp aggravation of class struggle connected with this are inevitable. But the forms of social revolution vary. It is not true that we regard violence and civil war as the only way to remake society . . .

Leninism teaches us that the ruling classes will not surrender their power voluntarily. And the greater or lesser degree of intensity which the struggle may assume, the use or the nonuse of violence in the transition to socialism depends on the resistance of the exploiters, on whether the exploiting class itself resorts to violence, rather than on the proletariat.

In this connection the question arises of whether it is possible to go over to socialism by using parliamentary means. No such course was open to the Russian Bolsheviks, who were the first to effect this transition. Lenin showed us another road, that of the establishment of a republic of Soviets, the only correct road in those historical conditions. Following that course we achieved a victory of history-making significance.

Since then, however, the historical situation has undergone radical changes which make possible a new approach to the question. The forces of socialism and democracy have grown immeasurably throughout the world, and capitalism has become much weaker. The mighty camp of socialism with its population of over 900 million is growing and gaining in strength. Its gigantic internal forces, its decisive advantages over capitalism, are being increasingly revealed from day to day. Socialism has a great power of attraction for the workers, peasants, and intellectuals of all countries. The ideas of socialism are indeed coming to dominate the minds of all toiling humanity.

At the same time the present situation offers the working class in a number of capitalist countries a real opportunity to unite the overwhelming majority of the people under its leadership and to secure the transfer of the basic means of production into the hands of the people. The Right-wing bourgeois parties and their governments are suffering bankruptcy with increasing frequency.

In these circumstances the working class, by rallying around itself the toiling peasantry, the intelligentsia, all patriotic forces, and resolutely repulsing the opportunist elements who are incapable of giving up the policy of compromise with the capitalists and landlords, is in a position to defeat the reactionary forces opposed to the popular interest, to capture a stable majority in parliament, and transform the latter from an organ of bourgeois democracy into a genuine instrument of the people's will. (*Applause*) In such an event this institution, traditional in many highly developed capitalist countries, may become an organ of genuine democracy, democracy for the working people.

The winning of a stable parliamentary majority backed by a mass revolutionary movement of the proletariat and of all the working people could create for the working class of a number of capitalist and former colonial countries the conditions needed to secure fundamental social changes.

In the countries where capitalism is still strong and has a huge military and police apparatus at its disposal, the reactionary forces will of course inevitably offer serious resistance. There the transition to socialism will be attended by a sharp class, revolutionary struggle.

Whatever the form of transition to socialism, the decisive and indispensable factor is the political leadership of the working class headed by its vanguard. Without this there can be no transition to socialism. . . .

5. CRISIS OF WORLD CAPITALISM—PROGRAM OF THE COMMUNIST PARTY OF THE SOVIET UNION*

1961

Imperialism has entered the period of decline and collapse. An inexorable process of decay has seized capitalism from top to bottom—its economic and political system, its politics and ideology. Imperialism has for ever lost its power over the bulk of mankind. The main content, main trend and main features of

* Moscow: Foreign Languages Publishing House, 1961, pp. 25-34, *excerpts*.

the historical development of mankind are being determined by the world socialist system, by the forces fighting against imperialism, for the socialist reorganisation of society.

The First World War and the October Revolution ushered in the general crisis of capitalism. The second stage of this crisis developed at the time of the Second World War and the socialist revolutions that took place in a number of European and Asian countries. World capitalism has now entered a new, third stage of that crisis, the principal feature of which is that its development was not connected with a world war.

The break-away from capitalism of more and more countries; the weakening of imperialist positions in the economic competition with socialism; the break-up of the imperialist colonial system; the intensification of imperialist contradictions with the development of state-monopoly capitalism and the growth of militarism; the mounting internal instability and decay of capitalist economy evidenced by the increasing inability of capitalism to make full use of the productive forces (low rates of production growth, periodic crises, continuous undercapacity operation of production plant, and chronic unemployment); the mounting struggle between labour and capital; an acute intensification of contradictions within the world capitalist economy; an unprecedented growth of political reaction in all spheres, rejection of bourgeois freedoms and establishment of fascist and despotic regimes in a number of countries; and the profound crisis of bourgeois policy and ideology—all these are manifestations of the *general crisis of capitalism.*

In the imperialist stage *state-monopoly capitalism* develops on an extensive scale. The emergence and growth of monopolies lead to the direct intervention of the state, in the interests of the financial oligarchy, in the process of capitalist reproduction. It is in the interests of the financial oligarchy that the bourgeois state institutes various types of regulation and resorts to the nationalisation of some branches of the economy. World wars, economic crises, militarism, and political upheavals have accelerated the development of monopoly capitalism into state-monopoly capitalism. . . .

State-monopoly capitalism stimulates militarism to an unheard of degree. The imperialist countries maintain immense armed forces even in peacetime. Military expenditures devour an ever-growing portion of the state budgets. The imperialist countries are turning into militarist, military-police states. Militarization pervades the life of bourgeois society . . .

The uneven development of capitalism alters the balance of forces between countries and makes the contradictions between

them more acute. The economic and with it the political and
military centre of imperialism has shifted from Europe to the
United States. U.S. monopoly capital, gorged on war profits and
the arms race, has seized the most important sources of raw
materials, the markets and the spheres of investment, has built
up a unique kind of colonial empire and become the biggest
international exploiter. Taking cover behind spurious professions
of freedom and democracy, U.S. imperialism is in effect performing the function of *world gendarme*, supporting reactionary dictatorial regimes and decayed monarchies, opposing democratic,
revolutionary changes and launching aggressions against peoples
fighting for independence.

*The U.S. monopoly bourgeoisie is the mainstay of international
reaction*. It has assumed the role of "saviour" of capitalism. The
U.S. financial tycoons are engineering a "holy alliance" of imperialists and founding aggressive military blocs. American troops
and war bases are stationed at the most important points of the
capitalist world . . .

The basic contradiction of the contemporary world, that between socialism and imperialism, does not eliminate the *deep
contradictions* rending the capitalist world. The aggressive military blocs founded under the aegis of the U.S.A. are time and
again faced with crises. The international state-monopoly organizations springing up under the motto of "integration," the mitiga-
tion of the market problem, are in reality new forms of the
redivision of the world capitalist market and are becoming seats
of acute strain and conflict.

The contradictions between the principal imperialist powers
are growing deeper. The economic rehabilitation of the imperialist
countries defeated in the Second World War leads to the revival
of the old and the emergence of new knots of imperialist rivalry
and conflict . . .

The American monopolies and their British and French allies
are openly assisting the West German imperialists who are cyni-
cally advocating aggressive aims of revenge and preparing a war
against the socialist countries and other European states. A dangerous centre of aggression, imperilling the peace and security of
all peoples, is being revived in the heart of Europe . . .

*The world imperialist system is rent by deep-rooted and acute
contradictions*. The antagonism of labour and capital, the contradictions between the people and the monopolies, growing militarism, the break-up of the colonial system, the contradictions
between the imperialist countries, conflicts and contradictions
between the young national states and the old colonial powers,
and—most important of all—the rapid growth of world socialism,

are sapping and destroying imperialism, leading to its weakening and collapse.

FOR FURTHER STUDY

Brzezinski, Zbigniew K., "Communist Ideology and International Affairs," *The Journal of Conflict Resolution*, Vol. IV, No. 3 (1960).

Burin, Frederic S., "The Communist Doctrine of the Inevitability of War," *The American Political Science Review*, Vol. LVII, No. 2 (June 1963).

Dallin, Alexander (ed.), *Soviet Conduct in World Affairs*. New York: Columbia University Press, 1960.

Diplomaticus, "Stalinist Theory and Soviet Foreign Policy," *The Review of Politics*, Vol. XIV (1952).

Garthoff, Raymond L., "The Concept of the Balance of Power in Soviet Policy-Making," *World Politics*, Vol. IV (1951).

Historicus, "Stalin on Revolution," *Foreign Affairs*, Vol. XXVII, No. 2 (1949).

Hunt, R. N. C., *The Theory and Practice of Communism*, 5th ed. New York: The Macmillan Company, 1957.

————, "The Importance of Doctrine," *Problems of Communism*, Vol. VII (1958).

Kennan, George F., "The Sources of Soviet Conduct," *Foreign Affairs*, Vol. XXV, No. 4 (1947).

Leites, Nathan, *The Operational Code of the Politbureau*. New York: McGraw-Hill Book Company, 1951.

Meyer, Alfred G., *Leninism*. Cambridge, Mass.: Harvard University Press, 1957.

Moore, Barrington, Jr., *Soviet Politics: The Dilemma of Power*. Cambridge: Harvard University Press, 1950.

Mosely, Philip E., "Soviet Foreign Policy: New Goals or New Manners?" *Foreign Affairs*, Vol. XXXIV, No. 4 (1956).

————, "The Meanings of Coexistence," *Foreign Affairs*, Vol. XLI, No. 1 (1962).

Reshetar, John S., Jr., *Problems of Analyzing and Predicting Soviet Behavior*. New York: Random House, 1955.

Riefe, R. H., "Moscow and the Changing Nature of Communist Ideology," *Journal of International Affairs*, Vol. XII, No. 2 (1958).

Ulam, Adam B., "Soviet Ideology and Soviet Foreign Policy," *World Politics*, Vol. XI (1959).

Wetter, Gustav A., "The Soviet Concept of Coexistence," *Soviet Survey*, No. 30 (1959).

Wolfe, Bertram D., "Communist Ideology and Soviet Foreign Policy," *Foreign Affairs*, Vol. XLI, No. 1 (1962).

Zinner, Paul E., "Ideological Bases of Soviet Foreign Policy," *World Politics*, Vol. IV (1952).

CHAPTER II

THE FORMATIVE YEARS, 1917–1921

The revolutionary turned ruler confronts a galaxy of unknowns. When the Bolsheviks took power on November 7, 1917, they faced challenges for which their experiences as underground revolutionaries and exiled members of an obscure political faction had not prepared them. Expecting world revolution, they had no appreciation of the complexity of their problems. Trotsky tells of Lenin's comment: "What foreign affairs will we have now?" Time and events soon provided the answer.

Burdened with the Czarist legacy of a dispirited, disorganized army, a population weary of war and suffering, and an internal order on the brink of breakdown, the Bolsheviks considered that their initial task was to take Russia out of the war. "Peace" had been one of the main slogans in their drive for power. The promise of peace represented a major political commitment, one which they neither dared nor desired to break. The undoubted popularity of such a move attracted the Bolsheviks as a means of gaining popular support. Furthermore, viewing the struggle as an "imperialist" war, they were predisposed to regard the traditional methods of international law and diplomacy as alien to a proletarian state. Accordingly, on November 8, the day after the Bolsheviks seized power, the All-Russian Congress of Soviets of Workers', Soldiers', and Peasants' Deputies unanimously approved a "Decree of Peace," proposing "to all warring peoples and their

Governments to begin immediately negotiations for a just and democratic peace" (reading 6). The Congress defined such a peace as "an immediate peace without annexations (i.e. without seizure of territory, without the forcible annexation of foreign nationalities) and without indemnities." Since this appeal was directed to the peoples of Western Europe, as well as to their respective governments, it was the first use by the Bolsheviks of what was later to be known as "demonstrative diplomacy." George Kennan has explained this as "diplomacy designed not to promote freely accepted and mutually profitable agreement as between governments, but rather to embarrass other governments and stir up opposition among their own peoples."[1] The declaration caught Russia's allies unawares and their reaction was one of concern and confusion. This initial excursion into the realm of diplomacy presaged ill for future relations with the Bolsheviks.

It soon became apparent that the Bolsheviks were serious about their decision to remove Russia from the war. The issue for them was survival. Negotiations with the Germans resulted in a preliminary armistice agreement on December 15, 1917, the first step toward taking Russia out of the "imperialist" war. Russia's allies—France, Great Britain, and the United States—expressed alarm and sought to dissuade the Bolsheviks from their course. The "Decree of Peace" had also announced the Bolsheviks' intention to publish the secret treaties entered into by the Czarist government. This they proceeded to do, to the further consternation of the Allies. Publication in November and December of 1917 of these documents, which outlined the division of future spoils, caused a sensation in the United States and stimulated demands in Western circles for a redefinition of peace aims. It led Wilson to issue his celebrated Fourteen Points, the open declaration of Allied aims, on January 8, 1918.[2] Referring directly several times to the German-Bolshevik negotiations at Brest-Litovsk, Wilson declared that "the treatment accorded Russia by her sister nations in the months to come will be the acid test of their good will, of their comprehension of her needs as distinguished from their own interests, and of their intelligent and unselfish sympathy." Noble words. But subsequent events, particularly the Allied intervention, made a mockery of them. Indeed, there is little to indicate that Wilson's address ever had the remotest effect on Allied policy toward Russia.[3]

Meanwhile, the unorthodox delaying tactics of the Bolsheviks at the Brest-Litovsk negotiations irritated the Germans, who were eager for a speedy conclusion of peace. Only then could they transfer the bulk of their formidable army from the Eastern Front to the West and deal a knockout blow to the Allies before

American strength was felt. The Bolshevik negotiators, unable to obtain any assurance of Allied support in the event of a rupture with Germany, attempted to prolong the discussions. The impatient German military commander, Hoffmann, drawing a blue line on a map marking German demands, gave the alternatives: an unequivocal answer or an immediate resumption of the German offensive. Leon Trotsky, the chief Russian negotiator, requested a few days in which to consult with Party leaders. He returned to Petrograd (Leningrad) on January 20 to find that the Constituent Assembly, only recently convened, had been dissolved and that the Bolsheviks had assumed absolute power. Russia's fleeting flirtation with democracy had ended.

Now began the first momentous Bolshevik debate on foreign policy. The Bolsheviks had hitherto assumed that, after appropriate agitation and propagandizing, the German troops would revolt against their "imperialist" government and thereby spark a proletarian revolution in Germany, which would spread, in turn, to Western Europe, signifying the start of a new era. Indeed, most Bolsheviks shared the ideological assumption that the revolution in Russia could prove successful only if accompanied by revolutions elsewhere in Europe.

Lenin, ever the realist and tactician, though accepting this assumption, felt, nevertheless, that the situation required a different tactical approach. In his *Theses on the Question of the Immediate Conclusion of a Separate and Annexationist Peace* (reading 7), Lenin argued, with force and clarity, that the preservation of the revolution in Russia must outweigh the more uncertain prospects of world revolution: that, at least for the immediate future, the interests of the international proletariat must be subordinated; and, indeed, that the best way to ensure the eventual success of the world socialist revolution was first to safeguard the revolution in Russia. Therefore, he called for an immediate end to hostilities. Trotsky, on the other hand, argued that the German demands should be summarily rejected and no peace signed; other "Left Communists," including Radek, Pokrovsky, and Kollantai, went even further and called for a "holy war" against the Germans. In an attempt to reconcile these diverse approaches, the Central Committee agreed upon Trotsky's formula of "no war, no peace." This was designed to prolong the negotiations and was expected, along with the continued dissemination of propaganda, to arouse the proletariat and precipitate a revolution in Germany. However, in recognition of Lenin's objections, the Central Committee agreed that, should the Germans resume their advance, a peace treaty would be signed. Lenin concurred, adding facetiously that "for the sake of a good peace with Trotsky, Latvia and Estonia are worth losing."[4] On January 30, Trotsky returned to Brest-Litovsk. He found the Germans in a far less patient mood and in the process of recognizing as spokesman for the Ukraine a splinter anti-Bolshevik group, with whom they signed a separate peace treaty on February 9, thereby obtaining badly needed grain and raw materials.[5]

Confronted with German annexational demands, Trotsky, to the astonishment of the Germans and Austrians, put his "no war, no peace" policy into effect by announcing Russia's immediate withdrawal from the war, her refusal to sign any terms of peace, and her decision to end all negotiations.[6] The Germans responded quickly, determined now to force Russia to accede. On February 18, the Central Powers launched a general offensive, advancing rapidly against feeble Russian resistance. In Petrograd the Central Committee hurriedly convened and, after some heated discussion, voted to sue for peace. But the Germans rolled onward, eager for more conquest and, seemingly, for the capture of Petrograd itself and the overthrow of the Bolshevik regime.[7] The Bolsheviks were thoroughly alarmed. Trotsky proposed that aid be sought from the Allies. Lenin, though not present, gave his approval to seeking "potatoes and arms from the bandits of Anglo-French imperialism."[8] But Allied policy toward the Bolsheviks remained a jumble of suspicion, ignorance, and misunderstanding. The efforts of several junior Allied diplomatic representatives—Raymond Robins (American), Bruce Lockhart (British), and Jacques Sadoul (French)—received little encouragement from their respective governments and were either ignored or misinterpreted.

In the face of mounting German victories, the Bolshevik plenipotentiaries signed a "Carthaginian" peace on March 3, 1918. For the Germans, the fruits of victory represented a third of Russia's population, of her cultivated land, and of her industry. Meanwhile, Raymond Robins, the American Red Cross representative, tried to prevent the ratification of the Brest Treaty by promising Allied support. The Allies' growing hostility toward the Bolsheviks, however, intensified an already developed Bolshevik distrust, which was further aggravated by reports of an impending Japanese intervention in Siberia. At this vital moment, the Allied embassies moved to the small town of Vologda to avoid capture during the threatening German advance on Petrograd. There they remained, diplomatic orphans, isolated from the maelstrom of events in Petrograd and Moscow (the Bolsheviks moved the capital to Moscow on March 11). Thus, the essentials of policy were being formulated in the Allied capitals virtually without the benefit of reports from knowledgeable personnel at the scene.

On March 5, Trotsky handed a note to Robins in which he asked what Allied policy would be: (a) if the Soviets refused to ratify the peace treaty with Germany; (b) if the Soviets decided to renounce the treaty; or (c) if the Germans continued to advance despite the treaty. The key questions asked were:

1. Can the Soviet Government rely on the support of the United States of North America, Great Britain, and France in its struggle against Germany?
2. What kind of support could be furnished in the nearest future and on what conditions—military equipment, transportation supplies, living necessities?
3. What kind of support would be furnished particularly and especially by the United States?
   Should Japan . . . attempt to seize Vladivostok and the Eastern-Siberian Railway . . . what steps would be taken by the other Allies, particularly and especially by the United States . . . ?[9]

After an unavoidable three-day delay, the dispatch was forwarded to Washington. Meanwhile, David R. Francis, the American ambassador, cabled a report indicating support of Robins and adding that a Japanese landing in Siberia at this time would be a gross mistake. On March 14, 1918, the fourth All-Russian Congress of Soviets gathered to ratify the treaty. Lenin, who had agreed to a forty-eight hour delay at the urgent request of Robins, could wait no longer. After reading a telegram of greeting from President Wilson, which was dated March 11 but which did not answer Trotsky's questions, Lenin turned to Robins and Lockhart and asked what they had heard from their governments. Each could only answer "nothing." In the early hours of the morning of March 15, Lenin outlined the economic, military, and political necessity for taking Russia out of the war. Soon afterward, the Congress ratified the treaty, and Russia was out of the war. Whether a favorable reply from Washington could have prevented the ratification at that late date is, of course, open to conjecture. Describing these events, Mr. Kennan writes: "Once again, as so often in the course of these rapidly moving events, Washington—troubled, hesitant, and ill-informed —had spoken, reluctantly, into the past."[10]

The shape of the future was not long in developing.

For the Bolsheviks, the Brest-Litovsk crisis served as a crucible from which emerged the outlines of a foreign policy. During their early days in power they were busy consolidating the regime and had no real understanding of the nature of foreign policy.

Trotsky, in his autobiography, offers an interesting commentary on this prevailing naivete. Upon assuming the position of Commissar of Foreign Affairs, he states, the expectation was that "I will issue a few revolutionary proclamations to the peoples of the world and then shut up shop." The Bolshevik leaders, expecting the socialist revolution to spread throughout the world, saw no need to adhere to the traditional ways of international politics. But Brest-Litovsk convinced them that an adjustment had to be made. Three factors were paramount in their thinking. First, they recognized that military weakness left them prey to foreign attack and increased the likelihood of their deposition. Second, the absence of expected revolutions in Germany and Western Europe meant that they could not depend on world revolution to strengthen the socialist revolution in Russia; therefore, though continuing to anticipate world revolution as the only ultimate security, the Bolsheviks undertook the creation of a Red Army to provide for their short-term safety. Finally, the policies both of the Central Powers and of the Entente buttressed the Bolsheviks' conviction, held to this day, that the capitalist world, irrespective of its competing internal alliances, was hostile and would persist in its efforts to overthrow the Bolshevik regime. Only world revolution could guarantee national security; yet national security was essential for the eventual success of world revolution.[11] This dualism—the furthering of world revolution and the quest for national security—has remained a salient feature of Soviet foreign policy.

Soviet behavior in the international arena represents a unique adaptation to the existing pattern of world politics: it tends to rationalize actions of national self-interest in terms of the transcendent concerns of the international proletariat; and while using traditional balance-of-power politics to protect the revolution, it spares no effort to undermine this system and replace it with "an international proletarian community." The stress on fomenting world revolution developed out of initial military weakness and, having proved its effectiveness as a weapon, has remained an integral part of the Soviet diplomatic arsenal. (*Note:* After the Allied intervention, and the subsequent civil war, the use of subversion and revolutionary propaganda became increasingly important as a technique to defeat the enemy and consolidate the power of the regime.)

The landing of Japanese troops at Vladivostok on April 5, 1918, triggered by the murder of three Japanese shopkeepers, began the intervention. Before it ended, British, French, and American troops would be involved, a bitter, all-out civil war would run its course, and Bolshevism would emerge triumphant in Russia.

From the ratification of the Brest-Litovsk Treaty in March to the resumption of official German-Soviet relations in May, the Bolsheviks had toyed with the possibility of accepting Allied aid and continuing in the war against Germany. However, as relations with the Allies deteriorated, and as it became apparent that the Germans, engrossed in the struggle on the Western front, had neither the intent nor the strength to overthrow the Bolshevik regime, this alternative lost whatever likelihood it may have had. On the other hand, the Allies, confused and uncertain, were not yet committed to intervention against the Bolsheviks. Reasonable justification soon replaced this initial Allied hesitancy. The catalyst was the Czecho-Slovak revolt, one of the strangest episodes of the entire period.[12]

The Czechs and Slovaks, originally part of the Austro-Hungarian armies, had deserted by the thousands and looked forward to the establishment of an independent state. Their sentiments were unmistakably pro-Allies. Shortly after the overthrow of the Czar, Thomas Masaryk, the future president of Czechoslovakia, had journeyed to Russia to negotiate for the organization of the Czechs and Slovaks into a unified force and for their removal (by way of Siberia) to the Western front for use in fighting the Germans and Austrians. The Provisional Government approved and took measures to transport this force. However, with the Bolshevik decision to leave the war, and the increasingly obvious anti-Bolshevik trend of Allied policy, the Czech Legion's position became untenable. The Bolsheviks feared that the Legion would be used to overthrow them; indeed, they believed that the Czechs were acting in concert with the recently landed Japanese forces toward this end. The Legion, on the other hand, fearing imprisonment, refused to surrender its weapons during the trip across Siberia for trans-shipment to the Western front. Earlier, in March, the British had landed a small detachment at Murmansk, with the tacit consent of the Bolsheviks, to safeguard substantial Allied stores. The German advance heightened concern for the safety of these supplies, and the Allied command decided to employ part of the Czech Legion to strengthen the British force. The intricate pattern of subsequent events need not concern us here. Suffice it to note that the Allied decision to intervene was precipitated by the chance outbreak of fighting between the Czech Legion and the Bolsheviks.

The confusions of these months were many. But isolated events have a way, in periods of great stress and confusion, of encouraging certain policy decisions which seem for the moment to characterize the entire situation. The Allies had not planned to use the Czechs to overthrow the Bolsheviks, but the plight of the Czechs helped provide the necessary impetus for what was at best a haphazardly conceived policy. According to George Kennan, the immediate reasons for the Czech-Bolshevik fighting lie:

. . . primarily in the general climate of confusion and suspicion that prevailed at this culminating moment of war and revolution; in the extremely complex situation in which the Czech Corps then found itself; in the complicating factor of the presence of large numbers of the war prisoners of the Central Powers, partly Bolshevized and partly not so, all along the Siberian line; in the abundant rumors of German instigation of Soviet actions. . . .

Had the Corps succeeded in making its way peacefully through the vast tinderbox of central Siberia during the spring of 1918, striking no sparks and raising no crucial issues as it went along, this—rather than what actually occurred—would have been the true wonder.[13]

In late June, additional British forces landed at Murmansk, followed by British and French landings at Archangel. A few weeks later, American troops also came to North Russia; and in early August they joined the Japanese in Siberia. The intervention was now a reality, nourished by the seeming success of anti-Bolsheviks in these areas and by the desire of Allied strategists to re-create an Eastern front against the Germans. There was no longer any possibility of compromise. The mold of hostility hardened. Increasingly, Bolshevik statements reflected desperation. The summer of 1918 was their darkest hour. Hope of survival depended on their ability to sow discord among the Allies and foment world revolution (reading 8). As the intervention spread, Soviet relations with Germany improved—notwithstanding the assassination of German Ambassador Mirbach, on July 6, 1918, by a disgruntled left-wing Socialist Revolutionary who hoped to precipitate a break with Germany and thereby force Russia back into the war on the side of the Allies. Both the German and Soviet governments desired friendly relations, though for different reasons (the Germans were preoccupied with the fighting on the Western front and welcomed the respite in Russia; the Bolsheviks, increasingly threatened by the Allied intervention, were content to let the Brest boundaries remain in effect for the time being). Thus German-Soviet relations improved as Allied-Soviet relations deteriorated. This was to be a recurring pattern from 1918 to 1941—as Soviet relations with one deteriorated, a rapprochement was effected with the other.

World War I ended on November 11, 1918. Whatever rationale the intervention originally had was no longer valid. But conflicting national interests and growing British and French commitments to anti-Bolshevik forces precluded any immediate disengagement. The intervention had become involved in the civil war. An eminent student of the period has described the situation thus: "One searches in vain in the records of the time not only for a consistent Allied policy, but even for a steadfast policy on the part of the individual Allied powers."[14] Fear of Bolshevism's spread to the rest of Europe, resentment over the Bolshevik repudiation of the prewar Czarist debts, the growing influence of émigré and pro-White groups—all sustained the resolve of the interventionists.

On November 13, the Bolsheviks abrogated the Brest-Litovsk Treaty, declaring its provisions null and void. During the autumn and winter a Red Army was conscripted, trained, and toughened for battle. Under the driving leadership of Leon Trotsky, this organization proved itself superior to the smorgasbord of armies and leaders that comprised the White Guard interventionists. A centralized military command, a compact geographical base and internal lines of communication, effective appeals to patriotism against foreign enemies, and the inability of the Whites to coordinate their military activities or agree on a common political program, all worked to Bolshevik benefit. In addition, the Bolshevik promise of self-determination, including the right of secession, induced the national minorities in Armenia, Georgia, Central Asia, etc. to resist attempts by the White armies to reimpose *Russian* control. During the crucial 1918 to 1920 period, the unrest and revolts in these areas weakened the interventionists' attempts at a restoration, thus inadvertently aiding the Bolsheviks. Needless to add, once the Bolsheviks defeated the Whites, they proceeded to reincorporate the minorities in the Caucasus and Central Asia into the Russian orbit and suppress all separatist movements.

The year 1919 was crucial. At Versailles a treaty was summarily handed to the Germans and with it were sown the seeds of the next war in a Europe weakened beyond its realization; in Germany, revolution met defeat at the hands of the military, and the fledgling Weimar republic started its tragic, short life; in America, Wilson's dream was defeated in the Senate and soon gave way to a "return to normalcy"—a phrase symbolizing America's abdication of international responsibility for two decades; the "Balkanized" area of central and southeastern Europe had not yet been linked with France in the unstable network of military alliances that was to give the French an illusion of security; in Paris fear of Bolshevism dominated French policy, and émigré Russians pushed for all-out war against the Bolsheviks; and in Russia, after the excesses and suffering of the period of "War Communism," Bolshevism emerged victorious. The Allies, forced to compromise by the unwillingness of their armies to fight in Russia in a struggle they did not understand, reluctantly abandoned their interventionist adventures.

Bolshevik behavior strengthened the cause of the pro-interventionists. By their cynicism, lack of sincerity, and revolutionary agitation, they made negotiation in good faith virtually impossible. Encouraged by revolution in Hungary and Germany, unrest in France, and the illusions of ideology, they continued to anticipate world revolution. To hasten this objective, the Bolsheviks in March 1919 established the Communist International, thus providing the interventionists with an added pretext for military action. By the end of 1919, however, it was apparent that the anti-Bolshevik elements could neither defeat the Red Army by force, nor match Bolshevism's emotional appeal.

To the great mass, Bolshevism was part promise and part fulfillment. From the revolution had come peace, land, and a new form of ownership. But it also painted a glorious future which attracted and provoked. The enemies of Communism had nothing thrilling or inspiring to offer. Lenin operated on credit. His capital was a promissory note on coming years. The Whites on the other hand could appeal only to the record of the past which they wished to enthrone again. Psychologically, the position of the Bolsheviks was therefore stronger.[15]

Each generation must learn anew the adage that it is not by bread alone that man lives.

A confident Lenin delivered the key address to the seventh All-Russian Congress on December 5, 1919 (reading 9). His report marked a turning point in the period of "War Communism." The danger from the Allied intervention had been successfully met, and the civil war had passed its most acute phase. The principal White Guard armies, under Kolchak and Denikin, had been defeated, and the pressures for peace had increased, particularly among the small nations bordering on European Russia—in 1920, Finland, Latvia, and Estonia concluded peace treaties with the Bolsheviks. Cogently presenting his analysis of the main stages of the intervention and the civil war, Lenin set forth the underlying assumptions of Soviet foreign policy, assumptions significant to the future of Soviet relations with the capitalist world and valid, in great measure, to this day: the fundamental antagonism between the capitalist and socialist systems; the expectation that the capitalist countries would attempt another intervention (a factor leading the Soviet leaders to orient their foreign policy along traditional balance-of-power lines); and the inevitable linking of Soviet national security with the necessity for world revolution.

Tactically, Soviet policy was learning to emphasize the importance of the international proletariat as an instrument to safeguard the Soviet Union, to exploit antagonisms within the capitalist world, not only between the "great" and "lesser" powers but within the respective countries themselves, and to capitalize on the conciliatory, frequently sympathetic, tendencies of the petty bourgeoisie and intelligentsia toward the Soviet Union. Soviet leaders appealed to the workers in the Allied countries to defend the socialist revolution by bringing pressure to bear on their governments to stop the intervention. Propaganda assumed an increasing importance in the policy of a *militarily* inferior Soviet Russia.

The last serious military threat came from the Poles. On April 25, 1920, Marshal Pilsudski launched an offensive and advanced rapidly into the Ukraine. By May 6 the Poles were in Kiev. By mid-May, however, the Red Army had counterattacked and the Poles in turn were in rapid retreat. By late July and early August the Soviet armies were at the gates of Warsaw. The Bolshevik leaders, stressing the class character of the struggle, expected revolution at any moment. (Ironically, Pilsudski had refused to act in concert with the White general, Denikin, the previous year, under conditions offering greater promise of victory. His anti-Russianism recognized no distinction between Red or White, since both groups favored a strong Russia, an unquestioned anathema to Pilsudski.)

In Moscow the second Congress of the Communist International met from July 23 to August 7 in a buoyantly optimistic atmosphere stimulated by the continuous advance of the Red Army into Poland. Zinoviev later described the scene and the mood:

> In the hall of congress hung a large map. Every day we marked on it the advance of our forces, and every day with breathless interest the delegates examined the map. . . . All of them understood that if the military objectives of our troops were reached it would mean an immense acceleration of the international proletarian revolution. All of them understood that on every step forward of our Red Army depended in the literal sense of the word the fate of the international proletarian revolution.[16]

Hopes ran high for the International. No longer was it to be a mere propaganda association, as at its foundation in March 1919; it was now to be tempered into a "fighting organ of the international proletariat." To ensure a high degree of centralization and discipline, the Congress revised its structure and adopted new operating procedures (reading 10). The Congress also prescribed conditions of admission to the Comintern (reading 11). These "21 conditions" made certain that the Comintern would, in fact, be "a single Communist Party having branches in different countries."

The emergence of the Kremlin as the undisputed spokesman and policy-maker for world communism can be traced to this Congress. First, it established a world-wide system of Moscow-controlled Communist Parties; second, it laid down the fundamentals of Communist policy on all significant questions. Other important resolutions adopted at the second Congress, particularly theses concerning the national and colonial question, will be discussed in a future chapter. By the late 1920s the struggle for power *within* the Kremlin having ended, all foreign Communist Parties acknowledged the primacy of the Communist Party of the Soviet Union and accepted Kremlin injunctions without question; the Comintern became a docile instrument of Soviet foreign policy.

Shortly after the Congress adjourned, the Poles, aided by the French, launched a powerful counteroffensive, and the over-extended Red Army retreated in haste. Contrary to Lenin's expectations, the Polish proletariat did not revolt, but fought as Poles against the historic and hated enemy—Russia. With this defeat of the Red Army, Russian expectations of an imminent world revolution ended. An armistice, negotiated on October 12, 1920, led to a treaty of peace signed on March 18, 1921 at Riga,* which governed Polish-Soviet relations until the partition of September 1939. After the armistice the Soviets threw the bulk of their forces against von Wrangel, the last of the White generals, and by mid-November 1920, successfully ended this campaign. Subsequently, the intervention collapsed in Siberia and the Caucasus. The Bolsheviks now turned to the problems of reshaping Russian society and "coexisting" in a hostile world.

Lenin outlined the essentials of Soviet policy in two speeches delivered in December of 1920 (readings 12 and 13). Tracing the phases of the intervention and the civil war, he reaffirmed the belief in the inevitability of world revolution and the triumph of communism, but held that a period of accommodation with the capitalist world, Party reorganization, and economic development was first necessary. By the time of the Tenth Party Congress (March 1921), the need for a temporary truce with the

* The Soviets, imperiled by von Wrangel's White army in southern Russia, agreed to Polish demands and ceded part of Byelorussia, as well as a strip of territory serving to separate Russia from Lithuania.

capitalist world was accepted and a rapprochement sought in the economic and political spheres.

Thus ended Bolshevism's first period of trial. A civil war and a foreign intervention had been successfully fought. The Communist Party was firmly entrenched. Thenceforth, Soviet foreign policy focused on the preservation of the Soviet Union, the improvement of its international position, and the spread of Communist influence and power. With the end of "War Communism," one period of Soviet foreign policy came to a successful conclusion. A second was about to begin.

NOTES

1. George F. Kennan, *Russia Leaves the War* (Princeton, N.J.: Princeton University Press, 1956), pp. 75–76.
2. Edward Hallett Carr, *The Bolshevik Revolution, 1917–1923* (New York: The Macmillan Company, 1953), Vol. III, p. 13.
3. Louis Fischer, *The Soviets in World Affairs* (London: Jonathan Cape, 1930), Vol. I, p. 42.
4. Leon Trotsky, *My Life: An Attempt at an Autobiography* (New York: Charles Scribner's Sons, 1930), p. 383.
5. Robert D. Warth, *The Allies and the Russian Revolution* (Durham, N.C.: Duke University Press, 1954), p. 225.
6. *Ibid.*, p. 226.
7. Fischer, *op. cit.*, pp. 60–61.
8. Warth, *op. cit.*, p. 231.
9. *The Congressional Record* (January 29, 1919), p. 2336.
10. Kennan, *op. cit.*, p. 517.
11. Carr, *op. cit.*, p. 57.
12. Fischer, *op. cit.*, p. 108.
13. George F. Kennan, *The Decision to Intervene* (Princeton, N.J.: Princeton University Press, 1958), p. 165.
14. William Henry Chamberlin, *The Russian Revolution, 1917–1921* (New York: The Macmillan Company, 1935), Vol. II, p. 151.
15. Fischer, *op. cit.*, pp. 234–235.
16. Jane Degras, *The Communist International, 1919–1943, Documents* (New York: Oxford University Press, 1956), Vol. I, pp. 110–111.

6. DECREE OF PEACE*

November 8, 1917

The Workers' and Peasants' Government, created by the revolution of October 24th and 25th [November 6th and 7th] and based on the Soviet of Workers', Soldiers', and Peasants' Deputies, proposes to all warring peoples and their Governments to begin immediately negotiations for a just and democratic peace.

An overwhelming majority of the exhausted, wearied, and war-tortured workers and the laboring classes of all the warring countries are longing for a just and democratic peace—a peace which in the most definite and insistent manner was demanded by Russian workers and peasants after the overthrow of the Tsar's monarchy. Such a peace the Government considers to be an immediate peace without annexations (i.e. without seizure of foreign territory, without the forcible annexation of foreign nationalities) and without indemnities.

The Government of Russia proposes to all warring peoples immediately to conclude such a peace. It expresses its readiness to take at once without the slightest delay, all the decisive steps until the final confirmation of all terms of such a peace by the plenipotentiary conventions of the representatives of all countries and all nations. . . .

The Government considers it to be the greatest crime against humanity to continue the war for the sake of dividing among the powerful and rich nations the weaker nationalities which were seized by them, and the Government solemnly states its readiness to sign immediately the terms of peace which will end this war, on the basis of the above-stated conditions, equally just for all nationalities without exception. At the same time the Government announces that it does not consider the above-stated conditions of peace as in the nature of an ultimatum, that is, it is ready to consider any other terms of peace, insisting, however, that such be proposed as soon as possible by any one of the warring countries and on condition of the most definite clarity and absolute exclusion of any ambiguousness, or any secrecy when proposing the terms of peace.

* U.S. House of Representatives, Committee on Un-American Activities, *The Communist Conspiracy*, House Report No. 2241, 84th Congress, 2nd session (1956), Part I, pp. 8–10, *excerpts*. The "Decree of Peace" was adopted at a Meeting of the All-Russian Congress of Soviets of Workers', Soldiers', and Peasants' Deputies on November 8, 1917.

The Government abolishes secret diplomacy and on its part expresses the firm intention to carry on all negotiations absolutely openly before all the people, and immediately begins to publish in full the secret treaties concluded or confirmed by the Government of landowners and capitalists from February up to November 7th, 1917. The Government abrogates absolutely and immediately all the provisions of these secret treaties in as much as they were intended in the majority of cases for the purpose of securing profits and privileges for Russian landowners and capitalists and retaining or increasing the annexations by the Great Russians.

While addressing the proposal to the Governments and peoples of all countries to start immediately open negotiations for the conclusion of peace, the Government expresses its readiness to carry on these negotiations by written communications, by telegraph, as well as by parleys of the representatives of various countries, or at a conference of such representatives. To facilitate such negotiations the Government appoints a plenipotentiary representative in neutral countries.

The Government proposes to all the Governments and peoples of all the warring countries to conclude an armistice immediately; at the same time, it considers desirable that this armistice should be conducted for a period of not less than three months— that is, a period during which it would be fully possible to terminate the negotiations for peace with the participation of the representatives of all peoples and nationalities drawn into the war or compelled to participate in it, as well as to call the plenipotentiary conventions of people's representatives of all countries for the final ratification of the terms of peace.

While addressing this proposal of peace to the Governments and peoples of all warring countries, the Provisional Workers' and Peasants' Government of Russia appeals also in particular to the class-conscious workers of the three most forward nations of the world and the largest states participating in the present war— England, France, and Germany. The workers of these countries have been of the greatest service to the cause of progress and socialism. We have the great example of the Chartist movement in England, several revolutions which were of universal historic importance accomplished by the French proletariat, and finally the heroic struggle against the *exclusive* law in Germany and the prolonged, stubborn, disciplined work—a work setting an example for the workers of the whole world—of creating mass proletarian organizations in Germany. All these examples of proletarian heroism and historic creative work serve as a guarantee that the workers of the above-mentioned countries understand the duties which devolve upon them now in the cause of the liberation of humanity from the horrors of war and its consequences, a cause which these workers by their resolute and energetic activity will help us to bring to a successful end—the cause of peace, and together with this, the cause of the liberation of the laboring and exploited.

The Brest-Litovsk Crisis

7. THESES ON THE QUESTION OF THE IMMEDIATE CONCLUSION OF A SEPARATE AND ANNEXATIONIST PEACE*

January 20, 1918

V. I. LENIN

1. The position of the Russian revolution at the present moment is that almost all the workers and the vast majority of the peasants undoubtedly support the Soviet Government and the Socialist revolution which it has started. To that extent the success of the Socialist revolution in Russia is assured.

2. At the same time, the civil war, provoked by the frantic resistance of the wealthy classes, who fully realize that the last and decisive fight for the preservation of private ownership of the land and means of production is before them, has not yet reached its climax. The victory of Soviet power in this war is assured, but some time must inevitably pass, no little exertion of effort will inevitably be demanded, a known period of acute devastation and chaos, usually associated with all wars, and civil war in particular, is inevitable before the resistance of the bourgeoisie will be crushed.

3. Besides, this resistance, in its less active and nonmilitary forms—sabotage, corruption of the deposed groups and of agents

* V. I. Lenin, *Sochinenia*, 2nd ed. (Moscow: State Publishing House, 1930), Vol. xxii, pp. 193–199, *excerpts*. Editor's translation.

of the bourgeoisie, who worm their way into the ranks of the socialists in order to ruin their cause, and so on and so forth— has proved so stubborn and capable of assuming so many diversified forms, that the struggle to counter it will inevitably take some time, and, in its main forms, is scarcely likely to end before several months. And without a decisive victory over the passive and covert resistance of the bourgeoisie and its supporters, the success of the socialist revolution cannot be possible.

4. Finally, the organizational problems of the Socialist transformation of Russia are so great and difficult that their solution . . . will demand a fairly long time.

5. All these circumstances taken together are such as to make it perfectly clear that for the success of socialism in Russia a certain amount of time, not less than several months, will be necessary, during which time the Socialist Government must have a completely free hand for first vanquishing the bourgeoisie in our own country and for taking care of the widespread and far-reaching mass organizational work.

6. The situation of the Socialist revolution in Russia must be understood in terms of the international tasks of our Soviet state, for the international situation in the fourth year of the war is such that the probable moment of the outbreak of revolution or overthrow of any of the European imperialist governments (including the German) is quite impossible to estimate. That the Socialist revolution in Europe must come, and will come, is beyond doubt. All our hopes for the *final* victory of socialism are based on this certainty and on this scientific prediction. Our propagandist activities in general, and the organization of fraternization in particular, must be intensified and broadened. But it would be a mistake to predicate the tactics of the Socialist Government in Russia on attempts to determine whether the European, and especially the German, Socialist revolution will take place in the next six months (or a similarly short period) or not. As it is impossible to determine this, all such attempts, objectively speaking, would be but a blind gamble.

7. The peace negotiations in Brest-Litovsk have by this date —January 20, 1918—made it perfectly clear that in the German government (which leads the other governments of the Quadruple Alliance by the halter) there is no doubt that the upper hand has been gained by the military party, which has virtually presented Russia with an ultimatum (and it is expected, it is necessary to expect, that any day now it will be presented formally). The ultimatum is as follows: either the continuation of the war, or an annexationist peace, i.e. peace on the condition that we surrender all the territory we occupy, while the Germans

keep *all* the territory they occupy and impose upon us an indemnity (outwardly disguised as payment for the maintenance of prisoners), an indemnity of about three thousand million rubles, payable in several years.

8. The demanding question of whether to accept this annexationist peace now, or immediately to wage a revolutionary war, faces the Socialist Government of Russia. Actually, no middle course is possible. No further delay is feasible, for we have *already* tried everything possible and impossible artificially to protract the negotiations.

9. Examining the arguments for an immediate revolutionary war, we encounter first of all the argument that a separate peace now would be, objectively speaking, an agreement with the German imperialists, an "imperialist deal," and so forth, and that, consequently, would be at complete variance with the basic principles of proletarian internationalism.

But this argument is clearly incorrect. Workers, who lose a strike, signing terms for the resumption of work which are unfavorable to them and favorable to the capitalists, do not betray socialism. Only those betray socialism who barter advantages for part of the workers in exchange for advantages to the capitalists, only such agreements are in principle impermissible.

Whoever calls a war with German imperialism a defensive and just war, but actually receives support from the Anglo-French imperialists, and hides from the people secret treaties concluded with them, betrays socialism. Whoever does not conceal anything from the people, and does not conclude any secret treaties with the imperialists, but agrees to sign terms of peace unfavorable for the weak nation and favorable to the imperialists of one group, if at the given moment he has no strength to continue the war, he does not betray socialism in the slightest degree.

10. Another argument for immediate war is that, by concluding peace, we, objectively speaking, become agents of German imperialism, for we give it the opportunity to release troops from our front, surrender to it millions of prisoners, and the like. But this argument is also clearly incorrect, for a revolutionary war at the present moment would make us, objectively speaking, agents of Anglo-French imperialism, by giving it subsidiary forces. The British bluntly offered our commander in chief, Krylenko, one hundred rubles per month for every one of our soldiers provided we continued the war. Even if we did not take a single kopek from the Anglo-French, we would all, objectively speaking, be helping them by diverting part of the German army. From this point of view, we would not entirely escape some

sort of imperialist tie, and it is evident that it is impossible to do so entirely without overthrowing world imperialism. The correct conclusion from this is that with the victory of a Socialist Government in any one country, questions must be decided, not from the point of view of whether this or that imperialism is preferable, but exclusively from the point of view of the best conditions for the development and consolidation of the Socialist revolution which has already begun.

In other words, the underlying principle of our tactics must not be which of the two imperialisms is it now more profitable to assist, but rather, how can the Socialist revolution most faithfully and reliably ensure the possibility of strengthening itself, or, at least, of maintaining itself in one country until it is joined by other countries.

11. It is said that the German Social-Democratic opponents of the war have now become "defeatists" and are requesting us not to surrender to German imperialism. But we recognized defeatism only in respect to *one's own* imperialist bourgeoisie, and victory over an alien imperialism, which is achieved in formal or actual alliance with a "friendly" imperialism, we have always rejected as a method intolerable in principle and unworthy in general.

The present argument is therefore only a modification of the previous one. If the German Left Social-Democrats were proposing that we delay negotiating a separate peace for a *definite* period, guaranteeing revolutionary action in Germany in this period, the question *might* become a different matter for us. Not only do the German leftists not say this, but, on the contrary, they formally declare: "Hold out as long as you can, but decide the question from the standpoint of the state of affairs in the *Russian* Socialist revolution, for it is impossible to promise you anything positive regarding the German revolution."

12. It is said that we definitely "promised" a revolutionary war in a series of party declarations, and that by concluding a separate peace we would be betraying our word.

This is untrue. We spoke of the *necessity* for a Socialist Government in an era of imperialism *"to prepare for and wage"* a revolutionary war; we said this in order to fight abstract pacifism and the theory of "defense of the fatherland," and, finally, to counter the purely selfish instincts of part of the soldiers; but we never gave any pledge to start a revolutionary war without taking into consideration the extent to which it is possible to wage such a war at any given moment.

Unquestionably, we must *prepare* for a revolutionary war. We are carrying out this promise, as we have in general carried out all our promises which could be carried out at once; we abrogated the secret treaties, offered all nations a just peace, and several times tried to prolong the peace negotiations in order to give other nations a chance to join us.

But the question whether it is possible to wage a revolutionary war *now and at once* should be decided only from the standpoint of whether material conditions permit it, and of the interests of the Socialist revolution which has already begun.

13. Having considered the arguments in favor of an immediate revolutionary war, we are forced to the conclusion that such a policy might perhaps answer the human craving for the beautiful, the dramatic, and the vivid, but it would certainly ignore the objective relation of class forces and material factors at the present moment of the Socialist revolution.

14. There can be no doubt but that our army at the present, and for the next few weeks (and probably for the next few months) is absolutely in no condition to resist a German offensive successfully: first, due to the extreme fatigue and weariness of the majority of the soldiers and the incredible confusion relating to supply and replacement problems; second, due to the utter unfitness of our horses, which dooms our artillery to inevitable destruction; and third, due to the utter impossibility of defending the coast from Riga to Revel, which gives the enemy a great opportunity of capturing the rest of Livonia, then Estonia, and of outflanking a large part of our forces, and finally, of capturing Petrograd.

15. Further, there is no doubt that the peasant majority of our army would be at the present time unreservedly favor an annexationist peace, and not an immediate revolutionary war; for the Socialist reorganization of the army and the merging of the Red Guard detachments with it have only just begun.

With the complete democratization of the army, to wage war against the wishes of the majority of the soldiers would be sheer adventurism, while the creation of a really staunch and ideologically strong Socialist workers' and peasants' army will require months and months, at least.

16. The poor peasantry in Russia is able to support a Socialist revolution led by the working class, but it is presently incapable of a serious revolutionary war. It would be a fatal mistake to ignore this objective relation of class forces at this time.

17. The present situation in regard to a revolutionary war is as follows:

If the German revolution would break out and triumph in the coming three or four months, then, perhaps, the tactics of an immediate revolutionary war would not ruin our Socialist revolution.

If, however, the German revolution does not occur in the

next few months, the course of events, given the continuation of the war, will inevitably be such that a smashing defeat will force Russia to conclude a far more disadvantageous separate peace, a peace that would be concluded, not by a Socialist Government, but by some other . . . For the peasant army, which is unendurably exhausted by the war, will, after the first defeats —and probably, even within a matter not of months but of weeks—overthrow the Socialist workers' Government.

18. In such a situation it would be absolutely intolerable tactics to stake the fate of the Socialist revolution which has already begun in Russia on the mere chance that the German revolution may begin in the near future, within a period estimated in weeks. Such tactics would be reckless. We do not have the right to gamble thusly.

19. And the German revolution will not be made more difficult, as far as its objective foundations are concerned, if we conclude a separate peace. Probably, the chauvinist intoxication will weaken it for a time, but the position of Germany will remain extremely grave, the war with Britain and America will be a prolonged one, and the aggressive imperialism of both sides will be fully exposed. A Socialist Soviet Republic in Russia will stand as a living example to the peoples of all countries, and the propaganda and revolutionary effect of this example will be enormous. There—the bourgeois system and a naked war of aggrandizement by two groups of plunderers. Here—peace and a Socialist republic of Soviets.

20. In concluding a separate peace, we free ourselves *as much as is possible at the present time* from both hostile imperialist groups, exploiting their hostility and war—to thwart concerted action on their part against us—and use this period to advance and consolidate the Socialist revolution. The reorganization of Russia on the basis of the dictatorship of the proletariat, and on the basis of the nationalization of the banks and large-scale industry, coupled with the exchange of goods in kind between the towns and the small peasants' societies, is economically possible, provided we are assured a few months peace in which to work. And such a reorganization will make socialism invincible both in Russia and all over the world, creating with that a solid economic basis for a mighty workers' and peasants' Red Army.

21. A really revolutionary war at the present time would mean a war waged by the Socialist republic against the bourgeois countries, with the aim, clearly defined and completely approved by the Socialist army, of overthrowing the bourgeoisie in other countries. We *obviously* are unable to achieve this objective at this *given* moment. We would be fighting now, objectively speak-

ing, for the liberation of Poland, Lithuania and Courland. But no Marxist, without flouting the principles of Marxism and of socialism generally, can deny that the interests of socialism are higher than the interests of the right of nations to self-determination. Our Socialist republic has done all it could, and continues to do so, for the realization of the right of self-determination for Finland, the Ukraine, etc. But if the concrete position of affairs is such that the existence of the Socialist republic is endangered at the present moment because of the violation of the right of self-determination of several nations (Poland, Lithuania, etc.), then, naturally, the preservation of the Socialist republic has the higher priority . . .

The Allied Intervention and the
Beginnings of "War Communism"

8. REPORT ON SOVIET FOREIGN POLICY TO THE FIFTH ALL-RUSSIAN CONGRESS OF SOVIETS*

July 4, 1918

GEORGI V. CHICHERIN

During the period following the conclusion of the Brest treaty, Russia's foreign policy has gone along lines different from those followed in the first months after the October Revolution. At the end of 1917 and the beginning of 1918 the basic feature of our foreign policy was the revolutionary offensive. It took its bearings from the immediate prospect of the world revolution, for which the Russian revolution was to serve as the signal. It was directed, over the heads of Governments, to the revolutionary proletariat

* Jane Degras, *Soviet Documents on Foreign Policy* (New York: Oxford University Press, 1951), Vol. I, pp. 83–85, *excerpts*. Published by permission of the Oxford University Press and the Royal Institute of International Affairs.

of all countries, and both in its actions, sharply opposed to the entire nature of existing capitalist Governments, and in its words, its strongly agitational offensives were calculated to stir up the revolutionary proletariat of all countries to an international revolutionary struggle against imperialism, against the capitalist system.

When the failure of any immediate support from the proletariat of other countries led to the defeat of the revolutionary Russian forces by Austro-German imperialism, to the occupation of Finland, the Ukraine, the Baltic provinces, Poland, Lithuania, and White Russia by the armed forces of German and Austro-Hungarian imperialism, the setting of Soviet Russia's foreign policy changed radically. For the last four months it has been compelled to pursue the aim of pushing off and postponing the dangers threatening it from all sides, trying to gain as much time as possible, both in order to give the growing proletarian movement in other countries time to ripen, and to gain more time for the new forms of political and social relationships established by the Soviet Government to take root among the popular masses of Russia, and to tie them more closely to the Soviet program.

Not having yet succeeded in creating adequate fighting forces for the defense of the country, surrounded by enemies awaiting its ruin, suffering from the incredible destruction brought about by war and tsarism, Soviet Russia in its foreign policy had all the time to keep in mind the need of avoiding the dangers threatening its destruction at every step. This policy of delay was possible thanks to the conflict of interests not only between the two coalitions, but also within each of them, and even within the imperialist camp of each belligerent country. The struggle on the western front has for the present tied up the forces of both coalitions so much that neither has decided to go all out openly for the destruction of Russia. Some imperialists in both coalitions think of the future after the war, of economic relations with Russia, this world market most capable of expansion. Instead of a policy of robbery, these elements in both coalitions would prefer a policy of trade, of concessions and economic conquests. Some of the military elements think of the part Russia could play, even in the present war. The hope of dragging Russia into war, at a time when it is re-creating its military power, is a factor entering into the calculations of both coalitions. So, side by side with the war parties in both coalitions who advocate an offensive to crush Soviet Russia, there are other elements supporting this policy.

The Soviet Government, having decided to conduct a policy of waiting, of maneuvering, for it is not anxious for military revenge, but is convinced that the social changes called forth by the war will lead to new relations between the nations, was compelled to yield, even after Brest, to force of arms, and also to take into account in its foreign policy the influence of elements acting against the war parties. These elements are weak, and we are not yet in a position to reinforce their influence with our own military power; the revolutionary proletarian movement, which is growing everywhere, has not yet reached the point of explosion, and therefore the report which we have to give is a grave report, a report on our retreats, a report of great sacrifices made in order to give Russia the opportunity of recuperating, of organizing its forces, and awaiting the moment when the proletariat of other countries will help us to complete the socialist revolution we began in October. . . .

9. REPORT TO THE SEVENTH ALL-RUSSIAN CONGRESS OF SOVIETS OF WORKERS', PEASANTS', RED ARMY, AND COSSACK DEPUTIES*

December 5, 1919

V. I. LENIN

We have always said, both before the October Revolution and during the October Revolution, that we consider ourselves, and can consider ourselves, only as one of the detachments of the international army of the proletariat, a detachment which assumed an advanced position not only because of the development and training it had received, but because of the unique conditions existing in Russia; and that, therefore, the victory of the socialist revolution can be regarded as final only when the proletariat has triumphed at least in several of the advanced countries. And it is in this respect that we experienced most

* V. I. Lenin, *Sochinenia*, 4th ed. (Moscow: Institute of Marx-Engels-Lenin, 1950), Vol. xxx, pp. 185–197, *excerpts*. Editor's translation.

difficulty . . . We found out that the development of the revolution in the more advanced countries is much slower, much more difficult and much more complex. This should not astonish us, for it was naturally far easier for a country like Russia to begin the socialist revolution than it is for advanced countries. But, at any rate, this slower, more complex, more zigzag type of development of the socialist revolution in Western Europe has confronted us with incredible difficulties. And first of all, one is inclined to ask: How can we explain the miracle that Soviet authority has managed to maintain itself in power for two years in a backward, poverty-stricken, and war-weary country, in spite of the obstinate struggle waged against it first by German imperialism, which was then considered as omnipotent, and then by the imperialism of the Entente, which a year ago settled accounts with Germany, knew no competitors, and lorded it over every country of the world without the smallest exception. Considered from the point of a simple calculation of forces, from the point of military strength, that is indeed a miracle, because the Entente was, and is, immeasurably more powerful than we. Nevertheless, what more than anything else distinguished the year under review is the fact that we gained a gigantic victory— so great a victory, that one might perhaps, without exaggeration, say that *our main difficulties are already behind us.* However great may be the dangers and difficulties that still lie before us, the greatest are apparently behind us. We must clearly understand the reason for this, and, what is more important, correctly define our policy in the future, for the future will no doubt see other attempts by the Entente to repeat its intervention and, perhaps, there will again appear the old predatory alliance between international and Russian capitalists for the restoration of the power of the landlords and capitalists and for the overthrow of Soviet authority in Russia—in a word, an alliance whose aim will be to extinguish the hearth of the world socialist conflagration which the RSFSR has become.

When the history of the Entente intervention and the political lesson which we received are considered from this point of view, I can say that this period of history is divided into three main stages, in each of which we secured a profound and lasting victory.

The first stage, and the one that was naturally most accessible and easy for the Entente, was its attempt to defeat Soviet Russia by means of its own troops. Of course, after the Entente had defeated Germany it had armies of millions of men at its disposal, armies that had not yet openly declared for peace and had not yet recovered from the bugbear of German imperialism with which they had been frightened in every Western country. Of course, at that time, from the military point of view and from the point of view of foreign policy, it meant nothing for the Entente to take a tenth of its armies and send it to Russia. You must note that it had complete control over the seas, complete control over the navy. The transport of troops and supplies was entirely in its hands. Had the Entente, which hated us as only the bourgeoisie can hate a socialist revolution, succeeded at that time in throwing one-tenth of its armies against us there is not the slightest doubt that the fate of Soviet Russia would have been sealed and would have had the same fate as befell Hungary [an attempted Communist coup failed in 1919].

Why did the Entente fail to do this? It landed troops in Murmansk. The campaign in Siberia was undertaken with the aid of Entente troops, and Japanese troops still occupy a remote part of eastern Siberia, while the troops of all the states of the Entente were to be found, although not in large numbers, in every part of western Siberia. Then French troops landed in the south of Russia. This was the first stage of the international intervention in our affairs, the first attempt, so to speak, to strangle Soviet power with troops which the Entente took from its own armies, i.e., the workers and peasants of the more advanced countries; and these troops, moreover, were well-equipped, and, in general, as regards the technical and material conditions of the campaign, there was no demand that the Entente was not in a position to satisfy. There were no obstacles in its way. How then is one to explain the failure of this attempt? In the end the Entente was obliged to withdraw its troops from Russia, because these troops proved unfit to carry on a struggle against revolutionary Soviet Russia. That, comrades, has always been our chief and fundamental argument. From the very beginning of the revolution we have said that we represent the party of the international proletariat, and that, no matter how great the difficulties of the revolution were, a time would come—and at the most crucial moment—when the sympathy and the solidarity of the workers oppressed by international imperialism would make themselves felt. For this we were accused of utopianism. But experience has shown that if we cannot always depend on action being taken by the proletariat, and if we cannot always depend on all the actions it takes, it can nevertheless be said that these two years of world history have proven that we were a thousand times right . . . in spite of our backwardness, in spite of the difficulties accompanying our struggle, the workers and peasants of England and France have shown themselves incapable of fighting us on our soil. . . .

After this first victory came the second stage in the intervention of the Entente in our affairs. At the head of every nation is a group of politicians who possess splendid experience, and who therefore, having lost one card, put their stakes on another, utilizing their domination over all the world. There is not a single country, there is not a single corner of the globe left where British, French, and American finance capital is not in fact in complete control. On this was based their new attempt. They attempted to compel the small states surrounding Russia, many of which had emancipated themselves and had received the opportunity of declaring their independence only during the period of the war—Poland, Estonia, Finland, Georgia, the Ukraine, etc.—to wage war on Russia with the assistance of British, French, and American money. . . . The Entente met resistance bringing pressure on the small countries. The Finnish bourgeoisie (for example) which has stifled tens of thousands of Finnish workers during the White terror and knows that it will never be forgiven for having done so, and that it is no longer supported by the German bayonets which gave it the opportunity to do so—this Finnish bourgeoisie hates the Bolsheviks with all the passion with which a plunderer of workers hates those who have thrown him off. Nevertheless, the Finnish bourgeoisie said to itself: "If we follow the instructions of the Entente, it means losing absolutely all hope of independence." And this independence had been granted them by the Bolsheviks in November 1917, when there was a bourgeois government in Finland. Thus, wide circles of the Finnish bourgeoisie wavered. We won the contest against the Entente because it had counted upon the small nations, yet, at the same time it had antagonized them . . . the small countries acted as we wanted them to act not because the Polish, Finnish, Lithuanian, and Latvian bourgeoisie derived any satisfaction in conducting their policy to the advantage of the Bolsheviks—that, of course, is nonsense—but because we were right in our definition of the universal-historical forces, namely, that either bestial capital would triumph, and, in such circumstances, no matter how democratic the republic—it would strangle every small nation of the world; or else the dictatorship of the proletariat would triumph, and only in this was there hope for the toilers and for all small, downtrodden, and weak nations. We showed that we were right not only in the theory, but also in the practice of world politics. . . .

This, comrades, the second stage of the international intervention, was our second historic triumph. In the first place, we deprived England, France, and America of their workers and peasants. Their troops would not fight against us. In the second place, we deprived them of these small countries, which are all against us and in every one of which a bourgeois government and not a Soviet government rules. . . .

But our successes did not stop with this . . . thirdly, within the Entente countries themselves we have started to deprive the Entente of the petty bourgeoisie and the educated middle classes which were formerly entirely hostile to us. [Lenin then read a declaration, signed by several leading French intellectuals, calling for an end to the Allied intervention in Russia.] . . . This is perhaps but a verbal expression of feeling on the part of a representative of the intelligentsia; but it may be said that this is our third victory over imperialist France, a victory won on French territory. That is what is shown by this declaration, a faltering and pitiful declaration in itself, but a declaration of the intelligentsia, who, as we have seen in tens and hundreds of instances, can make a million times more noise than their strength warrants, and who possess the ability of serving as a good barometer and of indicating whither the petty bourgoisie is tending. . . .

Organizing for World Revolution

10. STATUTES OF THE COMMUNIST INTERNATIONAL*

*Adopted at the Second Comintern Congress,
August 4, 1920*

The Communist International fully and unreservedly upholds the gains of the great proletarian revolution in Russia, the first victorious socialist revolution in the world's history, and calls upon all workers to follow the same road. The Communist International makes it its duty to support with all the power at its disposal every Soviet Republic, wherever it may be formed.

The Communist International is aware that for the purpose of a speedy achievement of victory the International Association of

* U.S. House of Representatives, Committee on Un-American Activities, *The Communist Conspiracy*, House Report No. 2242, 84th Congress, 2nd session (1956), Part I, Section C, pp. 25–28, *excerpts*.

Workers, which is struggling for the abolition of capitalism and the establishment of Communism, should possess a firm and centralized organization. To all intents and purposes the Communist International should represent a single universal Communist Party, of which the parties operating in every country form individual sections. The organized apparatus of the Communist International is to secure to the toilers of every country the possibility at any given moment of obtaining the maximum of aid from the organized workers of the other countries.

For this purpose the Communist International confirms the following items of its statutes:

1. The new International Association of Workers is established for the purpose of organizing common activity of the workers of various countries who are striving towards a single aim: the overthrow of capitalism; the establishment of the dictatorship of the proletariat and of the International Soviet Republic; the complete abolition of classes; and the realization of socialism—the first stage of Communist society.

2. The new International Association of Workers has been given the name of The Communist International.

3. All the parties and organizations comprising the Communist International bear the name of the Communist Party of the given country (section of the Communist International).

4. The World Congress of all parties and organizations which form part of the Communist International is the supreme organ of this International. The World Congress confirms the programs of the various parties comprising the Communist International. The World Congress discusses and decides the more important questions of program and tactics, which are connected with the activity of the Communist International. . . .

5. The World Congress elects an Executive Committee of the Communist International which serves as the leading organ of the Communist International in the interval between the convention of World Congresses, and is responsible only to the World Congress.

6. The residence of the Executive Committee of the Communist International is every time decided at the World Congress of the Communist International.

7. A special World Congress of the Communist International may be convened either by regulation of the Executive Committee, or at the demand of one-half of the number of the parties which were part of the Communist International at the last World Congress.

8. The chief bulk of the work and greatest responsibility in the Executive Committee of the Communist International lie with

the party of that country where, in keeping with the regulation of the World Congress, the Executive Committee finds its residence at the time. . . .

9. The Executive Committee is the leading organ of the Communist International between the conventions; the Executive Committee publishes in no less than four languages the central organ of the Communist International [the periodical *The Communist International*]. The Executive Committee makes the necessary appeals on behalf of the Communist International, and issues instructions obligatory on all the parties and organizations which form part of the Communist International. The Executive Committee of the Communist International enjoys the right to demand from the affiliated parties the exclusion of groups of members who are guilty of the infringement of international proletarian discipline, as well as the exclusion from the Communist International of parties guilty of the infringement of the regulations of the World Congress. In the event of necessity the Executive Committee organizes in various countries its technical and auxiliary bureaus, which are entirely under the control of the Executive Committee.

10. The Executive Committee of the Communist International enjoys the right to include in its ranks representatives of organizations and parties not accepted in the Communist International, but which are sympathetic towards communism; these are to have a consultative vote only.

11. The organs of all the parties and organizations forming part of the Communist International as well as of those which are recognized sympathizers of the Communist International, are obliged to publish all official regulations of the Communist International and of its Executive Committee.

12. The general state of things in the whole of Europe and of America makes necessary for the Communists of the whole world an obligatory formation of illegal Communist organizations along with those existing legally. The Executive Committee should take charge of the universal application of this rule.

13. All the most important political relations between the individual parties forming part of the Communist International will generally be carried on through the medium of the Executive Committee of the Communist International. In cases of exigency direct relations will be established, with the provision, however, that the ECCI shall be informed of them at the same time.

14. The Trade Unions that have accepted the Communist platform and are united on an international scale under the control of the ECCI, form Trade Union Sections of the Communist International. . . .

11. CONDITIONS OF ADMISSION TO THE COMMUNIST INTERNATIONAL*

Approved by the Second Comintern Congress,
August 6, 1920

The Communist International is being threatened with the danger of dilution with the fluctuating and half-and-half groups which have as yet not abandoned the ideology of the Second International. . . .

In view of this the Second World Congress finds it necessary to establish more definite conditions for the joining of new parties, as well as to point out to such parties as have already joined the Communist International the duties which are laid upon them.

The Second Congress of the Communist International rules that the conditions for joining the Communist International shall be as follows:

1. The general propaganda and agitation should bear a really Communist character, and should correspond to the program and decisions of the Third International. The entire party press should be edited by reliable Communists who have proved their loyalty to the cause of the proletarian revolution. The dictatorship of the proletariat should not be spoken of simply as a current hackneyed formula, it should be advocated in such a way that its necessity should be apparent to every rank-and-file working man and woman, to each soldier and peasant, and should emanate from everyday facts systematically recorded by our press day by day.

All periodicals and other publications, as well as all party publications and editions, are subject to the control of the presidium of the party, independently of whether the party is legal or illegal. The editors should in no way be given an opportunity to abuse their autonomy and carry on a policy not fully corresponding to the policy of the party.

Wherever the followers of the Third International have access, and whatever means of propaganda are at their disposal, whether the columns of newspapers, popular meetings, labor unions or

* U.S. House of Representatives, Committee on Un-American Activities, *The Communist Conspiracy,* House Report No. 2242, 84th Congress, 2nd session (1956), Part I, Section C, pp. 40–44, *excerpts.*

cooperatives—it is indispensable for them not only to denounce the bourgeoisie, but also its assistants and agents—reformists of every color and shade.

2. Every organization desiring to join the Communist International shall be bound systematically and regularly to remove from all the responsible posts in the labor movement (party organizations, editors, labor unions, etc.) all reformists and followers of the "center," and to have them replaced by Communists, even at the cost of replacing at the beginning "experienced" men by rank-and-file working men.

3. The class struggle in almost every country of Europe and America is entering the phase of civil war. Under such conditions the Communists can have no confidence in bourgeois laws. They should create everywhere a parallel illegal apparatus, which at the decisive moment should do its duty by the party, and in every way possible assist the revolution. In every country, where in consequence of martial law or of other exceptional laws, the Communists are unable to carry on their work lawfully, a combination of lawful and unlawful work is absolutely necessary.

4. A persistent and systematic propaganda and agitation is necessary in the army, where Communist groups should be formed in every military organization. Wherever, owing to repressive legislation, agitation becomes impossible, it is necessary to carry on such agitation illegally. But refusal to carry on or participate in such work should be considered equal to treason to the revolutionary cause, and incompatible with affiliation with the Third International.

5. A systematic and regular propaganda is necessary in the rural districts. The working class can gain no victory unless it possesses the sympathy and support of at least part of the rural workers and of the poor peasants, and unless other sections of the population are equally utilized. . . .

6. Every party desirous of affiliating with the Third International should renounce not only avowed social patriotism, but also the falsehood and the hypocrisy of social pacifism; it should systematically demonstrate to the workers that without a revolutionary overthrow of capitalism no international arbitration, no talk of disarmament, no democratic reorganization of the League of Nations will be capable of saving mankind from new imperialist wars.

7. Parties desirous of joining the Communist International must recognize the necessity of a complete and absolute rupture with reformism and the policy of the "centrists," and must advocate this rupture amongst the widest circles of the party membership, without which condition a consistent Communist

policy is impossible. The Communist International demands unconditionally and peremptorily that such rupture be brought about with the least possible delay. . . .

8. Every party desirous of belonging to the Third International should be bound to denounce without any reserve all the methods of "its own" imperialists in the colonies, supporting not only in words but practically a movement of liberation in the colonies. It should demand the expulsion of its own imperialists from such colonies . . . and carry on a systematic agitation in its own army against every kind of oppression of the colonial population.

9. Every party desirous of belonging to the Communist International should be bound to carry on systematic and persistent Communist work in the labor unions, cooperatives and other labor organizations of the masses. It is necessary to form Communist groups within the organizations, which by persistent and lasting work should win over labor unions to Communism . . . These Communist groups should be completely subordinated to the party in general.

10. Any party belonging to the Communist International . . . should support by all means in its power the international unification of Red labor unions, adhering to the Communist International. . . .

11. Parties desirous of joining the Third International shall be bound to inspect the personnel of their parliamentary factions, to remove all unreliable elements therefrom, to control such factions, not only verbally but in reality, to subordinate them to the Central Committee of the party, and to demand from each proletarian Communist that he devote his entire activity to the interests of real revolutionary propaganda.

12. All parties belonging to the Communist International should be formed on the basis of the principle of democratic centralization. At the present time of acute civil war the Communist Party will be able fully to do its duty only when it is organized in a sufficiently thorough way, when it possesses an iron discipline, and when its party center enjoys the confidence of the members of the party, who are to endow this center with complete power, authority and ample rights.

13. The Communist parties of those countries where the Communist activity is legal, should make a clearance of their members from time to time, as well as those of the party organizations, in order systematically to free the party from the petty bourgeois elements which penetrate into it.

14. Each party desirous of affiliating with the Communist International should be obliged to render every possible assistance to the Soviet Republics in their struggle against all counter-

revolutionary forces. The Communist parties should carry on a precise and definite propaganda to induce the workers to refuse to transport any kind of military equipment intended for fighting against the Soviet Republics, and should also by legal or illegal means carry on a propaganda amongst the troops sent against the workers' republics.

15. All those parties which up to the present moment have stood upon the old social and democratic programs should, within the shortest time possible, draw up a new Communist program in conformity with the special conditions of their country, and in accordance with the resolutions of the Communist International . . .

16. All the resolutions of the congresses of the Communist International, as well as the resolutions of the Executive Committee are binding for all parties joining the Communist International . . .

17. Each party desirous of joining the Communist International should bear the following name: Communist Party of such and such a country, section of the Third Communist International. The question of the renaming of a party is not only a formal one, but is a political question of great importance. The Communist International has declared a decisive war against the entire bourgeois world, and all the yellow Social Democratic parties. It is indispensable that every rank-and-file worker should be able clearly to distinguish between the Communist parties and the old official "Social Democratic" or "Socialist" parties, which have betrayed the cause of the working class.

18. All the leading organs of the press of every party are bound to publish all the most important documents of the Executive Committee of the Communist International.

19. All those parties which have joined the Communist International, as well as those which have expressed a desire to do so, are obliged in as short a space of time as possible, and in no case later than four months after the Second Congress of the Communist International, to convene an Extraordinary Congress in order to discuss these conditions. . . .

20. All those parties which at the present time are willing to join the Third International, but have so far not changed their tactics in any radical manner, should, prior to their joining the Third International, take care that not less than two-thirds of their committee members and of all their central institutions should be composed of comrades who have made an open and definite declaration prior to the convening of the Second Congress, as to their desire that the party should affiliate with the Third International . . .

21. Those members of the party who reject the conditions and the theses of the Third International, are liable to be excluded from the party.

The End of Intervention: The
Beginning of Accommodation

12. SPEECH AT A MEETING OF ACTIVISTS OF THE MOSCOW ORGANIZATION*

December 6, 1920

V. I. LENIN

Are there any radical antagonisms in the contemporary capitalist world that must be utilized? There are three principal antagonisms which I should like to enumerate. First, the one nearest to us, is the relationship between Japan and America. War is brewing between them. They cannot live in peace on the shores of the Pacific, although these shores are separated by three thousand versts. This rivalry is unquestionably due to the relations between their capitalisms. . . . The practical task of Communist policy is to take advantage of this hostility and to incite one against the other. . . .

Another antagonism is the one between America and the rest of the capitalist world. Nearly the whole of the capitalist world of "victors" emerged from the war with enormous gains. America is strong; everybody is now in debt to her, everything depends on her, she is more hated, she robs everybody, and is doing so in a very original way. She has no colonies. England emerged from the war with vast colonies, as did France. England offered America a mandate—that is the language they use nowadays—over one of the seized colonies, but America refused. Evidently American merchants reason somewhat differently. They saw that

* V. I. Lenin, *Sochinenia*, 4th ed. (Moscow: Institute of Marx-Engels-Lenin, 1950), Vol. xxxi, pp. 414–427, *excerpts*. Editor's translation.

war plays a definite part both as regards the resulting ruin and as regards the temper of the workers, and they came to the conclusion that there was no profit in accepting a mandate. But, naturally, they will not allow this colony to be used by other states . . . America cannot come to terms with Europe—that is a fact proven by history . . .

And the third rift is between the Entente and Germany. Germany has been vanquished, crushed by the Versailles Treaty, but she possesses enormous economic potentialities. Germany is the second country in the world in the level of economic development, if America is considered as the first. The experts even say that in the electrical industry she is superior to America, and you know that the electrical industry has tremendous importance. America is superior with respect to the application of electricity, but in technical perfection Germany is superior. And on such a country has been imposed the Versailles Treaty, a Treaty under which she cannot possibly live. Germany is one of the most powerful and advanced of the capitalist countries; she cannot tolerate the Versailles Treaty, and Germany must seek an ally against world imperialism, for, although she is herself imperialist, she has been oppressed.

These are the three tangles that are hopelessly confusing the entire game of the imperialists. That is the crux of the matter. And that is why from the political point of view we must with all our heart—or without any heart, but calculatingly—favor concessions . . .

But, of course, it would be a great mistake to think that concessions imply peace. Nothing of the kind. Concessions are nothing but a new form of war. Europe fought us, and now the war is entering a new stage. Formerly, the war was carried on in the field in which the imperialists were infinitely stronger, in the military field . . . we undoubtedly should have been crushed in two weeks. Nevertheless, we held our own and now we seek to continue the fight and pass to an economic war . . . This will also be a war in which not the slightest concession will be permissible. This war will be useful for us in all respects; and the transition from the old war to the new war will also be useful, not to mention the fact that there is a certain indirect guarantee of peace . . . but . . . as long as capitalism and socialism exist, we cannot live in peace; in the end, one or the other will triumph—a funeral dirge will be sung over either the Soviet Republic or world capitalism. This is a respite in the war. The capitalists will seek excuses for fighting. If they accept the proposal and agree to concessions, it will be harder for them. On the one hand, in case of war we shall have the best conditions; on the other hand, those who want to go to war will not agree to concessions. The existence of concessions is an economic and political argument against war. The states that might make war on us will not do so if they take concessions. From the point of view of the danger of a collision between capitalism and Bolshevism, it must be said that concessions are a continuation of the war, but in a different sphere.

13. ON FOREIGN TRADE CONCESSIONS*

December 21, 1920

V. I. LENIN

Comrades, the question of concessions (to foreign countries) has created considerable excitement and even apprehension everywhere, not only in party circles and among the workers, but among the peasants as well. . . .

I think we must realize that on the question of concessions we cannot be guided only by revolutionary instinct. Weighing all sides of the question, we shall be convinced of the correctness of the policy which we have adopted—which consists of a continuation of concessions. . . .

If we look back at the past three years, from the point of view of the international situation of the Soviet republic, then we shall see clearly that we have been able to hold on and to win victories over the unprecedentedly powerful alliance of the Entente powers, supported by the White Guards, only because unity has never existed among these powers. We have been able to triumph till now only thanks to the serious disagreements among the imperialist powers, and only because these disagreements have not been accidental party and domestic disagreements, but the result of deep-rooted, permanent differences of economic interests between the imperialist countries, which, standing firmly on the principle of private ownership of land

    * V. I. Lenin, *Sochinenia*, 2nd ed. (Moscow: State Publishing House, 1930), Vol. XXVI, pp. 5–14, *excerpts*. From Report on Concessions to the Communist Party Faction at the Eighth Congress of Soviets of the RSFSR, December 21, 1920. Editor's translation.

and capital, cannot but follow a predatory policy designed to overthrow Soviet Russia. . . .

Our policy is to use the differences of the imperialist powers in order to make agreement difficult, or to make such agreement temporarily impossible. This has been the basic line of our policy for the past three years, which necessitated the signing of the Brest peace and an agreement with Bullitt—treaties concerning the peace and the armistice which were both extremely disadvantageous to us. This is the same policy line that has determined for us the decision to continue to use concessions. We are now giving America concessions in Kamchatka [Far Eastern province] which is not actually ours at present since it is occupied by Japanese troops. At the present moment we are not in a position to fight Japan. We are giving America a territory for economic utilization which is useless to us and where we lack naval and armed forces. By giving this we set American imperialism against Japan and the Japanese bourgeoisie which are nearest to us and which still control the Far Eastern Republic. [The Far Eastern Republic consisted of what are now the Maritime and Khabarovsk provinces of the Soviet Union and existed from April 1920 to November 1922. It was controlled by the Communist Party and was designed to serve as a buffer state between Communist Russia and the noncommunist powers in the Far East, particularly the United States and Japan. With the end of the Allied intervention, and the departure of Japanese troops from Vladivostok, the Far Eastern Republic was dissolved and reincorporated into the RSFSR.]

Our main interests in negotiating concessions are political. And recent events have shown that we have profited greatly from these concessions. . . .

We have a whole line of information showing that some capitalist countries are taking preparatory steps (to launching an attack against us), and one might say that the White Guards are laying the preliminary groundwork in all nations. Therefore, our main task is to reestablish trade relations, and to do this we must have at least part of the capitalists on our side.

In England the struggle has been going on for a long time. We have already profited, for representatives of this worst of all capitalist exploiting countries have come out in favor of a trade agreement with Russia . . . Our direct interest and our immediate duty is to support in every way the parties and groups that seek the negotiation with us of this agreement. . . .

Experience has shown only too well that only a socialist revolution can put an end to eternal wars. Thus, our policy does

not attempt to incite war. We have done nothing, either directly
or indirectly, that would justify war between Japan and America.
All our propaganda and newspaper articles continually emphasize the truth, that war between America and Japan will be an
imperialist war, as was the war between the English alliance and
the German alliance in 1914; and that the socialists should not be
concerned with the defense of the fatherland, but with the
overthrow of the power of the capitalists and with the workers'
revolution. But if we, who are doing all that we can to accelerate
this revolution, find ourselves a weak socialist republic attacked
by imperialist brigands, is it not correct to utilize the differences
between them in order to make it difficult for them to unite
against us? Of course such a policy is correct. We have followed
it during the course of the past four years. The Brest treaty was
the main manifestation of this policy. While German imperialism
was fighting, we, utilizing the antagonisms among the imperialists, were able to hold on even when the Red Army had not been
created. . . .

Our objective now is to obtain a trade agreement with England
and start regular trade in order to purchase as soon as possible
the machinery needed for our broad plan to rehabilitate our
national economy. The sooner we do this, the greater will be our
bases for becoming economically independent of the capitalist
countries. Precisely now, when they burned themselves in the
military invasion against Russia, they cannot think of quickly
resuming the war; we must use the moment and direct our
energy toward the objective of obtaining trade relations with the
imperialist powers, even if the terms are high. We do not for a
second believe that this will be but a temporary interruption.
The experience of the history of revolutions, of large-scale
conflicts, teaches us that wars, a series of wars, are inevitable.
Such a question, as the existence of the Soviet republic side by
side with the capitalist countries—the Soviet republic, surrounded by capitalist states—is so inadmissible from the capitalist viewpoint that all these countries will seize the first
opportunity to resume the war. The peoples are now tired of
the imperialist war, they threaten to revolt when a continuation
of the war is suggested; but this does not preclude the possibility
that the capitalists may resume their plan in a number of years.
For this reason we must apply all our efforts to using the
opportunity presented to us to conclude trade agreements. . . .

Our foreign policy, while we are alone and the capitalist world
is strong, consists in utilizing existing antagonisms (of the
capitalist world).

FOR FURTHER STUDY

Carr, Edward Hallett, *The Bolshevik Revolution, 1917–1923*, Vols. I–IV. New York: The Macmillan Company, 1950, 1952, 1953, 1954.

Carroll, E. Malcolm, *Soviet Communism and Western Opinion, 1919–1921*. Chapel Hill: University of North Carolina Press, 1965.

Chamberlin, William Henry, *The Russian Revolution, 1917–1921*, 2 vols. New York: The Macmillan Company, 1935.

Deutscher, Isaac, *The Prophet Armed: Trotsky, 1879–1921*. New York: Oxford University Press, 1954.

Gankin, Olga H. and Harold H. Fisher, *The Bolsheviks and the World War: The Origin of the Third International*. Stanford: Stanford University Press, 1940.

Hulse, James W., *The Forming of the Communist International*. Stanford: Stanford University Press, 1964.

Kennan, George F., *Russia Leaves the War*. Princeton, N.J.: Princeton University Press, 1956.

———, *The Decision to Intervene*. Princeton, N.J.: Princeton University Press, 1958.

Page, Stanley W., *The Formation of the Baltic States: A Study of the Effects of Great Power Politics upon the Emergence of Lithuania, Latvia, and Estonia*. Cambridge, Mass.: Harvard University Press, 1959.

Pipes, Richard, *The Formation of the Soviet Union: Communism and Nationalism, 1917–1923*, 2nd ed. Cambridge, Mass.: Harvard University Press, 1964.

Reed, John, *Ten Days That Shook the World*. New York: Modern Library, 1935.

Smith, C. Jay, Jr., *Finland and the Russian Revolution, 1917–1922*. Athens, Ga.: University of Georgia Press, 1958.

Trotsky, Leon, *The History of the Russian Revolution*. Ann Arbor: University of Michigan Press, 1955.

Warth, Robert D., *The Allies and the Russian Revolution*. Durham, N.C.: Duke University Press, 1954.

Wheeler-Bennett, John W., *The Forgotten Peace: Brest-Litovsk, March 1918*. New York: William Morrow & Co., 1939.

White, John Albert, *The Siberian Intervention*. Princeton, N.J.: Princeton University Press, 1950.

Zeman, Z. A. B. (ed.), *Germany and the Russian Revolution, 1915–1918: Documents from the Archives of the German Foreign Ministry*. New York: Oxford University Press, 1958.

CHAPTER III

ACCOMMODATION AND CONSOLIDATION, 1921–1934

In the spring of 1921, the new period of Soviet foreign policy was initiated by three crucial events:

. . . one affecting the domestic policy of the RSFSR, the second its foreign policy, and the third the prospects of revolution in the country where they had hitherto appeared brightest and most certain. In March 1921, after the Kronstadt rising, Lenin introduced the New Economic Policy; a trade agreement was concluded between the RSFSR and Great Britain; and a communist rising in Germany was heavily and ignominiously defeated.[1]

Desperately in need of time to rebuild their disrupted economy, and frustrated by the failure of the Communist uprising in Germany, the Bolsheviks conceded that the revolutionary tide in Europe had ebbed and that capitalism was entering an era of stabilization. They hoped to use this interregnum to develop Russia's strength for the uncertain future. To promote economic development, the New Economic Policy was instituted, foreign

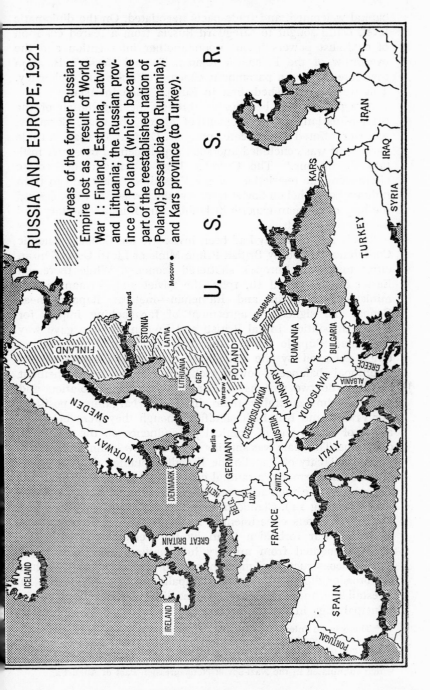

RUSSIA AND EUROPE, 1921

Areas of the former Russian Empire lost as a result of World War I: Finland, Esthonia, Latvia, and Lithuania; the Russian province of Poland (which became part of the reestablished nation of Poland); Bessarabia (to Rumania); and Kars province (to Turkey).

capital welcomed, and trade pacts negotiated. On the diplomatic level, Lenin sought to safeguard Russia from a feared coalition of capitalist powers intent upon another intervention and the overthrow of the Bolshevik regime. To end Russia's isolation therefore became a paramount concern of Bolshevik diplomacy. This was accomplished, first in Europe, then in Asia.

A beginning had been made through the negotiation of the British-Russian trade agreement of March 16, 1921. Germany, however, offered even greater promise. On May 6, 1921, a trade agreement was concluded and soon supplemented by secret military discussions.* The German High Command desired to circumvent the restrictions of the Versailles Treaty and to train military personnel on Soviet territory; the Soviets, in turn, desired the help of German experts in building up Russia's military and industrial strength.

Russia and Germany had been invited to the Genoa Economic Conference, called by British Prime Minister Lloyd George in an effort to restore Europe's shattered economy. While there, on Easter Sunday, April 16, 1922, the Soviet and German foreign ministers—Chicherin and Rathenau—met at Rapallo, near Genoa, and signed an agreement of far-reaching import for European politics. Initial British and French surprise gave way to dismay. Rapallo marked the first significant diplomatic triumph achieved by the Bolsheviks through the astute use of traditional balance-of-power techniques. This rapprochement between the two pariahs of Europe ended their isolation and enhanced immeasurably their diplomatic bargaining position. For France and Britain it signified, though they were not then aware of it, the end of political pre-eminence on the continent of Europe. The scale was shifting toward a new balance of power.

By the Treaty of Rapallo the Kremlin obtained *de jure* recognition from Germany, a mutual cancellation of existing financial claims, and the regularization and expansion of German-Soviet trade (reading 14). Clandestine military collaboration followed.[2] German missions experimented in Russia with advanced techniques of war forbidden them by the Versailles Treaty. The Soviets benefited from military information, from loans, and from the construction of modern tank and plane factories. Within the broader diplomatic struggle, Rapallo enabled the Soviets to forestall the anticipated capitalist coalition against them, their principal bogy in the interwar period.

* There is an interesting parallel between the events of 1921–1922 and those of 1939. For just as the commercial agreement of May 1921 was the forerunner of the Rapallo Treaty, so did the discussions for an economic accord in the summer of 1939 serve to veil the preliminary conversations which culminated in the Nazi-Soviet Nonaggression Pact of August 23.

The Versailles Treaty system had left both Germany and Russia isolated, the French-inspired *cordon sanitaire* (which consisted of French alliances with the small nations of Eastern Europe) being directed as much against the one as against the other. Each felt a strong need for an ally. At Rapallo each found a measure of strength and security. German-Soviet relations remained friendly until the rise of Hitler in 1933, though with fluctuating degrees of cordiality. For the Soviets in the 1920s Rapallo was particularly significant: in addition to ending their diplomatic isolation and ensuring their security against attack from a united capitalist world, it provided tangible economic and military benefits. For the Germans, bitter over the restrictive provisions of the Versailles Treaty, the loss of territory in the East, the harsh schedule of reparations, and the "war guilt" clause, it was a means of developing economic and military strength. General von Seeckt's secret negotiations during the crucial 1920-1922 period received the support of various influential factions and even the tacit approval of the antimilitaristic Social Democrat President, Ebert. Power politics outweighed ideological and political differences and made the Rapallo agreement a necessity for both.

Rapallo also spotlighted ideological differences between the left and right wings of the Russian Communist Party—between the school of permanent revolution and that of temporary stabilization. Both schools believed that a Communist Germany was necessary for Soviet survival, but differed over the tactics to be used. The Comintern, headed by Zinoviev, who was supported by Trotsky and Kamenev, advocated a more aggressive policy of promoting revolution by the German Communist Party, with a concomitant de-emphasis of the Rapallo Treaty. Lenin, Chicherin, and Radek, on the other hand, favored more elaborate negotiations with the German Government and reliance on Rapallo. The German Communist Party's failure at revolution in 1923 split that Party and laid it open to unquestioned domination by the Kremlin-controlled Comintern. It also contributed to Zinoviev's downfall in his power struggle with Stalin. The once powerful German Communist Party became, as other foreign Communist Parties were to become under Stalin, a docile, expendable instrument to be manipulated by Moscow.

On October 5, 1925, with the signing of the Locarno Treaty, a pact of mutual security with France and Britain, Germany embarked on Foreign Minister Stresemann's pro-Western policy of "fulfillment." To quiet Moscow's alarm, specifically her fears of German entry into an anti-Soviet bloc, Germany signed the Berlin Treaty of April 24, 1926 with Russia. It ran for five years and was subsequently extended for an additional three-year period. Friendship with the USSR continued to have a strong attraction for the German military and the big Ruhr industrialists. The Soviets, however, insisted on according to Rapallo an importance unwarranted in view of Europe's fluctuating politics. For them, it seemed to provide the firmest guarantee for their national security among the available political alternatives. It did remain a vital security link, but only until the advent of Hitler's aggressive expansionist policies.

In addition to relying upon friendly relations with Germany, the Soviet leaders endeavored to establish close relations with other nations on a bilateral basis. Shunned by the League of Nations, they did not rest their security upon that organization's ability to preserve the peace. On the contrary, the Soviets regarded the League as a "masked league of the so-called Great Powers, who have appropriated to themselves the right of disposing of the fate of weaker nations" and as serving as "a cover for the preparation of military action for the further suppression of small and weak nationalities" (reading 15). Even after joining the League in 1934, the Kremlin appeared to base its principal hopes for a viable collective security system on direct agreement with France and Britain, rather than on any multilateral League action.

In quest of allies, two approaches were utilized. First, the Soviet Government sought to obtain diplomatic recognition. Of particular significance was the *de jure* recognition granted by Britain's first Labour Cabinet on February 2, 1924.* This set off a chain reaction, and by late 1924 every major power except the United States had recognized the Soviets. Second, to ensure that the nations on her western borders would not serve as a staging ground for an interventionist-minded capitalist coalition, the Soviet Government sought to neutralize them by treaties of nonaggression and nonintervention. It desired, in effect, to undermine the French alliance system in Eastern Europe. Aided by Poland's grandiose pretensions to great power status and the fears these engendered among the Baltic countries, Moscow succeeded in negotiating a treaty of friendship and neutrality with Lithuania in 1926 and a trade pact with Latvia in 1927. Not until after the Kellogg-Briand Pact of 1928 outlawing war,

---

* In November of the same year, a successor Conservative Party Cabinet temporarily broke off diplomatic relations and denounced all existing treaties with the USSR over an alleged plot by Zinoviev to take advantage of British labor troubles and foment revolution. Though the "Zinoviev letter" was never proven to be authentic, it took a return to power of the Labour Party to bring about a resumption of diplomatic relations in December 1929.

however, were the Soviets also able to induce Poland, Rumania, and Estonia to agree to treaties of nonaggression. On February 9, 1929, the East Pact, or oft-called Litvinov Protocol, was signed with these nations in Moscow. At the time Soviet diplomats considered it a signal achievement, for it ensured that no aggressive bloc would use Eastern Europe as a base for an invasion of the Soviet Union. The East Pact, however, did little in a positive sense to promote Soviet power in the area.

Soviet influence in Eastern Europe was of little consequence prior to 1939. The countries of Eastern Europe were united in their mistrust and fear of Bolshevik policy, ideology, and objectives, but in little else. The Versailles system of economic and political fragmentation in Eastern Europe did little to encourage cooperative approaches to mutual problems; and since the USSR did not pose any immediate military threat, being preoccupied with grave internal problems, the nations of the area took no important measures to improve relations with the neighboring colossus. Trade between the USSR and Eastern Europe remained insignificant; political ties were weak and proved incapable of fostering a common front against the resurgence of an aggressive Germany. Russia's traditional interests in Eastern Europe were ignored in the councils of Europe, and all major steps affecting the area in the interwar period were taken without Soviet participation. This legacy Stalin was so tragically to reverse in the post-World War II era.

The Soviets also sought to strengthen their national security through use of the Comintern. Local Communist Parties tried to undermine legitimate governments, agitate against groups deemed hostile by Moscow, and promote revolutionary activities. At times this presented the Kremlin with a basic policy dilemma: Soviet diplomacy sought to take advantage of divisions within the capitalist world and to produce such splits where possible and, at the same time, to acquire allies in the very capitalist countries it was alienating through the revolutionary activities of the Comintern.

> In this fashion the goal of ultimate and complete security, to be gained after the victory of the proletarian revolution in the more important capitalistic countries, came into conflict with the goal of immediate security, to be obtained only with the acceptance of questionable allies.[3]

In Asia, meanwhile, revolutionary developments attracted Bolshevik attention, particularly to China. The Bolshevik revolution and Communist ideology introduced a new, dynamic force into the Far Eastern scene. Its impact was widespread and profound, especially in China where the breakdown of central government authority and the mushrooming political ferment among the intellectuals assured an eager receptivity for ideas promising national independence, rapid industrialization and transformation of society, and liberation from foreign domination. Bolshevik propaganda sedulously cultivated these aspirations.

In July 1919 the Bolsheviks in a general declaration to the Chinese people had solemnly renounced all former Czarist privileges in China.* Because of unsettled conditions in Siberia, the declaration did not reach China until March 1920, but its impact then was enormous, especially among the intelligentsia and students who were openly disgruntled over the arbitrary assignment at Versailles of former German interests in Shantung to Japan.[4]

Contact between Sun Yat-sen, founder of the Kuomintang, who had established a regime in Canton rivaling that of Peking, and the Comintern was affected briefly in 1921. Bolshevik efforts to obtain diplomatic recognition from Peking had foundered in the previous year over Soviet reluctance to relinquish all claims to Outer Mongolia and northern Manchuria, areas of former Czarist interest and control over which Moscow had succeeded in re-establishing a semblance of authority.[5] The Bolsheviks therefore, directed closer attention to the revolutionary Sun Yat-sen and the Kuomintang, which offered the promise of a richer political harvest. Accordingly, it was in China that cooperation with bourgeois national movements, a policy advocated by Lenin at the second Comintern Congress in 1920, was given its first test.

By 1923 the Soviet position in the Far East had been improved, albeit inadvertently, as a consequence of the Washington Conference (November 12, 1921–February 6, 1922). Though not invited, despite its protest that as a Far Eastern Power it should have a voice in matters affecting the area's future, Moscow, in a twist of irony for which history is often noted, emerged as the principal beneficiary. The Conference persuaded the Japanese to withdraw their remaining troops from Siberia and also effected the termination of the Anglo-Japanese alliance. The result was a shift in the Far Eastern balance of power in Russia's favor.

In January 1923 Moscow sent A. A. Joffe, the peripatetic Comintern agent, to Sun Yat-sen. They met in Shanghai and

---

* However, the Bolsheviks were careful to remain vague about the future status of the Chinese Eastern Railway which had been Russian owned since the 1890s. For an excellent article on this issue see Allen S. Whiting, "The Soviet Offer to China of 1919," in *Far Eastern Quarterly* (August 1951).

issued a Joint Manifesto (reading 16). This marked the start
of the period of collaboration between the Soviet Union and the
Kuomintang. The Manifesto acknowledged that "because of the
nonexistence of conditions favorable to their successful application in China, it is not possible to carry out either Communism
or even the Soviet system in China . . . and [China's] most
pressing problems are the completion of national unification and
the attainment of full national independence." It also postponed
final disposition of the Chinese Eastern Railway and Outer Mongolia. In general, the Joffe-Sun agreement guided Soviet policy
in China until 1927, and, at the behest of Stalin and Bukharin,
Moscow henceforth supported Canton against Peking. Soviet
advisers flocked to aid the Kuomintang (known as the KMT):
General Blucher (Galen) helped found the Whampoa Military
Academy; and Michael Borodin, perhaps the most important of
all the Soviet agents in China, revitalized the Kuomintang party
apparatus along Bolshevik lines. The organizational and political
techniques introduced by the Soviets overshadowed their meager
financial and material aid. In a preview of the future "popular
front" tactic, Moscow sanctioned membership by Chinese Communists in the Kuomintang, but only as individuals. The
Communist Party preserved its identity and continued to exist
as a party within a party.* Though the partnership proved to
be fleeting, Russia succeeded in entering the mainstream of the
Chinese revolution.

In May 1924, Moscow and Peking negotiated a series of diplomatic agreements, covering a wide range of issues which were
later upheld by the Kuomintang when it extended its control
over North China. They called among other things for Soviet
troop withdrawal from Outer Mongolia, recognition of the area
as an integral part of China, and joint administration of the
Chinese Eastern Railway pending a permanent settlement.† The
Soviets also renounced extraterritoriality and other formerly

---

* The Chinese Communist movement was founded by two Peking University professors, Chen Tu-hsiu and Li Ta-chao, who were attracted to
Marxism and Lenin's doctrine of imperialism because they provided the
means of "judging and criticizing the capitalist West from a western point
of view." For a superb, sophisticated discussion see Benjamin L. Schwartz,
Chinese Communism and the Rise of Mao (Cambridge: Harvard University
Press, 1951). The Chinese Communist Party itself was officially established
in July 1921.

† The Soviets, in implementing this phase of the agreement, managed
to obtain operational control of the Chinese Eastern Railway, and thus
preserved their interests in Manchuria. Fighting broke out in 1929 along
the railroad between Soviet and Chinese troops in a test of Soviet determination to remain in North China. Finally, in 1935, Moscow sold its interest in the Railway to Japan as part of its policy of appeasement in the Far
East.

held special privileges. Notwithstanding these concessions, the Soviet Union forced Chinese recognition of autonomy for Outer Mongolia, thus giving new expression to former Czarist interests in the area. (Indicative of Kremlin control was the fact that after 1928 Outer Mongolia was included in the Soviet Five Year Plan.) A Moscow-sponsored "People's Republic" was proclaimed shortly thereafter. In addition, "by providing the sole military and financial support for the fledgling regime, Russia assured itself of a loyal area on its vastly extended, poorly protected Asian flank."[6] Hence, Moscow's policy in Outer Mongolia, as in Manchuria, was an amalgam of security considerations and imperialist ambitions.

A vital conciliatory link with the Kuomintang disappeared when Sun Yat-sen died on March 12, 1925, and was quickly succeeded by Chiang Kai-shek. A year later, concerned over the growing influence of the left and Communist wings of the Kuomintang and intent upon ending the confusion of competing factions, Chiang Kai-shek acted suddenly, arresting and executing several key Communists. Within a month he moved in a similar fashion against the right. Throughout this purge of the opposition, he took care to reaffirm his continued fidelity to the alliance with Moscow. Despite the open plight of the Chinese Communists, Stalin did nothing. Thus local Communist Party interests were once again sacrificed, as they had been in Germany, in order to promote Soviet interests and security. The possibility that China's national renaissance and "1917" might be at hand, and the decidedly pro-Marxist sympathies of many Kuomintang leaders, encouraged Stalin to consider the situation more favorable to the cause of communism than it actually was. This self-imposed myopia could no longer be justified, however, after the even harsher crackdown on the Communists in April and May 1927, which presaged the eclipse of Soviet influence in China for more than a generation.*

In his military campaign to unify China, Chiang Kai-shek captured Nanking and Shanghai in April 1927. A few days later he arrested local Shanghai Communist leaders and brutally suppressed the attempt of the city's proletariat to establish a Communist government. Moscow maintained its silence and per-

---

* The story of the Soviet decline in China is a complex one, involving a number of interrelated conflicts—"the conflict between Chiang Kai-shek and Borodin, the conflict between the left and the right wings of the Kuomintang, the conflict between the Kuomintang as a whole and the Chinese Communists, the conflicts between the Comintern agents in China (notably Borodin and Roy), the conflict between Peking and Moscow, the conflict between Stalin and Trotsky, and the conflict between Soviet Russia and the Western Powers in China." Henry Wei, *China and Soviet Russia* (Princeton, N.J.: D. Van Nostrand Company, 1956), p. 64.

sisted in efforts to continue the alliance with the Kuomintang. Mass revolutionary action was discouraged. But new suppressions in May finally ended the collaboration. Thus, Moscow's initial attempt to communize China was thwarted, as had been earlier similar efforts in Turkey and Iran.

The Peking Government, meanwhile, suspecting Soviet intrigue, had searched the Soviet embassy compound in April, and discovered a number of highly subversive documents which spelled out in great detail the scope of Comintern conspiratorial activities. They contained a list of Comintern agents, a resolution relating to the Chinese question passed earlier in the year by the Executive Committee of the Comintern (reading 17), and an analysis of the Chinese situation as viewed by Moscow. According to the Chinese Government, the captured documents proved: (*a*) that the Soviet embassy had an extensive political and military secret service organization in China, which conducted espionage everywhere, even in the foreign legations in Peking; (*b*) "that the so-called Soviet advisers and military instructors in the south are members of the various Councils of the Kuomintang and the Communists . . . and that they were paid by the Soviet Government through the Military Attaché in Peking"; and (*c*) that the Soviet Government with its embassy in Peking acting as an intermediate agency was furnishing arms and munitions to the enemies of the (Peking) Government to which its embassy was accredited. Publication of these documents occasioned sharp Soviet protests and denials concerning their authenticity.

By November Chiang Kai-shek had consolidated his control over the various dissident KMT factions, including the Communists. The Soviet Government responded by breaking off diplomatic relations with Chiang's government in December 1927. Stalin, whose alliance with the Kuomintang not only had brought disaster to the Party in China but threatened to undermine his position in the struggle for power with Trotsky, declared to a surprised Fifteenth Party Congress that capitalism's period of "stabilization" had come to an end and that the period of "peaceful coexistence" had been replaced by one of ominous and increased imperialist intervention against the USSR (reading 18). This interpretation, adopted and expanded by the sixth Congress of the Communist International in September 1928, signified a return to a revolutionary line by the Comintern, and to a lesser extent by the Soviet Union.

Soviet historians have since adjusted the pattern of events to cast Stalin's policy in a "correct" light, but whatever the interpretation, the fact remains that Comintern policy in China, as well

as in other areas of Asia, was a failure. The year 1929 witnessed
outbreaks of fighting in Manchuria, and war with China came
dangerously close. By the end of the 1920s the Kremlin was on
the defensive in Indonesia, India, Japan, and French Indo-China,
and Communist influence in these areas remained marginal
until the outbreak of World War II.

After the disappointments in China and elsewhere in Asia,
and the rupture with Great Britain, the Soviets searched abroad
for new means of assuring their security. Internally they intensified the drive to develop "socialism in one country" and to
accelerate industrial growth. Interpretations of international
events continued to be presented (and formulated) within the
Leninist framework, but "the Soviet Union proceeded to follow
the typical balance of power pattern of cooperating with one
power or group of powers against an opposing group, and shifting its alliances in accord with obvious national interests." [7]

Successive setbacks abroad, coupled with economic and party
demands at home, led Stalin to adopt a cautious foreign policy
for the Soviet Union, though at the same time he launched the
Comintern on an ultra-revolutionary tack. These seemingly con-
tradictory and confusing approaches were designed to promote
Soviet security at a moment of increasing isolation. In September
1928, the Comintern elaborated the "hard" line at its Sixth
Congress, which formulated the position of international communism in relation to the world situation (reading 19). The
main principles enunciated remain in effect to this day. Specifically, they held that: (1) the Soviet Union is the citadel of
world revolution—"she is the international driving force of
proletarian revolution that impels the proletariat of all countries
to seize power . . . she is the prototype of the fraternity of
nationalities in all lands united in the World Union of Socialist
Republics and of the economic unity of the toilers of all countries
in a single world socialist economic system that the world proletariat must establish when it has captured political power"; (2)
the preservation of the Soviet Union must be the primary concern
of the international proletariat—"In the event of the imperialist
states declaring war upon and attacking the USSR, the international proletariat must retaliate by organizing bold and determined mass action and struggle for the overthrow of the
imperialist governments"; (3) all Communist Parties owe
exclusive allegiance to Moscow. Local interests must be subordinated to the line set forth by the Comintern and the Soviet
Union. The Congress concluded on an uncompromising note:

The Communists disdain to conceal their views and aims. They
openly declare that their aims can be attained only by the forcible

overthrow of all the existing social conditions. Let the ruling class
tremble at a Communist revolution. The proletarians have nothing to
lose but their chains. They have a world to win.

By eschewing all cooperation with reformist Social Democratic
parties, now labeled "fascist" and considered the most dangerous
foes of communism, Stalin introduced a disastrous exclusiveness
which mortally split the German left and helped bring Hitler to
power. His policy "paralyzed the political strength of the German
working class when it alone could have barred Hitler's road to
power." [8] Stalin, failing completely to comprehend the destructive
dynamism of the Nazi movement, must bear considerable
responsibility for what happened in Germany.

Militarily weak, and burdened with serious internal difficulties,
the Soviet Union sought security in various ways. In the early
1930s, the USSR attempted to draw closer to the nations of Eastern Europe by negotiating nonaggression pacts with them. It also
signed one, on November 29, 1932, with a France alarmed at
the rising temper of German nationalism. These accords, however, did not provide any real measure of security for the Soviets;
they merely provided the illusion of better relations. None ever
developed into significant instruments of collective security. Russia still needed peace and this often-proclaimed desire was
undoubtedly genuine. Though not a member of the League, it
participated in several League-sponsored commissions seeking
ways to decrease international tension.[9] At the Sixteenth Party
Congress in June 1930, Stalin expressed what probably remained
the *leitmotif* of his policy until 1939:

. . . a result of this policy (of negotiating nonaggression and trade
pacts) is the fact that we have succeeded in maintaining peace, in not
allowing the enemy to draw us into conflicts, in spite of a number of
provocative acts and adventurist attacks on the part of the warmongers. We will continue to pursue this policy of peace with all our
might and with all the means at our disposal. We do not want a single
foot of foreign territory; but of our territory we will not surrender a
single inch to anyone.

The desire for peace encompassed not only the absence of war
but an expansion of economic relations as well. Having launched
an ambitious Five Year Plan that involved collectivization and
industrialization crises, the Soviet Union looked to the West for
the machinery and material required to build up its military and
industrial strength. But the world depression bred an egocentric
economic nationalism that militated against any really rational
analysis of Soviet needs by the powers best equipped to help.
Unable to rely on the United States, Great Britain, or France for

expanded trade or loans, the USSR turned increasingly to Germany during the 1931–1934 period. But two events beyond the control of the Soviet leadership shaped its future and its foreign policy—the Japanese invasion of Manchuria and the triumph of Hitler in Germany. The latter was particularly crucial for it was to threaten the very existence of the Soviet State.

Faithful to the 1928 Comintern line, the German Communists joined the ultra-nationalists in denouncing all efforts by the Weimar Government to effect a rapprochement with the Western Powers. They aimed their heaviest fire at the Social Democrats and assisted the Nazis in undermining the operation of constitutional government by obstructionism and rowdyism in the Reichstag. Indeed, according to Max Beloff, "There is some evidence that early in 1931 a deliberate decision was taken to cooperate in the country with the Nazis in order to accelerate the destruction of the Social-Democratic Party and its organizations." [10] Hitler came to power, in great measure, through the assistance of the Communists. After January 30, 1933, the policy of friendship with the Soviet Union was abandoned by Hitler until August 1939.

Moscow at first viewed Hitler's victory with mingled uncertainty, misunderstanding, and self-deception. It deluded itself as to the nature of Hitler's objectives and their implications for German foreign policy. While the Comintern talked of the imminence of proletarian revolution, Moscow carefully avoided giving the slightest provocation. The German Communist Party was meekly surrendered as a sacrificial offering in a vain and costly attempt to convince Hitler of Russia's intent to remain aloof from any interference in German affairs. Rapallo was still formally operative, but German ratification, on May 5, 1933, of the protocol prolonging the 1926 Berlin Treaty was only partially reassuring. Stalin waited in silence and with growing anxiety, refraining for almost a year from any comment about events in Germany, thus adding to the confusion of an already sorely bewildered Comintern.

The German ambassador in Moscow, Herbert von Dirksen, favored friendship with the Soviet Union and repeatedly urged Berlin to allay Moscow's rising insecurity by a forthright statement of peaceful intent. In a secret dispatch to the Foreign Ministry on February 20, 1933, he wrote:

An attitude of watchful waiting is being taken toward the new German Cabinet here. Basically it is hoped that the strength of their mutual interests will make possible the continuance of the present friendly policy. But the foundations of their mutual relations are felt to be unstable, both in a juridical and in a political respect; in a juridical respect, because the Berlin Treaty and the Conciliation Convention are not in force because they were not ratified; in a political respect because there have for some time been no statements of political intention on the part of the Reich Government with respect to its Russian policy, while toward France very positive statements have been made by Germany in the past year. They are still haunted here by the story of the military alliance offered to France. The statements made by influential Germans privately to Soviet politicians regarding the unaltered course of Germany's Russian policy have, it is true, assuaged the strongest fears. But they could not take the place of the positive effect of a public statement by the German Government. There is also disappointment here over the fact that even the substitutes for such official government statements, such as friendly telegrams on special occasions or interviews of a positive nature on the part of Germany, have been omitted.[11]

His successor, Rudolf Nadolny, similarly urged cooperation with the Soviet Union—in vain. By late 1933 the Soviet Union had become sufficiently disenchanted and concerned over German policy to begin exploring ways of moving closer to the West. It signed a treaty of friendship with Italy, established diplomatic relations with the United States (which finally accorded recognition in November), and developed more cordial contacts with the French; and Foreign Minister Maxim Litvinov increasingly appeared at international conferences. Japanese expansion in the Far East, and indications of Hitler's uncompromising anti-Soviet attitude, had led the Kremlin to turn to the West.

At the Seventeenth Party Congress in January 1934, Stalin at last commented publicly on developments in Germany as well as on the over-all international situation (reading 20). His analysis, however, stopped far short of the harsh conclusions demanded by the events of the previous year. He appeared insensitive to the inherent threat posed by Nazism, preferring to regard it as likely to be short-lived. Throughout his speech, Stalin proffered the olive branch to Germany and tried to make unmistakable his desire for continued relations in the tradition of Bismarck and Rapallo.

In this connection some German politicians say that the USSR has now taken on orientation towards France and Poland; that from an opponent of the Versailles Treaty it has become a supporter of it, and that this change is to be explained by the establishment of the fascist regime in Germany. That is not true. Of course, we are far from being enthusiastic about the fascist regime in Germany. But fascism is not the issue here, if only for the reason that fascism in Italy, for example, has not prevented the USSR from establishing the best relations with that country. Nor is it a question of any alleged change in our attitude towards the Versailles Treaty. It is not for us, who have experienced the shame of the Brest Peace, to sing the praises of the Versailles Treaty. We merely do not agree to the world being flung into the abyss of a new war on account of that treaty. The same must be said of the alleged new orientation taken by the USSR. We never had any orientation towards Germany, nor have we any orientation towards Poland and France. Our orientation in the past and our orientation at the present time is towards the USSR, and towards the USSR alone. . . . And if the interests of the USSR demand rapprochement with one country or another which is not interested in disturbing peace, we adopt this course without hesitation.

But events soon compelled the Soviet Union to follow another path. The course of the next five years was determined not in Moscow or Paris or London, but in Berlin.

Hitler ignored Stalin's overtures. He proceeded to conclude a nonaggression pact with Poland, thus laying the diplomatic groundwork for the Nazi expansion of 1938–1939. This treaty bred suspicion and sharpened tension between France and Poland, between Czechoslovakia and Poland, and between Poland and the Soviet Union (which feared that Hitler was tempting the Poles with the old Pilsudski dream of annexing the Ukraine). It accelerated the increasingly evident withdrawal of France from Central Europe. In mid-1934, Hitler's purge of Roehm, his former co-conspirator, the death of Marshal Hindenburg, that senile fragment of Weimar legitimacy, and the Nazi assassination of the Austrian Chancellor Dollfuss, all denoted Hitler's growing dictatorial power. The shadows darkened ominously over Europe, and in the Kremlin fear of Germany forced Stalin to reappraise the course of Soviet foreign policy. It is interesting, in retrospect, to reread a statement written for a Western audience in 1934 by a prominent Soviet spokesman on the objectives of Soviet foreign policy (reading 21). His indignant denial of any imperial ambitions on the part of the Soviet Union contrasts sharply with Stalin's actions, once circumstances and a second world war afforded the opportunity for expansion.

NOTES

1. Edward Hallett Carr, *The Bolshevik Revolution, 1917–1923* (New York: The Macmillan Company, 1953), Vol. III, p. 225. The Riga Peace Treaty with Poland and a friendship pact with Turkey were also concluded at this time.
2. John W. Wheeler-Bennett, *The Nemesis of Power* (New York: St. Martin's Press, 1954), p. 130.
3. Barrington Moore, Jr., *Soviet Politics: The Dilemma of Power* (Cambridge, Mass.: Harvard University Press, 1950), p. 215.
4. Henry Wei, *China and Soviet Russia* (Princeton, N.J.: D. Van Nostrand Company, Inc., 1956), p. 18.

5. David J. Dallin, *The Rise of Russia in Asia* (New Haven, Conn.: Yale University Press, 1949), pp. 187–199.
6. Allen S. Whiting, *Soviet Policies in China, 1917–1924* (New York: Columbia University Press, 1954), pp. 250–251.
7. Moore, *op. cit.*, p. 214.
8. Isaac Deutscher, *Stalin: A Political Biography* (New York: Oxford University Press, 1949), p. 406.
9. *Infra*, Chapter IX. The Soviet attitude toward the problem of disarmament is treated separately.
10. Max Beloff, *The Foreign Policy of Soviet Russia, 1929–1936* (New York: Oxford University Press, 1947), Vol. i, p. 62.
11. *Documents on German Foreign Policy: The Third Reich: The First Phase* (Washington, D.C.: Government Printing Office, 1957), Vol. i, p. 64.

The Soviet-German Rapprochement

14. TREATY REGARDING SOLUTION OF GENERAL PROBLEMS*

Rapallo, April 16, 1922

The German Government, represented by Reichsminister Dr. Walther Rathenau, and the Government of the RSFSR, represented by People's Commissar Chicherin, have agreed upon the following provisions:

I. The two Governments agree that all questions resulting from the state of war between Germany and Russia shall be settled in the following manner:

(a) Both Governments mutually renounce repayment for their war expenses and for damages arising out of the war, that is to say, damages caused to them and their nationals in the zone of war operations by military measures, including all requisitions effected in a hostile country. They renounce in the same way repayment for civil damages inflicted on civilians, that is to say, damages caused to the nationals of the two countries by exceptional war legislation or by violent measures taken by any authority of the state of either side.

(b) All legal relations concerning questions of public or private law resulting from the state of war, including the question

* Leonard Shapiro, *Soviet Treaty Series* (Washington, D.C.: Georgetown University Press, 1950), Vol. i, pp. 168–169, *excerpts*. Reprinted by permission of the Georgetown University Press.

of the treatment of merchant ships which fell into the hands of the one side or the other during the war, shall be settled on the basis of reciprocity.

(c) Germany and Russia mutually renounce repayment of expenses incurred for prisoners of war. The German Government also renounces repayment of expenses for soldiers of the Red Army interned in Germany. The Russian Government for its part, renounces repayment of the sums Germany has derived from the sale of Russian Army material brought into Germany by these interned troops.

II. Germany renounces all claims resulting from the enforcement of the laws and measures of the Soviet Republic as it has affected German nationals or their private rights or the rights of the German state itself, as well as claims resulting from measures taken by the Soviet Republic or its authorities in any other way against subjects of the German state or their private rights, provided that the Soviet Government shall not satisfy similar claims made by any third state.

III. Consular and diplomatic relations between Germany and the Federal Soviet Republic shall be resumed immediately. The admission of consuls to both countries shall be arranged by special agreement.

IV. Both Governments agree, further, that the rights of the nationals of either of the two Parties on the other's territory as well as the regulation of commercial relations shall be based on the most favored nation principle. This principle does not include rights and facilities granted by the Soviet Government to another Soviet state or to any state that formerly formed part of the Russian Empire.

V. The two Governments undertake to give each other mutual assistance for the alleviation of their economic difficulties in the most benevolent spirit. In the event of a general settlement of this question on an international basis, they undertake to have a preliminary exchange of views. The German Government declares itself ready to facilitate, as far as possible, the conclusion and the execution of economic contracts between private enterprises in the two countries.

VI. Article I, Paragraph (b), and Article IV of this Agreement will come into force after the ratification of this document. The other Articles will come into force immediately.

The USSR and the League of Nations

15. PRESS STATEMENT ON THE SOVIET UNION AND THE LEAGUE OF NATIONS*

November 23, 1925

MAXIM LITVINOV

We regard the League of Nations, as before, not as a friendly association of peoples working for the general good, but as a masked league of the so-called Great Powers, who have appropriated to themselves the right of disposing of the fate of weaker nations. The fact that Germany, a defeated country that is in the military sense weak, is now entering the League, does not imply a change in the character of the League; it only means that certain Powers are counting on using Germany to assist in carrying out their plans in general, and their hostile designs against the USSR in particular.

More than any other Government, the Soviet Government is interested in strengthening peace, on the basis of independence and self-determination for all nations. That is why it would welcome the creation of an international organization in which and through which every nation could realize its national sovereign rights and all nations could settle the differences arising between them by peaceful and friendly means. But less than any other Government does the Soviet Government see in the existing League of Nations an approximation to such an organization. Up to now the League of Nations has not in the slightest degree justified the hopes and expectations placed in it by its protagonists. It has not only failed even once to protect the rights and security of a small or weak nationality against coercion and the military verdict of stronger Powers, but on the chief question which is of vital interest to all mankind, and in particular to us, on the question of disarmament, it has not yet taken one single serious step.

The League is a cover for the preparation of military action

* Jane Degras, *Soviet Documents on Foreign Policy* (New York: Oxford University Press, 1952), Vol. II, pp. 65–66, *excerpts*. Reprinted by permission of the Oxford University Press and the Royal Institute of International Affairs.

for the further suppression of small and weak nationalities. To a considerable degree it is only a diplomatic *bourse,* where the strong Powers arrange their business and conduct their mutual accounts behind the back and at the expense of the small and weak nations. The USSR, as a state of the working masses, cannot take responsibility for the League of Nations, which sanctifies the enslavement and exploitation of foreign nations. Inspired solely by the desire to avoid any complications which might break the general peace, and in particular the progress of its great work of internal construction, and pursuing its policy of nonintervention in the internal affairs of other nations, the USSR does not feel the slightest desire to enter an organization in which it would have to play the part either of hammer or of anvil. In particular, the Soviet Government knows that it would then be confronted, in the form of partners or even of judges, with states, many of which have not even recognized it, and consequently do not even conceal their enmity toward it, and with others, even among those which have recognized it, which even now behave toward it with ill-concealed hostility.

You may therefore inform the public in your country that all the rumors of some kind of change in the Soviet Government's attitude to the League of Nations, and incidentally to Locarno, are without foundation, and that the Government of the USSR, like the Government of the United States, is firmly determined in the future as in the past, to stand aside from such organization.

Promise and Disaster in China

16. JOINT MANIFESTO*

January 26, 1923

SUN YAT-SEN AND A. A. JOFFE

1. Dr. Sun is of the opinion that, because of the nonexistence of conditions favorable to their successful application in China,

* Reprinted by permission of the publishers from *A Documentary History of Chinese Communism* by Conrad Brandt, Benjamin Schwartz, and John K. Fairbank (Cambridge, Mass.: Harvard University Press, 1952), pp. 70–71, *excerpts.*

it is not possible to carry out either Communism or even the Soviet system in China. M. Joffe agrees entirely with this view; he is further of the opinion that China's most important and most pressing problems are the completion of national unification and the attainment of full national independence. With regard to these great tasks, M. Joffe has assured Dr. Sun of the Russian people's warmest sympathy for China, and of (their) willingness to lend support.

2. In order to eradicate misunderstandings, Dr. Sun has requested M. Joffe to reaffirm the principles enunciated by Russia in its Note to the Chinese Government of September 27, 1920. M. Joffe accordingly reaffirmed these principles, and categorically declared to Dr. Sun that Russia is willing and ready to enter into negotiations with China on the basis of Russia's abandonment of all treaties, and of the rights and privileges (conceded by China) under duress, secured by the Tsarist Government from China. Among the above-mentioned treaties are included the treaties and agreements concerning the Chinese Eastern Railway.

3. Dr. Sun holds that the Chinese Eastern Railway question in its entirety can be satisfactorily settled only by a competent Sino-Russian Conference. But the key to the current situation lies in the fact that a *modus vivendi* ought to be devised for the administration of the said railway at present. Dr. Sun and M. Joffe are of the same opinion that the administration of this railway should be temporarily reorganized after an agreement has been reached between the Chinese and Russian Governments, but (on condition) that the real rights and special interests of either party are not injured. Dr. Sun also holds that the matter should be discussed with Chang Tso-lin.

4. M. Joffe categorically declares to Dr. Sun (and Dr. Sun is entirely satisfied with regard to this point): that it is not, and never has been, the intention or the objective of the present Russian Government to carry out imperialistic policies in Outer Mongolia, or to work for Outer Mongolia's independence from China. Dr. Sun therefore does not deem the immediate evacuation of Russian troops from Outer Mongolia to be urgently necessary or to the real advantage of China. This is due to the fact that, the present Peking Government being weak and impotent, after the withdrawal of the Russian troops it would most likely be unable to prevent the activities of the Russian Whites from causing fresh difficulties for the Russian Government, thereby creating a situation even graver than that which exists at present.

17. RESOLUTION RELATING TO THE CHINESE QUESTION CARRIED AT THE SEVENTH EXTENDED PLENARY SESSION OF THE EXECUTIVE COMMITTEE OF THE INTERNATIONAL COMMUNIST PARTY*

Moscow, March 1927

1. Imperialism and the Chinese Revolution

1. The Chinese revolution is one of the most important and powerful factors which disturbs the stabilization of capitalism. During the last two years imperialism has suffered in China considerable defeats, the results of which will produce a considerable influence on the exacerbation of the crisis of the world capitalism. In consequence of the victorious advance of the National Army towards North China, the domination of the imperialists was practically undermined in half of the country. . . .

2. The fundamental power of imperialism in China consists in the actual monopoly of everything that concerns the financial and industrial life of the country (the salt tax, the mortgage of the customs revenues, railways, waterways, mines, heavy industry—all this belongs chiefly to foreign capital). Should capitalism keep this solid base, it will find in China a serious support in the matter of stabilization of capitalism. Owing to its huge population, China is a market with boundless possibilities. It may become a most profitable field for the investment of capital, provided the necessary political guarantees are secured. The enormous resources of raw materials are hardly touched in China. Therefore imperialism will make desperate efforts to crush the Chinese revolution which threatens to overthrow it. If it does not succeed in crushing the latter by means of its traditional method—the provocation of civil war—or possibly

---

* This document was received by the Soviet Military Attaché in Peking on March 28, 1927. The translation was made from a copy not damaged by fire, which was discovered after photographs of the damaged document had been made. See *Chinese Social and Political Science Review*, Vol. XI (1927), Public Documents Supplement, pp. 169–177, *excerpts*.

by means of armed intervention, imperialism will try to frustrate the national movement of liberation which develops alongside the revolution. . . .

3. From the international point of view the Chinese revolution, be it but for its anti-militaristic character, is an essential part of the international revolution. This fact is connected in China with the following most important circumstances which favor the further development and deepening of the Chinese revolution:

(a) The competition of the imperialistic powers in China which weakens the position of world imperialism.

(b) The crisis of world capitalism.

(c) The growth of the proletarian movement in Western Europe. . . .

(d) The development of the national-revolutionary movement in the colonies which doubtless will still more increase under the influence of the further development of the Chinese revolution.

(e) The fact that proletarian dictatorship exists in the USSR in connection with close geographical proximity of the latter to China and the geographical remoteness of China from the basic centers of the economic and military-political power of the imperialistic powers.

4. Parallel with the rapid development of the national revolutionary movement, the social forces participating in it are involved in a no less rapid process of regrouping.

The national revolution in China develops under such peculiar conditions that it differs substantially from the classical bourgeois revolutions of the Western European states of the past century, as well as from the revolution of 1905 in Russia. The chief of these peculiarities is the semi-colonial position of China, which is dependent on foreign imperialism. Another difference between the Chinese revolution and the bourgeois-democratic revolutions of the past consists in that the Chinese revolution is taking place in the period of the world revolution and forms an integral part of the world's movement tending to destroy the capitalistic regime. This factor will define the history of the Chinese revolution and the grouping of the social forces that participate in it. . . .

5. The consecutive stages of development of the revolutionary movement in China are characterized by serious regrouping of the social forces. During the first stage one of the chief motive powers consisted of the national bourgeoisie and the bourgeois intelligentsia who sought the support of the proletariat and the petty bourgeoisie.

In the second stage the character of the movement changes

and its social base is shifted to another grouping of classes. New and more revolutionary forms of the struggle are developing. On the Chinese area a new factor of the highest order appears in the person of the laboring class.

The economic strikes grow into a political struggle against imperialism and become most important from the historic point of view. The proletariat forms a bloc with the peasantry, which enters into an active struggle for its interests, as well as with the petty town bourgeoisie and a part of the capitalistic bourgeoisie. This combination of forces brought about a politically corresponding grouping of parties in the Kuomintang and the Canton Government. At present the movement is on the threshold of the third stage and on the eve of a new regrouping of the classes. At this stage of the development the motive forces of the movement will be a bloc—of a still greater revolutionary character—the bloc of the proletariat, the peasantry and the petty town bourgeoisie, while the greater part of the big capitalistic bourgeoisie will be excluded. . . .

6. Parallel to the grouping of the class forces of the revolution the forces of the counterrevolution also take shape. . . .

The proletariat and its party must tactically take advantage of all dissensions among the strata of the bourgeoisie which recede from the revolution, as well as of the dissensions among the different imperialistic groups, by no means forgetting their fundamental aim and conforming to the latter all their strategical maneuvers and tactical measures.

General Prospects of the Chinese Revolution

7. The general prospects of the Chinese revolution become very clear when the grouping of the classes is considered from this point of view. Although, historically speaking, the Chinese revolution at its present stage of development bears a bourgeois democratic character, it must get the character of a wider social movement. It is essential that the Chinese revolution should not result in the creation of such social-political conditions as would lead to a capitalistic development of the country. The Chinese revolution which is effected in the period of collapse of capitalism, is a part of the general struggle tending to overthrow capitalism and introduce socialism. The structure of a revolutionary state is defined by the class on which it is based. It will not be purely that of a bourgeois-democratic state. The state will be a democratic dictatorship of the proletariat, the peasantry and other classes that are being exploited. It will be a revolutionary anti-imperialistic government up to the time when it will develop into a noncapitalistic (socialistic) one.

The Chinese Communist Party must strain every nerve to realize in the end this revolutionary aim of taking the way to a noncapitalistic development. Otherwise, i.e., if the bourgeoisie obtains victory over the proletariat and the bourgeoisie that leads it, the power in the country will practically fall again into the hands of the foreign imperialists, even though in new forms of domination.

8. The further development of the prospects of the Chinese revolution depends, in the first place, on the part which is played by the proletariat. The events of the last years have shown that a militarist revolutionary national front can be organized only under the leadership of the proletariat. The struggle against the hegemony of capitalists is successfully carried out only under the hegemony of the proletariat. This is a fundamental principle on which depend the tactics of the Chinese revolution.

The Line Changes

18. POLITICAL REPORT OF THE CENTRAL COMMITTEE AT THE FIFTEENTH CONGRESS OF THE CPSU*

December 1927

JOSEPH STALIN

The International Policy of Capitalism and the Preparation of New Imperialist Wars

In this connection, the question of redividing the world and spheres of influence, which constitute the basis of foreign markets, is today the principal question in the policy of world capitalism. I have already said that the existing distribution of colonies and spheres of influence brought about as a result of the last imperialist war has already become obsolete. It now fails to satisfy either the United States, which, not being content

* Joseph Stalin, *Works* (Moscow: Foreign Languages Publishing House, 1954), Vol. x, pp. 282–298, *excerpts*.

with South America, is trying to penetrate Asia (primarily China); or Britain, whose dominions and a number of whose most important Eastern markets are slipping from her hands; or Japan, which every now and again is "obstructed" in China by Britain and America; or Italy and France, which have an incalculable number of "points of dispute" in the Danubian countries and in the Mediterranean; and least of all does it satisfy Germany, which is still bereft of colonies. . . .

Have attempts been made during the period under review to bring about a "peaceful settlement" of the maturing military conflicts? Yes, there have been more of them than might have been expected; but they have led to nothing, absolutely nothing. Not only that; those attempts have turned out to be merely a screen for the preparations that the "powers" are making for new wars, a screen intended to deceive the people, to deceive "public opinion." Take the League of Nations, which, according to the mendacious bourgeois press, and the no less mendacious Social-Democratic press, is an instrument of peace. What has all the League of Nations' talk about peace, disarmament, reduction of armaments led to? To nothing, except the deception of the masses, except new spurts in armaments, except a further aggravation of the maturing conflicts. Can it be regarded as accidental that although the League of Nations has been talking about peace and disarmament for three years, and although the so-called Second International has been giving its support to this mendacious talk for three years, the "nations" are continuing to arm more and more, expanding the old conflicts among the "powers," piling up new conflicts, and thus undermining the cause of peace? . . .

Is it not obvious that the growth of armaments is dictated by the inevitability of new imperialist wars between the "powers," that the "spirit of war" is the principal content of the "spirit of Locarno"?

I think that the present "peaceful relations" could be likened to an old, worn-out shirt consisting of patches held together by a thin thread. It is enough to pull this thread fairly hard, to break it in some place or other, for the whole shirt to fall to pieces, leaving nothing but patches. It is enough to shake the present "peaceful relations" somewhere in Albania or Lithuania, in China or North Africa, for the whole "edifice of peaceful relations" to collapse.

That is how things were before the last imperialist war, when the assassination in Sarajevo led to war.

That is how things are now.

Stabilization is inevitably giving rise to new imperialist wars.

The State of the World Revolutionary Movement and the Harbingers of a New Revolutionary Upsurge

. . . the revolutionary awakening of the colonial and dependent countries presages the end of world imperialism. The fact that the Chinese revolution has not yet led to direct victory over imperialism cannot be of decisive significance for the prospects of the revolution. Great popular revolutions never achieve final victory in the first round of their battles. They grow and gain strength in the course of flows and ebbs. That has been so everywhere, including Russia. So it will be in China.

The most important result of the Chinese revolution is the fact that it has awakened from agelong slumber and has set in motion hundreds of millions of exploited and oppressed people, has utterly exposed the counter-revolutionary character of the cliques of generals, has torn the mask from the faces of the Kuomintang servitors of counterrevolution, has raised the prestige of the Communist Party among the masses of the common people, has raised the movement as a whole to a higher stage and has roused new hope in the hearts of the millions of the oppressed classes in India, Indonesia, etc. Only the blind and the faint-hearted can doubt that the Chinese workers and peasants are moving towards a new revolutionary upsurge. . . .

The Stabilization of Capitalism Is Becoming More and More Putrid and Unstable

Whereas a couple of years ago it was possible and necessary to speak of the ebb of the revolutionary tide in Europe, today we have every ground for asserting that *Europe is obviously entering a period of new Revolutionary upsurge;* to say nothing of the colonies and dependent countries, where the position of the imperialists is becoming more and more catastrophic. . . . Whereas a year or two ago it was possible and necessary to speak of a period of a certain equilibrium and "peaceful coexistence" between the USSR and the capitalist countries, today we have every ground for asserting that *the period of "peaceful coexistence" is receding into the past,* giving place to a period of imperialist assaults and preparation for intervention against the USSR.

True, Britain's attempts to form a united front against the USSR have failed so far. The reasons for this failure are: the contradiction of interests in the camp of the imperialists; the fact that some countries are interested in economic relations with the USSR; the peace policy of the USSR; the counteraction of the working class of Europe; the imperialists' fear of unleashing revolution in their own countries in the event of war against the USSR. But this does not mean that Britain will abandon her efforts to organize a united front against the USSR, that she will fail to organize such a front. The threat of war remains in force, despite Britain's temporary setbacks.

Hence the task is to take into account the contradictions in the camp of the imperialists, to postpone war by "buying off" the capitalists and to take all measures to maintain peaceful relations.

We must not forget Lenin's statement that as regards our work of construction very much depends upon whether we succeed in postponing war with the capitalist world, which is inevitable, but which can be postponed either until the moment when the proletarian revolution in Europe matures, or until the moment when the colonial revolutions have fully matured, or, lastly, until the moment when the capitalists come to blows over the division of the colonies. . . .

To sum up, we have:

Firstly, the growth of the contradictions within the capitalist encirclement; the necessity for capitalism of a new redivision of the world by means of war; the interventionist tendencies of one part of the capitalist world headed by Britain; the reluctance of the other part of the capitalist world to become involved in war against the USSR, preferring to establish economic relations with it; a conflict between these two tendencies and a certain possibility for the USSR to turn these contradictions to account for the purpose of maintaining peace.

Secondly, we have the collapsing stabilization; the growth of the colonial-revolutionary movement; the signs of a new revolutionary upsurge in Europe; the growth of the prestige of the Comintern and its sections throughout the world; the obvious growth of the sympathy of the working class of Europe for the USSR; the growing might of the USSR and the growing prestige of the working class of our country among the oppressed classes throughout the world.

19. THE PROGRAM OF THE COMMUNIST INTERNATIONAL*

September 1928

The USSR [is] the base of the world movement of all oppressed classes, the center of international revolution, the greatest factor in world history. In the USSR, the world proletariat for the first time acquires a country that is really its own, and for the colonial movements the USSR becomes a powerful center of attraction. Thus, the USSR is an extremely important factor in the general crisis of capitalism, not only because she has dropped out of the world capitalist system and has created a basis for a new socialist system of production but also because she plays an exceptionally great revolutionary role generally; she is the international driving force of proletarian revolution that impels the proletariat of all countries to seize power; she is the living example proving that the working class is not only capable of destroying capitalism, but of building up Socialism as well; she is the prototype of the fraternity of nationalities in all lands united in the World Union of Socialist Republics and of the economic unity of the toilers of all countries in a single world socialist economic system that the world proletariat must establish when it has captured political power. . . .

In view of the fact that the USSR is the only fatherland of the international proletariat, the principal bulwark of its achievements and the most important factor for its international emancipation, the international proletariat must on its part facilitate the success of the work of socialist construction in the USSR and defend her against the attacks of the capitalist powers by all the means in its power. . . .

In the event of the imperialist states declaring war upon and attacking the USSR, the international proletariat must retaliate by organizing bold and determined mass action and struggle for the overthrow of the imperialist governments with the slogan of: Dictatorship of the Proletariat and alliance with the USSR.

In the colonies, and particularly the colonies of the imperialist country attacking the USSR, every effort must be made to take

* U.S. House of Representatives, Committee on Foreign Affairs, *The Strategy and Tactics of World Communism*, House Document No. 619, 80th Congress, 2nd session (1948), pp. 121–140, *excerpts.*

advantage of the diversion of the imperialist military forces to develop an anti-imperialist struggle and to organize revolutionary action for the purpose of throwing off the yoke of imperialism and of winning complete independence. . . .

In order that it may fulfill its historic mission of achieving the dictatorship of the proletariat, the Communist Party must first of all set itself and accomplish the following fundamental strategic aims:

Extend its influence over the majority of the members of its own class, including working women and the working youth. To achieve this the Communist Party must secure predominant influence in the broad mass proletarian organizations (Soviets, trade unions, factory councils, cultural organizations, etc.). . . . To work in reactionary trade unions and skillfully to capture them, to win the confidence of the broad masses of the industrially organized workers, to change and "remove from their posts" the reformist leaders, represent important tasks in the preparatory period. . . .

The Communist Party must extend its influence over the masses of the urban and rural poor, over the lower strata of the intelligentsia and over the so-called "small man," i.e. the petty-bourgeois strata generally. It is particularly important that work be carried on for the purpose of extending the Party's influence over the peasantry. . . .

The tasks of the Communist International connected with the revolutionary struggle in colonies, semi-colonies and dependencies are extremely important strategical tasks in the world proletarian struggle. The colonial struggle presupposes that the broad masses of the working class and of the peasantry in the colonies be rallied round the banner of the revolution; but this cannot be achieved unless the closest cooperation is maintained between the proletariat in the oppressing countries and the toiling masses in the oppressed countries. . . .*

In order that revolutionary work and revolutionary action may be coordinated and in order that these activities may be guided most successfully, the international proletariat must be bounden by international class discipline. . . . This international Communist discipline must find expression in the subordination of the partial and local interests of the movement to its general and lasting interests and in the strict fulfillment, by all members, of the decisions passed by the leading bodies of the Communist International.

Unlike the Social-Democratic, Second International, each

* For further information on this Comintern statement concerning developing areas see Chapter X.

section of which submits to the discipline of "its own" national bourgeoisie and of its own "fatherland," the sections of the Communist International submit to only one discipline, i.e. international proletarian discipline, which guarantees victory in the struggle of the world's workers for world proletarian dictatorship. . . .

The Communists disdain to conceal their views and aims. They openly declare that their aims can be attained only by the forcible overthrow of all the existing social conditions. Let the ruling class tremble at a Communist revolution. The proletarians have nothing to lose but their chains. They have a world to win.

"Workers of all countries, unite!"

1934: The End of an Era

20. REPORT TO THE SEVENTEENTH CONGRESS OF THE CPSU*

January 26, 1934

JOSEPH STALIN

Comrades, more than three years have passed since the Sixteenth Congress. That is not a very long period. But it has been fuller in content than any other period. I do not think that any period in the last decade has been so rich in events as this one.

In the *economic* sphere these years have been years of continuing world economic crisis . . . While formerly people here and there still disputed whether there was a world economic crisis or not, now they no longer do so, for the existence of the crisis and its devastating effects are only too obvious. Now the controversy centers around another question: Is there a way out of the crisis or not; and if there is, then what is to be done?

In the *political* sphere these years have been years of further tension both in the relations between the capitalist countries

* Joseph Stalin, *Works* (Moscow: Foreign Languages Publishing House, 1955), Vol. XIII, pp. 288–312, *excerpts*.

and in the relations within them. Japan's war against China and the occupation of Manchuria, which have strained relations in the Far East; the victory of fascism in Germany and the triumph of the idea of revenge, which have strained relations in Europe; the withdrawal of Japan and Germany from the League of Nations, which has given a new impetus to the growth of armaments and to the preparations for an imperialist war; the defeat of fascism in Spain [the monarchy had been overthrown in 1931 and a republic set up], which is one more indication that a revolutionary crisis is maturing and that fascism is far from being long-lived—such are the most important events in the period under review. It is not surprising that bourgeois pacifism is breathing its last and that the trend toward disarmament is openly and definitely giving way to a trend towards armament and rearmament.

It is easy to understand how difficult it has been for the USSR to pursue its peace policy in this atmosphere poisoned with the miasma of war schemes. . . .

What did the USSR rely on in this difficult and complicated struggle for peace?

(a) On its growing economic and political might.

(b) On the moral support of the vast masses of the working class of all countries, who are vitally interested in the preservation of peace.

(c) On the prudence of those countries which for one motive or another are not interested in disturbing the peace, and which want to develop trade relations with such a punctual client as the USSR.

(d) Finally—on our glorious army, which stands ready to defend our country against assaults from without.

It was on this basis that we began our campaign for the conclusion with neighboring states of pacts of nonaggression and of pacts defining aggression. You know that this campaign has been successful. As you know, pacts of nonaggression have been concluded not only with the majority of our neighbors in the West and in the South, including Finland and Poland, but also with such countries as France and Italy; and pacts defining aggression have been concluded with those same neighboring states, including the Little Entente (Czechoslovakia, Rumania, and Yugoslavia).

On the same basis the friendship between the USSR and Turkey has been consolidated; relations between the USSR and Italy have improved and have indisputably become satisfactory; relations with France, Poland, and other Baltic states have improved; relations have been restored with the USA, China, etc.

Of the many facts reflecting the successes of the peace policy of the USSR two facts of indisputably material significance should be noted and singled out.

1. I have in mind, firstly, the change for the better that has taken place recently in the relations between the USSR and Poland and between the USSR and France. In the past, as you know, our relations with Poland were not at all good. Representatives of our state were assassinated in Poland. Poland regarded herself as the barrier of the Western states against the USSR. All the various imperialists counted on Poland as their advanced detachment in the event of a military attack on the USSR. The relations between the USSR and France were no better . . . But now those undesirable relations are gradually beginning to disappear. They are giving way to other relations, which can only be called relations of rapprochement . . . the atmosphere of mutual distrust is beginning to be dissipated. This does not mean, of course, that the incipient process of rapprochement can be regarded as sufficiently stable and as guaranteeing ultimate success. Surprises and zigzags in policy, for example in Poland, where anti-Soviet sentiments are still strong, can as yet by no means be regarded as out of the question. But the change for the better in our relations, irrespective of its results in the future, is a fact worthy of being noted and emphasized as a factor in the advancement of the cause of peace.

What is the cause of this change? What stimulates it?

Primarily, the growth of the strength and might of the USSR.

In our times it is not the custom to take any account of the weak—only the strong are taken into account. Furthermore, there have been some changes in the policy of Germany which reflect the growth of revanchist and imperialist sentiments in Germany.

In this connection some German politicians say that the USSR has now taken an orientation towards France and Poland; that from an opponent of the Versailles Treaty it has become a supporter of it, and that this change is to be explained by the establishment of the fascist regime in Germany. That is not true. Of course, we are far from being enthusiastic about the fascist regime in Germany. But it is not a question of fascism here, if only for the reason that fascism in Italy, for example, has not prevented the USSR from establishing the best relations with that country. Nor is it a question of any alleged change in our attitude towards the Versailles Treaty. It is not for us, who have experienced the shame of the Brest Peace, to sing the praises of the Versailles Treaty. We merely do not agree to the world being flung into the abyss of a new war on account of that treaty. The same must be said of the alleged new orientation taken by the USSR. We never had any orientation towards Germany, nor have we any orientation towards Poland and France. Our orientation in the past and our orientation at the present time is towards the USSR, and towards the USSR alone. (*Stormy applause*) And if the interests of the USSR demand rapprochement with one country or another which is not interested in disturbing peace, we adopt this course without hesitation.

No, that is not the point. The point is that Germany's policy has changed. The point is that even before the present German politicians came to power, and particularly after they came to power, a contest began in Germany between two political lines: between the old policy, which was reflected in the treaties between the USSR and Germany, and the "new" policy, which, in the main, recalls the policy of the former German Kaiser, who at one time occupied the Ukraine and marched against Leningrad, after converting the Baltic countries into a *place d'armes* for this march; and this "new" policy is obviously gaining the upper hand over the old policy. The fact that the advocates of the "new" policy are gaining supremacy in all things, while the supporters of the old policy are in disfavor, cannot be regarded as an accident. . . .

2. I have in mind, secondly, the restoration of normal relations between the USSR and the United States of America. There cannot be any doubt that this act is of very great significance for the whole system of international relations. The point is not only that it improves the chances of preserving peace, improves the relations between the two countries, strengthens trade connections between them, and creates a basis for mutual collaboration. The point is that it forms a landmark between the old position, when in various countries the USA was regarded as the bulwark for all sorts of anti-Soviet trends, and the new position, when that bulwark has been voluntarily removed, to the mutual advantage of both countries.

Such are the two main facts which reflect the successes of the Soviet policy of peace.

It would be wrong, however, to think that everything went smoothly in the period under review. . . .

Recall, say, the pressure that was brought to bear upon us by Britain; the embargo on our exports, the attempt to interfere in our internal affairs and to use this as a probe—to test our power of resistance. True, nothing came of this attempt, and later the embargo was lifted; but the unpleasant aftereffect of these sallies still makes itself felt in everything connected with the relations between Britain and the USSR. . . .

Nor must we lose sight of the relations between the USSR and Japan, which stand in need of considerable improvement. Japan's refusal to conclude a pact of nonaggression, of which Japan stands in no less need than the USSR, once again emphasizes the fact that all is not well in the sphere of our relations. . . . It is not difficult to understand that such circumstances cannot but create an atmosphere of uneasiness and uncertainty. Of course, we shall persistently continue to pursue a policy of peace and strive for an improvement in our relations with Japan, because we want to improve these relations. But it does not depend entirely upon us. That is why we must at the same time take all measures to guard our country against surprises, and be prepared to defend it against attack. . . . Those who want peace and seek business relations with us will always have our support. But those who try to attack our country will receive a crushing repulse to teach them in the future not to poke their pig snouts into our Soviet garden. (*Thunderous applause*)

21. THE BASES OF SOVIET FOREIGN POLICY*

KARL RADEK

The attempt to represent the foreign policy of the Soviet Union as a continuation of Tsarist policy is ridiculous. Bourgeois writers who do so have not grasped even the purely external manifestations of this policy. It used to be an axiom of Tsarist policy that it should strive by every available means to gain possession of the Dardenelles and of an ice-free port on the Pacific. Not only have the Soviets not attempted to seize the Dardenelles, but from the very beginning they have tried to establish the most friendly relations with Turkey; nor has Soviet policy ever had as one of

* Karl Radek, "The Bases of Soviet Foreign Policy," *Foreign Affairs*, Vol. XII (January 1934), pp. 193–206, *excerpts.* The material is copyrighted by, and published with the permission of, the Council on Foreign Relations. At this time, Karl Radek was the editor of *Izvestia* (official organ of the Soviet Government), a member of the Central Committee of the Communist Party, and a former Secretary of the Executive Committee of the Communist International. Radek was purged several years later. However, the ideas he developed in this article were officially sanctioned at the time they were published.

its aims the conquest of Port Arthur or of Dairen. Again, Tsarism, or any other bourgeois regime in Russia, would necessarily resume the struggle for the conquest of Poland and of the Baltic states, as is doubtless clear to any thoughtful bourgeois politician in those countries. The Soviet Union, on the contrary, is most anxious to establish friendly relations with these countries, considering their achievement of independence a positive and progressive historical factor.

It is silly to say that geography plays the part of fate, that it determines the foreign policy of a state. Tsarist policy originated not in geographical conditions, but in the privileges of the Russian nobility and the demands of young Russian capitalism. . . .

The Soviet Union is opposed to imperialism. It is opposed to an imperialistic war. It recognizes as equitable only one war, the war for the defense of socialism, the war of the enslaved peoples for their liberation. This point of view determines our attitude toward imperialism, as a system, and toward the consequences of its policy which finds their expression in the preparation of a new war. It also dictates our attitude toward imperialistic alliances which evolve during the process of preparing a new war for the redistribution of the world.

The Soviet Union takes no part in the struggle for the redistribution of the world.

The words of Stalin at the Sixteenth Congress of the Communist Party of the Soviet Union—"We do not want a single bit of foreign land; but at the same time not an inch of our land shall ever be yielded to anyone else"—these words are the exact expression of the policy of the Soviet Union. . . .

Nonparticipation in imperialistic alliances having for their purpose the plundering of foreign lands is the second leading principle of the foreign policy of the Soviet Union.

But the preparation of an imperialistic war is a fact, the existence of imperialistic alliances is a fact, and the Soviet Union can not limit itself to a mere expression of its negative attitude toward the objects of imperialism and toward imperialistic alliances. The Soviet Union must do everything to protect itself against the attack of the capitalist Powers who intend to conquer a portion of the Soviet territory or to overthrow the political framework of the socialist state.

The peace policy of the Soviet manifests itself not only in the struggle for disarmament, the struggle for the maximum reduction in armaments, but also in nonaggression pacts. In any given concrete case such a pact means a guarantee of Soviet neutrality in conflicts which may arise among the capitalist nations, conceded in exchange for the undertaking by the latter to refrain from attacking the Soviet Union or intervening in its domestic affairs. . . .

The Soviet Union is confronted both in Europe and the Far East with hostile camps which are preparing war against one another. It holds toward them a position of neutrality, and endeavors to guarantee its own peace by a policy of noninterference in their affairs and by entering into mutual obligations of non-aggression with all sides. These obligations have been stated concretely and precisely in the pact containing the definition of the aggressor. The Soviet Government has definitely undertaken not to move its armed forces by land, sea, or air across the frontiers of states which have assumed similar obligations, and also not to intervene directly or indirectly in their domestic affairs. All this indicates to the world that the policy of peace and neutrality on which the Soviet Union has embarked is not a mere diplomatic gesture, but a concrete political obligation the earnestness of which should be beyond question. . . .

The Soviet Union does not close the door to the possibility of a deal, an agreement, with imperialistic Powers which are waging a struggle against other imperialist Powers, if the latter attack the Soviet Union; but in entering into such an agreement the Soviet Union would not accept any responsibility for the specific purposes pursued by the imperialistic Power parties to the agreement. Never and under no conditions would it participate in the plundering of other nations, because participation in such a plunder would be contrary to the international solidarity of the workers. But against attacking imperialism an agreement is permissible with any opponent in order to defeat an enemy invading Soviet territory. . . .

And we are convinced that, irrespective of what might be the course of the war and who might be responsible for its origins, the only victor that would emerge from it would be the Soviet Union leading the workers of the whole world; for it alone has a banner which, in case of a war, can become the banner of the masses of the entire world.

FOR FURTHER STUDY

Angress, Werner T., *Stillborn Revolution: The Communist Bid for Power in Germany, 1921–1923*. Princeton, N.J.: Princeton University Press, 1963.

Beloff, Max, *The Foreign Policy of Soviet Russia, 1929–1936*, Vol. I. New York: Oxford University Press, 1947.

Borkenau, Franz, *World Communism*. Ann Arbor: University of Michigan Press, 1962.

Brandt, Conrad, *Stalin's Failure in China, 1924–1927*. Cambridge, Mass.: Harvard University Press, 1958.

Carr, Edward Hallett, *German-Soviet Relations Between the World Wars, 1919–1939*. Baltimore: Johns Hopkins Press, 1951.

————, *Socialism in One Country 1924–1926*, Part 3, Vol. II. New York: The Macmillan Company, 1964.

Dallin, David J., *The Rise of Russia in Asia*. New Haven, Conn.: Yale University Press, 1949.

Deutscher, Isaac, *Stalin: A Political Biography*. New York: Oxford University Press, 1949.

Eudin, Xenia and Harold H. Fisher (eds.), *Soviet Russia and the West, 1920–1927*. Stanford: Stanford University Press, 1957.

————— and Robert C. North (eds.), *Soviet Russia and the East, 1920–1927*. Stanford: Stanford University Press, 1957.

Fischer, Louis, *The Soviets in World Affairs*, 2 vols. New York: Vintage Books, 1960.

Freund, Gerald, *Unholy Alliance: Russian-German Relations from the Treaty of Brest-Litovsk to the Treaty of Berlin*. New York: Harcourt, Brace & World, 1957.

Hilger, Gustav and Alfred G. Meyer, *The Incompatible Allies*. New York: The Macmillan Company, 1953.

Kochan, Lionel, *Russia and the Weimar Republic*. Cambridge, Eng.: Bowes and Bowes, 1954.

McKenzie, Kermit E., *Comintern and World Revolution, 1928–1943*. New York: Columbia University Press, 1964.

Rosenbaum, Kurt, *Community of Fate: German-Soviet Diplomatic Relations, 1922–1928*. Syracuse, N.Y.: Syracuse University Press, 1965.

Schwartz, Benjamin, *Chinese Communism and the Rise of Mao*. Cambridge, Mass.: Harvard University Press, 1951.

Scott, William Evans, *Alliance Against Hitler: The Origins of the Franco-Soviet Pact*. Durham, N.C.: Duke University Press, 1962.

Whiting, Allen S., *Soviet Policies in China, 1917–1924*. New York: Columbia University Press, 1954.

CHAPTER IV

THE SEARCH FOR
SECURITY, 1934–1941

Soviet entry into the League of Nations on September 18, 1934, marked a basic shift in Soviet foreign policy. It was one of the early manifestations of a determined effort to meet the growing threat of an expansionist-minded Germany and Japan, and to end the increasing sense of isolation, through a system of collective security. The military resurgence of Germany in particular drew the USSR and the Western democracies closer in the face of the common danger. Cooperation foundered, however, on misunderstandings rooted in past antagonisms and suspicions, and on a mutual ideological hostility that virtually precluded politically necessary adjustments. This failure was to bring tragedy to the Soviet Union and to all of Europe.

In the next few years the Soviet Government emerged as a leading advocate of united League action. The address of Soviet Foreign Minister Litvinov, before the Assembly on the occasion of the USSR's becoming a member, set the pattern for subsequent Soviet disquisitions on the potential role of the League (reading 22). Litvinov acknowledged the early Soviet fear that the nations of the League "might give collective expression to their hostility towards the Soviet Union and combine their anti-Soviet activities," and he added that many of the League's decisions and activities were not looked upon with favor by the Soviet Government. The Soviet Union, however, cognizant of the ominous danger posed by aggressive fascism, appreciated the urgent need to organize an effective collective security system and was convinced that, "with the firm will and close cooperation of all its Members a great deal could be done at any given moment for the utmost diminution of the danger of war."

But though using the League to mobilize resistance to aggressive fascism, the Soviet Union sought, at the same time, to vitalize its bilateral agreement with France. On December 5, 1934, a protocol—preliminary to a more extensive security agreement—was signed.

The departure of Germany from the League of Nations on October 14, 1933, and its unconcealed hostility toward the Soviet Union had forced the Soviet Government to revise its previous assumption that only a Germany friendly to the Versailles victors threatened Soviet security.

The rapprochement between the Soviet Union and the Western democracies proceeded promisingly during the spring of 1935, with Anthony Eden's visit to Moscow in March and Pierre Laval's in May. Meanwhile, Hitler's courtship of Poland had added to Soviet fears. Moscow openly acknowledged the seriousness of the deterioration of relations with Germany. To cement the budding alliance system, the Soviet Union signed a Treaty of Mutual Assistance with France on May 2, 1935, and one with Czechoslovakia on May 16. France and the USSR pledged themselves to come to one another's assistance in the event of an unprovoked aggression.

The crucial treaty, on which so much of Europe's subsequent tragic history hinged, was that between the Soviet Union and Czechoslovakia. It contained a provision obligating the Soviet Government to come to the aid of Czechoslovakia *only* if France acted similarly in fulfillment of its responsibility. Thus, the Czechoslovak-Soviet agreement stated that "The two Governments recognize that the undertakings to render mutual assistance will operate between them only in so far as the conditions laid down in the present Treaty may be fulfilled and in so far as assistance may be rendered by France to the Party victim of the aggression."[1] In 1938–1939, this escape clause, invoked apparently by France's failure to fulfill its written pledge to Prague, was instrumental in the capitulation and collapse of Czechoslovakia. Legally, the provision freed the Soviet Union from any obligation to aid Czechoslovakia; morally, it placed the burden of shame upon France.

Soviet entry into the League, implying a willingness to conform to the accepted pattern of international politics, required a shift in policy by the Communist International, because Soviet leaders were unwilling to dispense with so valuable an asset. At the seventh (and last) Comintern Congress, in July and August of 1935, the Soviet Government preserved the Comintern by altering its policy in the interests of expediency and alliance with the Western democracies.

The main report was delivered by Georgi Dimitrov, the Bulgarian Communist who had won world renown in 1933 for his courageous defense against the Nazi-manufactured charge that he was responsible for the burning of the Berlin Reichstag. Condemning fascism as the most reactionary and dangerous brand of imperialist capitalism, Dimitrov declared that no techniques should be overlooked in striving for its defeat. He turned to classical literature for an appropriate example of the new tactic of the "Popular Front."

Comrades, you remember the ancient tale of the capture of Troy. Troy was inaccessible to the armies attacking her, thanks to her impregnable walls. And the attacking army, after suffering many sacrifices, was unable to achieve victory until with the aid of the famous Trojan horse it managed to penetrate to the very heart of the enemy camp.

We revolutionary workers, it appears to me, should not be shy about using the same tactics with regard to our Fascist foe, who is defending himself against the people with the help of the living wall of his cutthroats.

Dimitrov discarded the thesis, adopted in 1928, that fascism and social democracy were twin evils and called for the creation of a Popular Front of all parties opposed to fascism (reading 23) —a radical departure from the previous injunction against cooperation with bourgeois parties. But the growing threat from an aggressive Germany overruled all possible objections, and a collective security system embracing the Soviet Union and the Western democracies was pushed. Dimitrov did emphasize, however, that all Communist Parties were to maintain their identities within the framework of the various Popular Fronts. The Comintern Congress adopted Dimitrov's report on August 20, 1935, and all Communist Parties moved to act in concert with antifascist parties, regardless of their ideological or political coloration. The Comintern also sought to blame Hitler's advent to power on the shortsightedness of the German Social-Democrats. Thus, the "big lie" was used to gloss over grievous errors of Communist strategy, to nurture the myth of Stalin's infallibility, and to associate the Communist Party with the popular struggle against fascism. But the tactical switch adopted by Moscow in no way repudiated the revolutionary doctrines of the sixth Comintern Congress of 1928. These remained the accepted tenets of world communism, awaiting new "objective situations" for their further utilization.*

The Popular Front policy and the collective security system were soon tested in the crucible of international politics. Both were found wanting. In October 1935, Italy invaded Ethiopia, as part of Mussolini's course of expansion. Litvinov called upon the League to punish the aggressor. But the Western democracies, fearful of pushing Italy into an alliance with Germany, refrained from any forceful action. As with Manchuria, the League failed to cope with aggression. Scarcely had the furor over Ethiopia subsided than there was a more direct challenge to the European system of collective security.

On March 7, 1936, Hitler marched into the Rhineland in violation of the Locarno Treaty (1925). That treaty's so-called corollary, the Rhine Pact, granted to France and Great Britain specific authority to act without awaiting League approval. But France was beset with one of its perennial cabinet crises and did nothing, despite offers of support from Britain and Poland. Hitler, with his uncanny political insight and sense of timing, had won his great gamble.† This move not only set Germany firmly upon the path to conquest and war, but also strengthened Hitler's power in Germany. The last potential restraint—the German General Staff—was cowed into silence and submission by his stunning success. The Kremlin undoubtedly viewed the French paralysis with concern, for it highlighted the lack of determination of the West to resist German remilitarization and expansion. Russia may also have begun to reappraise the attractiveness of the alliance with France. There is evidence that Moscow, at the time, surreptitiously renewed its efforts to negotiate a Rapallo-type treaty with Nazi Germany.

Events in Spain soon revealed still further the appalling vacil-

---

* The Popular Front failed for a variety of reasons: the appeasement policy practiced by France and Great Britain at a time when resistance might have resulted in a meaningful cooperation with the USSR; the legacy of suspicion between the Communists and their partners against fascism, which precluded any positive or extensive cooperation; the impact of the Soviet purges; and, finally, the sellout at Munich.

† The German General Staff opposed Hitler's march into the Rhineland at this time, fearing French retaliation would lead to a reoccupation of the Ruhr and destroy the new Wehrmacht in its infancy. From captured Government documents we know that the German Army had orders to withdraw at once if the French gave any indication of opposition. Paul Otto Schmidt, Hitler's personal interpreter, quotes him as saying that "If the French had marched into the Rhineland then we should have had to retreat with ignominy, for we had not the military resources at our disposal for even feeble resistance." Indeed, if France had acted otherwise, how different might have been the subsequent history of Europe!

lation and feebleness of the French and British. On July 19, 1936, with the newly formed French Popular Front Government of Léon Blum scarcely two months old, General Franco rose against the Spanish Republic. The Spanish Civil War of 1936–1939 accelerated the disintegration of the Popular Front, provided the first European battleground for World War II, and split Western European political circles so grievously that the effects are still evident today. It confronted Soviet leaders with a serious dilemma. Another fascist country bordering France might push Paris into more intimate ties with Moscow. On the other hand, though a Loyalist victory achieved with open Communist support would undoubtedly enhance Soviet prestige, it might paradoxically frighten France and lead her to view Hitler less belligerently.* Stalin moved cautiously, preferring French, rather than Soviet, involvement.† Furthermore, the Soviet Union was committed to supporting the League of Nations. As in the Manchurian and Ethiopian crises, the League proved unable to agree upon effective counter-measures. France and Britain, beset by serious internal problems, did not assist the Spanish Republic but used the League as a crutch to gain meaningless acceptance for an unenforceable policy of nonintervention in Spain by the major European Powers, the Soviet Union included. But the open secret of German and Italian support of Franco with men and equipment induced Stalin to take measures designed to preserve the Popular Front policy, though he maintained the official pretense of nonintervention. By October 1936, increasingly worried by reports of an impending German-Italian-Japanese alliance, the Soviet Union embarked on a program of limited intervention.

Several interpretations of the Soviet move are possible: According to Germany and Italy, the USSR intervened with the

---

* A quite different interpretation is suggested by General W. G. Krivitsky, at that time Chief of Soviet Military Intelligence in Western Europe. He believed that Stalin wanted to establish a Soviet controlled regime in Spain. "That done he could command the respect of France and England, win from them the offer of a real alliance, and either accept it or—with that as a bargaining point—arrive at his underlying steady aim and purpose, a compact with Germany." *I Was Stalin's Agent* (London: Hamish Hamilton, 1939), p. 99.

† According to Franz Borkenau, a leading analyst of Soviet policy, Stalin's initial reaction was to try to involve France, not the Soviet Union, in the Spanish struggle, for "French intervention on the republican side would have eliminated any possibility of a four-power pact (involving Germany, and Britain, and France and Italy), would have driven France into the arms of Russia, would have sharpened the antagonism between the Axis and the West, while Russia could safely remain outside all serious commitments; and it would have redounded to the glory of the French Communists and would have strengthened their position with the Popular Front." *European Communism* (New York: Harper & Row, Publishers, 1953), p. 167.

specific intent of establishing a Soviet republic. This view received support in many conservative and reactionary European circles. Other elements, only slightly less suspicious of Kremlin motives, felt that Moscow wanted to involve the Western democracies in a war with the fascist states in order to forestall any Nazi expansion in the East. The pro-Communists attributed Soviet support of the Loyalists to a desire to strengthen the principle of collective security and thereby halt the spread of fascism.

Each contention contains some validity. However, according to one leading student of the period, the *primary* objective of the Soviet Union at that time was to put up "as strong a resistance against Franco and his allies as possible in order to support Russia's foreign policy of defense against fascism,"[2] and thus forestall any Nazi move against Russia itself.

The Spanish Civil War was one of the major tragedies of the twentieth century. Like any civil war it involved great bitterness and bloodshed. The Communists took advantage of the situation to increase their influence in Loyalist circles and then initiated a purge of all opposition elements comparable to the one then going on in the Soviet Union. In the final analysis, Soviet intervention intensified the distrust between the Soviet Union and the Western democracies.[3]

By 1938, however, Soviet attention was diverted to matters of more immediate concern. The formation of the Rome-Berlin Axis in October 1936 had been followed by the negotiation of the German-Japanese Anti-Comintern Pact in November. As the danger from Germany and Japan became more acute, Soviet apprehension grew.

Just as fear of Germany motivated the Popular Front policy in Europe, so in the Far East did the specter of an expansionist Japan encourage a rapprochement with China. Soviet-Japanese relations had a checkered history. During the Russian Civil War and the Allied intervention Japan took possession of eastern Siberia, including the Vladivostok region. However, as a result of the Washington Conference (1922) and Russia's gradual recovery, the Japanese withdrew. When Japanese relations with Russia were re-established in January 1925, Japan agreed to evacuate the northern half of Sakhalin Island. The two nations remained passively friendly during the 1925–1931 period, despite their rivalry in Manchuria and recurring difficulties about Japanese fishing rights in the north Pacific. After the Japanese invasion of Manchuria, on September 18, 1931, and subsequent occupation of it, relations deteriorated. The Soviet Union was confronted with a new challenge to its security. Its initial policy was one of strict neutrality, of watch and wait; it fully expected that the Japanese action was but a prelude to a strike against Siberia.

Soviet relations with China, severed since late 1927 and further strained by the 1929 fighting in Manchuria for control of the Chinese Eastern Railway, took a turn for the better after the Japanese invasion of Manchuria. Diplomatic relations were restored on December 12, 1932. Since none of the difficulties that had originally precipitated the break proved amenable to negotiation, however, their agreement merely affirmed the status quo before 1929.[4]

Throughout 1932, the Soviet Union observed the ineffectiveness of the League and the Lytton Commission, the manifest unwillingness of the Great Powers to resist Japan with anything stronger than a stream of protest notes, and the growing indications of its strategic isolation. Fear of attack by a coalition of capitalists became acute. Accordingly, Moscow tried a direct settlement with Japan. Litvinov proposed a nonaggression pact several times but was repeatedly rebuffed, though the Japanese did evince a strong desire to purchase the northern lines of the Manchurian railroad, which were still controlled by the Soviet Union. Negotiations began in Tokyo in June 1933 and continued intermittently for almost two years until, in March 1935, Moscow finally agreed, over bitter Chinese protests, to sell its interests in the railroad. Though Russian relations with the Western democracies had improved, Chinese weakness, anxiety over Hitler's anti-Bolshevik declarations, and indications of closer collaboration between Japan and Germany led the Russians to settle with Japan. During the negotiations to sell the Chinese Eastern Railway, however, they also strengthened their military position along the Amur River and in Outer Mongolia.

This effort at appeasement did not satisfy Japan's expansionist appetite. Japanese forces soon moved into the Inner Mongolian provinces of Jehol and Chahar, seeking to establish a puppet state—as they had established Manchukuo in Manchuria—and thereby to threaten the Soviet position in Outer Mongolia. A mutual assistance treaty was concluded between the USSR and Outer Mongolia in March 1936, despite Chinese protests that the area was juridically under Chinese sovereignty (though controlled by Russia since 1924). The Soviets replied that the treaty, which was obviously designed to bolster Soviet hegemony in this increasingly crucial area, in no way compromised Chinese sovereignty, which they still claimed to recognize. They further exploited Chinese weakness by extending their influence into the sparsely settled, strategic province of Sinkiang. Meanwhile, relations with Japan continued to deteriorate. Through the maze of fisheries disputes, border incidents, and debt difficulties associated with the Chinese Eastern Railway settlement, two traditional enemies were feeling out each other's strength in preparation for the final test which might come at any moment.

It must not be overlooked that Soviet policy in the Far East is conditioned, and even controlled, by developments in Europe and by their effect on the security of the Soviet homeland. Indeed, this integral relationship is often neglected in analyses of Soviet foreign policy.

As for the Chinese, their protests against the none-too-subtle extension of Soviet influence gave way to an urgent need for Soviet help following the full-scale Japanese invasion of July 1937. During the preceding year Moscow, concerned over the implications of the Anti-Comintern Pact, had pushed for a Popular Front in China. In December 1936, Chiang Kai-shek was dramatically kidnapped. His captors insisted that he stop the enervating punitive expeditions against the Communists, husband his strength, and devote himself to leading the struggle against Japan.* Reluctantly, he consented. The introduction of the Popular Front policy in China benefited Moscow, for the renewed Communist-Kuomintang collaboration strengthened China's capacity to resist Japan; it also helped promote the security of Soviet Far Eastern frontiers from possible Japanese attack at a time when developments in Europe were taking an increasingly ominous course. In addition, it enabled the Chinese Communists to consolidate their position in northwest China in preparation for the postwar struggle for power with the Kuomintang.

The Japanese launched their second invasion of China on July 7, 1937. Appreciating the potential threat to its security, yet not fearing any immediate attack, the Soviet Union signed a nonaggression pact with China on August 21, though she well knew that this would adversely affect relations with Japan. In time, the USSR provided China with important, though limited, quantities of military supplies, particularly during the period between the fall of France and Hitler's invasion of the Soviet Union.

China appealed to the League for help against Japan. The signers of the Nine-Power Treaty of 1922 met in Brussels to

* Some experts on the Far East believe that the Soviet Government was instrumental in organizing the plot from the beginning. Or, there may not have been any connection. Rather, the absence of efforts to establish a Popular Front in China immediately after the 1935 Comintern pronouncement may have resulted from Stalin's reluctance to commit himself until it had become an accomplished fact in Europe. It may have also indicated a lack of interest or knowledge of the situation in China, not in itself surprising given the growing threats in Europe, and the trials and purges in the Soviet Union, which dominated Stalin's attention.

discuss what action, if any, to take. Russia, having accepted an invitation, was momentarily encouraged by President Roosevelt's speech calling for a quarantine against the aggressors. But the conference ended in failure. The concept of collective security had suffered another blow. Events at Munich were shortly to complete Soviet disenchantment and lead to accord with Hitler.

Meanwhile, Soviet supplies were delivered to China via Sinkiang. And farther to the east, along the Manchurian-Mongolian frontier, an increasing number of border "skirmishes" broke out between Japanese and Soviet troops, often involving half a million men. The clashes at Changkufeng, a pivotal area near the Soviet, Manchurian, and Korean borders, in July 1938, and at Nomonhan, on the Mongolian frontier, in May 1939, were of particular importance. The Soviets repulsed the Japanese in both battles. Not until after the signing of the Nazi-Soviet pact in August 1939, which apparently caught the Japanese by surprise, did an uneasy quiet settle along the entire border as Japanese expansion took a southern course and the USSR concentrated on problems of expansion and conflict in Europe. To safeguard their northern flank, the Japanese concluded a Neutrality Pact with the Soviet Union in April 1941.

Western writers seeking to understand Stalin's reasons for signing with Hitler have generally overlooked the crucial importance for Soviet leaders of the undeclared war with Japan, and particularly the degree to which the massive battles fought with armor and aircraft from May through August 1939 influenced Stalin's policy in Europe.* Emphasizing the momentous events in Europe, these writers have underestimated the role that fear of an imminent major war with Japan played in Soviet thinking. The recent outpouring of Soviet military memoirs and histories provides us with much new information on Soviet Far Eastern developments and should result in Western re-evaluations of the factors conditioning Soviet policy in Europe at this time.

Throughout the period before 1941, Soviet policy in the Far East aimed principally at preserving Soviet security by the use of balance-of-power politics. Changes in political alignment were undertaken as they served Soviet national interest. The shift to a policy of expansion in the Far East developed out of the new international situation resulting from the defeat of Japan and the triumph of the Chinese Communists in 1949.

* Western military experts, in assessing the ability of the Soviet Union to resist the Nazi onslaught, chose to take as their point of departure the weakening of the Red Army as a result of the 1936–1938 purges and its poor showing in the winter war against Finland, ignoring its impressive performance against Japan in the Far East.

By early 1938 Hitler's activities dominated the international stage. For Russia, Spain had become a diversionary theater, and the immediate threat from Japan had receded as a result of the war in China. After the occupation of Austria on March 12, Hitler turned to Czechoslovakia, the next steppingstone to German conquest of Europe. His ostensible objective was the reincorporation of the Sudetenland into Germany. But Hitler's appetite, increased by Western weakness and retreat, would be satisfied only with the reduction of Czechoslovakia to the status of a German province. Five days after the Austrian anschluss Litvinov held a press conference in which he emphasized that the latest aggression was no longer in a remote area: "this time the violence has been perpetrated in the center of Europe and has created an indubitable menace not only for the eleven countries now contiguous with the aggressor, but also for all European states, and not only European ones." After referring to the Czechoslovak and Polish-Lithuanian crises, he proceeded to outline the Soviet position:

The Soviet Government being cognizant of its share in this responsibility and being also cognizant of its obligations ensuing from the League Covenant, from the Briand-Kellogg Pact, and from the treaties of mutual assistance concluded with France and Czechoslovakia, I can state on its behalf that on its part it is ready as before to participate in collective actions, which would be decided upon jointly with it and which would aim at checking the further development of aggression and at eliminating the increased danger of a new world massacre. It is prepared immediately to take up in the League of Nations or outside of it the discussion with other Powers of the practical measures which the circumstances demand. It may be too late to-morrow, but to-day the time for it is not yet gone if all the States, and the Great Powers in particular, take a firm and unambiguous stand in regard to the problem of the collective salvation of peace.[5]

Britain and France, however, failed to respond to this Soviet invitation to organize against Germany. Moscow felt a growing sense of isolation, which was to reach its peak after Munich. From March to September the Sudeten crisis continued to mount in intensity. The Western democracies tried to placate Hitler, while they virtually ignored the Soviet Union. On June 23, 1938, Litvinov spoke in Moscow on the ominous international situation, the imminent demise of the League, and the abjectness of Western diplomacy.

The League of Nations is stricken with paralysis and unless urgent measures be taken to restore it, it will fall to pieces completely at the moment the conflict begins. With the exception of Czechoslovakia, the Western European Powers have no longer any allies among the middle and small States of Europe. Some of these States have openly entered the orbit of the aggressor countries, others, for fear of the latter, are mumbling about neutrality. . . .

Such are the results of the "realistic" policy of the Western European Powers counterposed by them to the system of collective security we uphold together with the strengthening of the League of Nations, which might, perhaps, even now be able to save the situation . . .[6]

By mid-September Hitler's crescendo of invective against Czechoslovakia alarmed the British and French Governments enough to cause British Prime Minister Chamberlain to fly to Berchtesgaden. There on September 15, Britain, France, and Germany reached an agreement calling upon Czechoslovakia to accede to Hitler's demands. At first Prague refused. But British and French pressure reversed Czech determination. According to President Eduard Beneš:

We were informed that if we did not accept their plan for the cession of the so-called Sudeten regions, they would leave us to our fate, which, they said, we had brought upon ourselves. They explained that they certainly *would not go to war with Germany just "to keep the Sudeten Germans in Czechoslovakia."*[7]

On September 30, the dismemberment of Czechoslovakia began. The Munich agreement, ceding the Sudetenland to Germany, was signed without the participation of the victim or of the Soviet Union. A tragic mandate was imposed upon a hapless nation.

Throughout the crisis the Soviet Government affirmed its willingness to support the League in any collective action and to live up to its obligation to come to the aid of Czechoslovakia, provided France did likewise. On September 21, at the Nineteenth Session of the Assembly of the League of Nations, Litvinov stated that:

. . . the Soviet Union has . . . expressed its readiness to perform all the decisions and even recommendations of the League which were directed to preserving peace and combating the aggressors, irrespective of whether those decisions coincided with its immediate interests as a State. . . .

It was only two days ago that the Czechoslovak Government addressed a formal enquiry to my Government as to whether the Soviet Union is prepared, in accordance with the Soviet-Czech pact, to render Czechoslovakia immediate and effective aid if France, loyal to her obligations, will render similar assistance, to which my Government gave a clear answer in the affirmative.[8]

To what extent were Soviet offers of aid genuine? Were the Soviets prepared to cooperate in good faith in a collective security system designed to halt Nazi aggression? The answers must for-

ever remain matters of controversy and conjecture. Many critics
of official British and French policy, such as Churchill and Paul-
Boncour, insisted that a unique opportunity was lost when the
Soviet offers of cooperation were rebuffed.[9] On the other hand,
it may be argued that France and Great Britain were not ready
for war.* In addition, in the minds of their leaders "any suspicion that the Soviet Government might be less anxious than
they were themselves to avoid war, because the USSR might
expect to profit from it, was counterbalanced by the suspicion
that the Red Army (weakened by the purge) was in no shape in
1938 to enter upon a war against Germany."[10] In any event,
Soviet leaders had legitimate grounds for criticizing the Western
policy of appeasement, and given their ideological biases, they
drew the worst possible conclusions from Munich (reading 24).
Hitler had succeeded at one stroke in securing the betrayal of
Czechoslovakia, virtually rupturing relations between the Soviet
Union and the Western democracies, and undermining France's
entire security system in Eastern Europe. The tragedy of Munich
was the tragedy of men of little vision, politically inept and
plagued by domestic crises, which rendered them helpless in the
surging tide of historic forces over which no one individual or
party had any control.

In March 1939, contrary to his solemn declaration at Munich
that he had no further territorial demands, Hitler occupied all
of Czechoslovakia. A few days earlier, Stalin had delivered a
major address on the international situation to the Eighteenth
Party Congress (reading 25). Though he flailed both the Western
democracies for their uncertain policy of neutrality and nonintervention and Germany for its aggressive posture, Stalin did
not elaborate on the future orientation of Soviet foreign policy.
Rather, he contented himself with the statement that the USSR
must be cautious and not allow itself "to be drawn into conflicts
by warmongers who are accustomed to have others pull the chest-

---

* A number of works have appeared, written by insiders at Munich, to
support the thesis that the sellout of Czechoslovakia was prompted by a
need for time in which to prepare for the coming war. For example, Commander P. K. Kemp, the Admiralty archivist and head of the Historical
Section, writes that the Chiefs of Staff warned Prime Minister Chamberlain,
at the time of Munich, that "the country was not ready for war, that no
measures of force, whether alone or in alliance with other European countries, could now stop Germany from inflicting a crushing defeat on Czechoslovakia, and that any involvement in war with Germany at this stage could
well lead to an ultimate defeat, through her unpreparedness, of the country
[Great Britain] herself." This bleak report, he states, forced Chamberlain
into a position from which there was no escape; "national prestige, national
honor, the obliquy of future generations, none of these could weigh against
his overriding duty to his country, to gain time." *Key to Victory: The Triumph of British Sea Power in World War II* (Boston: Little, Brown and
Company, 1958), p. 26.

nuts out of the fire for them." The general tenor of his speech was anti-Nazi, but the price for Soviet agreement with either coalition was left open for negotiation.

At last convinced that Hitler's ambitions could not readily be curbed, the British Government belatedly undertook to organize resistance and, quite unexpectedly, extended a unilateral guarantee to Poland on March 31, 1939, which stated that:

> . . . in the event of any action which clearly threatened Polish independence, and which the Polish Government accordingly considered vital to resist with their national forces, His Majesty's Government would feel themselves bound at once to lend the Polish Government all support in their power.

Poland, a minor and pathetic villain during the Czech crisis,* found itself without friendly neighbors, sandwiched between an opportunistic, insecure Russia and an aggressive, expansionist Germany. After the absorption of Czechoslovakia, Hitler directed his invective against Poland, demanding that the Polish corridor and the port of Danzig, separating Germany from East Prussia, be incorporated into the Greater Reich. Despite the growing German threat, Poland balked at any meaningful cooperation with its historic nemesis, Russia. In view of Stalin's subsequent policy of aggrandizement, it is evident that Polish fears were warranted. Hungary and Rumania also refused to cooperate with Moscow. On April 19 a report emanating from Warsaw stated that:

> Poland has informed Great Britain and Russia that she refuses to participate in any efforts to draw the Soviet Union into the anti-aggression "peace front" being organized by Britain, it was announced officially tonight. Poland has a "negative attitude" toward permitting Soviet troops or planes to march or fly over Polish territory, the announcement said.[11]

At the same time, the German Foreign Office responded quickly to the Soviet ambassador's remark that he saw no reason why relations between their countries might not "become better and better." The Kremlin regarded both Western and fascist coalitions as anathemas, but sought a rapprochement with one or the other, irrespective of ideological or political differences. It maneuvered (a) to prevent either coalition from making possible an aggression against the Soviet Union and (b) to obtain the highest price for its support. To this end Moscow was prepared to follow any course.

---

* At the time of Munich, the Poles had refused to discuss the possible passage of Soviet troops across Polish territory in the event that aid was to be rendered Czechoslovakia; afterward, they participated in the mutilation of Czechoslovakia by occupying the Teschen district in Silesia.

On May 3, 1939, a date which may be regarded as a turning point for Soviet policy, Molotov succeeded Litvinov as Foreign Minister.* This move signified the abandonment of efforts to promote a collective security system and to rely upon the League of Nations—a policy associated by Western leaders with Litvinov —and the start of active work toward an agreement with Germany. Yet in his first report to the Supreme Soviet on May 31, Molotov acknowledged indications that Britain and France were now prepared to counteract fascist expansion.

> How serious these changes are still remains to be seen. As yet it cannot even be said whether these countries are seriously desirous of abandoning the policy of non-intervention, the policy of non-resistance to the further development of aggression. May it not turn out that the present endeavor of these countries to resist aggression in *some* regions will serve as no obstacle to the unleashing of oppression in *other* regions?

This scarcely veiled allusion reflected Soviet distrust and the belief that the Western democracies were still trying to induce Hitler to expand to the East.†

The events of the next three months are too complex and involved to be recounted here.[12] Hitler, faced with the British guarantee to Poland, unilaterally abrogated the 1934 Polish-German treaty and moved to ensure his eastern flank by an accord with the USSR. Negotiations concentrated on the price of Soviet neutrality. During this period Western concern mounted. The German-Soviet rapprochement became a virtual certainty as a result

---

* There have thus far been but seven Foreign Ministers: Leon Trotsky (November 1917–April 1918); Georgi Chicherin (1918–1929); Maxim Litvinov (1929–1939); Vyacheslav M. Molotov (1939–1949; 1953–1956); Andrei Vyshinsky (1949–1953); Dimitri Shepilov (1956); Andrei Gromyko (1957–?).

† For a Soviet interpretation of the British policy of appeasement of Germany, Italy, and Japan, during the pre-Munich (1935–1938) period see *A Short History of the Communist Party of the Soviet Union* (New York: International Publishers, 1939): "The 'democratic' states are, of course, stronger than the fascist states. The one-sided character of the developing world war is due to the absence of a united front of the 'democratic' states against the fascist powers. The so-called democratic states, of course, do not approve of the 'excesses' of the fascist states and fear any accession of strength to the latter. But they fear even more the working class movement in Europe and the movement of national emancipation in Asia, and regard fascism as an 'excellent antidote' to these 'dangerous' movements. For this reason the ruling circles of the 'democratic' states, especially the ruling Conservative circles of Great Britain, confine themselves to a policy of pleading with the overweening fascist rulers 'not to go to extremes', at the same time giving them to understand that they 'fully comprehend' and on the whole sympathize with their reactionary police policy towards the working class movement and the national emancipation movement." (English edition, 1939), p. 334.

of discussions on August 2–4, when Germany decided to meet
Moscow's terms. A British and French *military* mission, with no
formal written powers to make *political* decisions, left for Moscow
by sea on August 5. This seeming lack of urgency on the part of
Britain and France was not lost on the Soviet leaders. By the
time discussions opened on August 12, it was too late. The
Western democracies were unwilling (and unable) to meet
Stalin's price—a free hand in the Baltic states and the right to
send troops into Poland in the event of attack by Germany.

On August 19, Germany and the Soviet Union signed a trade
agreement. Four days later, Ribbentrop, the German Foreign
Minister, flew to Moscow and the fateful ten-year Nonaggression
Pact was signed the same day (reading 26). The agreement
obligated each partner to absolute neutrality "should one of the
High Contracting Parties become the object of belligerent action
by a third power." In reality, it gave the green light to Hitler's
invasion of Poland. The secret protocol called for the partition of
Poland and placed Estonia, Latvia, Finland, and Bessarabia within
the Soviet sphere of influence, assigning Lithuania to Germany.

The Nazi-Soviet pact differed in two notable ways from previous nonaggression pacts signed by the USSR.[13] First, it had no
stipulation that "if one of the contracting parties should commit
an act of aggression against a third party the other contracting
party would be entitled to denounce the pact." Second, the last
article of the Treaty stated that it was to "enter into force as
soon as it is signed," an unusual diplomatic provision. These
departures from tradition constituted a tacit Soviet acknowledgment of the character of Nazi intentions—indeed, they openly
encouraged Germany's aggressive designs. On August 31, at a
special session of the Supreme Soviet convened to ratify the
treaty, Molotov delivered a lengthy speech in which he defended
the Soviet Union in its negotiations with the Western Powers
(reading 27).

At dawn, on September 1, 1939, Nazi legions rolled into Poland.
Two days later, true to their word, Britain and France declared
war on Germany. World War II was a reality. The new war was
an imperialist one to Moscow, in whose view "international war
and peace are not two diametrically opposed and mutually exclusive phenomena, but two equally important means, supple-
menting each other in the communist's advance toward their
final revolutionary goal."[14] It never clearly said so, but it undoubtedly wished a plague on both sides and tended "to view
the Second World War through the prism of the first one, and to
hope that the working classes of the warring countries could
revolt as the Russian working class had done."[15] Stalin hoped to

remain a spectator, ready to profit from the mutual exhaustion of the competing coalitions.

With the outbreak of war, the Soviet Union abandoned its previous policy of nonaggression for a course of aggression and territorial expansion. It rationalized its actions in terms of national security, exploiting, in true Machiavellian fashion, the preoccupation elsewhere of the other European powers. Soviet imperialism, by whatever name and however legitimatized, was, with the subsequent defeat of Germany, to move Soviet power into the heart of Europe and thus give rise to the cold war. Meanwhile, on September 17, 1939, Red Army troops marched into eastern Poland; on September 28, Germany and the Soviet Union formally partitioned the country by secret agreement. The protocol also transferred most of Lithuania to the Soviet sphere "in return for the emphatic shift eastward in the Soviet-Polish demarcation line, which now followed the Bug instead of the Vistula for most of its length."[16]

Stalin wasted little time in extending Soviet influence into the Baltic states. Mutual assistance agreements with Estonia, Latvia, and Lithuania were only preliminaries to the formal incorporation of these states into the Soviet Union in August 1940. Finland was next on the Soviet list. Negotiations during October and November (1939) failed to bring about the desired result. Accordingly, on November 29, Soviet troops attacked Finland. Mounting Western sympathy for the Finns developed into unstinting admiration as the numerically superior and better-equipped Soviet troops were stymied and outmaneuvered on the wintry wastes of the Karelian Isthmus and central Finland. The League of Nations condemned the Soviet aggression and evicted the USSR from the organization on December 14. Western support, however, did not crystallize into material assistance for the beleaguered, gallant Finns, who finally had to capitulate. A treaty of peace was signed on March 12, 1940. Reviewing the reasons for the Finnish campaign in his speech of March 29, Molotov emphasized, among other considerations, the paramountcy of security (reading 28).

The successful Nazi blitzkrieg in April and May and the astonishing, unexpected French collapse in June, accelerated Soviet efforts to bolster its position vis-a-vis Germany. Soviet pressure was put on Rumania to relinquish Bessarabia and northern Bukovina. With evident reluctance, Germany accepted the Soviet annexation, at the same time taking measures to consolidate its own influence in the rest of Rumania. Difficulties also developed over Bulgaria and Yugoslavia; the expansionist appetites of Germany and the Soviet Union sharpened their rivalry in the Balkans and in Finland; other strains appeared in the economic sphere. By September 1940, Hitler became convinced that Russia would have to be subjugated if his conquest of Europe was to be safeguarded.

Portentous Soviet-German conversations were held in Berlin on November 12–13, 1940, concerning the shape of the "new order" wrought by the supposed defeat of the British Empire.[17] Ribbentrop referred to the fruitful results of German-Soviet collaboration and asked "whether in the long run the most advantageous access to the sea for Russia could not be found in the direction of the Persian Gulf and the Arabian Sea, and whether at the same time certain other aspirations of Russia in this part of Asia—in which Germany was comfortably disinterested—could not also be realized." He also supported revision of the Montreux Convention (governing access through the Dardanelles and the Bosporus) to make it more favorable to the Soviet Union. A protocol was drawn up, but never signed, between Germany, Italy, and Japan on the one side and the Soviet Union on the other, by which the USSR was to obtain recognition of its recent territorial acquisitions and a promise of peace with Japan; and a secret protocol, assigning spheres of influence among the four powers, declared that Soviet "territorial aspirations center south of the national territory of the Soviet Union in the direction of the Indian Ocean." Molotov's intransigence and his expressed desire for further expansion in the Balkans, Finland, and the Straits area angered Hitler and confirmed his resolve to subjugate the Soviet Union. It is interesting to note that Molotov's demands were set forth in non-Marxist, openly power-political terms, and clearly coincided with traditional Czarist territorial objectives (reading 29). The limits of compatibility had been exceeded. On December 18, 1940, the Führer issued the order to prepare for the attack on the USSR (Operation Barbarossa). Preparations were to be completed by May 15, 1941.

For the next six months the Soviet Union tried to maintain friendly relations with Germany, honoring all economic agreements scrupulously. Relations with the United States and Great Britain were correct, but little else. In February 1941, German troops completely occupied Rumania, and in March, Bulgaria as well, thus outflanking Yugoslavia. Meanwhile, Mussolini's invasion of Greece turned into a rout—of the Italian Army. To extricate his partner, and safeguard his own Balkan flank, Hitler invaded Yugoslavia on April 6—two days *after* Molotov had informed the German Government of his intention to conclude a nonaggression pact with Belgrade. The Soviet leaders retreated. They did not sign the treaty with Yugoslavia, nor did they make any effort to aid the Yugoslavs, and within two weeks Nazi forces occupied all of Yugoslavia. But Hitler's original date for the invasion of the Soviet Union had to be postponed until June 22. On May 6, Stalin assumed the office of Chairman of the Council of People's Commissars (equivalent to Prime Minister). This, his first formal *Government* position since his rise to undisputed leadership in the USSR, revealed the Kremlin's growing concern over German intentions. Outwardly, German-Soviet relations remained unchanged as the Soviet Union tried in every way to appease Hitler. Time, however, had run out on the "unholy alliance."

NOTES

1. Leonard Shapiro, *Soviet Treaty Series* (Washington, D.C.: Georgetown University Press, 1955), Vol. II, p. 131.
2. David T. Cattell, *Communism and the Spanish Civil War* (Berkeley: University of California Press, 1956), p. 211. This provides an excellent account of events in Spain and analyzes the extent to which the Communist Party affected developments in Spain. He stresses "the importance of the defensive motive rather than the offensive motive in the Soviet Union's intervention in Spain. She was not interested in a satellite in Spain at this time but only in a tool to stop the aggression of the Fascist states against herself." Dr. Cattell's companion volume, *Soviet Diplomacy and the Spanish Civil War* (1957), gives a valuable account of the relationship between Soviet foreign policy and the Soviet attitude toward events in Spain.
3. Max Beloff, *The Foreign Policy of Soviet Russia, 1936–1941* (New York & London: Oxford University Press, 1949), Vol. II, p. 38.
4. Harriet L. Moore, *Soviet Far Eastern Policy, 1931–1945* (Princeton, N.J.: Princeton University Press, 1945), p. 19.
5. *Documents on International Affairs, 1938* (London: Oxford University Press, 1942), Vol. I, pp. 314–315.
6. *Ibid.*, p. 322.
7. Dr. Eduard Beneš, *Memoirs of Eduard Beneš: From Munich to New War and New Victory* (Boston: Houghton Mifflin Company, 1954), p. 43.
8. Maxim Litvinov, *Against Aggression* (New York: International Publishing Co., 1939). pp. 128–130.
9. *Survey of International Affairs, 1938* (London: Oxford University Press, 1953), Vol. III, p. 408.
10. *Ibid.*, p. 409.
11. *The New York Herald Tribune* (April 20, 1939), quoted by V. A. Yakhontoff, *USSR Foreign Policy* (New York: Coward-McCann, Inc., 1945), p. 201.
12. For an excellent treatment of this period see David J. Dallin, *Soviet Russia's Foreign Policy, 1939–1942* (New Haven, Conn.: Yale University Press, 1942), chaps. I–IV.
13. *Ibid.*, pp. 55–56.
14. T. A. Taracouzio, *War and Peace in Soviet Diplomacy* (New York: The Macmillan Company, 1940), p. 295.
15. Isaac Deutscher, *Stalin: A Political Biography* (New York: Oxford University Press, 1949), p. 411.
16. Beloff, *op. cit.*, Vol. II, p. 284.
17. *Nazi-Soviet Relations, 1939–1941* (Washington, D.C.: Department of State, 1948), pp. 217–260.

The USSR and the League of Nations

22. SPEECH ON THE OCCASION OF THE SOVIET ENTRY INTO THE LEAGUE OF NATIONS*

September 18, 1934

MAXIM LITVINOV

I will speak with that frankness and moderation which many of you, knowing me of old, will, I am sure, grant me, and which can only be helpful to our mutual understanding and our future cooperation.

We represent here a new state—new, not geographically, but new in its external aspects, its internal political and social structure, and its aspirations and ideals. The appearance in the historical arena of a new form of state has always been met with hostility on the part of old state formations. It is not surprising that the phenomenon of a new state with a social-political system radically different from any heretofore known should come up against intense hostility from without and manifested by literally all other countries in the world. This hostility has been not merely theoretical, but has found expression even in military action, assuming the form of prolonged externally organized attempts to interfere in the internal affairs of the new state for the purpose of getting it back to the old lines. At the time when the League of Nations was being formed to proclaim the organization of peace, the people of our country had as yet not been enabled to enjoy the blessings of peace. They still had to defend their internal peace with arms, and to contend for long their right to internal self-determination and their external independence. Even after the most extreme forms of intervention in the affairs of our state were over, the hostility of the outer world continued to be manifested in the most varying degrees and forms . . . people in the Soviet Union naturally feared that these nations united in the

* League of Nations, *Official Journal*, Special Supplement No. 125 (September 1934), pp. 66–69, *excerpts*.

League might give collective expression to their hostility towards the Soviet Union and combine their anti-Soviet activities. It can hardly be denied that at that time, and even very much later, there were still statesmen who thought or at least dreamed, of such collective action. . . .

Today we are happy to be able to state that . . . the advocates of the policy of ignoring and isolating the Soviet Union are no longer to be met among broad-minded statesmen, among the representatives of the more important states molding international life who think on realistic lines and understand the needs of the present day, but must be searched for among narrow-minded politicians unable to rise above their petty political passions and strong prejudices and deriving their knowledge of countries and peoples from muddied sources. . . .

In order to make our position quite clear, I should like further to state that the idea in itself of an association of nations contains nothing theoretically inacceptable for the Soviet state and its ideology . . . The Soviet state has . . . never excluded the possibility of some form or other of association with states having a different political and social system, so long as there is no mutual hostility and if it is for the attainment of common aims. For such an association it considers that the essential conditions would be, first, the extension to every state belonging to such an association of the liberty to preserve what I might call its state personality and the social-economic system chosen by it—in other words, reciprocal noninterference in the domestic affairs of the States therein associated; and, secondly, the existence of common aims. As to the first condition, which we have named the peaceful coexistence of different social-political systems at a given historical stage, we have advocated it again and again at international conferences. . . . The invitation to the Soviet Union to join the League of Nations may be said to represent the final victory of this principle.

For its part, the Soviet Government, following attentively all developments of international life, could not but observe the increasing activity in the League of Nations of States interested in the preservation of peace and their struggle against aggressive militarist elements . . . The organization of peace! Could there be a loftier and at the same time more practical and urgent task for the cooperation of all nations? The words used in political slogans have their youth and their age. If they are used too often without being applied, they wear themselves out and end by losing potency. Then they have to be revived and instilled with new meaning. The sound and the meaning of the words "organization of peace" ought now to be different from their sound and meaning twelve or fifteen years ago. Then, to many Members of the League of Nations, war seemed to be a remote theoretical danger, and there seemed to be no hurry as to its prevention. Now, war must appear to all as the threatening danger of to-morrow. Now, the organization of peace, for which so far very little has been done, must be set against the extremely active organization of war. Then, many believed that the spirit of war might be exorcised by adjurations, resolutions and declarations. Now, everybody knows that the exponents of the idea of war, the open promulgations of the refashioning of the map of Europe and Asia by the sword, are not to be intimidated by paper obstacles. Members of the League of Nations know this by experience. We are now confronted with the task of averting war by more effective means. . . .

We must accept the incontestable fact that, in the present complicated state of political and economic interests, no war of any serious dimensions can be localized, and any war, whatever its issue, will turn out to have been but the first of a series. We must also tell ourselves that sooner or later any war will bring misfortune to all countries, whether belligerents or neutrals. . . .

Finally, we must realize once and for all that no war with political or economic aims is capable of restoring so-called historical justice, and that all it could do would be to substitute new and perhaps still more glaring injustices for old ones, and that every new peace treaty bears within it the seeds of fresh warfare. . . .

I do not consider it the moment to speak in detail about effective means for the prevention of impending and openly promulgated war. One thing is quite clear for me, and that is that peace and security cannot be organized on the shifting sands of verbal promises and declarations. The nations are not to be soothed into a feeling of security by assurances of peaceful intentions, however often they are repeated, especially in those places where there are grounds for expecting aggression or where, only the day before, there have been talk and publications about wars of conquest in all directions, for which both ideological and material preparations are being made. We should establish that any state is entitled to demand from its neighbors, near and remote, guarantees for its security, and that such a demand is not to be considered as an expression of mistrust. Governments with a clear conscience and really free from all aggressive intentions, cannot refuse to give, in place of declarations, more effective guarantees which would be extended to themselves and give them also a feeling of complete security.

Far be it from me to overrate the opportunities and means of the League of Nations for the organization of peace. I realize, better perhaps than any of you, how limited these means are. I am aware that the League does not possess the means for the complete abolition of war. I am however convinced that, with the firm will and close cooperation of all its Members, a great deal could be done at any given moment for the utmost diminution of the danger of war, and this is a sufficiently honorable and lofty task, the fulfillment of which would be of incalculable advantage to humanity.

The Comintern, the Popular Front, and Soviet Policy

23. REPORT TO THE SEVENTH CONGRESS OF THE COMMUNIST INTERNATIONAL*

August 1935

Comrades, millions of workers and toilers of the capitalist countries ask the question: How can fascism be prevented from coming to power and how can fascism be overthrown after being victorious? To this the Communist International replies: *The first thing that must be done, the thing with which to commence, is to form a united front, to establish unity of action of the workers in every factory, in every district, in every region, in every country, all over the world. Unity of action of the proletariat on a national and international scale is the mighty weapon which renders the working class capable not only of successful defense but also of successful counter-offensive against fascism, against the class enemy . . .* a powerful united front of the proletariat would exert tremendous influence in *all other strata of the toiling people,* on the peasantry, on the urban petty bourgeoisie, on the intelligentsia. A united front would inspire the wavering groups with faith in the strength of the working class.

But even this is not all. The proletariat of the imperialist countries has possible allies not only in the toilers of its own countries

* U.S. House of Representatives, Committee on Un-American Activities, *The Strategy and Tactics of World Communism; The World Congress of the Communist International,* 84th Congress, 2nd session (1956), pp. 308–313, *excerpts.*

but also in the *oppressed nations of the colonies and semi-colonies . . .* [and] if, finally, we take into consideration that international unity of action by the proletariat relies on the *steadily growing strength of a proletarian state, a land of socialism, the Soviet Union,* we see that broad perspectives are revealed by the realization of united action on the part of the proletariat on a national and international scale. . . .

Is it possible to realize this unity of action by the proletariat in the individual countries and throughout the whole world? Yes, it is. And it is possible at this very moment. The Communist International *attaches no conditions to unity of action except one, and that an elementary condition acceptable for all workers, viz. that the unity of action be directed against fascism, against the offensive of capital, against the threat of war, against the class enemy.*

What objections can the opponents of the united front have and how do they voice their objections?

Some say: "To the Communists the slogan of the united front is merely a maneuver." But if it is a maneuver, we reply, why don't you expose the "Communist maneuver" by your honest participation in a united front? We declare frankly: We want unity of action by the working class, so that the proletariat may grow stronger in its struggle against the bourgeoisie, in order that while defending today its current interests against attacking capital, against fascism, the proletariat may be in a position tomorrow to create the preliminary conditions for its final emancipation.

"The Communists attack us," say others. But listen, we have repeatedly declared: We shall not attack anyone, neither persons nor organizations nor parties that stand for the united front of the working class against the class enemy. . . .

"We cannot form a united front with the Communists, since they have a different program," says a third group. But you yourselves say that your program differs from the program of the bourgeois parties, and yet this did not and does not prevent you (Social-Democrats) from entering into coalitions with these parties. . . .

"If we establish a united front with the Communists, the petty bourgeoisie will take fright at the 'Red Danger' and will desert to the fascists," we hear it said quite frequently. But does the united front represent a threat to the peasants, the petty traders, the artisans, the toiling intellectuals? No, the united front is a threat to the big bourgeoisie, the financial magnates, the *junkers* and other exploiters, whose regime brings complete ruin to all these strata.

"Social-Democracy is for democracy, the Communists are for dictatorship, therefore we cannot form a united front with the Communists," say some of the Social-Democratic leaders. But are we offering you now a united front for the purpose of proclaiming the dictatorship of the proletariat? We make no such proposal for the time being.

"Let the Communists recognize democracy, let them come out in its defense, then we shall be ready for a united front." To this we reply: We are adherents of Soviet democracy, the democracy of the toilers, the most consistent democracy in the world. But in the capitalist countries we defend and shall continue to defend every inch of bourgeois-democratic liberties which are being attacked by fascism and bourgeois reaction, because the interests of the class struggle of the proletariat so dictate. . . .

"The Communists act like dictators, they want to prescribe and dictate everything to us." No. We prescribe nothing and dictate nothing. We only make proposals concerning which we are convinced that if realized they will meet the interests of the toiling people. . . .

Thus all these arguments against the united front *will not bear the slightest criticism*. They are rather the flimsy excuses of the reactionary leaders of Social-Democracy, who prefer their united front with the bourgeoisie to the united front of the proletariat. . . .

What is and ought to be the basic content of the united front at the present stage? The defense of the immediate economic and political interests of the working class, the defense of the working class against fascism, must form the *starting point* and *main content* of the united front in all capitalist countries. . . . This means:

First, joint struggle really to shift the burden of the consequences of the crisis onto the shoulders of the ruling classes . . . to the shoulders of the rich.

Second, joint struggle against all forms of the fascist offensive, in defense of the gains and the rights of the toilers, against the liquidation of bourgeois-democratic liberties.

Third, joint struggle against the approaching danger of imperialist war, a struggle that will impede the preparations for such a war. . . .

Communists of course cannot and must not for a moment abandon their own independent work of Communist education, organization and mobilization of the masses. However, for the purpose of ensuring that the workers find the road to unity of action, it is necessary to strive at the same time both for short-term and for long-term agreements providing for *joint action* with Social-Democratic Parties, Reformist Trade Unions and other organizations of the toilers against the class enemies of the proletariat. The chief stress in all this must be laid on developing mass action locally, *to be carried out by the local organizations* through local agreements. . . .

It goes without saying that the concrete realization of the united front will take *various* forms in various countries, depending upon the condition and character of the workers' organizations and their political level, upon the concrete situation in the particular country, upon the changes in progress in the international labor movement, etc. . . .

Soviet Diplomacy and the Munich Crisis

24. THE SOVIET VIEW OF MUNICH*

Returning from Munich, Chamberlain claimed in one of his public addresses that "henceforth peace was assured for a generation." Churchill appraised the results of Munich quite differently. "England," he said with bitterness and indignation, "had to choose between war and shame. Its ministers chose shame, and thereby received war itself."

. . . [on the eve of Munich] from Paris and London urgent warnings went to Prague: Czechoslovakia must not count on the Soviet Union, which is too far away, does not have a common frontier with Czechoslovakia, and finally, does not want to enter in a war regardless of its treaty obligations concerning aid to Czechoslovakia. In this way the diplomacy of the French and British Governments sought to weaken the resolve of the Czechoslovak people and discredit the Soviet Union in the eyes of the democrats of the entire world. It also indicated the other motives of bourgeois diplomacy. To the [bourgeois] leaders, the thought of joint action with the Soviet Union against Hitler was an unpleasant one. The former head of the French military mission in

* V. P. Potemkin (ed.), *Istoriia Diplomatii* [History of Diplomacy] (Moscow: Government Publication of Foreign Literature, 1945), Vol. III, pp. 643–646, *excerpts*. This work, which appeared shortly after the end of the war, was edited by a former member of the Soviet foreign service and represents a rather serious, relatively nonpolemical treatment of the interwar period. Editor's translation.

Czechoslovakia, General Foch, expressed this attitude with a soldier's bluntness in conversations with certain politicians in Prague.

Foch declared that France would be unwilling to smash Hitler through the help of the Soviet Union. For first of all, world public opinion would accord the honor for this victory to the Red Army. This would painfully affect the national honor of France. But there was still a more important reason.

The destruction of Hitler in cooperation with the Bolsheviks would evoke a stormy wave of sympathy for the Soviet Union. This would promote a dangerous growth in the revolutionary workers' movement. Such a prospect was by no means pleasing to the French Government. "In short," concluded General Foch, "we do not want to come out against Hitler, united with the Bolsheviks." By slanderous inventions anti-Soviet diplomacy opposed all known facts. The whole world knew that the Soviet Government considered the demands on its honor fulfilled by assuming treaty obligations for itself and by tirelessly struggling for collective security and mutual cooperation by the democratic countries against the inciters of war.

The Soviet Union proved to be the only government which kept faith with its international obligations in relations with Czechoslovakia. . . . At the beginning of September 1938 the French Government turned to the USSR Government with the question of what its position would be in the event that Czechoslovakia was subjected to attack. The answer of the Soviet Government was clear and unequivocal; to convene quickly the governments of the USSR, England and France; to issue a declaration in the name of these powers which would state that Czechoslovakia will be rendered aid in case of an unprovoked attack on it by Germany; to bring this question to the League of Nations for consideration of the measures to take for its (Czechoslovakia's) defense; finally, to organize a technical consultation among the representatives of the General Staffs of the USSR, France, and Czechoslovakia in order to work out a plan of mutual military cooperation. Such were the proposals of the Soviet Government. From this it was shown that the USSR would render Czechoslovakia help by all available means and by all accessible paths, if, as was established by its treaty with Czechoslovakia, France itself came to her defense.

In the middle of September the Czechoslovak Government asked the USSR Government whether it was prepared to render rapid and effective aid to Czechoslovakia in accordance with the Czech-Soviet pact, if such aid came from the side of France. To this inquiry the Soviet Government quickly replied in the affirmative. As is known, the Czech-Soviet pact stipulated that the USSR will render aid to Czechoslovakia only in the event that France does exactly the same thing. At any rate it was understood that, by compelling Czechoslovakia to accept the German-English-French ultimatum, France was in fact breaking its promise of aid to Czechoslovakia, as stipulated by the Czech-French pact.

By that very action the Soviet Government was formally freed from the obligation to render aid to Czechoslovakia in accordance with the Czech-Soviet pact. None the less, the Soviet Government did not take advantage of its right to leave Czechoslovakia to its fate. The Czech-Soviet pact was not declared inoperative. The USSR was ready as before to provide support to Czechoslovakia if its government wished it. . . .

Between them the reactionary press of Britain and France intensively spread fabrications about the Soviet Union, intimating that it did not intend to fulfill its treaty obligations with respect to Czechoslovakia. The machinations of the slanderers were exposed: in Geneva, in the Assembly of the League of Nations, the reply of the Soviet Government on the inquiries of France and Czechoslovakia was announced. So was torn away the provocative intentions of the reactionaries. On the other hand, the USSR appeared before the world as the only country which, in a moment of universal panic, desertion and treachery, maintained complete calm, demonstrated its unswerving faith to treaty obligations, and showed a strong determination to defend international peace and democracy against the instigators of war. . . . As to the Munich conference and its decision, the USSR Government in no way had, nor does it now have, anything to do with it.

25. REPORT TO THE EIGHTEENTH CONGRESS OF THE CPSU*

March 10, 1939

JOSEPH STALIN

Comrades, five years have elapsed since the Seventeenth Party Congress. No small period, as you can see. During this period the world has undergone considerable changes. . . . What changes exactly have taken place in this period in the international situa-

* Joseph Stalin, *Problems of Leninism* (Moscow: Foreign Languages Publishing House, 1953), p. 746, pp. 751–759, *excerpts*.

tion? In what way exactly has the external and internal position of our country changed? . . .

The new imperialist war became a fact.

It is not so easy in our day suddenly to break loose and plunge straight into war without regard for treaties of any kind or for public opinion. Bourgeois politicians know this quite well. So do the fascist rulers. That is why the fascist rulers decided, before plunging into war, to mold public opinion to suit their ends, that is, to mislead it, to deceive it.

A military bloc of Germany and Italy against the interests of Britain and France in Europe? Bless us, do you call that a bloc? "We" have no military bloc. All "we" have is an innocuous "Berlin-Rome axis"; that is, just a geometrical equation for an axis. (Laughter)

A military bloc of Germany, Italy, and Japan against the interests of the United States, Britain, and France in the Far East? Nothing of the kind! "We" have no military bloc. All "we" have is an innocuous "Berlin-Rome-Tokyo triangle"; that is, a slight penchant for geometry. (General laughter)

A war against the interests of Britain, France, the United States? Nonsense! "We" are waging war on the Comintern, not on those states. If you don't believe it, read the "anti-Comintern pact" concluded between Italy, Germany, and Japan.

That is how Messieurs the aggressors thought to mold public opinion, although it was not hard to see how preposterous this clumsy game of camouflage was; for it is ridiculous to look for Comintern "hotbeds" in the deserts of Mongolia, in the mountains of Abyssinia, or in the wilds of Spanish Morocco. (Laughter)

But war is inexorable. It cannot be hidden under any guise. For no "axes," "triangles," or "anti-Comintern pacts" can hide the fact that in this period Japan has seized a vast stretch of territory in China, that Italy has seized Abyssinia, that Germany has seized Austria and the Sudeten region, that Germany and Italy together have seized Spain, and all this in defiance of the interests of the nonaggressive states. The war remains a war; the military bloc of aggressors remains a military bloc; and the aggressors remain aggressors. It is a distinguishing feature of the new imperialist war that it has not yet become a universal, a world war. The war is being waged by aggressor states, who in every way infringe upon the interests of the nonaggressive states, primarily Britain, France, and the USA, while the latter draw back and retreat, making concession after concession to the aggressors.

Thus we are witnessing an open redivision of the world and spheres of influence at the expense of the nonaggressive states, without the least attempt at resistance, and even with a certain connivance, on their part. Incredible, but true. To what are we to attribute this one-sided and strange character of the new imperialist war? How is it that the nonaggressive countries, which possess such vast opportunities, have so easily and without resistance abandoned their positions and their obligations to please the aggressors? Is it to be attributed to the weakness of the nonaggressive states? Of course not! Combined, the nonaggressive, democratic states are unquestionably stronger than the fascist states, both economically and militarily. To what then are we to attribute the systematic concessions made by these states to the aggressors?

It might be attributed, for example, to the fear that a revolution might break out if the nonaggressive states were to go to war and the war were to assume world-wide proportions. The bourgeois politicians know, of course, that the first imperialist world war led to the victory of the revolution in one of the largest countries. They are afraid that a second imperialist world war may also lead to the victory of the revolution in one or several countries.

But at present this is not the sole or even the chief reason. The chief reason is that the majority of the nonaggressive countries, particularly Britain and France, have rejected the policy of collective security, the policy of collective resistance to aggressors, and have taken up a position of nonintervention, a position of "neutrality." Formally speaking, the policy of nonintervention might be defined as follows: "Let each country defend itself against the aggressors as it likes and as best it can. That is not our affair. We shall trade both with the aggressors and with their victims." But actually speaking, the policy of nonintervention means conniving at aggression, giving free rein to war, and, consequently, transforming the war into a world war. The policy of nonintervention reveals an eagerness, a desire, not to hinder the aggressors in their nefarious work: not to hinder Japan, say, from embroiling herself in a war with China, or, better still, with the Soviet Union; not to hinder Germany, say, from enmeshing herself in European affairs, from embroiling herself in a war with the Soviet Union; to allow all the belligerents to sink deeply into the mire of war, to encourage them surreptitiously in this; to allow them to weaken and exhaust one another; and then, when they have become weak enough, to appear on the scene with fresh strength, to appear, of course, "in the interests of peace," and to dictate conditions to the enfeebled belligerents.

Cheap and easy!

Take Japan, for instance. It is characteristic that before Japan invaded North China (1937) all the influential French and

British newspapers shouted about China's weakness and her inability to offer resistance, and declared that Japan with her army could subjugate China in two or three months. Then the European and American politicians began to watch and wait. And then, when Japan commenced military operations, they let her have Shanghai, the vital center of foreign capital in China; they let her have Canton, a center of Britain's monopoly influence in South China; they let her have Hainan, and they allowed her to surround Hongkong. Does not this look very much like encouraging the aggressor? It is as though they were saying: "Embroil yourself deeper in war; then we shall see."

Or take Germany, for instance. They let her have Austria, despite the undertaking to defend her independence; they let her have the Sudeten region; they abandoned Czechoslovakia to her fate, thereby violating all their obligations; and then they began to lie vociferously in the press about "the weakness of the Russian army," "the demoralization of the Russian air force," and "riots" in the Soviet Union, egging on the Germans to march farther east, promising them easy pickings, and prompting them: "Just start war on the Bolsheviks, and everything will be all right." It must be admitted that this looks very much like egging on and encouraging the aggressor. . . .

Far be it from me to moralize on the policy of nonintervention, to talk of treason, treachery, and so on. It would be naive to preach morals to people who recognize no human morality. Politics are politics, as the old, case-hardened bourgeois diplomats say. It must be remarked, however, that the big and dangerous political game started by the supporters of the policy of nonintervention may end in serious fiasco for them. . . .

The war has created a new situation with regard to the relations between countries. It has enveloped them in an atmosphere of alarm and uncertainty. By undermining the basis of the postwar peace regime and overriding the elementary principles of international law, it has cast doubt on the value of international treaties and obligations. Pacifism and disarmament schemes are dead and buried. Feverish arming has taken their place. Everybody is arming, small states and big states, including primarily those which practice the policy of nonintervention. Nobody believes any longer in the unctuous speeches which claim that the Munich concessions to the aggressors and the Munich agreement opened a new era of "appeasement." They are disbelieved even by the signatories to the Munich agreement, Britain and France, who are increasing their armaments no less than other countries.

Naturally, the USSR could not ignore these ominous developments . . . while our country is unswervingly pursuing a policy of maintaining peace, it is at the same time working very seriously to increase the preparedness of our Red Army and our Red Navy. At the same time, in order to strengthen its international position, the Soviet Union decided to take certain other steps. At the end of 1934 our country joined the League of Nations, considering that despite its weakness the League might nevertheless serve as a place where aggressors could be exposed, and as a certain instrument of peace, however feeble, that might hinder the outbreak of war. The Soviet Union considers that in alarming times like these even so weak an international organization as the League of Nations should not be ignored. In May 1935 a treaty of mutual assistance against possible attack by aggressors was signed between France and the Soviet Union. A similar treaty was simultaneously concluded with Czechoslovakia. In March 1936 the Soviet Union concluded a treaty of mutual assistance with the Mongolian People's Republic. In August 1937 the Soviet Union concluded a pact of nonaggression with the Chinese Republic. . . .

The foreign policy of the Soviet Union is clear and explicit.

1. We stand for peace and the strengthening of business relations with all countries. That is our position; and we shall adhere to this position as long as these countries maintain like relations with the Soviet Union, and as long as they make no attempt to trespass on the interests of our country.

2. We stand for peaceful, close and friendly relations with all the neighboring countries which have common frontiers with the USSR. That is our position; and we shall adhere to this position as long as these countries maintain like relations with the Soviet Union, and as long as they make no attempt to trespass, directly or indirectly, on the integrity and inviolability of the frontiers of the Soviet state.

3. We stand for the support of nations which are the victims of aggression and are fighting for the independence of their country.

4. We are not afraid of the threats of aggressors, and are ready to return two blows for every one delivered by warmongers who attempt to violate our Soviet frontiers. . . .

The Tasks of the Party in the sphere of foreign policy are:

1. To continue the policy of peace and of strengthening business relations with all countries;

2. To be cautious and not allow our country to be drawn into conflicts by warmongers who are accustomed to have others pull the chestnuts out of the fire for them;

3. To strengthen the might of our Red Army and Red Navy to the utmost . . .

The Unholy Alliance

26. TREATY OF NONAGGRESSION BETWEEN GERMANY AND THE UNION OF SOVIET SOCIALIST REPUBLICS*

August 23, 1939

The Government of the German Reich and the Government of the Union of Soviet Socialist Republics desirous of strengthening the cause of peace between Germany and the USSR, and proceeding from the fundamental provisions of the Neutrality Agreement concluded in April 1926 between Germany and the USSR, have reached the following agreement:

ARTICLE I
Both High Contracting Parties obligate themselves to desist from any act of violence, any aggressive action, and any attack on each other, either individually or jointly with other powers.

ARTICLE II
Should one of the High Contracting Parties become the object of belligerent action by a third power, the other High Contracting Party shall in no manner lend its support to this third power.

ARTICLE III
The Governments of the two High Contracting Parties shall in the future maintain continual contact with one another for the purpose of consultation in order to exchange information on problems affecting their common interests.

ARTICLE IV
Neither of the two High Contracting Parties shall participate in any grouping of powers whatsoever that is directly or indirectly aimed at the other party.

ARTICLE V
Should disputes or conflicts arise between the High Contracting Parties over problems of one kind or another, both parties shall

* R. J. Sontag and J. S. Beddie (eds.), *Nazi-Soviet Relations 1939–1941: Documents from the Archives of the German Foreign Office* (Washington, D.C.: Department of State, 1948), pp. 76–78, *excerpts.*

settle these disputes or conflicts exclusively through friendly exchange of opinion, or, if necessary, through the establishment of arbitration commissions.

ARTICLE VI

The present treaty is concluded for a period of ten years, with the proviso that, in so far as one of the High Contracting Parties does not denounce it one year prior to the expiration of this period, the validity of this treaty shall automatically be extended for another five years.

ARTICLE VII

The present treaty shall be ratified within the shortest possible time. The ratifications shall be exchanged in Berlin. The agreement shall enter into force as soon as it is signed.

Done in duplicate, in the German and Russian languages.

Moscow, August 23, 1939

For the Government   With full power of the
of the German Reich: Government of the USSR:

V. Ribbentrop   *V. Molotov*

[SECRET ADDITIONAL PROTOCOL]

On the occasion of the signature of the Nonaggression Pact between the German Reich and the Union of Soviet Socialist Republics the undersigned plenipotentiaries of each of the two parties discussed in strictly confidential conversations the question of the boundary of their respective spheres of influence in Eastern Europe. These conversations led to the following conclusions:

1. In the event of a territorial and political rearrangement in the areas belonging to the Baltic States (Finland, Estonia, Latvia, Lithuania) the northern boundary of Lithuania shall represent the boundary of the spheres of influence of Germany and the USSR. In this connection the interest of Lithuania in the Vilna area is recognized by each party.

2. In the event of a territorial and political rearrangement of the areas belonging to the Polish state the spheres of influence of Germany and the USSR shall be bounded approximately by the line of the rivers Narew, Vistula, and San.

The question of whether the interests of both parties make desirable the maintenance of an independent Polish state and how such a state should be bounded can only be definitely determined in the course of further political developments.

In any event both Governments will resolve this question by means of a friendly agreement.

3. With regard to Southeastern Europe attention is called by the Soviet side to its interest in Bessarabia. The German side declares its complete political disinterestedness in these areas.

4. This protocol shall be treated by both parties as strictly secret.

Moscow, August 23, 1939

For the Government   Plenipotentiary of the
of the German Reich: Government of the USSR:

V. *Ribbentrop*   V. *Molotov*

27. THE MEANING OF THE SOVIET-GERMAN NONAGGRESSION PACT—SPEECH TO THE SUPREME SOVIET*

August 31, 1939

V. M. MOLOTOV

Comrades: Since the third session of the Supreme Soviet the international situation has shown no change for the better. On the contrary, it has become even more tense. The steps taken by various governments to put an end to this state of tension have obviously proved inadequate. They met with no success. This is true of Europe.

Nor has there been any change for the better in East Asia. Japanese troops continue to occupy the principal cities and a considerable part of the territory of China. Nor is Japan refraining from hostile acts against the USSR. Here, too, the situation has changed in the direction of further aggravation.

In view of this state of affairs, the conclusion of a pact of nonaggression between the USSR and Germany is of tremendous positive value, eliminating the danger of war between Germany

* U.S. House of Representatives, Committee on Foreign Affairs, *The Strategy and Tactics of World Communism*, House Document No. 619, 80th Congress, 2nd session (1948), pp. 158–165, *excerpts*.

and the Soviet Union. In order more fully to define the significance of this pact, I must first dwell on the negotiations which
have taken place in recent months in Moscow with representatives of Great Britain and France. As you know, Anglo-French-
Soviet negotiations for conclusion of a pact of mutual assistance
against aggression in Europe began as far back as April.

True, the initial proposals of the British Government were, as
you know, entirely unacceptable. They ignored the prime requi-
sites for such negotiations—they ignored the principle of
reciprocity and equality of obligations. In spite of this, the Soviet
Government did not reject the negotiations and in turn put
forward its own proposals. We were mindful of the fact that
it was difficult for the Governments of Great Britain and France
to make an abrupt change in their policy from an unfriendly
attitude towards the Soviet Union which had existed quite
recently to serious negotiations with the USSR based on the
condition of equality of obligation.

However, the subsequent negotiations were not justified by
their results. The Anglo-French-Soviet negotiations lasted four
months. They helped to elucidate a number of questions. At the
same time they made it clear to the representatives of Great
Britain and France that the Soviet Union has to be seriously
reckoned with in international affairs. But these negotiations
encountered insuperable obstacles. The trouble, of course, did
not lie in individual "formulations" or in particular clauses in the
draft of the pact. No, the trouble was much more serious.

The conclusion of a pact of mutual assistance against aggression would have been of value only if Great Britain, France, and
the Soviet Union had arrived at agreement as to definite military
measures against the attack of an aggressor. Accordingly, for
a certain period not only political but also military negotiations
were conducted in Moscow with representatives of the British
and French armies. However, nothing came of the military
negotiations.

They encountered the difficulty that Poland, which was to be
jointly guaranteed by Great Britain, France, and the USSR,
rejected military assistance on the part of the Soviet Union.
Attempts to overcome the objections of Poland met with no success. More, the negotiations showed that Great Britain was not
anxious to overcome these objections of Poland, but on the
contrary encouraged them. It is clear that, such being the attitude
of the Polish Government and its principal ally towards military
assistance on the part of the Soviet Union in the event of aggression, the Anglo-French-Soviet negotiations could not bear fruit.
After this it became clear to us that the Anglo-French-Soviet
negotiations were doomed to failure.

What have the negotiations with Great Britain and France shown? The Anglo-French-Soviet negotiations have shown that the position of Great Britain and France is marked by howling contradictions throughout. Judge for yourselves. On the one hand, Great Britain and France demanded that the USSR should give military assistance to Poland in case of aggression. The USSR, as you know, was willing to meet this demand, provided that the USSR itself received like assistance from Great Britain and France. On the other hand, precisely Great Britain and France brought Poland on the scene, who resolutely declined military assistance on the part of the USSR. Just try under such circumstances to reach an agreement regarding mutual assistance, when assistance on the part of the USSR is declared beforehand to be unnecessary and intrusive.

Further, on the one hand, Great Britain and France offered to guarantee the Soviet Union military assistance against aggression in return for like assistance on the part of the USSR. On the other hand, they themselves displayed extreme dilatoriness and an absolutely light-minded attitude towards the negotiations, entrusting them to individuals of secondary importance who were not invested with adequate powers.

It is enough to mention that the British and French military missions came to Moscow without any definite powers and without the right to conclude any military convention.

More, the British military mission arrived in Moscow without any mandate at all (*general laughter*), and it was only on the demand of our military mission that on the very eve of the breakdown of the negotiations they presented written credentials. But even these credentials were of the vaguest kind, that is, credentials without proper weight. Just try to distinguish between this light-minded attitude towards the negotiations on the part of Great Britain and France and frivolous make-believe at negotiations designed to discredit the whole business of negotiations. . . .

I shall now pass to the Soviet-German Nonaggression Pact. The decision to conclude a nonaggression pact between the USSR and Germany was adopted after military negotiations with France and Great Britain had reached an impasse owing to the insuperable differences I have mentioned. As the negotiations had shown that the conclusion of a pact of mutual assistance could not be expected, we could not but explore other possibilities of ensuring peace and eliminating the danger of war between Germany and the USSR. If the British and French Governments refused to reckon with this, that is their affair. It is our duty to think of the interests of the Soviet people, the interests of the Union of Soviet Socialist Republics. (*Prolonged applause*) . . . it is clear that the commercial and credit agreement [concluded on August 19] with Germany is fully in accord with the economic interests and defense needs of the Soviet Union. This agreement is fully in accord with the decision of the Eighteenth Congress of our Party, which approved Stalin's statement as to the need for "strengthening business relations with all countries."

When, however, the German government expressed the desire to improve political relations as well, the Soviet government had no grounds for refusing. This gave rise to the question of concluding a nonaggression pact. Voices are now being heard testifying to the lack of understanding of the most simple reasons for the improvement of political relations between the Soviet Union and Germany which has begun. For example, people ask with an air of innocence how the Soviet Union could consent to improve political relations with a state of a fascist type. "Is that possible?" they ask. But they forget that this is not a question of our attitude towards the internal regime of another country but of the foreign relations between the two states. They forget that we hold the position of not interfering in the internal affairs of other countries and, correspondingly, of not tolerating interference in our own internal affairs. Furthermore, they forget the important principle of our foreign policy which was formulated by Stalin at the Eighteenth Party Congress as follows:

> We stand for peace and the strengthening of business relations with all countries. That is our position; and we adhere to this position as long as these countries maintain like relations with the Soviet Union, and as long as they make no attempt to trespass on the interests of our country.

The meaning of these words is quite clear: the Soviet Union strives to maintain friendly relations with all non-Soviet countries, provided that these countries maintain a like attitude towards the Soviet Union. In our foreign policy towards non-Soviet countries, we have always been guided by Lenin's well-known principle of the peaceful coexistence of the Soviet state and of capitalist countries. A large number of examples might be cited to show how this principle has been carried out in practice. But I will confine myself to only a few. We have, for instance, a nonaggression and neutrality treaty with Fascist Italy ever since 1933. It has never occurred to anybody as yet to object to this treaty. And that is natural. Inasmuch as this pact meets the interests of the USSR, it is in accord with our principle of the peaceful coexistence of the USSR and the capitalist countries. We have nonaggression pacts also with Poland and certain other countries whose semi-fascist system is known to all. These pacts have not given rise to any misgivings either. . . .

August 23, 1939, the day the Soviet-German Nonaggression

Pact was signed, is to be regarded as a date of great historical importance. . . .

The art of politics in the sphere of foreign relations does not consist in increasing the number of enemies for one's country. On the contrary, the art of politics in this sphere is to reduce the number of such enemies and to make the enemies of yesterday good neighbors, maintaining peaceable relations with one another. (*Applause*)

History has shown that enmity and wars between our country and Germany have been to the detriment of our countries, not to their benefit. Russia and Germany suffered most of all countries in the war of 1914–1918. Therefore the interests of the peoples of the Soviet Union and Germany stand in need of peaceable relations. The Soviet-German Nonaggression Pact puts an end to enmity between Germany and the USSR and this is in the interests of both countries. The fact that our outlooks and political systems differ must not and cannot be obstacles to the establishment of good political relations between both states, just as like differences are not impediments to good political relations which the USSR maintains with other non-Soviet capitalist countries. Only enemies of Germany and the USSR can strive to create and foment enmity between the peoples of these countries. We have always stood for amity between the peoples of the USSR and Germany, for the growth and development of friendship between the peoples of the Soviet Union and the German people. (*Loud and prolonged applause*)

The importance of the Soviet-German Nonaggression Pact lies in the fact that the two largest states of Europe have agreed to put an end to the enmity between them, to eliminate the menace of war and live at peace one with the other, making narrow thereby the zone of possible military conflicts in Europe. Even if military conflicts in Europe should prove unavoidable, the scope of hostilities will now be restricted. Only the instigators of a general European war can be displeased by this state of affairs, those who under the mask of pacifism would like to ignite a general conflagration in Europe.

The Soviet-German Pact has been the object of numerous attacks in the English, French, and American press. . . . Attempts are being made to spread the fiction that the signing of the Soviet-German Pact disrupted the negotiations with England and France on a mutual assistance pact. In reality, as you know, the very reverse is true. The Soviet Union signed the Nonaggression Pact with Germany, for one thing, in view of the fact that the negotiations with France and England had run into insuperable differences and ended in failure through the fault of the ruling classes of England and France.

Further, they go so far as to blame us because the pact, if you please, contains no clause providing for its denunciation in case one of the signatories is drawn into war under conditions which might give someone an external pretext to qualify this particular country as an aggressor. But they forget for some reason that such a clause and such a reservation is not to be found either in the Polish-German Nonaggression Pact signed in 1934 and annulled by Germany in 1939 against the wishes of Poland, or in the Anglo-German declaration on nonaggression signed only a few months ago. The question arises: Why cannot the USSR allow itself the same privilege as Poland and England allowed themselves long ago?

Finally, there are wiseacres who construe from the pact more than is written in it. (*Laughter*) For this purpose, all kinds of conjectures and hints are mooted in order to cast doubt on the pact in one or another country. But all this merely speaks for the hopeless impotence of the enemies of the pact who are exposing themselves more and more as enemies of both the Soviet Union and Germany, striving to provoke war between these countries.

In all this, we find fresh corroboration of Stalin's warning that we must be particularly cautious with warmongers who are accustomed to have others pull the chestnuts out of the fire for them. We must be on guard against those who see an advantage to themselves in bad relations between the USSR and Germany, in enmity between them and [those] who do not want peace and good neighborly relations between Germany and the Soviet Union.

We can understand why this policy is being pursued by out-and-out imperialists. But we cannot ignore such facts as the especial zeal with which some leaders of the Socialist parties of Great Britain and France have recently distinguished themselves in this matter. And these gentlemen have really gone the whole hog, and no mistake. (*Laughter*) These people positively demand that the USSR get itself involved in war against Germany on the side of Great Britain. Have not these rabid warmongers taken leave of their senses? (*Laughter*) Is it really difficult for these gentlemen to understand the purpose of the Soviet-German Nonaggression Pact, on the strength of which the USSR is not obligated to involve itself in war either on the side of Great Britain against Germany or on the side of Germany against Great Britain? Is it really difficult to understand that the USSR is pursuing and will continue to pursue its own independent policy, based on the interests of the peoples of the USSR and only their interests? (*Prolonged applause*)

If these gentlemen have such an uncontrollable desire to fight, let them do their own fighting without the Soviet Union. We would see what fighting stuff they are made of . . . The Soviet Union signed a pact with Germany, fully assured that peace between the peoples of the USSR and Germany is in the interests of all peoples, in the interests of universal peace. Every sincere supporter of peace will realize the truth of this. This pact corresponds to the fundamental interests of the working people of the Soviet Union and cannot weaken our vigilance in defense of these interests . . .

This pact, like the unsuccessful Anglo-French-Soviet negotiations, proves that no important questions of international relations, and questions of Eastern Europe even less, can be settled without the active participation of the Soviet Union, that any attempts to shut out the Soviet Union and decide such questions behind its back are doomed to failure.

The Soviet Attack on Finland

28. THE MEANING OF THE WAR IN FINLAND—SPEECH TO THE SUPREME SOVIET*

March 29, 1940

V . M . M O L O T O V

What was the meaning of the war that has taken place in Finland during the last nearly three and a half months? As you know the meaning of these events lay in the necessity for safeguarding the security of the northwestern frontiers of the Soviet Union, and above all the safeguarding of the security of Leningrad. All through October and November of last year the Soviet Government discussed with the Finnish Government proposals which, in view of the existing international situation— a situation that was growing more and more inflammable—we considered absolutely essential and urgent for safeguarding the security of our country and especially of Leningrad. Nothing

* *Soviet Peace Policy* (London: Lawrence & Wishart, Ltd., 1941), pp. 52-62, *excerpts*. Reprinted by permission of the publisher.

came of these negotiations because of the unfriendly attitude adopted by the Finnish representatives. The decision of the issue passed to the field of war.

It may safely be said that had Finland not been subjected to foreign influences, had Finland been less incited by certain third States to adopt a hostile policy towards the USSR, the Soviet Union and Finland would have arrived at a peaceful understanding last autumn, and matters would have been settled without war. But in spite of the fact that the Soviet Government reduced its request to a minimum, a settlement could not be reached by diplomatic means.

Now that hostilities in Finland have ceased and a peace treaty between the USSR and the Republic of Finland has been signed, it is necessary and possible to judge the significance of the war in Finland in the light of incontrovertible facts. And these facts speak for themselves. They show that in the neighborhood of Leningrad, all over the Karelian Isthmus to a depth of fifty to sixty kilometers, the Finnish authorities had erected numerous powerful ferroconcrete and granite and earth fortifications armed with artillery and machine guns. . . .

In short, hostilities in Finland have shown that already by 1939 Finland, and especially the Karelian Isthmus, had been converted into a *place d'armes* ready for an attack by third Powers on the Soviet Union, for an attack on Leningrad.

Incontrovertible facts have shown that the hostile policy which we encountered on the part of Finland last autumn was no fortuitous thing. Forces hostile to the Soviet Union had prepared in Finland such a *place d'armes* against our country and in the first place against Leningrad, which, should a foreign situation arise unfavorable to the USSR, was to play its part in the plans of the anti-Soviet forces of the imperialists and their allies in Finland. Not only has the Red Army smashed the Mannerheim Line and thereby covered itself with glory as the first army to force its way under most difficult conditions through a deep, powerful zone of perfectly modern military fortification, not only has the Red Army together with the Red Fleet destroyed the Finnish *place d'armes* which has been made ready for an attack on Leningrad, but it has also put an end to certain anti-Soviet plans which some third countries had been hatching during the past few years. . . .

It is not difficult to see that the war in Finland was not merely an encounter with Finnish troops. No, the matter was more complicated than that. It was not merely Finnish troops whom our troops encountered here but the combined forces of the imperialists of a number of countries, including British, French, and others who assisted the Finnish bourgeoisie with every form of weapon, especially artillery and aircraft as well as with men in the guise of "volunteers," with gold and every kind of supplies, and with their frenzied propaganda all over the world for the purpose of instigating war against the Soviet Union in every way. . . .

What is the basic idea of the Peace Treaty? It is that it *properly ensures the safety of Leningrad and of Murmansk and the Murmansk Railway.* This time we could not confine ourselves merely to the desires we expressed last autumn, acceptance of which by Finland would have averted war. After the blood of our men had been spilt, through no fault of our own, and after we had become convinced that the hostile policy of the Finnish Government towards the Soviet Union had gone very far indeed, we were obliged to put the question of the security of Leningrad on a more reliable basis, in addition we could not but raise the question of the security of the Murmansk railway and Murmansk which is our only ice-free ocean port in the west and is therefore of extreme importance for our foreign trade and for communication between the Soviet Union and other countries generally. . . .

Soviet Strategic Objectives (1940)

29. MOLOTOV'S DEMANDS ON HITLER*

November 1940

[*The German Ambassador in the Soviet Union (Schulenburg) to the German Foreign Office*]

TELEGRAM

VERY URGENT   Moscow, November 26, 1940—5:34 a.m.
STRICTLY SECRET   Received November 26, 1940—8:50 a.m.
No. 2362 of November 25

For the Reich Minister in person.

Molotov asked me to call on him this evening and in the presence of Dekanosov stated the following:

---

* R. J. Sontag and J. S. Beddie (eds.), *Nazi-Soviet Relations 1939–1941: Documents from the Archives of the German Foreign Office* (Washington, D.C.: Department of State, 1948), pp. 258–259, *excerpts.*

The Soviet Government has studied the contents of the statements of the Reich Foreign Minister in the concluding conversation on November 13 and takes the following stand:

"The Soviet Government is prepared to accept the draft of the Four Power Pact which the Reich Foreign Minister outlined in the conversation of November 13, regarding political collaboration and reciprocal economic [support] subject to the following conditions:

"(1) Provided that the German troops are immediately withdrawn from Finland, which, under the compact of 1939, belongs to the Soviet Union's sphere of influence. At the same time the Soviet Union undertakes to ensure peaceful relations with Finland and to protect German economic interests in Finland (export of lumber and nickel).

"(2) Provided that within the next few months the security of the Soviet Union in the Straits is assured by the conclusion of a mutual assistance pact between the Soviet Union and Bulgaria, which geographically is situated inside the security zone of the Black Sea boundaries of the Soviet Union, and by the establishment of a base for land and naval forces of the U.S.S.R. within range of the Bosporus and the Dardanelles by means of a long-term lease.

"(3) Provided that the area south of Batum and Baku in the general direction of the Persian Gulf is recognized as the center of the aspirations of the Soviet Union.

"(4) Provided that Japan [renounces] her rights to concessions for coal and oil in Northern Sakhalin.

"In accordance with the foregoing, the draft of the protocol concerning the delimitation of the spheres of influence as outlined by the Reich Foreign Minister would have to be amended so as to stipulate the focal point of the aspirations of the Soviet Union south of Batum and Baku in the general direction of the Persian Gulf.

"Likewise, the draft of the protocol or agreement between Germany, Italy, and the Soviet Union with respect to Turkey should be amended so as to guarantee a base for light naval and land forces of the U.S.S.R. on [am] the Bosporus and the Dardanelles by means of a long-term lease, including—in case Turkey declares herself willing to join the Four Power Pact— a guarantee of the independence and of the territory of Turkey by the three countries named.

"This protocol should provide that in case Turkey refuses to join the Four Powers, Germany, Italy, and the Soviet Union agree to work out and to carry through the required military and diplomatic measures, and a separate agreement to this effect should be concluded.

"Furthermore there should be agreement upon:

"(a) a third secret protocol between Germany and the Soviet Union concerning Finland (see Point 1 above).

"(b) a fourth secret protocol between Japan and the Soviet Union concerning the renunciation by Japan of the oil and coal concession in Northern Sakhalin (in return for an adequate compensation).

"(c) a fifth secret protocol between Germany, the Soviet Union, and Italy, recognizing that Bulgaria is geographically located inside the security zone of the Black Sea boundaries of the Soviet Union and that it is therefore a political necessity that a mutual assistance pact be concluded between the Soviet Union and Bulgaria, which in no way shall affect the internal regime of Bulgaria, her sovereignty or independence."

In conclusion Molotov stated that the Soviet proposal provided for five protocols instead of the two envisaged by the Reich Foreign Minister. He would appreciate a statement of the German view.

Schulenburg

FOR FURTHER STUDY

Beloff, Max, *The Foreign Policy of Soviet Russia, 1929–1941*, 2 vols. New York: Oxford University Press, 1947, 1949.

Budurowycz, Bohdan B., *Polish-Soviet Relations, 1932–1939*. New York: Columbia University Press, 1963.

Cattell, David T., *Communism and the Spanish Civil War*. Berkeley: University of California Press, 1956.

———, *Soviet Diplomacy and the Spanish Civil War*. Berkeley: University of California Press, 1957.

Dallin, David J., *Soviet Russia's Foreign Policy, 1939–1942*. New Haven, Conn.: Yale University Press, 1942.

Gafencu, Grigoire, *Prelude to the Russian Campaign*. London: Victor Gollancz, 1945.

Jakobson, Max, *The Diplomacy of the Winter War: An Account of the Russo-Finnish Conflict, 1939–1940*. Cambridge, Mass.: Harvard University Press, 1961.

Johnson, Chalmers, *An Instance of Treason: Ozaki Hotsumi and the Sorge Spy Ring*. Stanford: Stanford University Press, 1964.

Kennan, George F., *Russia and the West Under Lenin and Stalin*. Boston: Little, Brown & Company, 1960.

McLane, Charles B., *Soviet Policy and the Chinese Communists, 1931–1946*. New York: Columbia University Press, 1958.

Maisky, Ivan, *Who Helped Hitler?* London: Hutchinson & Co., 1964.

Moore, Harriet L., *Soviet Far Eastern Policy, 1931–1945*. Princeton, N.J.: Princeton University Press, 1945.

Rossi, Angelo, *The Russo-German Alliance, 1939–1941*. Boston: Beacon Press, 1951.

Sontag, Raymond I. and James S. Beddie (eds.), *Nazi-Soviet Relations: 1939–1941, Documents from the Archives of the German Foreign Office*. Washington, D.C.: Government Printing Office, 1948.

Tarulis, Albert N., *Soviet Policy Toward the Baltic States, 1918–1940*. Notre Dame, Ind.: University of Notre Dame Press, 1958.

Wheeler-Bennett, John W. *Munich: Prologue to Tragedy*. New York: Duell Sloan & Pearce, 1948.

_____, *The Nemesis of Power*. New York: St. Martin's Press, 1953.

CHAPTER V

THE WARTIME ALLIANCE

The Nazi-Soviet honeymoon ended on June 22, 1941, as German troops swept into the USSR on an eighteen-hundred-mile front. Later that day, V. M. Molotov, the People's Commissar for Foreign Affairs, made the announcement to the Soviet people:

Citizens of the Soviet Union! The Soviet Government and its head, Comrade Stalin, have instructed me to make the following statement:

Today, at 4 A.M., without any complaints having been presented to the Soviet Union, without a declaration of war, German troops attacked our country, attacked our borders at many points, and bombed from their airplanes our cities of Zhitomir, Kiev, Sevastopol, Kaunas, and some others, killing and wounding over 200 persons. There were also enemy air raids and artillery shelling from Rumanian and Finnish territory.

This unheard of attack upon our country is perfidy unparalleled in the history of civilized nations. The attack on our country was perpetrated despite the fact that a Treaty of non-aggression had been signed between the USSR and Germany, and that the Soviet Government was most faithfully abiding by all the provisions of this Treaty. The attack upon our country was perpetrated despite the fact that during the entire period of the operation of this Treaty the German Government could not find grounds for a single complaint to the USSR concerning observance of the Treaty. The entire responsibility for this brigand attack upon the Soviet Union falls fully and completely upon the German-Fascist rulers.

Twice within a generation were the Bolsheviks engaged in a struggle for survival. This time, however, they were to have powerful allies. A common cause—the destruction of Hitlerism—submerged ideological differences and political antagonisms. Winston Churchill, long an open opponent of Bolshevism, cast aside politics and personal feelings and offered the Soviets friendship and alliance. The day after the Nazi invasion, he made his intentions clear in a broadcast to the British people:

No one has been a more consistent opponent of Communism than I have for the last twenty-five years. I will unsay no word that I have spoken about it. But all this fades away before the spectacle which is now unfolding. The past, with its crimes, its follies, and its tragedies, flashes away. . . .

We have but one aim and one single, irrevocable purpose. We are resolved to destroy Hitler and every vestige of the Nazi regime. From this nothing will turn us—nothing. We will never parley, we will never negotiate with Hitler or any of his gang. We shall fight him by land, we shall fight him by sea, we shall fight him in the air, until, with God's help, we have rid the earth of his shadow and liberated its peoples from his yoke. Any man or state who fights on against Nazidom will have our aid. Any man or state who marches with Hitler is our foe. . . . That is our policy and that is our declaration. It follows, therefore, that we shall give whatever help we can to Russia and the Russian people. . . .

Soon afterward, the British and Soviet Governments entered into negotiations and, on July 12, signed a protocol in which both agreed not "to negotiate nor conclude an armistice or treaty of peace except by mutual agreement" and "to render each other assistance and support of all kinds in the present war against Hitlerite Germany." On July 18, Stalin replied directly to Churchill. Thus began the forging of "The Grand Alliance" against Hitler.

As Nazi Panzer divisions rolled farther into Russia, Western military experts predicted the collapse of the Soviet Union within a matter of weeks.[1] Their appraisal of Soviet military power was influenced by the known weakening of the Red Army caused by the 1937 purges, the poor performance of Soviet forces in the Finnish winter campaign of 1939–1940, and, perhaps most important of all, the impressive record of Nazi successes in the West and in the Balkans.

On July 3, Stalin made a momentous radio appeal to the Soviet people (reading 30). With rare candor, no doubt dictated by the extreme gravity of the situation, he admitted that the country was in mortal peril, that there was no time for comforting words. Sensing a need to justify his pro-Nazi policy orientation of

1939–1941, he held that this course had afforded the Soviets time to strengthen their defenses. For reasons of his own, Stalin did not mention the territorial acquisitions of that period—the Baltic states, the eastern part of Poland, and Bessarabia. He emphasized instead the initial German advantage from the "treacherous" attack, and appealed for the people to unite to defeat the invader as their ancestors before them had triumphed over Napoleon and Kaiser Wilhelm II, both of whom had enjoyed a reputation of invincibility.

(*Note:* Stalin did not tell the Soviet people that he had ignored repeated warnings from Churchill in April and May of the impending German invasion;[2] nor did he assume responsibility for the nation's unpreparedness. Indeed, if we are to believe Khrushchev's revelations, made at the Twentieth Party Congress in February 1956, about Stalin's shortcomings, it was Stalin's refusal to heed well-founded and persistent intelligence and diplomatic reports of imminent German invasion that cost the Soviets so heavily and facilitated the rapidity and extent of the initial Nazi advances. According to Khrushchev:

> Despite these particularly grave warnings, the necessary steps were not taken to prepare the country properly for defense and to prevent it from being caught unawares.
> Did we have time and the capabilities for such preparations? Yes, we had the time and capabilities. . . .
> Had our industry been mobilized properly and in time to supply the Army with the necessary material, our wartime losses would have been decidedly smaller. Such mobilization had not been, however, started in time. . . .
> When the fascist armies had actually invaded Soviet territory and military operations began, Moscow issued the order that the German fire was not to be returned. Why? It was because Stalin, despite evident facts, thought that the war had not yet started, that this was only a provocative action on the part of several undisciplined sections of the German Army, and that our reaction might serve as a reason for the Germans to begin the war.
> As you see, everything was ignored: warnings of certain Army commanders, declarations of deserters from the enemy army, and even the open hostility of the enemy. Is this an example of the alertness of the Chief of the Party and of the State at this particularly significant historical moment?[3])

The complete truth may never be known.

As the Nazis penetrated deeper into Russia, even to the outskirts of Leningrad and Moscow, the Soviets relied on their traditional scourges for any would-be conqueror—the vastness of their country and the severity of its winters. They also adopted a "scorched earth" policy, leaving nothing of use to the invader.

At first the Germans were greeted as liberators in many *non-Russian* areas of the Soviet Union, such as the Ukraine—an illuminating testament to a generation of Communist rule. But the Nazis, themselves captives of their racist ideology, came as self-proclaimed conquerors, intent upon colonizing the country and brutally exploiting its manpower and resources.[4] They thus wasted, politically and psychologically, the strong vein of anti-Communist sentiment, and by this blunder contributed greatly to their eventual defeat.

While the Nazis continued to advance into Russia, anticipating the victory that would make them masters of the Eurasian land mass, the newly formed Allied coalition sought to establish a firm basis for military cooperation. Churchill had promised to render all possible aid, but obviously only the United States could meet the enormous needs of the Soviet Union. In America, as in Great Britain, all hostility toward the Soviet Union was overshadowed by the resolve to work together in the common interest. President Roosevelt immediately moved to extend lend-lease aid. This aspect of cooperation with the Soviets proved successful, though not without frequent difficulties. Harry Hopkins, President Roosevelt's trusted adviser and trouble-shooter, flew to Moscow in July 1941 to assess the Soviet capacity and determination to resist Hitler. His favorable report helped convince Roosevelt, and shipments to Russia, under an interim lend-lease agreement, began almost immediately. In 1942, though understandably eager to take the offensive against the Japanese, the United States undertook to deliver more than a billion dollars worth of war material and supplies to the Soviet Union. Subsequently, other lend-lease agreements were concluded. The Soviet's contact with its Allies was effected via Murmansk, Iran, and Vladivostok, particularly the first two. America eventually supplied the USSR with approximately 11 billion dollars in vitally needed goods of every description: trucks, tanks, rolling stock, machine tools, textiles, shoes, oil, and food.

British-Soviet cooperation first developed in Iran, where events impelled them to act in concert. Confronted with an imminent pro-Nazi coup in Teheran, the British and Soviets occupied the country. In its note of August 25 (reading 31), the Soviet Government justified the Allied action on the basis of the pertinent provision of its 1921 treaty with Iran which held that:

... if a third party should attempt to carry out a policy of usurpation by means of armed intervention in Persia, or if such power should desire to use Persian territory as a base for operations against the Russian Socialist Federal Soviet Republic, or if a foreign power should threaten the frontiers of the Russian Socialist Federal Soviet Republic, or those of its allies, and if the Persian Government should not be able to put a stop to such a menace after having been once called upon to do so by the Russian Socialist Federal Soviet Republic, the Russian Socialist Federal Soviet Republic shall have the right to advance its troops into the Persian interior for the purpose of carrying out the military operations necessary for its defense. The Soviet Government undertakes, however, to withdraw its troops from Persian territory as soon as the danger has been removed.

By mid-September 1941, the Shah capitulated and abdicated in favor of his son, the present ruler of Iran. The joint Allied occupation was followed by a Treaty of Alliance with Iran, signed on January 29, 1942, and Iran soon became a main Allied artery of supplies for the Soviet war effort. In addition to outlining Allied prerogatives, including the right to "maintain in Iranian territory land, sea, and air forces in such numbers as they consider necessary," the treaty assured Iran that the Allies would withdraw their forces "from Iranian territory not later than six months after all hostilities between the Allied Powers and Germany and her associates have been suspended by the conclusion of an armistice or armistices, or on the conclusion of peace between them, whichever date is the earlier."[5] Soviet failure to abide by the terms of this provision precipitated one of the early crises of the postwar period—one involving Iran, the Great Powers, and the United Nations.

Meanwhile, the German advance overran the Soviet economic and industrial heartland. It failed, however, to attain its principal strategic objective: the destruction of the Red Army. Moscow and Leningrad held firm, and by the beginning of December it was apparent that Hitler would not winter in the Kremlin. As in 1812, winter providently came early.* Furthermore, the Japanese surprise attack on Pearl Harbor on December 7, 1941 meant that the Soviets no longer had to fear a two-front war. Nonetheless, the danger to the Allied cause was never greater than during the bleak winter of 1941–1942—a winter of successive defeats and disasters—and the summer of 1942. But when the Nazis and the

* The need to postpone the invasion of Russia from May 15 to June 22, which was occasioned by the resistance of Yugoslavia in April 1941, cost the Germans dearly. One astute observer commenting on this development observed that: "The winter had fallen three weeks earlier than usual; and it is one of the many ironies of the war, that the Yugoslav defiance, which had produced so little immediate impression on the Germans, may have paid compound interest in the end by delaying the onset of the attack on Russia just long enough to permit the Russian winter to intervene decisively. The Russian historic stubbornness, flair for strategy, and enlightened adoption of the mechanical developments of modern warfare, with the appropriate tactical implications, had done the rest." Strategicus, *A Short History of the Second World War* (London: Faber & Faber Ltd., n.d.), p. 117,

Japanese failed to attain victory by late 1942, their ultimate defeat was assured. Time and resources favored the Allies.

In November 1942, the British and Americans landed in North Africa, while the Soviets engaged the Germans in the epic struggle for Stalingrad. The battle-to-the-death for this vital industrial center on the lower Volga was a symbol of Soviet determination to retreat no further. The grim struggle for the city continued for weeks, fought street by street, house by house. On February 2, 1943, the Nazi forces surrendered. Stalingrad was saved. The defeat was one from which the Nazis never recovered, and the Allied cause received an incalculable boost of morale.

On all fronts 1943 marked the turning of the tide. Now, political differences within the strange alliance between Communist Russia and the Western democracies assumed added dimensions. All had shared the resolve to defeat the Axis Powers, subordinating other war aims to this overriding objective. However, as *military* victory approached, the *political* dilemmas and disagreements over the postwar settlement sharpened. The post-1945 "Cold War" was rooted in the conflicting, incompatible objectives of the Allies. Each understandably sought greater security against a possible German revival. But this meant different things to each. Subsequent Soviet maneuvering for power, position, and economic advantage rendered impossible the task of formulating a postwar settlement. Throughout the war, even during the darkest days of the Nazi invasion, Stalin was more concerned with political issues than were Churchill or Roosevelt. Certainly he had a clearer idea, politically and otherwise, of what he wanted as a victor, but for the time being military necessities overshadowed political differences. Defeat of the Axis Powers took precedence over all other considerations. At the Inter-Allied Conference in London in late September 1941, Soviet Ambassador Maisky pledged his Government's adherence to the principles of the Atlantic Charter (drawn up by Churchill and Roosevelt at their mid-Atlantic meeting of August 14, 1941), called for Allied unity in the struggle against Germany, and announced Soviet support for the right of every nation "to establish such a social order and to choose such a form of government as it deems opportune and necessary for the better promotion of its economic and cultural prosperity." As long as specific political questions did not intrude upon the straightforward task of destroying Nazism, Allied unity held firm.

From the first forging of the coalition, the Soviet Union pressed for the launching of a second front in Europe that would draw forty to sixty German divisions away from the East. This demand was repeated again and again and proved a "constant dissonance

in the theme of coalition."[6] Stalin broached the issue in his first
direct communication to Churchill on July 18, 1941, and many
times again (see pertinent sections in readings 32, 33, and 34).
Stalin's xenophobia toward the West reflected his uncompromising ideological hostility and his memory of two trying decades
of Soviet-Western diplomatic relations. He was particularly critical of what he regarded as Allied unwillingness to make military
efforts comparable to those being made by the Red Army and
the Soviet people. This remained a sore point in Allied relations.
To cement closer ties and to try to overcome such attitudes, the
British signed a twenty-year treaty of alliance with the Soviets on
May 26, 1942. Led by earlier talks, first with Churchill and then
with Roosevelt, to expect a second front in France in 1942, Molotov, in his speech calling upon the Supreme Soviet to ratify the
Soviet-British alliance, announced this as a promised certainty
rather than as an eventual intention (reading 35). The result
was Soviet disappointment, open skepticism of Allied ability, and
continued suspicion. At no time during the war did Stalin show
a real understanding or appreciation of the unique logistic and
military problems involved in a projected invasion across the
English Channel—the mammoth amount of shipping required to
transport millions of men and many more millions of tons of
equipment—or of America's need to fight an additional war
against a powerful foe in the Pacific. Patient Allied efforts at
compromise with their distrustful partner proved largely futile,
for Stalin invariably interpreted such Allied efforts in the worst
possible light.

Of the many political problems besetting Soviet-Western wartime relations, none assumed more dramatic proportions or
proved more elusive of accord than that of the future of Poland.
Since the Nazi-Soviet partition of 1939, there had been no diplomatic relations between the Soviet Union and Poland. As far as
the Soviet Government was concerned, Poland no longer existed.
With the advent of the Nazi attack, however, Stalin adopted a
conciliatory position with respect to the Polish question, a gesture
designed to strengthen the newly formed bonds of friendship
with the West. On July 30, 1941, an agreement was reached in
London between the Soviet and Polish Governments which was
supposed to serve as a basis for future amicable relations (reading 36). In a fundamental reversal of policy, the Soviets conceded that the territorial changes of 1939 were no longer valid.
Diplomatic relations between Poland and the USSR were
re-established and plans made for training and equipping a
Polish army on Soviet soil from among the thousands of Poles
imprisoned after the 1939 partition.

Several days later, a portentous article appeared in *Pravda*. Though applauding the Soviet-Polish pact, it justified Soviet action in the 1939 partition on the grounds that Moscow was "duty bound to give a helping hand to the Ukrainians and Byelorussians who made up most of the population in the eastern regions of Poland."[7] *Pravda* also asserted that although the time was not suitable for discussion of final frontier lines, there was nothing "immutable" in the Polish-Soviet frontier as established by the 1921 Treaty of Riga: "The question of future Soviet-Polish borders is a matter for the future." Thus did the Soviets dilute the sense of their signed word, even as the ink dried on the agreement. Similar occurrences were to mar future Allied unity.

During British Foreign Minister Anthony Eden's visit to Moscow in December 1941, Stalin insisted on recognition for the Soviet frontiers as they existed in June 1941, which would sanction all Soviet territorial acquisitions since September 1939. Though evaded at the time, this frequently repeated demand became, with the change in Allied fortunes, a growing source of discord. The Allies opposed Soviet claims to eastern Poland, as well as any prospective incorporation of the Baltic states into the Soviet Union. Tension between the Polish Government-in-exile and the Soviet Government reached the breaking point over the Katyn Forest controversy.* On April 13, 1943, the Nazis reported the "discovery" of the mass grave of Polish officers and blamed the Soviets for the atrocity. The Polish Government-in-exile proposed an impartial investigation of this allegation. Stalin's reply was quick and harsh: he severed diplomatic relations with the Polish Government, holding that Polish belief in the Nazi accusations indicated a lack of faith in the integrity of the Soviet Government; he also charged the Poles with exploiting the "Hitlerite slanderous fake" in order to force territorial concessions from the Soviet Government (reading 37). Though the ostensible cause of the breach was the Polish request for an investigation of the German charges, in the background was the continued insistence of the Poles upon a restoration of their 1939 frontier with the Soviet Union. The Poles refused to settle for territorial compensation at the expense of Germany. This Katyn incident was most convenient for Stalin. Eager to ensure a pro-Soviet

---

* After the partition of Poland the Soviets interned, among others, some 15,000 Polish officers and men, the elite of the defunct Polish army. By the spring of 1940 their whereabouts were a mystery. With the resumption of Polish-Soviet diplomatic relations in July 1941, the Polish Government-in-exile repeatedly requested information concerning the fate of these Poles. Soviet officialdom maintained an ominous silence. The Nazis placed the blame for the murder on the Soviet Government. Meanwhile, the Polish Government-in-exile reacted with honorable intent but little political prudence and requested the International Red Cross to conduct an investigation.

(Communist) regime in postwar Poland, he announced the establishment of an organization known as the "Union of Polish Patriots" a few days later. This group later served as the basis for the Soviet puppet Lublin Government. As a postscript to the Katyn Forest controversy, it may be noted that upon reconquering the area, the Soviets conducted their own investigation, and "conclusively" placed the blame on the Nazis. The issue was later raised at the Nuremberg war crimes trials, but the Soviet representatives chose neither to refute the German accusation of 1943 nor to take advantage of the opportunity to clear themselves of the widely believed charge. In such circumstances, silence decrees a presumption of Soviet guilt.*

The Soviet-Polish rupture seriously tried Allied unity. The Allies, reluctant to jeopardize the alliance, beset by continual Soviet demands for a second front, and increasingly indignant at Soviet disparagement of their war effort and aid, did not wish to press the Polish issue too far. The possibility that Stalin might conclude a sudden and separate agreement with Hitler as in 1939 also concerned Allied leaders.[8] The temper eased noticeably when Moscow announced the dissolution of the Communist International on May 22, 1943. In reply to a question from a British correspondent, Stalin expressed the hope that this action would end all fears that the Soviet Union "intends to intervene in the life of other nations and to 'Bolshevize' them" and that it would promote the unity of all groups fighting Hitlerism (reading 38). Undoubtedly a dramatic gesture aimed at assuaging Western feelings and at obscuring the Polish question, the announced dissolution of the Comintern seemed to herald the Kremlin's abandonment of its global apparatus designed to subvert existing governments and serve Soviet interests. We now know that the Comintern was never really dissolved; it merely functioned in secret.†

The growing complex of political problems convinced the heads

* The House of Representatives Select Committee to Conduct an Investigation and Study of the Facts, Evidence, and Circumstances of the Katyn Forest Massacre concluded, in its Interim Report of July 2, 1952 (82nd Congress, 2nd session, House Rept. No. 2430) that "the Soviet NKVD committed the mass murders . . . as a calculated plot to eliminate all Polish leaders who subsequently would have opposed the Soviets' plans for communizing Poland." A dispassionate study by J. K. Zawodny, *Death in the Forest* (Notre Dame: University of Notre Dame Press, 1962), places the responsibility conclusively on the Soviet Union.

† See Wolfgang Leonhard, *Child of the Revolution* (Chicago: Henry Regnery Company, 1957). In this personal account of life as a professional Communist Party functionary, the author tells of his assignment to the German section of the Comintern in Moscow after its "dissolution" in May 1943. There he was trained for future political tasks in Germany. The Comintern apparatus was kept intact, merely moving its headquarters to an anonymous section of Moscow.

of state that a meeting was necessary. Accordingly, at a preliminary conference of Foreign Ministers—Hull, Eden, Molotov—
in Moscow from October 15 to 30, 1943, an agenda was prepared,
and on November 28, 1943, Stalin, Churchill, and Roosevelt met
at Teheran. A broad range of topics was discussed: the makeup
of the proposed United Nations Organization; Soviet interests
in the Far East; the future of Germany; the Polish question; and
Soviet objectives in Eastern Europe. Shortly after the conference
ended, one of the American participants summed up in a memorandum what the full application of Stalin's desires could mean:

> Germany is to be broken up and kept broken up. The states of
> eastern, southeastern, and central Europe will not be permitted to
> group themselves into any federations or association. France is to be
> stripped of her colonies and strategic bases beyond her borders and
> will not be permitted to maintain any appreciable military establish-
> ment. Poland and Italy will remain approximately their present terri-
> torial size, but it is doubtful if either will be permitted to maintain
> any appreciable military force. The result would be that the Soviet
> Union would be the only important military and political force on the
> continent of Europe. The rest of Europe would be reduced to military
> and political impotence.[9]

Western leaders considered this statement unnecessarily pessimistic.

Meanwhile, the military picture progressively brightened.
Soviet offensives drained Nazi strength and drove the Germans
from Soviet soil. By January 1944 the Red Army had crossed
the former Polish frontier. On January 10, 1944, the Soviet news
agency, *Tass*, contradicted Polish claims to the 1939 boundary
(reading 39) and accused the Polish Government of deliberately
falsifying the frontier question. The incorporation of the western
Ukraine and western Byelorussia, according to *Tass*, reflected
the wishes of the peoples living in these areas. The Soviet Government continued to favor the existence of a strong, independent, friendly Polish state, whose western frontier should be
extended "through incorporation with Poland of ancient Polish
lands previously wrested by Germany."

The intransigence both of the leaders of the Polish Govern-
ment-in-exile and of Stalin, and the fear on the part of the
Western Powers of prejudicing postwar cooperation with the
Soviets, precluded an acceptable settlement. At the urging of both
Churchill and Roosevelt, however, Mikolajczyk, the Polish Prime
Minister, journeyed to Moscow in a desperate effort to reach an
agreement. He arrived on July 30, 1944, on the eve of the tragic
attempt by the Polish underground to expel the Nazis and liberate
Warsaw. Four days earlier, the Soviet Government had signed
an agreement with a puppet creation of the Kremlin, the Com-

mittee of National Liberation, which became the core of the
postwar Communist regime. This Committee declared Lublin the
capital of Poland. The Soviet statement only heightened an
already tense situation:

> The Soviet Government declares that it considers the military opera-
> tions of the Red Army on the territory of Poland as operations on the
> territory of a sovereign, friendly, allied state. In connection with this,
> the Soviet Government does not intend to establish on the territory of
> Poland organs of its own administration, considering this the task
> of the Polish people.
>
> It has decided, in view of this, to conclude with the Polish Com-
> mittee of National Liberation an agreement on relations between the
> Soviet Government and the Polish administration.
>
> The Soviet Government declares that it does not pursue aims of
> acquiring any part of Polish territory or of a change of social structure
> in Poland, and that the military operations of the Red Army on the
> territory of Poland are dictated solely by military necessity and by the
> striving to render the friendly Polish people aid in its liberation from
> German occupation.[10]

This assertion, that the Soviets had no territorial ambitions nor
desire to alter existing institutions, had previously been made by
Molotov on April 2, 1944, as the Red Army approached the
Rumanian frontier. However, he referred specifically to the
Soviet-Rumanian frontier as it existed in 1941, thus making it
indisputably clear that the 1940 Soviet annexation of Bessarabia
was not open for negotiation. The full extent of Soviet objectives
in Eastern Europe was to become tragically evident in the next
few years.

Another source of dissension among the Allies, Finland, had
proved particularly embarrassing in the early days of the war.
Western sympathy toward Finland was long standing, and Finland's joining (voluntarily or not) the Nazi attack on the USSR
had placed American policy-makers in a quandary. Prior to United
States entry into the war, the Finns attempted to rationalize their
behavior; the Soviet Government had acted immediately to refute
Finnish contentions. Once America entered the war, its treatment
of Finland as a belligerent was but a matter of time. Efforts to
induce Finland to disengage itself from German domination
failed. By the summer of 1944, Finland stood alone with no
prospects of help from any quarter, not even from Germany.
On September 19, 1944, an armistice was signed with the Soviet
Union, and Finland was out of the war.* Under the final treaty

* The terms imposed on Finland were harsh, but they did ensure that its
independence would be preserved. They provided that: (1) Finland would
withdraw her troops behind the Soviet-Finnish frontier line of March 12,
1940. (2) This would continue as the boundary except that in the far north

of peace signed in 1947, Finland's independence was preserved, but its foreign policy orientation understandably reflected the prevailing attitudes of its powerful neighbor.

The year 1944 was one of Allied victories. On June 6, Anglo-American-Canadian forces landed in France—the long-awaited second front was a reality. By the end of the year France had been liberated and the final preparations for the invasion of Germany itself were under way. On the Eastern Front Soviet military leaders shifted their offensives "with astonishing regularity, power and circumspection, like a boxer who systematically covers his opponent with telling blows without expecting that one single blow will knock him down."[11] With the approach of victory the unresolved political problems could no longer be evaded. The future of Poland and of all of Eastern Europe, the division of Germany, the role of the Soviet Union in the war against Japan, the coordination of the final assault on Germany, and the preparations for the establishment of the United Nations Organization—all had to be discussed and agreements reached. To facilitate solutions to these knotty problems, Roosevelt and Churchill expressed a willingness to meet with Stalin, and so, once again, the Western leaders embarked on a long journey, this time to the Crimea, in an attempt to ensure the peace. The Yalta Conference was held in the former Czarist palace of Livadia from February 4 to 10, 1945.

Much has been written about this conference. Some insist that Eastern Europe and China were here "sold out" to the Soviets; others argue that the agreements reached were justifiable under existing circumstances and information known, and that they reflected military realities. In any honest effort at appraisal one must remember that differences in the relative weights accorded the same "facts" will result in strikingly different final judgments. Before examining the Yalta deliberations, it is useful to review the military-political picture of February 1945.

Allied troops were at the Rhine; Soviet forces prepared to cross the Oder and launch the final attack on Berlin, some forty miles away. The Red Army already controlled most of Eastern Europe; Tito's Partisans dominated the political scene in Yugoslavia. In the Far East, despite major victories over the Japanese at Iwo Jima and Okinawa, American military experts expected a difficult

---

Finland agreed to cede Petsamo to the Soviets and granted them a naval base at Porkkala-Udd; in return, the Soviets agreed to relinquish their previously held lease on the peninsula of Hangoe. (3) Finland would pay a 300-million-dollar indemnity in kind in six years. (4) Soviet forces would not occupy Finland; the administration was to remain in control of Finnish authorities.

fight before Japan's final surrender. In November 1944, the Joint Chiefs of Staff had weighed the pros and cons of Soviet participation in the war against Japan and concluded that:

(a) We desire Russian entry at the earliest possible date consistent with her ability to engage in offensive operations and are prepared to offer the maximum support possible without prejudice to our main effort against Japan.

(b) We consider that the mission of Russian Far Eastern Forces should be to conduct an all-out offensive against Manchuria to force the commitment of Japanese forces and resources in North China and Manchuria that might otherwise be employed in the defense of Japan, to conduct intensive air operations against Japan proper and to interdict lines of communication between Japan and the mainland of Asia.[12]

On the eve of the conference most Western leaders firmly believed and hoped that it would be possible to extend the unity forged in wartime to the postwar period.* Suspicion of Soviet intentions did exist among some professional diplomats, but popular sentiment in the West favored continued collaboration with the Soviet Union. Admiration for the courage displayed by the Soviet people and sympathy for their suffering and sacrifice were widespread. It remained for political developments and Stalin's blatant disregard of his pledged word to bring about a fundamental shift in climate and to trigger the "Cold War." But this was still in the future.

The most important political discussions at Yalta focused on the Polish and German questions and on the conditions under which the Soviet Union would later enter the war against Japan.

The discussions between Western and Soviet military staffs gave no evidence of competition or distrust in their planning for the final assault on Germany. According to the eminent historian Herbert Feis:

Each showed a wish to have the other push its attack with all possible speed and vigor so that the Germans would not be able to transfer troops between east and west and their reserves would the sooner be used up. Thus no attempt was made to reach agreement as to the places or lines along which the armies coming from the east and from the west should stop. Their destination was to be decided by the course of battle; the question of where and how long the armies of each would *remain* was left to the makers of political arrangements.[13]

---

* However, it should be noted that on January 8, 1945, Churchill, in writing to Roosevelt about their coming meeting with Stalin, prophetically wrote: "This may well be a fateful Conference, coming at a moment when the Great Allies are so divided and the shadow of the war lengthens out before us. At the present time I think the end of this war may well prove to be more disappointing than was the last." Winston S. Churchill, *Triumph and Tragedy* (Boston: Houghton Mifflin Company, 1953), p. 341.

However, the political issues affecting the fate of postwar Europe did not fare so well. The Polish question figured "at no fewer than seven out of the eight plenary meetings of the Yalta Conference."[14] Attention centered on four key aspects of this perhaps most vexing of all existing questions: (a) a formula for establishing a single Provisional Government for Poland; (b) how and when to hold free elections; (c) possible solutions to the future of Poland's frontiers, both in the east and the west; (d) steps designed to safeguard the security of the Soviet rear.

The communique issued at the end of the Yalta Conference, on February 12, 1945, took note of these and other problems and sketched solutions which, if applied with fidelity and good faith, might have served the interests of all (reading 40). But it was evident, even before the war was won, that Stalin intended to interpret the Yalta Declaration in a manner most apt to enhance Soviet security and power. A prime catalyst in the disintegration of the wartime alliance, the Polish question represented, in a larger sense, a barometer recording the peril points of two incompatible conceptions of security.

Agreement on Germany's immediate future came more readily. All parties agreed that Germany must surrender unconditionally. Upon the termination of hostilities an Allied Control Council was to serve as the top coordinating and policy organ of the occupying powers; three zones of occupation were established, a fourth later being allocated to France from the American and British zones; the Soviets agreed that the Western Powers were to have free and unhampered access to Berlin, which was situated deep inside the Soviet zone of occupation; and the basic principles guiding reparations arrangements were reached. Accord was also achieved on the proposed organization of the United Nations and on the broad approaches determining future political actions in Eastern Europe and the Balkans. The stage was well set at Yalta to sustain concerted military action against Germany until final victory and to manage the German surrender smoothly.

The Far East played no part in the published formal deliberations at Yalta; a secret protocol was drawn up. No mention of it, therefore, appeared in the public statement issued at the end of the conference. Throughout the war the Soviet Union maintained strictly correct relations with Japan in accordance with the five-year neutrality pact of April 13, 1941. Only in the last days of the war did Soviet forces become involved in the Pacific conflict. Moscow had departed slightly from its posture of neutrality and associated itself with the Chinese Government by signing the Four Power Declaration of November 1, 1943, under which the United States, Great Britain, China, and the Soviet

Union pledged themselves to cooperate against all their common enemies. More significantly, as early as August 1942 Stalin had assured Harriman of Soviet help in the war against Japan at the appropriate time and had specifically repeated this assurance in November 1943 and in September and October 1944. There had been some informal discussion at Teheran of Soviet territorial objectives in the Far East, with Stalin expressing interest in a warm-water port, the return of southern Sakhalin, and the acquisition of the Kuril Islands, but nothing definite was settled at the time. In October 1944, at the Moscow Conference, Stalin reaffirmed to Churchill his willingness to enter the war against Japan three months after the defeat of Germany, subject to certain conditions, which were presented to the American Government in December and served as the basis for the secret agreement on the Far East which was concluded at Yalta (reading 41). They provided for the preservation of the status quo in Outer Mongolia (Mongolian People's Republic), the return of southern Sakhalin, the internationalization of the port of Dairen, the annexation of the Kuril Islands, and the restoration of former Russian rights in Manchuria. These stipulations were later accepted by China and incorporated into the Sino-Soviet Treaty of Friendship and Alliance, signed on August 14, 1945, which contained a Soviet promise "to render to China moral support and aid in military supplies and other material resources, such support and aid to be entirely given to the National Government as the Central Government of China."

Was the price paid for Soviet participation excessive considering the dividends expected? Would the United States Government have accepted Stalin's conditions had it realized the imminence of Japan's surrender? Indeed, in view of traditional Russian Far Eastern objectives, would Stalin not have entered the war even without the Yalta concessions? Ironically, it was the American military experts, with their estimates of another eighteen months of war after the defeat of Germany and anticipated casualties approaching the million mark in any invasion of the Japanese home islands, who influenced the political decision at Yalta to grant Soviet demands; these concessions helped restore the USSR to a position of power in the Far East comparable to that which it held in 1904, on the eve of the Russo-Japanese war.

The intricate and fascinating story of all the controversies, discussions, and deals that marked the Yalta deliberations,[15] and their implications for the postwar period, will long be debated by historians. We who examine the record in retrospect would do well to ponder the afterthoughts on Yalta so eloquently expressed by Sir Winston Churchill:

It is not permitted to those charged with dealing with events in times of war or crisis to confine themselves purely to the statement of broad general principles on which good people agree. They have to take definite decisions from day to day. They have to adopt postures which must be solidly maintained, otherwise how can any combinations for action be maintained? It is easy, after the Germans are beaten, to condemn those who did their best to hearten the Russian military effort and to keep in harmonious contact with our great Ally, who had suffered so frightfully. What would have happened if we had quarrelled with Russia while the Germans still had three or four hundred divisions on the fighting front? Our hopeful assumptions were soon to be falsified. Still, they were the only ones possible at the time.[16]

With the approach of victory the tide of trust that had flowed at Yalta ebbed fast; "Stalin was giving way to suspicion of the American-British conduct of the war and to resentment at their attempts to maintain influence in any region near Soviet frontiers. To the Western Allies it seemed that under the spell of victory the Russians were becoming indifferent to their wartime vows."[17]

On May 8, 1945, Germany surrendered unconditionally. Japan collapsed quickly thereafter.* The dropping of the atomic bomb on Hiroshima on August 6, 1945, and the entry of the USSR two days later into the war, sealed Japan's fate. She capitulated on August 14; the formal signing was aboard the battleship *Missouri* in Tokyo Bay on September 2.

The war was over. The challenge of the peace remained.

* During the late spring and early summer the Japanese Government sought to enter into surrender negotiations with the West, hopeful that the Soviet Government would act as a disinterested intermediary. For an excellent account of these negotiations and Soviet behavior as seen from the Japanese position see Toshikazu Kase, *Journey to the Missouri* (New Haven: Yale University Press, 1950).

NOTES

1. Robert E. Sherwood, *Roosevelt and Hopkins* (New York: Harper & Row, Publishers, 1948), pp. 303–305.
2. Winston S. Churchill, *The Grand Alliance* (Boston: Houghton Mifflin Company, 1950), pp. 358–361.
3. Nikita S. Khrushchev, *Special Report to the Twentieth Congress of the Communist Party of the Soviet Union* (February 1956).
4. For a superb scholarly account of this phase of Nazi policy see Alexander Dallin, *German Rule in Russia, 1941–1945: A Study of Occupational Policies* (New York: St. Martin's Press, 1957); also of particular interest is the story of Soviet General Andrei Vlasov, a hero of the battle of Moscow who defected to the Germans, as told by George Fischer in *Soviet Opposition to Stalin* (Cambridge: Harvard University Press, 1952). According to the author, General Vlasov organized an army of almost 600,000 from among the captive Soviets and offered to fight under German control. But the Nazis never used this "Russian

Liberation Army" to advantage. Fischer believes that Vlasov was not so much pro-Hitler as anti-Stalin.

5. Andrew Rothstein (tr.), *Soviet Foreign Policy During the Patriotic War: Documents and Materials* (New York: Hutchinson and Company, n.d.), Vol. I, p. 129.

6. Herbert Feis, *Churchill-Roosevelt-Stalin* (Princeton, N.J.: Princeton University Press, 1957), p. 15.

7. *Pravda*, August 4, 1941.

8. Sherwood, *op. cit.*, p. 734.

9. Feis, *op. cit.*, p. 275.

10. *USSR Information Bulletin*, Vol. IV, No. 86 (July 29, 1944).

11. Isaac Deutscher, *Stalin: A Political Biography* (New York: Oxford University Press, 1949), p. 512.

12. U. S. Department of Defense, *The Entry of the Soviet Union into the War Against Japan: Military Plans, 1941–1945* (Washington, D.C., 1955).

13. Feis, *op. cit.*, p. 498.

14. Winston S. Churchill, *Triumph and Tragedy* (Boston: Houghton Mifflin Company, 1953), p. 365.

15. For a full account of the Conference see *Foreign Relations of the United States: The Conferences of Malta and Yalta, 1945* (Washington, D.C.: Government Printing Office, 1955).

16. Churchill, *Triumph and Tragedy*, p. 402.

17. Feis, *op. cit.*, p. 562.

Forging the Alliance

30. BROADCAST SPEECH *

July 3, 1941

J O S E P H   S T A L I N

Comrades, citizens, brothers, and sisters, men of our Army and Navy! I am addressing you, my dear friends!

The perfidious military attack on our Motherland begun on June 22 by Hitler Germany is continuing. In spite of the heroic resistance of the Red Army, and although the enemy's finest divisions and finest air force units have already been smashed and have met their doom on the field of battle, the enemy continues to push forward, hurling fresh forces into the attack. . . . A grave danger hangs over our country.

How could it have happened that our glorious Red Army sur-

* *Soviet War Documents:* Special Supplement to *USSR Information Bulletin* (Washington, D.C.: USSR Embassy, December 1943), *excerpts*.

rendered a number of our cities and districts to the Fascist armies? Is it really true that the German-Fascist troops are invincible, as is ceaselessly trumpeted by boastful fascist propagandists? Of course not! History shows that there are no invincible armies and never have been. Napoleon's army was considered invincible but it was beaten successively by Russian, English, and German armies. Kaiser Wilhelm's German army in the period of the first imperialist war was also considered invincible, but it was beaten several times by Russian and Anglo-French forces and was finally smashed by the Anglo-French forces. The same must be said of Hitler's German-Fascist army today. This army has not yet met with serious resistance on the continent of Europe. Only on our territory has it met serious resistance. . . .

As to part of our territory having nevertheless been seized by German-Fascist troops, this is chiefly due to the fact that the war of Fascist Germany on the USSR began under conditions favorable for the German forces and unfavorable for the Soviet forces. The fact of the matter is that the troops of Germany, as a country at war, were already fully mobilized, and the 170 divisions hurled by Germany against the USSR and brought up to the Soviet frontiers were in a state of complete readiness, only awaiting the signal to move into action, whereas the Soviet troops had still to effect mobilization and to move up to the frontiers. Of no little importance in this respect is the fact that Fascist Germany suddenly and treacherously violated the nonaggression pact she concluded in 1939 with the USSR, disregarding the fact that she would be regarded as the aggressor by the whole world. Naturally, our peace-loving country, not wishing to take the initiative in breaking the pact, could not resort to perfidy.

It may be asked: how could the Soviet Government have consented to conclude a nonaggression pact with such treacherous fiends as Hitler and Ribbentrop? Was this not an error on the part of the Soviet Government? Of course not! Nonaggression pacts are pacts of peace between two states. It was such a pact that Germany proposed to us in 1939. Could the Soviet Government have declined such a proposal? I think that not a single peace-loving state could decline a peace treaty with a neighboring state, even though the latter was headed by such fiends and cannibals as Hitler and Ribbentrop. But that, of course, only on the one indispensable condition, namely, that this peace treaty did not infringe, either directly or indirectly on the territorial integrity, independence and honor of the peace-loving state. As is well known, the nonaggression pact between Germany and the USSR was precisely such a pact.

What did we gain by concluding the nonaggression pact with Germany? We secured our country peace for a year and a half and the opportunity of preparing its forces to repulse Fascist Germany should she risk an attack on our country despite the pact. This was a definite advantage for us and a disadvantage for Fascist Germany.

What has Fascist Germany gained and what has she lost by treacherously tearing up the pact and attacking the USSR? She has gained certain advantageous positions for her troops for a short period, but she has lost politically by exposing herself in the eyes of the entire world as a bloodthirsty aggressor. There can be no doubt that this shortlived military gain for Germany is only an episode, while the tremendous political gain of the USSR is a serious and lasting factor that is bound to form the basis for the development of decisive military successes of the Red Army in the war with Fascist Germany. . . .

What is required to put an end to the danger hovering over our country, and what measures must be taken to smash the enemy? Above all, it is essential that our people, the Soviet people, should understand the full immensity of the danger that threatens our country and abandon all complacency, all heedlessness, all those moods of peaceful constructive work which were so natural before the war, but which are fatal today when the war has fundamentally changed everything. The enemy is cruel and implacable. He is out to seize our lands watered with our sweat, to seize our grain and oil secured by our labor. He is out to restore the rule of the landlords, to restore Tsarism, to destroy the national culture and the national state existence of the . . . free peoples of the Soviet Union, to Germanize them, to convert them into the slaves of the German princes and barons. Thus the issue is one of life or death for the Soviet State, of life or death for the peoples of the USSR. . . .

All our work must be immediately reconstructed on a war footing, everything must be subordinated to the interests of the front and the task of organizing the demolition of the enemy. . . . We must wage a ruthless fight against all disorganizers of the rear, deserters, panic-mongers, and rumor-mongers, we must exterminate spies, diversionists, and enemy parachutists, rendering rapid aid in all this to our destroyer battalions. . . . In case of forced retreat of Red Army units, all rolling stock must be evacuated, the enemy must not be left a single engine, a single railway car, not a single pound of grain or gallon of fuel. Collective farmers must drive off all their cattle and turn over their grain to the safe keeping of the State authorities for transportation to the rear. All valuable property, including nonferrous metals, grain, and fuel, which cannot be withdrawn, must be destroyed without fail. In areas occupied by the enemy, guerrilla units, mounted and foot, must be formed, diversionist groups must be organized to combat the enemy troops, to foment guerrilla warfare everywhere, to blow up bridges and roads, to damage telephone and telegraph lines, to set fire to forests, stores and transports. In the occupied regions conditions must be made unbearable for the enemy and all his accomplices. They must be hounded and annihilated at every step, and all their measures frustrated. . . .

31. NOTE OF THE SOVIET GOVERNMENT TO THE GOVERNMENT OF IRAN[*]

August 25, 1941

In the Soviet-Iranian Treaty of February 26, 1921, the Soviet Government declared null and void the treaties and agreements between the Government of Tsarist Russia and the Iranian Government violating the sovereignty of Iran. . . . Later, for a period of many years, the Soviet Government constantly rendered assistance to Iran in the field of economic development. . . .

The Soviet Government, however, as well as the Government of Iran, had at the time of the conclusion of the principal Soviet-Iranian Treaty of February 26, 1921, already clearly realized the special difficulties which might be encountered in the course of strengthening friendly relations between the Soviet Union and Iran in case the territory of Iran should be used by elements hostile both to the USSR and to Iran itself, and in case these elements should try to use Iran as a base for aggression against the USSR.

With a view to averting such danger, Article VI of the Soviet-Iranian Treaty provided as follows:

"Both High Contracting Parties agree that if a third party should attempt to carry out a policy of usurpation by means of armed intervention in Persia, or if such power should desire to use Persian territory as a base for operations against the Russian Socialist Federal Soviet Republic, or if a foreign power should

[*] V. M. Molotov, Deputy Chairman of the Council of People's Commissars of the USSR, handed this note to the Iranian Ambassador on August 25, 1941. *USSR Information Bulletin*, No. 37 (August 26, 1941), pp. 5–12, *excerpts.*

threaten the frontiers of the RSFSR, or those of its allies, and if the Persian Government should not be able to put a stop to such a menace after having been once called upon to do so by the Russian Socialist Federal Soviet Republic, the Russian Socialist Federal Soviet Republic shall have the right to advance its troops into the Persian interior for the purpose of carrying out the military operations necessary for its defense. The Soviet Government undertakes, however, to withdraw its troops from Persian territory as soon as the danger has been removed."

Thus the Soviet Government, in full agreement with the Iranian Government, undertook to protect the interests of the USSR in Iran should the danger mentioned in the Treaty of 1921 occur, and at the same time confirmed its obligation immediately to withdraw its troops from the territory of Iran after the danger had passed. It is well known that the Soviet Government for a period of 20 years of the operation of the 1921 Treaty did not consider it necessary to invoke Article 6 of the 1921 Treaty in order to protect its interests.

Recently, however, and particularly since the beginning of the perfidious aggression of Hitlerite Germany against the USSR, the activity of German-Fascist conspiratorial groups on the territory of Iran, hostile both to the USSR and to Iran, has assumed a menacing character. Having made their way into important official posts in more than 50 Iranian Departments, German agents are trying by every means to provoke disorder and disturbance in Iran, to violate the peaceful life of the Iranian people, to instigate Iran against the USSR and to involve Iran in a war with the USSR. . . . [specific instances of German activity given at length]

The situation in Iran, resulting from the above-mentioned conditions, is fraught with extreme dangers. The Soviet Government is thus obliged to carry out immediately all measures which it is not only entitled to take but is bound to take for self-defense in strict conformity with Article 6 of the Treaty of 1921.

During the period since the German aggression against the USSR the Soviet Government has thrice—on June 26, July 19, and August 16 of this year—drawn the attention of the Iranian Government to the danger which the subversive and espionage activities of German agents in Iran constitute.

On June 26 of this year the Soviet Government informed the Shah of Iran that the Soviet Government had at its disposal reliable information concerning a coup d'état being prepared by Germans in Iran. On July 19 of this year the Soviet Government, together with the British Government, again raised before the Iranian Government the question of putting an end to the hostile activities conducted by the Germans and of troubles being prepared by them which threaten the interests not only of Iran itself but also of neighboring states. At the same time the Government of the Soviet Union and the Government of Great Britain insisted upon the expulsion from Iran of Germans whose presence in Iran is incompatible with the interests of Iran itself as well as with the interests of the Soviet Union and Great Britain.

Finally, on August 16 of this year, the Soviet Government, as well as the Government of Great Britain, for the third time, raised before the Iranian Government the necessity of taking urgent measures to put an end to activities of German agents in Iran directed against the interests of Iran as well as of the Soviet Union and Great Britain, and once more insisted upon the speediest expulsion of these Germans from Iran. . . .

Unfortunately, the Iranian Government has refused to take measures which would put an end to the troubles and disorders fomented by German agents on the territory of Iran, thus encouraging German agents in their criminal activities. As a result of this, the Soviet Government has been forced to take necessary measures and to avail itself immediately of the right belonging to the Soviet Union in virtue of Article 6 of the Treaty of 1921, namely, the right to advance its troops into the territory of Iran for the purpose of self-defense.

These measures are in no way directed against the Iranian people. The Soviet Government has no designs affecting the territorial integrity and the independence of the Iranian State. The military measures which the Soviet Government is undertaking are directed exclusively against the danger created by hostile activities of Germans in Iran. As soon as this danger, threatening the interests of Iran and the USSR has been removed, the Soviet Government, in compliance with its obligation under the Soviet-Iranian Treaty of 1921 will immediately withdraw Soviet troops from Iranian territory.

Moscow, August 25, 1941.

32. SPEECH TO THE MOSCOW SOVIET ON
THE ANNIVERSARY OF THE
OCTOBER REVOLUTION*

November 6, 1941

JOSEPH STALIN

Never before has the Soviet rear been as stable as it is now. It is quite likely that any other state having sustained such territorial losses as we have now, would not stand the test and would suffer a decline. If the Soviet system has so easily withstood the test and has consolidated its rear still more, it means that the Soviet system is now the most stable system. . . . [Stalin then developed the situation at the front.] Along with the favorable conditions, there are also a number of conditions unfavorable for the Red Army, as a consequence of which our Army has suffered temporary reverses, has been compelled to withdraw, and compelled to give up to the enemy a number of regions of our country. What are these unfavorable conditions? What are the causes of the temporary military reverses of the Red Army?

One of the causes of the reverses is the absence of a second front in Europe against the German Fascist armies. The fact is that at the present time there are on the continent of Europe no armies of Great Britain or of the United States which could wage war against the German Nazi troops. Therefore, the Germans do not have to split their forces and wage war on two fronts—in the west and in the east. This situation means that the Germans, considering their rear in the West secure, are free to move all their troops and the troops of their European allies against our country. The situation is now such that our country is waging the war of liberation alone, without anybody's assistance, against the combined forces of the Germans, Finns, Rumanians, Italians, and Hungarians. . . .

We have not nor can we have such war aims as the seizure of foreign territories or the conquest of other peoples, irrespective of whether European peoples and territories or Asiatic peoples or territories, including Iran, are concerned. . . . We have not nor

* USSR *Information Bulletin*, No. 127, Special Supplement (December 13, 1941), *excerpts*.

can we have such war aims as the imposition of our will and regime on the Slavic and other enslaved peoples of Europe who are waiting for our help. Our aim is to help these peoples in their struggle for liberation from Hitler's tyranny, and then to accord them the possibility of arranging their lives on their own land as they think fit, with absolute freedom. No interference of any kind with the domestic affairs of other nations!

The Second Front and the Turning of the Tide

33. REPORT ON THE OCCASION OF THE TWENTY-FIFTH ANNIVERSARY OF THE OCTOBER REVOLUTION*

November 6, 1942

JOSEPH STALIN

[*Stalin started his speech by outlining the activities undertaken to strengthen the economy and armed forces. After presenting an analysis of military operations on the Soviet-German front, he proceeded to raise the question of the Second Front in Europe.*]

. . . How are we to explain the fact that the Germans this year were still able to take the initiative of operations into their hands and achieve substantial tactical successes on our front?

It is to be explained by the fact that the Germans and their allies succeeded in mustering all their available reserves, hurling them onto the Eastern Front and creating a big superiority of forces in one of the directions. There can be no doubt that but for these measures the Germans could not have achieved any success on our front.

But why were they able to muster all their reserves and hurl them onto the Eastern Front? Because the absence of a second front in Europe enabled them to carry out this operation without

* *USSR Information Bulletin*, No. 135 (November 12, 1946), *excerpts*.

any risk to themselves. Hence the chief reason for the tactical successes of the Germans on our front this year is that the absence of a second front in Europe enabled them to hurl onto our front all their available reserves and to create a big superiority of forces in the southwestern direction.

Let us assume that the second front existed in Europe as it existed in the first World War, and that the second front diverted, let us say, sixty German divisions and twenty divisions of Germany's allies. What would have been the position of the German troops on our front then?

It is not difficult to guess that their position would be deplorable. More, it would have been the beginning of the end of the German-Fascist troops, for in that case the Red Army would not be where it is now, but somewhere near Pskov, Minsk, Zhitomir, and Odessa. That means that in the summer of this year the German-Fascist army would already have been on the verge of disaster. If that has not occurred, it is because the Germans were saved by the absence of a second front in Europe.

Let us examine the question of a second front in Europe in its historical aspect. In the first World War Germany had to fight on two fronts: in the west chiefly against Great Britain and France, and in the east against the Russian troops. Thus in the first World War there existed a second front against Germany. Of the 220 divisions which Germany had then, not more than 85 German divisions were stationed on the Russian front. If to this we add the troops of Germany's allies then facing the Russian front, namely 37 Austro-Hungarian divisions, 2 Bulgarian divisions, and 3 Turkish divisions, we get a total of 127 divisions facing the Russian troops. The rest of the divisions of Germany and her allies chiefly held the front against the Anglo-French troops, while a part of them performed garrison service in the occupied territories of Europe. Such was the position in the first World War.

What is the position now, in the second World War, in September of this year, let us say? According to authenticated information which is beyond all doubt, of 256 divisions which Germany now has, not less than 179 German divisions are on our front. If to this we add 22 Rumanian divisions, 14 Finnish divisions, 10 Italian divisions, 13 Hungarian divisions, 1 Slovak and 1 Spanish division, we get a total of 240 divisions which are now fighting on our front. The remaining divisions of Germany and her allies are performing garrison service in the occupied countries of France, Belgium, Norway, Holland, Yugoslavia, Poland, Czechoslovakia, etc. while part of them are fighting in Libya or Egypt against Great Britain, the Libyan front diverting in all 4 German divisions and 11 Italian divisions.

Hence, instead of the 127 divisions as in the first World War, we are now facing on our front no less than 240 divisions, and instead of 85 German divisions we now have 179 German divisions fighting the Red Army. There you have the chief reason and foundation for the tactical success of the German-Fascist troops on our front in the summer of this year.

The German invasion of our country is often compared to Napoleon's invasion of Russia. But this comparison will not bear criticism. Of the 600,000 troops which began the campaign against Russia, Napoleon scarcely brought 130,000 or 140,000 as far as Borodino. That was all he had at his disposal at Moscow.

Well, we now have over 3,000,000 troops facing the front of the Red Army and armed with all the implements of modern warfare. What comparison can there be here?

The German invasion of our country is also sometimes compared to the German invasion of Russia at the time of the first World War. But neither will this comparison bear criticism. First, in the first World War there was a second front in Europe which rendered the German position very difficult, whereas in this war there is no second front in Europe.

Secondly, in this war, twice as many troops are facing our front as in the first World War. Obviously the comparison is not appropriate. You can now conceive how serious and extraordinary are the difficulties confronting the Red Army, and how great is the heroism displayed by the Red Army in its war of liberation against the German-Fascist troops. . . .

34. REPORT AT THE MEETING OF THE SOVIET OF DEPUTIES ON THE TWENTY-SIXTH ANNIVERSARY OF THE OCTOBER REVOLUTION*

November 6, 1943

JOSEPH STALIN

The past year has marked a turn not only in the patriotic war of the Soviet Union but also in the whole World War. The changes which have taken place during this year in the military

* *USSR Information Bulletin*, No. 125 (November 11, 1943), *excerpts.*

and international situation have been favorable to the USSR and the Allied countries friendly to it, and detrimental to Germany and her accomplices in brigandage of Europe. . . .

Of course, the present actions of the Allied armies in the south of Europe cannot yet be regarded as a second front. But still it is something like a second front. Obviously the opening of a real second front in Europe, which is not so distant, will considerably hasten the victory over Hitlerite Germany and will consolidate even more the fighting partnership of the Allied countries. . . .

The victory of the Allied countries over Hitlerite Germany will put on the agenda the important questions of organizing and rebuilding of the state, economic, and cultural life of the European peoples. The policy of our Government in these questions remains unchanging. Together with our Allies we shall have to:

First: Liberate the peoples of Europe from the Fascist invaders and help them rebuild their national states dismembered by the Fascist enslavers. The peoples of France, Belgium, Yugoslavia, Czechoslovakia, Poland, Greece, and other states now under the German yoke must again become free and independent.

Second: Grant the liberated peoples of Europe the full right and freedom to decide for themselves the question of their own form of government.

Third: Take measures that all Fascist criminals responsible for this war and the sufferings of the people bear stern punishment and retribution for all the crimes they committed, no matter in what country they may hide.

Fourth: Establish such an order in Europe as will completely preclude the possibility of new aggression on the part of Germany.

Fifth: Establish lasting economic, political, and cultural collaboration among the peoples of Europe, based on mutual confidence and mutual assistance, for the purpose of rehabilitating the economic and cultural life destroyed by the Germans.

35. REPORT TO THE SUPREME SOVIET*

June 18, 1942

V. M. MOLOTOV

Comrades, Deputies:

The Government has deemed it necessary to submit to the Supreme Soviet for examination and ratification the Anglo-Soviet Treaty concluded on May 26 in London, in view of the great political importance of the treaty. The treaty consolidates the friendly relations which have been established between the Soviet Union and Great Britain and their mutual military assistance in the struggle against Hitlerite Germany. It transforms these relations into a stable alliance. The treaty also defines the general line of our joint action with Great Britain in the postwar period. The entire tenor of the treaty bears out its great political significance not only for the development of Anglo-Soviet relations but also for the future development of the entire complex of international relations in Europe. . . .

The treaty consists of two parts: The first part contains two articles defining the relations between the USSR and Great Britain during the war against Hitlerite Germany, and the second part contains articles defining the relations between the two countries after the war.

Of the first part of the treaty it may be said that it repeats in general the tenor of the well known Anglo-Soviet Agreement of July 12 of last year, transforming this agreement into a formal treaty. Giving greater precision to last year's agreement, this part of the treaty provides for mutual military and other assistance and support not only against Germany, but also against "those states which are associated with her in acts of aggression in Europe."

The second part of the treaty is comparatively new. The significance of this part of the treaty consists, first, in the fact that it lays down for the first time basic principles for friendly collaboration between the USSR and Great Britain after the war. It also provides for collaboration by both countries with other United Nations in the peace settlement and in the postwar period.

* *USSR Information Bulletin*, No. 74 (June 20, 1942), *excerpts*.

This collaboration is conceived along the lines of the basic principles of the well-known Atlantic Charter, to which the USSR in good time adhered.

There can be no doubt that an agreement of this kind will be of great significance in the entire future development of Europe. Both countries agreed to work together after the reestablishment of peace "for the organization of security and economic prosperity in Europe." The treaty states that both countries "will take into account the interests of the United Nations in realizing this objective and will act in accord with the two principles of not seeking territorial aggrandizement for themselves and of noninterference in the internal affairs of other States." These principles of the treaty are in full accord with the well-known pronouncement by the head of the Government of the USSR, comrade Stalin, on 6 November last year:

We have not and cannot have any such war aims as the seizure of foreign territories and the subjugation of foreign peoples, whether it is a question of peoples and territories of Europe or of peoples and territories of Asia, including Iran.

Important as are the questions which are dealt with in the treaty and to which great attention was devoted in the London negotiations, these negotiations, as you know, were not confined to the aforementioned questions alone. Both in London and Washington other important questions were also discussed. I am referring chiefly to questions intimately bearing on the vital problems of our war against Hitlerite Germany.

Serious attention was naturally paid in our negotiations both in London and in Washington to the problems of the second front in Europe. The results of these negotiations are dealt with in similar words both in Anglo-Soviet and Soviet-American communiqués. Both communiqués declare that in the negotiations "complete understanding was reached with regard to the urgent tasks of the creation of a second front in Europe in 1942."

This statement is of great importance to the peoples of the Soviet Union, since the creation of a second front in Europe will make insuperable difficulties for Hitler's armies on our front. Let us hope that our common enemy will soon experience to his cost the results of the evergrowing military collaboration of the three Great Powers. . . .

The Problems of Poland and the Future of Eastern Europe

36. AGREEMENT BETWEEN THE GOVERNMENT OF POLAND AND THE UNION OF SOVIET SOCIALIST REPUBLICS*

London, July 30, 1941

ARTICLE 1. The Government of the USSR recognizes the Soviet-German treaties of 1939 as to territorial changes in Poland as having lost their validity. The Polish Government declares Poland is not bound by any agreement with any third power which is directed against the USSR.

ARTICLE 2. Diplomatic relations will be restored between the two Governments upon the signing of this agreement, and an immediate exchange of Ambassadors will be arranged.

ARTICLE 3. The two Governments mutually agree to render one to another aid and support of all kinds in the present war against Hitlerite Germany.

ARTICLE 4. The Government of the USSR expresses its consent to the formation on territory of the USSR of a Polish Army under a commander appointed by the Polish Government in agreement with the Soviet Government, the Polish Army on territory of the USSR being subordinated in an operational sense to the Supreme Command of the USSR, in which the Polish Army will be represented. All details as to command, organization and employment of this force will be settled in a subsequent agreement.

ARTICLE 5. This agreement will come into force immediately upon signature and without ratification. The present agreement is drawn up in two copies in the Russian and Polish languages. Both texts have equal force.

The Soviet Government grants amnesty to all Polish citizens now detained on Soviet territory either as prisoners of war or on other sufficient grounds, as from the resumption of diplomatic relations.

* *USSR Information Bulletin*, No. 123 (December 6, 1941), *excerpts.*

37. NOTE OF THE SOVIET GOVERNMENT ON ITS DECISION TO BREAK OFF RELATIONS WITH THE POLISH GOVERNMENT*

April 25, 1943

[*On April 25, 1943, V. M. Molotov, People's Commissar for Foreign Affairs, handed the Polish Ambassador, M. Romer, a Note of the Soviet Government as follows:*]

Mr. Ambassador,

On behalf of the Government of the Union of Soviet Socialist Republics, I have the honor to notify the Polish Government of the following:

The Soviet Government considers the recent behavior of the Polish Government with regard to the USSR as entirely abnormal, violating all regulations and standards of relations between two Allied States.

The slanderous campaign, hostile to the Soviet Union, launched by the German Fascists in connection with the murder of Polish officers which they themselves committed in the Smolensk area on territory occupied by German troops, was at once taken up by the Polish Government and is being fanned in every way by the Polish official press. Far from offering a rebuff to the vile Fascist slander of the USSR, the Polish Government did not even find it necessary to address to the Soviet Government with any inquiry or explanation on this subject.

Having committed a monstrous crime against the Polish officers, the Hitlerite authorities now stage a farcical investigation, and for this staging they have made use of certain Polish pro-Fascist elements whom they themselves picked in occupied Poland where everything is under Hitler's heel and where an honest Pole cannot openly have his say. For the "investigation" both the Polish Government and the Hitlerite Government invited the International Red Cross, which is compelled, in conditions of a terroristic regime with its gallows and mass extermination of the peaceful population, to take part in this investigation farce staged by Hitler. Clearly such an "investigation," conducted behind the back of the Soviet Government at that, cannot evoke the confidence of people possessing any amount of honesty.

The fact that the hostile campaign against the Soviet Union

---

* *USSR Information Bulletin,* No. 45 (April 29, 1943), *excerpts.*

commenced simultaneously in the German and Polish press and is conducted along the same lines—this fact leaves no doubt as to the existence of contact and accord in carrying out this hostile campaign between the enemy of the Allies—Hitler, and the Polish Government.

While the peoples of the Soviet Union are bleeding profusely in the hard struggle against Hitlerite Germany and strain every effort for the defeat of the common enemy of the Russian and Polish peoples and all freedom-loving, democratic countries, the Polish Government, to please Hitler's tyranny, deals a treacherous blow to the Soviet Union.

The Soviet Government is aware that this hostile campaign against the Soviet Union was undertaken by the Polish Government in order to exert pressure upon the Soviet Government by making use of the Hitlerite slanderous fake for the purpose of wresting from it territorial concessions at the expense of the interests of the Soviet Ukraine, Soviet Byelorussia and Soviet Lithuania.

All these circumstances compel the Soviet Government to recognize that the present Government of Poland, having slid to the path of accord with Hitler's Government, has actually discontinued allied relations with the USSR and has adopted a hostile attitude toward the Soviet Union.

On the strength of all the above, the Soviet Government has decided to sever relations with the Polish Government.

Please accept, Mr. Ambassador, assurances of my very high esteem.

V. Molotov

38. REPLY TO THE QUESTION ON THE DISSOLUTION OF THE COMINTERN[*]

May 28, 1943

JOSEPH STALIN

The dissolution of the Communist International is proper and timely because it facilitates the organization of the common onslaught of all freedom-loving nations against the common enemy

[*] *USSR Information Bulletin*, No. 60 (June 3, 1943), *excerpts*. Question posed by Mr. Harold King, Correspondent of Reuter's News Agency.

—Hitlerism. The dissolution of the Communist International is proper because:

(a) It exposes the lie of the Hitlerites to the effect that "Moscow" allegedly intends to intervene in the life of other nations and to "Bolshevize" them. An end is now being put to this lie;

(b) It exposes the calumny of the adversaries of Communism within the labor movement, to the effect that Communist Parties in various countries are allegedly acting not in the interest of their people but on orders from outside. An end is now being put to this calumny, too;

(c) It facilitates the work of patriots in freedom-loving countries for uniting the progressive forces of their respective countries, regardless of party or religious faith, into a single camp of national liberation—for unfolding the struggle against fascism;

(d) It facilitates the work of patriots of all countries for uniting all freedom-loving peoples into a single international camp for the fight against the menace of the world domination by Hitlerism, thus clearing the way to the future organization of a companionship of nations based upon their equality.

I think that all these circumstances taken together will result in a further strengthening of the united front of the Allies and other United Nations in their fight for victory over Hitlerite tyranny.

I feel that the dissolution of the Communist International is perfectly timely because it is exactly now, when the fascist beast is exerting its last strength—that it is necessary to organize the common onslaught of freedom-loving countries to finish off this beast and to deliver the peoples from fascist oppression.

> With Respect,
> J. Stalin

39. DECLARATION ON SOVIET-POLISH RELATIONS—*TASS* COMMUNIQUÉ*

January 10, 1944

On January 5 in London was published a declaration of the émigré Polish Government on Soviet-Polish relations which contains a number of incorrect assertions, including an incorrect assertion about the Soviet-Polish frontier.

As is well known, the Soviet Constitution established the Soviet-

* USSR *Information Bulletin*, Vol. IV, No. 7 (1944), p. 1.

Polish frontier in conformity with the will of the population of Western Ukraine and Western Byelorussia, as expressed through a plebiscite conducted on a broad democratic basis in 1939. Then the territories of the Western Ukraine in which Ukrainians form the overwhelming majority of the population were incorporated with the Soviet Ukraine, and the territories of Western Byelorussia in which Byelorussians form an overwhelming majority of the population were incorporated with Soviet Byelorussia. The injustice committed by the Riga Treaty of 1921, which was imposed upon the Soviet Union, in regard to the Ukrainians inhabiting the Western Ukraine and the Byelorussians inhabiting Western Byelorussia, was thus rectified.

The incorporation of Western Ukraine and Western Byelorussia with the Soviet Union not only did not violate the interests of Poland, but on the contrary created a reliable foundation for stable and permanent friendship between the Polish people and its neighbors—the Ukrainian and Byelorussian and Russian peoples.

The Soviet Government has repeatedly stated that it stands for the reestablishment of a strong and independent Poland and for friendship between the Soviet Union and Poland. The Soviet Government declares again that it seeks to establish friendship between the USSR and Poland on the basis of stable, good neighborly relations and mutual respect and, if the Polish people will so desire—on the basis of an alliance for mutual assistance against the Germans as the chief enemies of the Soviet Union and Poland. . . .

At present the possibility is opening for the rebirth of Poland as a strong and independent state. However, Poland must be reborn not through the seizure of Ukrainian and Byelorussian lands, but through the restoration to Poland of lands which belonged to Poland from time immemorial and were wrested by the Germans from her. Only in this way trust and friendship could be established between the Polish, Ukrainian, Byelorussian and Russian peoples.

The eastern frontiers of Poland can be established by agreement with the Soviet Union. The Soviet Government does not regard the frontiers of 1939 as unalterable. These frontiers can be modified in Poland's favor so that the areas in which the Polish population forms a majority be turned over to Poland. In this case the Soviet Polish frontier could pass approximately along the so-called Curzon line, which was adopted in 1919 by the Supreme Council of the Allied Powers, and which provides for inclusion of the Western Ukraine and Western Byelorussia into the Soviet Union.

The western frontiers of Poland must be extended through incorporation with Poland of ancient Polish lands previously wrested by Germany, without which it is impossible to unite the whole Polish people in its state, which thereby will receive a needed outlet to the Baltic Sea.

The just aspiration of the Polish people for its full reunion in a strong and independent state must receive recognition and support.

The émigré Polish government, isolated from its people, proved incapable of establishment of friendly relations with the Soviet Union. It also proved incapable of organizing active struggle against the German invaders within Poland herself. Furthermore, by its incorrect policy it not infrequently plays into the hands of the German occupationists.

However, the interests of Poland and the Soviet Union consist in that stable, friendly relations be established between our countries and that the people of Poland and the Soviet Union unite in struggle against the common external enemy, as demanded by the common cause of all the Allies.

The Yalta Conference

40. REPORT OF THE CRIMEA CONFERENCE*

February 12, 1945

For the past eight days, Winston S. Churchill, Prime Minister of Great Britain, Franklin D. Roosevelt, President of the United States of America, and Marshal J. V. Stalin, Chairman of the Council of Peoples' Commissars of the Union of Soviet Socialist Republics have met with the Foreign Secretaries, Chiefs of Staff and other advisors in the Crimea. . . .

The Defeat of Germany

We have considered and determined the military plans of the three Allied Powers for the final defeat of the common enemy.

* *Foreign Relations of the United States: The Conferences at Malta and Yalta, 1945* (Washington, D.C.: Government Printing Office, 1955), pp. 968–975, *excerpts.*

The military staffs of the three Allied nations have met in daily meetings throughout the Conference. These meetings have been most satisfactory from every point of view and have resulted in closer coordination of the military effort of the three Allies than ever before. The fullest information has been interchanged. The timing, scope, and coordination of new and even more powerful blows to be launched by our armies and air forces into the heart of Germany from the East, West, North, and South have been fully agreed and planned in detail . . . Nazi Germany is doomed. The German people will only make the cost of their defeat heavier to themselves by attempting to continue a hopeless resistance.

The Occupation and Control of Germany

We have agreed on common policies and plans for enforcing the unconditional surrender terms which we shall impose together on Nazi Germany after German armed resistance has been finally crushed. These terms will not be made known until the final defeat of Germany has been accomplished. Under the agreed plan, the forces of the Three Powers will each occupy a separate zone of Germany. Coordinated administration and control has been provided for under the plan through a central Control Commission consisting of the Supreme Commanders of the Three Powers with headquarters in Berlin. It has been agreed that France should be invited by the Three Powers, if she should so desire, to take over a zone of occupation, and to participate as a fourth member of the Control Commission. The limits of the French zone will be agreed by the four governments concerned through their representatives on the European Advisory Commission.

It is our inflexible purpose to destroy German militarism and Nazism and to ensure that Germany will never again be able to disturb the peace of the world. We are determined to disarm and disband all German armed forces; break up for all time the German General Staff that has repeatedly contrived the resurgence of German militarism; remove or destroy all German military equipment; eliminate or control all German industry that could be used for military production; bring all war criminals to just and swift punishment and exact reparation in kind for the destruction wrought by the Germans; wipe out the Nazi Party, Nazi laws, organizations and institutions, remove all Nazi and militarist influences from public office and from the cultural and economic life of the German people; and take in harmony such other measures in Germany as may be necessary to the future peace and safety of the world. It is not our purpose to destroy the people of Germany, but only when Nazism and militarism have been extirpated will there be hope for a decent life for Germans, and a place for them in the comity of nations.

Reparation by Germany

We have considered the question of the damage caused by Germany to the Allied Nations in this war and recognized it as just that Germany be obliged to make compensation for this damage in kind to the greatest extent possible. . . .

United Nations Conference

We are resolved upon the earliest possible establishment with our Allies of a general international organization to maintain peace and security. . . .

Declaration on Liberated Europe

We have drawn up and subscribed to a Declaration on Liberated Europe. This Declaration provides for concerting the policies of the Three Powers and for joint action by them in meeting the political and economic problems of liberated Europe in accordance with democratic principles. The text of the Declaration is as follows:

. . . The establishment of order in Europe and the rebuilding of national economic life must be achieved by processes which will enable the liberated peoples to destroy the last vestiges of Nazism and Fascism and to create democratic institutions of their own choice . . . the three governments will jointly assist the people in any European liberated state or former Axis satellite state in Europe . . . (a) to establish conditions of internal peace; (b) to carry out emergency measures for the relief of distressed people; (c) to form interim governmental authorities broadly representative of all democratic elements in the population and pledged to the earliest possible establishment through free elections of governments responsive to the will of the people; and (d) to facilitate where necessary the holding of elections. . . .

Poland

We came to the Crimea Conference resolved to settle our differences about Poland. We discussed fully all aspects of the question. We reaffirm our common desire to see established a strong, free, independent, and democratic Poland. As a result of our discussions we have agreed on the conditions in which a new Polish Provisional Government of National Unity may be formed in such a manner as to command recognition by the three major powers.

The agreement reached is as follows:

A new situation has been created in Poland as a result of her complete liberation by the Red Army. This calls for the establishment of a Polish Provisional Government which can be more broadly based than was possible before the recent liberation of western Poland. The Provisional Government which is now functioning in Poland should therefore be reorganized on a broader democratic basis with the inclusion of democratic leaders from Poland itself and from Poles abroad. . . . This Polish Provisional Government of National Unity shall be pledged to the holding of free and unfettered elections as soon as possible on the basis of universal suffrage and secret ballot. In these elections all democratic and anti-Nazi parties shall have the right to take part and to put forward candidates. . . .

The three Heads of Government consider that the eastern frontier of Poland should follow the Curzon Line with digressions from it in some regions of five to eight kilometres in favor of Poland. They recognize that Poland must receive substantial accessions of territory in the north and west. They feel that the opinion of the new Poland Provisional Government of National Unity should be sought in due course on the extent of these accessions and that the final delimitation of the western frontier of Poland should thereafter await the Peace Conference. . . .

Unity for Peace as for War

Our meeting here in the Crimea has reaffirmed our common determination to maintain and strengthen in the peace to come that unity of purpose and of action which has made victory possible and certain for the United Nations in this war. We believe that this is a sacred obligation which our Governments owe to our peoples and to all the peoples of the world.

41. SECRET AGREEMENT REGARDING ENTRY OF THE SOVIET UNION INTO THE WAR AGAINST JAPAN*

February 11, 1945

Agreement

The leaders of the three Great Powers—the Soviet Union, the United States of America, and Great Britain—have agreed that in two or three months after Germany has surrendered and the war in Europe has terminated the Soviet Union shall enter into the war against Japan on the side of the Allies on condition that:

1. The *Status Quo* in Outer Mongolia (The Mongolian People's Republic) shall be preserved;

2. The former rights of Russia violated by the treacherous attack of Japan in 1904 shall be restored, viz.:

(a) the southern part of Sakhalin as well as the islands adjacent to it shall be returned to the Soviet Union,

(b) the commercial port of Dairen shall be internationalized, the preeminent interests of the Soviet Union in this port being safeguarded and the lease of Port Arthur as a naval base of the USSR restored,

(c) the Chinese-Eastern Railroad and the South-Manchurian Railroad which provides an outlet to Dairen shall be jointly operated by the establishment of a joint Soviet-Chinese Company, it being understood that the preeminent interests of the Soviet Union shall be safeguarded and that China shall retain full sovereignty in Manchuria;

3. The Kuril Islands shall be handed over to the Soviet Union.

It is understood, that the agreement concerning Outer Mongolia and the ports and railroads referred to above will require concurrence of Generalissimo Chiang Kai-shek. The President will take measures in order to obtain this concurrence on advice from Marshal Stalin.

The Heads of the three Great Powers have agreed that these claims of the Soviet Union shall be unquestionably fulfilled after Japan has been defeated.

* *Foreign Relations of the United States: The Conferences at Malta and Yalta, 1945* (Washington, D.C.: Government Printing Office, 1955), p. 984, *excerpts.*

This top-secret document was made public by the Department of State on February 11, 1946.

For its part the Soviet Union expresses its readiness to conclude with the Nationalist Government of China a pact of friendship and alliance between the USSR and China in order to render assistance to China with its armed forces for the purpose of liberating China from the Japanese yoke.

J. Stalin
Franklin D. Roosevelt
Winston S. Churchill

FOR FURTHER STUDY

Butow, Robert J. C., *Japan's Decision to Surrender*. Stanford: Stanford University Press, 1954.

Churchill, Winston S., *The Second World War*, 6 vols. Boston: Houghton Mifflin Company, 1948–1953.

Clark, Alan, *Barbarossa: The Russian-German Conflict, 1941–1945*. New York: William Morrow & Co., 1964.

Deane, John R., *The Strange Alliance: The Story of Our Efforts at Wartime Cooperation with Russia*. New York: The Viking Press, 1947.

Djilas, Milovan, *Conversations with Stalin*. New York: Harcourt, Brace & World, 1962.

Feis, Herbert, *Churchill-Roosevelt-Stalin*. Princeton, N.J.: Princeton University Press, 1957.

————, *Between War and Peace: The Potsdam Conference*. Princeton, N.J.: Princeton University Press, 1960.

Gallagher, Matthew P., *The Soviet History of World War II: Myths, Memories, and Realities*. New York: Frederick R. Praeger, 1963.

Kase, Toshikazu, *Journey to the Missouri*. New Haven, Conn.: Yale University Press, 1950.

Kot, Stanislaw (ed.), *Conversations with the Kremlin and Dispatches from Russia*. New York: Oxford University Press, 1963.

Lundin, Charles L., *Finland in the Second World War*. Bloomington: Indiana University Press, 1957.

McNeill, William H., *America, Britain, and Russia: Their Cooperation and Conflict, 1941–1946*. New York: Oxford University Press, 1954.

Rozek, Edward J., *Allied Wartime Diplomacy: A Pattern in Poland*. New York: John Wiley & Sons, 1958.

Stettinius, Edward R., Jr., *Roosevelt and the Russians: The Yalta Conference*. New York: Doubleday & Company, 1949.

Umiastowski, Roman, *Poland, Russia, and Great Britain, 1941–1945*. London: Hollis and Carter, 1946.

Werth, Alexander, *Russia at War: 1941–1945*. New York: E. P. Dutton & Co., 1964.

Xydis, Stephen G., *Greece and the Great Powers, 1944–1947: Prelude to the "Truman Doctrine."* Thessaloniki: Institute for Balkan Studies, 1963.

CHAPTER VI

SOVIET POLICY
AND THE ROOTS
OF THE COLD WAR

The inability of the victors to maintain their wartime cooperation—and the consequent division of the world into two hostile camps—overshadowed all else in the immediate postwar period. Within months after the defeat of the Axis Powers this failure was revealed by fundamental disagreements over Eastern Europe, Germany, Iran, and the Far East. Pre-1939 power relationships significantly changed: Germany and Japan had been defeated; Britain and France were seriously weakened; and Soviet forces occupied all Eastern Europe. The sharply delineated bipolarity of world power soon exacerbated the situation.

The investigation into the "causes" of the Cold War involves several factors, each important as a historical determinant, though its relative significance is subject to disagreement. First, there are these constants: the enduring legacy of Soviet-Western suspicion, only partially mitigated by wartime collaboration;* the quest of the Soviet Union for security, which, though understand-

* Distrust was a continuing feature of the alliance. Muted during the war, it crystallized clearly after victory and revealed its deep-rooted character. For manifestations of wartime distrust among the Big Three see *Stalin's Correspondence with Churchill, Attlee, Roosevelt and Truman, 1941–1945.* (New York: E. P. Dutton & Co., 1958.)

able, required an extension of its frontier and sphere of influence westward into the center of Europe where it conflicted with the security interests of the Western Powers; the tendency of Soviet leaders, reared in the Marxist-Leninist tradition, to regard the West again as an enemy, once the common foe had been beaten; and, above all, the theme of territorial expansion so manifest in Czarist, as well as in Bolshevik, foreign policy.

Second, there are the fortuitous and unpredictable components of historical events. Thus, there may have been a strong Soviet expectation, based on remarks of American officials at Yalta, of a rapid American military withdrawal from Europe. Soviet leaders could, and did, "treat with contempt American protests, even President Roosevelt's personal appeals to Stalin, concerning the open and frequent violations of the Yalta agreement on eastern Europe."[1] One may also muse over the probable effect on the Kremlin of the sudden American decision in August 1945 to end all lend-lease aid. Coming so soon after the military victory, it may have dispelled any Soviet hopes of basing its recovery and reconstruction at least partially on continued American assistance. This, in turn, may have lessened the possibility of a more moderate policy toward the West and the problems of postwar settlement.* Coupled with the fresh disclosure of America's monopoly possession of the atom bomb (a factor in itself having enormous military-political implications), this may have magnified Soviet suspicions of American intentions—particularly when viewed through the prism of Marxist-Leninist assumptions.

Finally, the inexorable drift in the 1945–1947 period toward a bipolarity of power and politics must also be attributed to the xenophobia, imperial ambitions, and sense of insecurity of Joseph Stalin, and to his resolve to ensure Soviet security by establishing Moscow's hegemony over all of Europe east of the Stettin-Trieste line. At Yalta Stalin had expressed particular concern over the orientation of postwar Poland's government and politics. In response to Churchill's assertion that for Britain the matter of Polish independence was a question of honor, Stalin replied that:

Throughout history, Poland has been the corridor through which the enemy has passed into Russia. Twice in the last thirty years our enemies, the Germans, have passed through this corridor. It is in

---

* Certainly, subsequent events added to the Soviet impression of Western antagonism. For example, on December 6, 1945, the United States Government wrote off 25 billion dollars of lend-lease aid to Britain and the Commonwealth, and agreed to lend the British Government 4.4 billion dollars. A few months later France received 1.4 billion dollars. An earlier Soviet request for a loan remained unanswered by the State Department; it supposedly "got lost" in the Department. While too much need not be made of such incidents, they must, nonetheless, be weighed in the balance.

Russia's interest that Poland should be strong and powerful, in a position to shut the door of this corridor by her own force. . . . it is necessary that Poland should be free, independent in power. Therefore, it is not only a question of honor but of life and death for the Soviet state itself.[2]

The line between legitimate security needs and openly expansionist objectives is not easily drawn. C. E. Black, appraising Soviet aims in Europe, has stated that:

What is important is that regardless of whether Soviet Russia merely wants friendly states on her border or in fact desires to use eastern Europe as a springboard of aggression, the same revolutionary method will be employed. The theoretical basis of this policy is that only countries as fully sovietized as Russia itself can be regarded as safe neighbors and reliable friends.[3]

Certainly, the post-World War II expansion of Soviet power into the heart of Europe exceeded the wildest dreams of the most imperialistic Czar. For the first time in European history one Great Power dominated the entire area between the Soviet Union and Western Europe, an area extending from the Baltic to the Black Sea (reading 42). The Western Powers, on the other hand, regarded this expansion of Soviet influence as a lasting threat to their safety. The roots of the "Cold War" lay in this fundamental conflict between incompatible concepts of national security.

The difficulties of the postwar period may conveniently be dated from the Potsdam Conference of July 1945. Relations between the USSR and the Western Powers had deteriorated noticeably since Yalta. Discord developed over the reconstitution of the Polish Government, the heavy-handedness of Soviet rule in Bulgaria and Rumania, the disposition of Trieste, the reparations issue, and the Allied administration of Germany.* The Conference failed to dispel the bitterness resulting from the Soviet Union's installation in Eastern Europe of governments in which Communists were assured strategic posts (such as control of the all-important Ministries of Interior and of the Courts). While conflicting interpretations of what constituted "democratic" government aggravated suspicion and augured ill for the future, America's rapid demobilization encouraged Stalin to act without fear of effective resistance.

---

* On June 5, 1945, the United States, France, Great Britain, and the Soviet Union negotiated an agreement calling for the division of Germany into separate zones which were to be administered by each of the Great Powers. Berlin was treated as a separate zone and similarly partitioned. Finally, responsibility for policy decisions affecting Germany as a whole was vested in the Allied Control Council.

The Council of Foreign Ministers met formally for the first time in London from September 11 to October 2, 1945, primarily to draft peace treaties with Finland, Italy, and the Balkan countries. But the old problems remained unsolved, and new ones appeared, such as Soviet demands for a trusteeship over one of the former Italian colonies and for the establishment of an Allied Control Council in Japan, comparable to the one operating in Germany, which would have given the Soviet Government a veto over American occupation policy. The Foreign Ministers adjourned without reaching agreement on any substantive issue. They convened again in late December, this time in Moscow, at the behest of Secretary of State Byrnes, who had been informed by Ambassador Harriman that "the breakdown of the London Conference had been stimulated by the Russians' belief that they were not being consulted adequately by our [American] officials in Japan"[4]—a cogent example, if this was the actual cause of the impasse, of the hypersensitivity of the Soviets to imagined slights in the diplomatic arena.

As a compromise, the Soviet Union was made a member of the Far Eastern Commission (meeting in Washington) and the Allied Control Council for Japan (Toyko). However, since these organs had only advisory functions, the Soviet Government could not interfere with the conduct of American occupation policy. A breakthrough was also achieved on other issues, and the Foreign Ministers agreed to convene a peace conference in Paris not later than May 1, 1946. The question of free elections in Bulgaria, Poland, and Rumania, however, and the character of the governments established there under Soviet aegis, continued to plague the discussants. Finally before the conference ended, controversy flared up over Iran.

Amid this rising tide of dissension, suspicion, and frustration, Premier Stalin delivered a pre-election speech on February 9, 1946, that presaged a resurgence of Marxist-Leninist orthodoxy in domestic affairs, as well as in official Soviet pronouncements on international matters. Again he emphasized the Leninist thesis that the uneven development of capitalism leads to war. He noted that "that group of capitalist countries which considers itself worse provided than others with raw materials and markets usually [makes] attempts to alter the situation and repartition the 'spheres of influence' in its favor by armed force. The result is a splitting of the capitalist world into two hostile camps and war between them." In reaffirming the fundamental postulates of Communist theory on the causes and nature of capitalist wars, Stalin blamed the West for World War II. He insisted that the defeat of Germany did not necessarily eliminate the danger of war and, lauding the superiority of the Soviet system, called for a "new mighty upsurge in the national economy" that would treble prewar production and guarantee the Soviet Union against another invasion. His gloomy outlook on relations with the capitalist world dominated Soviet behavior and hastened the Cold War. Stalin spoke six weeks before the Iranian crisis reached its critical phase and almost a month *before* Churchill, at Fulton, Missouri, on March 5, 1946, called for a strengthening of Anglo-American ties in the face of growing Soviet expansion. Churchill pointed out that:

> From Stettin in the Baltic to Trieste in the Adriatic an iron curtain has descended across the Continent. All these famous cities and the populations around them lie in the Soviet sphere and are subject, in one form or another, not only to Soviet influence but to a very high and increasing degree of control from Moscow.

Stalin termed Churchill a "warmonger" and compared him to Hitler. Quite surprisingly, a number of students of Soviet affairs have echoed this theme, intimating that Churchill's speech helped intensify East-West hostility. But they ignore the implications of Stalin's speech made some four weeks earlier.[5]

By early 1946, Soviet power was entrenched in Eastern Europe and was threatening in the Middle East, especially in Iran. Occupied by the Allies during the war in order to safeguard the flow of supplies to the Soviet Union, Iran now could not obtain the promised evacuation of Soviet troops. During their occupation of northern Iran, Soviet authorities denied the central Government in Teheran access to the area and at the same time strengthened the local Communist (Tudeh) Party. In September 1945, the Tudeh Party sought increased autonomy for Azerbaijan, the Iranian province bordering on the Soviet Union. The central Government refused Tudeh demands for fear of augmenting Communist influence elsewhere in Iran. In December 1945 the Communists announced the creation of a new government in Tabriz, capital of Azerbaijan, under Ja'far Pishevari, a veteran Communist and Comintern agent; also, a "Kurdish People's Republic," with its capital in Mahabad, was proclaimed in western Azerbaijan, and the Communists intensified their efforts to kindle an irredentist movement among the Kurdish tribes of northern Iraq and eastern Turkey. This hastened the deterioration of Turkish-Soviet relations;* meanwhile Iranian troops seeking to re-enter Azerbaijan were turned back by the Red Army.

* The Soviet Government had terminated its 1925 treaty of friendship with Turkey in March 1945 and applied pressure for a revision of the Montreux Convention that would accord it military control over the Straits. The Soviet also demanded the return of Kars and Ardahan, provinces ceded

Despite Stalin's statement "that the Soviet Union had no designs, territorial or otherwise, against Iran and would withdraw its troops as soon as they felt secure about the Baku oil fields"[6] (a rather specious excuse for retaining troops in Iran in view of the obvious disparity of military power of the two countries), Soviet troops continued to occupy the northern provinces. Iran appealed to the United Nations on January 19, 1946, charging the Soviet Union with interference in its internal affairs and with endangering the peace. American efforts to effect a withdrawal of all foreign troops by January 1, 1946, were rejected by the Soviet Government, which reminded the Western Powers that under the Iranian-Soviet-British treaty of 1942 it was entitled to remain in Iran until March 2, 1946. During the often acrimonious negotiations in the Security Council, a cabinet crisis in Teheran led the Shah to appoint Qavam Saltaneh, generally regarded by Western officials as pro-Tudeh, as Premier. Qavam began direct talks with Soviet leaders and spent almost a month in Moscow attempting to negotiate a settlement. In the United Nations Soviet tactics thwarted every constructive effort at a solution—a portent of future behavior in the world organization. As the date for the departure of Soviet troops under the 1942 agreement came and went with no visible change in Soviet attitude, Western leaders grew profoundly disturbed, particularly in view of Stalin's speech of February 9, 1946. Churchill's speech at Fulton reflected this increasing anxiety over Soviet ambitions.

On April 4, the Soviet Government agreed to evacuate Iran in return for Iranian concessions, including the formation of a joint-stock Soviet-Iranian oil company and a degree of autonomy for Azerbaijan. Westerners viewed this as a Soviet triumph and glumly awaited Iran's early disappearance behind the "Iron Curtain," a view undoubtedly shared, but with more pleasure, by the Kremlin. Though the final decision of the Soviet Government to withdraw from Iran by May 9 is usually attributed primarily to pressure by the UN Security Council and world public opinion, some specialists credit it mainly to the astuteness and shrewdness of Premier Qavam. Richard N. Frye states that:

The Soviet evacuation of northern Iran was the result of a number of factors; probably the most important was the belief on the part of the Russians that Qavam had been won over to their side. He had suppressed the anti-Soviet elements and had agreed to a joint oil company, subject to ratification of parliament. The rebel government in

to Turkey in 1918. Soviet pressure on Turkey sharpened, and by late 1946 Bulgarian and Greek Communists were active in stirring up trouble along Turkey's exposed frontier. These activities were instrumental in the promulgation of the Truman Doctrine in March 1947.

Azerbaijan was growing in strength and there was every reason to suppose that it would maintain its position and even gain at the expense of the Teheran government. The pressure of world opinion and the debates in the United Nations, although they may have been responsible in influencing the Soviet government to evacuate Iran earlier than had been planned, were probably of much less significance than the factors mentioned above. When the Soviet government did announce that it had evacuated all its troops on May 9, 1946, it seemed as though Iran had fallen on the Soviet side of the curtain.[7]

Late that year, the Iranian parliament rejected the proposed economic treaty with the USSR. Qavam had actually outfoxed Moscow, and by the end of 1946 the immediate threat of a Communist coup had passed. Azerbaijan was once again under the control of the central Government.[8] Shortly after, in one of the ironies for which Middle Eastern politics are noted, Qavam was replaced as Premier and all but exiled.

Meanwhile, preparations for the Peace Conference dragged on through the spring of 1946. Not until the end of July did representatives of twenty-one nations meet in Paris. Though no agreement was reached over Germany or Austria, the Soviet Union yielded sufficiently on a number of peripheral issues, and seemed willing enough to accept compromises on others, to permit the conclusion of peace treaties with Italy, Finland, Hungary, and Rumania in February 1947. The West had the treaties it so coveted, but time quickly revealed how hollow they were. The Soviet Government soon repudiated its concessions and moved to complete its political domination of Eastern Europe. Stalin not only had an acute appreciation of the revolutionary conditions in Eastern Europe, but he pursued his principal political and strategic objectives in the area with a singleness of purpose that had become only too clear to the Western Powers by early 1947. He sought, first, to eliminate all Western influence from Eastern Europe and, concomitantly, to establish Soviet hegemony. These objectives superseded all others. The quest for control of Eastern Europe culminated in the setting up of "People's Democracies" in all these countries by the end of 1948. Though the pattern and the pace varied from country to country, the result was the same: complete Sovietization.*

* An outstanding account of the Soviet take-over in Eastern Europe, perhaps the best single volume in English on the subject, is Hugh Seton-Watson's *The East European Revolution* (New York: Frederick A. Praeger, 1956). Mr. Seton-Watson distinguishes three distinct stages in the Soviet pattern of satellitization: the genuine coalition, the bogus coalition, and the Communist-controlled monolith. Each of these stages is traced in the various countries of Eastern Europe during the 1945–1949 period. Another excellent work on this topic is Robert Lee Wolff's *The Balkans in Our Time* (Cambridge: Harvard University Press, 1956), chaps. 9 and 10.

Soviet diplomacy in microcosm may be seen in the approach to one aspect of the peace treaties: the provision affecting the free navigation of the Danube. Since 1815, with certain modifications, an international commission whose members included Europe's Great Powers had maintained the principle and practice of free navigation of this vital commercial artery. Russia, not a member of the commission, had traditionally sought to control the Danube valley and to deny any voice in Danubian affairs to states not bordering on the river. Therefore, as a necessary first step toward itself becoming a riparian state, Russia had long coveted Bessarabia. Having annexed it in 1940, the USSR insisted in 1945 on the exclusion of nonriparian powers from membership. At Paris the Soviets agreed, after lengthy negotiation, to specific clauses in the peace treaties assuring the international character of the Danube. Once the treaties were signed, however, they promptly proceeded to ignore their obligations in this matter. The denouement came with startling finality at the Belgrade Conference of July-August 1948—the most significant postwar incident in the international control of the Danube. Outnumbering the Western, nonriparian powers, the Soviet Union and its satellites arbitrarily and easily changed membership requirements to allow only riparian states on the commission. Through its annexation of Bessarabia, the USSR became the only Great Power on the commission. Its voice became dominant. This episode further diminished the West's fading influence in the Balkans and helped the USSR consolidate its Eastern European empire.

Throughout 1946 and 1947, the Soviet Government deliberately sought to curb all Eastern European contact with the non-Communist world, even excluding United Nations personnel from the area. Addressing the General Assembly on December 8, 1946, Soviet Foreign Minister Molotov proposed "that all states represented in the General Assembly should present information on their troops stationed in foreign territories belonging to other United Nations"—an effort to obtain data on United States forces in Western Europe. He fought, however, the American counterproposal that information be given "about troops stationed not only in territories of the United Nations *but in the territories of former enemy states as well,*" for this would have required the Soviets to reveal their troop dispositions in Bulgaria, Hungary, East Germany, and Rumania.

Of all postwar problems, none contributed more to East-West hostility than that of the future of Germany. In a sense, the German problem is *the* European problem. Economic, political, strategic, and technological power factors all coalesce in the struggle over Germany; and the present unchallenged position of the Soviet Union in Eastern Europe cannot be permanently assured as long as Germany, with its reservoir of skilled manpower, scientific tradition, and industrial strength, remains a potential opponent. International politics has frequently seen the victors disagree among themselves and end by courting the former enemy. Since 1946, this has been true with respect to Germany.

The Soviets at first had favored an exploitative policy, designed to weaken Germany industrially, aid Soviet reconstruction, and encourage instability in Western Europe. Excessive Soviet reparations demands ruined efforts to negotiate the German question. However, the Kremlin soon realized the folly of this course and shifted to a more accommodating, conciliatory policy toward Germany—though not toward Western attitudes on the issue of Germany. This Soviet policy was first expressed by Molotov at the July 1946 Paris meeting of Foreign Ministers (reading 43). Asserting that the spirit of revenge could not underlie negotiations with Germany, he acknowledged that it would be folly to seek to destroy Germany as a state or to agrarianize her and destroy her major industries. Molotov suggested instead that Germany be permitted to become "a democratic and peace-loving state which alongside of agriculture, would have its own industry and foreign trade, but which would be deprived of the economic and military potentiality to rise again as an aggressive force." He also proposed that the Ruhr, the key to German industrial power, be placed under inter-Allied control, and that a single German government be set up, willing to fulfill all its obligations, particularly those concerning reparations. Secretary of State Byrnes responded to this bid for German favor by making similar comments in his Stuttgart speech of September 6, 1946. He also, significantly, threw American support behind Germany in the question of a return of the "eastern territories." It will be remembered that before the Potsdam Conference, the Soviet Union had unilaterally transferred all German territory east of the Neisse River to Poland, thus strengthening Poland's claim to the area. This territory has served, to this day, to compensate Poland for the 180,000 square kilometers of eastern Poland taken over by the USSR and to bind her to the Soviet Union. The West, however, has never recognized Polish claims to this territory. According to Barrington Moore, Jr., "This pair of speeches by Byrnes and Molotov might be regarded as the unofficial funeral of the Potsdam agreement and the overt beginning of a race for Germany between the Western Powers and the USSR, though the roots of the split can be traced back to the divergent policies of the various powers from the first days of the occupation."[9] Byrnes' strategy forced the Soviets to choose between the Poles and the Germans, thus deflating Soviet prestige in Western Germany.

The long succession of Soviet vetoes in the Security Council in 1946–1947 also indicated the growing cleavage between the West and the Soviet Union. The Soviet representative cast his first veto on February 16, 1946, and cast eight more before the year was over. Most early Soviet vetoes dealt with the admission of new members, a recurring issue throughout the first decade of the United Nations. Though the proposal to amend the UN Charter and abolish the veto is often raised, there is little likelihood that any great power would support such a change. Molotov justified the veto right in a speech before the UN on September 14, 1946 (reading 44), and the defense has subsequently been reiterated.*

In Poland ill-disguised Communist manipulations of the general elections of January 19, 1947, convinced the West that the Soviets had no intention of permitting free elections as pledged at Yalta and Potsdam. The Polish Peasant Party of Mikolajczyk waged a hopeless struggle,[10] and the Democratic Bloc (composed of the Communists and their allies) not unexpectedly emerged victorious. Official British and American protests were futile.

After a year and a half of following a policy of "patience with firmness," the United States prepared to assume Western leadership and embark upon a positive program of checking Soviet expansion. In 1947 a fateful chain of policy decisions by the Soviet Union and the United States irrevocably decided their political estrangement and led from a period of simulated accord to the one of protracted hostility that still endures with varying degrees of intensity.

On March 12, 1947, President Truman announced the decision of the American Government to extend economic and military assistance to Greece and Turkey.[11] The immediate impetus behind this move was the expressed inability of Great Britain to continue the responsibility for the defense of these areas. British power in the eastern Mediterranean was replaced by that of the United States. Quite possibly, the Truman Doctrine came at an inopportune moment in international diplomacy, two days after the Moscow Conference of Foreign Ministers had convened to discuss a number of key questions, including the Soviet demand for reparations. Western rejection of these demands, coupled with the apparent American willingness to aid liberally two small, strategically located nations, seriously undermined any prospects the

* An added source of antagonism was the Soviet veto in August 1947 of a report submitted by the UN Commission of Investigation which had been set up to investigate guerrilla fighting in northern Greece. The General Assembly, however, established a UN Special Commission on the Balkans, boycotted by the USSR, which helped confine hostilities in the area (along the Greek-Yugoslav-Bulgarian frontier). The Titoist defection in June 1948, and Truman Doctrine aid, finally restored the peace.

conference may have had, and it ended in failure (March 10-April 24).

Moscow promptly denounced the Truman Doctrine as "but a smoke-screen for expansion" (reading 45). The criticisms against it were sharp and varied; it was characterized as an example of America's postwar policy of imperialism; the Soviets also insisted that it deliberately circumvented the UN, thereby undermining the world organization. The Soviet journal, *New Times*, held that:

The proposed measures for Greece and Turkey cannot be taken as a demonstration of the will of the American Government for international cooperation within the framework of the UN Charter. On the contrary, they confirm the suspicion of a desire to convert the United Nations Organization into a tool of American policy, and, since that does not succeed, to reduce its importance virtually to naught. The reference to the UNO in the message (Truman) cannot but serve as a reminder that the only lawful and sensible way to assist Greece and Turkey, if the need for that has arisen, is by action undertaken through the UNO.[12]

Once committed to recognizing Europe's vital relationship to American national interest, the United States supplemented the Truman Doctrine with a more permanent and far-reaching program of assistance. On June 5, 1947, Secretary of State Marshall, speaking at Harvard University, expressed America's willingness to help rebuild Europe and invited the European nations to draw up a list of their needs and to prepare the necessary machinery for the implementation of American assistance. Under the leadership of the British Foreign Secretary, Ernest Bevin, and the French Foreign Minister, Georges Bidault, a conference of all European nations, including the Soviet Union, was convened in Paris on June 27. Discussions were at first secret. Then, Moscow unexpectedly issued a statement on June 29 presenting its views and criticisms of the conference and of the British and French proposals (reading 46). The ostensible bases of the Soviet attack were then largely economic. To the Soviets, Western proposals seemed to entail an all-encompassing program of integration of the various national economies. They felt that this would have required abandonment of their plan to industrialize Eastern Europe and incorporate it in the Soviet Five Year Plans. They also intimated that Marshall Plan aid was to be used to promote the economic, and hence political, expansion of American influence. This soon became a dominant theme of Soviet propaganda. Molotov's suspicions on this point "were accentuated when he learnt that Marshall Aid was not to be administered through any machinery set up by the United Nations but through an independent medium, in which—he assumed—American influence would be unchallenged."[13] By July 2, Moscow withdrew from the conference.

For several days after the Soviet departure, the question of Eastern European participation remained open. Indeed, as late as July 8, the Czechoslovak Government indicated its willingness to attend the Paris meetings. However, this acceptance was soon withdrawn as a result of Soviet pressure.*

The Soviet refusal to participate in the Marshall Plan program accelerated the East-West estrangement. Many attempts have been made to explain the Soviet decision. Since it is unlikely that American aid would have been forthcoming had Moscow remained one of the proposed recipients, continued Soviet participation might well have sounded the death knell for the Marshall Plan and for European recovery. The Kremlin, however, committed a blunder, and the West benefited. Several interpretations may be noted at this time. They also represent the general policy alternatives available to the Kremlin in 1945, when cooperation with the West was still a distinct, if fading, possibility.

First, the Soviet leaders probably believed in an impending severe economic crisis in the United States. Early postwar Soviet periodicals stressed this theme. If Soviet leaders did indeed anticipate such a crisis, they could scarcely be expected, with their ideology and objectives, to join any plan specifically designed to stabilize the capitalist world. After Stalin's speech of February 9, 1946, Soviet society moved toward increased orthodoxy and conformity in all areas. Of particular pertinence was the denunciation, in May 1947, of Eugen Varga, a prominent Soviet economist, for asserting that a capitalist crisis was not imminent and that capitalism was entering an era of stabilization and expansion.

Second, Stalin's preoccupation with sovietizing Eastern Europe, and with integrating that area into a Soviet-controlled economic and political system, may have precluded any cooperation with Western Europe that would have interfered with this paramount strategic objective. Soviet leaders held that to have permitted these countries to maintain any but the most unavoidable economic ties with the West would have politically strengthened the pro-Western elements still operating in the coalition governments of Eastern Europe.

Third, Soviet lack of interest in European recovery was ap-

---

* At the time, the Czechoslovak Prime Minister, Klement Gottwald, an old-guard Communist, was in Moscow negotiating a new trade agreement. He ordered Czechoslovakia's withdrawal at Stalin's order. Gottwald's refusal, as well as those of most of the Eastern European Governments, was first announced by Moscow radio.

parent early in the postwar period. This is logical economically, in view of the Soviet need to attend its own wounds; it is also logical politically, since an unstable Europe gave added promise of succumbing to communism. This promise was particularly evident in Italy and France, countries whose Communist Parties had emerged from the war with enhanced prestige and with a broad base of voted support. More significantly, the perpetuation of unstable conditions in Western Europe decreased the likelihood of any Western interference with Stalin's policies in Eastern Europe. Thus, discouraging Europe's recovery would not only keep the West from challenging Soviet hegemony in Eastern Europe, but also would facilitate the spread of communism in Western Europe itself.

Fourth, Soviet mistrust of American motives may have underlain Stalin's reluctance to make any concessions in order to obtain American financial assistance. According to one analyst:

It [the Soviet Union] fears that this country, by offering loans to Russia's neighbors for the purchase of American goods, will not only make it difficult for the Russians to obtain the goods they need, but that the flag will follow, and American political influence will penetrate in the wake of loans and goods.[14]

Finally, an interpretation of a quite different stripe held that the Soviets chose not to participate because they then would have been required to divulge vital statistical data concerning their needs and shortages, information of military significance which the Kremlin preferred not to reveal.

Though there is wide disagreement over what motivated Soviet policy, there is no question that, during the summer and fall of 1947, East-West relations steadily deteriorated. Prospects for an over-all European political settlement disappeared, as Soviet attacks on the Marshall Plan intensified. The growing egocentricity of Stalinist policy can be seen in an editorial in *Izvestia* (September 3, 1947) which attributed the Allied victory in the Far East "primarily through the efforts of the Soviet people and its armies, led by the great Stalin." And on September 18, 1947, Andrei Y. Vyshinsky, the Soviet delegate to the United Nations, set the general tenor for official policy in a speech before the General Assembly (reading 47):

As is now clear, the Marshall Plan constitutes in essence merely a variant of the Truman Doctrine adapted to the conditions of postwar Europe.
    . . . Moreover, this Plan is an attempt to split Europe into two camps and, with the help of the United Kingdom and France, to complete the formation of a *bloc* of several European countries hostile to the

interests of the democratic countries of Eastern Europe and most particularly to the interests of the Soviet Union.

Stalin now moved to complete the breach by establishing a rival grouping of states controlled by the Soviet Union. The Comintern was resurrected as the Cominform (Communist Information Bureau) at a special conference of Communist Parties in Wiliza Gora (Upper Silesia) on September 22–23, 1947. Communist strategy changed significantly. The Kremlin formally revived the thesis of the capitalist menace, and policy statements emphasized the enduring and irreconcilable antagonism between the capitalist and Communist systems.*

Andrei Zhdanov's speech at the founding conference of the Cominform must be regarded as the most significant effort since the Comintern program of 1928 to formulate the position of international communism in the world and to integrate it into a unified whole[15] (reading 48). The speech was important not only because of its ambitious scope, but also because of the powerful position of the man charged with its presentation.† It represented the most comprehensive postwar statement of Soviet policy and tactics yet delivered.

Zhdanov began by announcing that the war had wrought fundamental changes in world power relationships.

A new alignment of political forces has arisen. The more the war recedes into the past, the more distinct become two major trends in postwar international policy, corresponding to the division of the political forces operating on the international arena into two major camps: the imperialist and antidemocratic camp, on the one hand, and the anti-imperialist and democratic camp, on the other.

Identifying the United States as the principal antagonist, he proceeded to interpret the economic, ideological, and military bases of its foreign policy. Expansionism was the theme common to all these factors. Zhdanov justified Soviet opposition to the Marshall Plan and, defending Soviet policy, made clear Moscow's determination to control Eastern Europe. In concluding, he called for concerted and active opposition by all Communist Parties to the Marshall Plan. In effect, Zhdanov's speech declared a permanent "Cold War" against the West. The tactical ramifications of this militant policy soon became apparent in France and Italy where

---

* In his speech of September 9, 1945, Stalin had indicated that the Soviet Union considered itself liberated from the capitalist menace. Two years later, this old thesis was revived. A. W. Just, "Moskaus neue These," *Aussenpolitik*, Vol. 1 (July 1950), pp. 103–109.

† Andrei Zhdanov ranked high in the upper echelons of the Soviet hierarchy. Indeed, many observers of the Soviet scene regarded him as second only to Joseph Stalin. Zhdanov, however, died in 1948.

general strikes, accompanied by labor violence, were instigated in November 1947 in an attempt to paralyze the nascent Marshall Plan program, and in Southern Asia, where Communist Parties split with bourgeois-nationalist movements and attempted to subvert existing regimes by direct revolutionary means.

In addition to mobilizing Communist Parties against the Marshall Plan and Western policy, the Cominform served manifold purposes. Ideologically, it demanded unquestioning adherence to the Moscow line. Organizationally, it facilitated the consolidation of Communist power, as purges swept the East European satellites. The Cominform became an instrument for ensuring a monolithic control over the various European Communist Parties. It was also a nucleus for future intra-Eastern European economic planning and integration. Politically, as a focal point for international communism, it not only crystallized opposition to Western policy, but symbolized Communist unity and cooperation. Whether Soviet motivation was primarily defensive or offensive, the establishment of the Cominform was a turning point in postwar international relations. Cooperation, accommodation, and collaboration with the non-Communist world —the official line in the early postwar period—were now dropped. Henceforth, Stalin concentrated on preserving the Soviet empire in Eastern Europe.

NOTES

1. Philip E. Mosely, "Soviet-American Relations Since the War," *Annals* (May 1949), p. 207.
2. James F. Byrnes, *Speaking Frankly* (New York: Harper & Row, Publishers, 1947), pp. 31-32.
3. C. E. Black, "Soviet Policy in Eastern Europe," *Annals* (May 1949), p. 153.
4. Byrnes, *op. cit.*, p. 108.
5. For example, such useful works as *A History of Soviet Russia* (New York: Frederick A. Praeger, 1957) by Georg von Rauch; Frederick L. Schuman, *Russia Since 1917* (New York: Alfred A. Knopf, 1957); and an otherwise particularly skillful presentation of the 1945–1947 period by Kenneth Ingram, *History of the Cold War* (New York: Philosophical Library, 1955).
6. Byrnes, *op. cit.*, p. 119.
7. Lewis V. Thomas and Richard N. Frye, *The United States and Turkey and Iran* (Cambridge, Mass.: Harvard University Press, 1951), pp. 239-240.
8. For an excellent account of this period see George Lenczowski, *Russia and the West in Iran, 1918–1948: A Study in Big Power Rivalry* (Ithaca, N.Y.: Cornell University Press, 1949), chap. XI.
9. Barrington Moore, Jr., *Soviet Politics—The Dilemma of Power* (Cambridge, Mass.: Harvard University Press, 1950), p. 378.
10. Stanislaw Mikolajczyk, *The Rape of Poland: The Pattern of Soviet Domination* (New York: McGraw-Hill Book Company, 1948). See chapter XIV for a description of the appalling difficulties devised by the Communists to deprecate and destroy the Peasant Party.

11. *Department of State Bulletin*, Vol. xvi (March 23, 1947), pp. 534–537.
12. "American Foreign Policy," *New Times* (March 21, 1947), p. 3.
13. Kenneth Ingram, *History of the Cold War* (New York: Philosophical Library, 1955), p. 61.
14. Vera M. Dean, "Russia's Foreign Economic Policy," *Foreign Policy Reports*, Vol. xxii (February 1, 1947), p. 267.
15. G. I., "The Evolution of the Cominform, 1947–1950," *World Today*, Vol. vi (May 1950), pp. 213–214.

Structural Changes in Postwar Europe

42. THE GEOPOLITICS OF THE PEACE SETTLEMENT*

HUEY LOUIS KOSTANICK

Soviet power has been extended westward through creation of a large bloc of satellite states and through Soviet military occupation of Eastern Germany and Eastern Austria. In conjunction with Soviet expansion has come a major Slavic westward movement, which has wiped out a thousand years of Germanic expansion.

The impact of Soviet power applies in almost as strong a measure in other countries of Eastern and Central Europe outside the Soviet sphere of influence, as it applies to the Soviet satellite states themselves. In the immediate postwar period, Greece was faced not only with the problems of postwar rehabilitation but also with the problems of Communist guerrilla warfare which threatened to split Greece through loss of the fertile plains of Macedonia and western Thrace. . . . Similarly, Turkey has been disquieted by Soviet demands for participation in military defense of the Turkish straits. These pressures have created severe drains on the economies of Greece and Turkey. As a direct result, the United States undertook the task of supplying economic and military aid to these countries and thus became the

* Huey Louis Kostanick, "The Significance of Geopolitical Changes in Eastern Europe," *Education*, Vol. LXXII (February 1952), pp. 381–387, *excerpts*. Reprinted with the permission of the author and the Palmer Publishing Company.

other major power actively participating in Eastern European affairs. . . .

Politically, the Soviet bloc has been formed of Poland, Czechoslovakia, Hungary, Rumania, Bulgaria, and Albania, while Estonia, Latvia, and Lithuania have been directly annexed to the USSR. The satellite countries are dominated by Communist governments, which have made political, economic, and military agreements with the Soviet Union and among themselves. . . .

Alliance with the Soviet Union has also reversed the traditional pattern of trade with Western Europe. Eastern Europe has, essentially, an agricultural economy, which must export agricultural commodities. . . . In the interwar period, Germany, which in turn needed agricultural products, became the major trader with almost all of the countries of the area. The Danube River played a major role in this trade and, in addition, northwestern European ports served as outlets for Eastern European exports to other areas of the world. In the postwar period, the trade of the satellites was reoriented toward the Soviet Union, whose economy could be bolstered by the valuable supplies of foods and industrial crops as well as Rumanian petroleum and other minerals. . . .

A basic realignment of Eastern Europe both politically and demographically has been created by the loss of German and Italian territories and the subsequent westward expansion of the Soviet Union and of other Slavic states. This expansion has taken place in different zones and in different fashions. The Soviet Union has advanced westward territorially through annexation of areas from each of the countries that bordered her on the West, and politically through creation of the Soviet bloc and through military occupation of Eastern Germany and of Eastern Austria. Poland and Yugoslavia have also gained territory at the expense of their western neighbors.

This westward expansion is most evident in the reversal of previous German expansion into Eastern Europe. Viewed broadly, this reversal may be expressed in terms of three successive "axes" having Trieste as the southern pivot. In 1939, the axis between Germanic and Slavic control extended roughly from Trieste to Königsberg (Kaliningrad) in German East Prussia. In the postwar period, through German losses of territory to Poland the line of German-Slav territorial and ethnic division swung westward to extend from Trieste to Stettin (Szczecin). But the ultimate Slavic political advance is more realistically marked by the western border of Soviet military occupation as represented by the Trieste-Lubeck axis, although the occupied territory is still German populated. . . .

The
SOVIET UNION
IN EUROPE
1966

NORWAY

SWEDEN

FINLAND

Murmansk

UNION OF

SOVIET

Leningrad

ESTONIA

LATVIA

Moscow

LITHUANIA

SOCIALIST

GT. BRIT.

DENMARK

REPUBLICS

NETH.

Berlin

Oder-Neisse Line

BELG.

EAST
GER.

WEST GERMANY

Warsaw

POLAND

LUX.

CZECHOSLOVAKIA

BESSARABIA

FRANCE

SWITZ.

AUSTRIA

HUNGARY

RUMANIA

YUGOSLAVIA

ITALY

BULGARIA

ALBANIA

GREECE

TURKEY

Recovered by the Soviet Union in its westward expansion: northern and southern
border regions in Finland (1940 and 1944); Estonia, Latvia, and Lithuania
(1940); and part of former East Prussia from Germany, eastern Poland, Ruthenia
from Czechoslovakia, and Bessarabia from Rumania (all after World War II).

- - - - - - -   Boundaries of Soviet Union before expansion.

▬▬▬▬▬   Present boundaries of Soviet Union.

Since 1939, approximately 187,000 square miles of territory with an estimated population of nearly 23 million have been annexed by the USSR. These territories are now administered as integral parts of the Soviet Union. . . . This expansion represents the greatest territorial change resulting from World War II, and was achieved at the expense of a number of East European countries.

In the Arctic zone, the Soviet Union gained from Finland the ice-free port of Petsamo, west of the Soviet port of Murmansk which in winter is kept open only by icebreakers. . . . Another zone of Soviet advance was the vital Baltic lowland, a portion of the North European Plain which has served as the invasion route to Western Europe for centuries. . . . [The] Baltic "window to the West" has been widened by the inclusion of Estonia, Latvia, and Lithuania in the USSR. Although their annexation is not recognized by the United States, they are Soviet republics, and their transportation facilities and ports form an additional link between the producing areas of western Russia and the Baltic Sea. . . .

The greatest loss of territory was by Poland, from whom the USSR annexed the entire eastern zone. Part of this territory, the Vilno area, was ceded to Lithuania, which had contested Polish possession of this historic Lithuanian capital. The annexation of southeastern Poland, of Ruthenia from Czechoslovakia, and of Northern Bucovina from Rumania gave control of strategic Carpathian passes, and, of greater importance, extended Russian territory over the Carpathians into the Danubian basin of Central Europe. A common border with Hungary was also secured.

In the Balkans, control of the northern distributory channel of the Danube was secured through the return of Bessarabia by Rumania, thus making the USSR a Danubian and Balkan power.

Through these territorial gains, the Soviet Union won an ice-free Arctic port, increased access to the Baltic Sea and the North European Plain, advanced into the Danubian basin, and secured a control point at the mouth of the Danube, as well as extending frontiers to Norway and Hungary. These are indeed significant geopolitical gains. . . .

Poland has been "moved" bodily westward in comparison to its prewar position. In the east, Poland had ceded to the USSR a 70,000 square-mile zone, thus placing its capital, Warsaw, only a hundred miles from the new eastern border. As compensation, Poland gained control of the southern portion of German East Prussia and of the international port of Danzig. Of even greater importance to Poland was the addition of 39,000 square miles of eastern Germany, which included the valuable industrial district of German Silesia. Thus, although Poland decreased from a total area of 150,000 to 121,000 square miles, its economy has been strengthened by additions of fertile agricultural land, a major industrial district, and the Baltic port of Stettin. Through this westward shift, a new position has been secured on the North European Plain. Expulsion of Germans and resettlement of Poles in the new areas poses a future problem should Germany seek the return of these territories. . . .

Axis defeat resulted in the elimination of Germany and Italy as Eastern European powers. Axis defeat also created another aspect of the new geopolitical situation—Soviet military occupation of Eastern Germany and of Eastern Austria. Under the division of Germany into four Allied occupational zones, Eastern Germany and Eastern Austria were placed under Soviet administration. Within these zones, the Berlin and Vienna enclaves were similarly subdivided. The western borders of these zones have come to mark the real frontiers of Soviet expansion. They are within the "Iron Curtain" of Europe, which separates differing ideologies, because in the Soviet zones Communist governments have come into power. In both countries, valuable agricultural land and industrial districts are included in the Soviet zones, and, from a strategic point of view, the Soviet position on the North European Plain has been extended westward to the Elbe River and further control of the Danubian gateway has been secured. . . .

The geopolitical changes that have taken place since the opening of World War II are indeed broad and sweeping and are evident in diverse aspects of the East European scene. Their scope ranges from the new political power of both the Soviet Union and of the United States and the new political and economic patterns to territorial shifts and population displacement. Through these changes, a new phase of the history of Eastern Europe has been created, a phase in which the Soviet Union has played a dominant role. The Axis defeat set the stage for the westward expansion of Eastern Europe and for new political and demographic alignments.

The Struggle for Germany

43. THE FUTURE OF GERMANY AND THE PEACE TREATY WITH GERMANY*

July 10, 1946

V. M. MOLOTOV

The time has come for us to discuss the future of Germany and the peace treaty with that country.

The Soviet Government has always held that the spirit of revenge is a poor counsellor in such affairs. Nor would it be correct to identify Hitler Germany with the German people, although the German people cannot divest themselves of responsibility for Germany's aggression and for its dire consequences.

The Soviet people experienced the unparalleled suffering of enemy occupation, as a result of the invasion of the Soviet Union by the German armies. Our losses are great and inestimable. Other peoples of Europe, and not of Europe alone, will long feel the heavy losses and hardships caused by the war which Germany imposed.

It is, therefore, understandable that the problem of Germany's future should be agitating the minds not only of the German people, who are anxious to safeguard themselves for the future and prevent a renewal of German aggression. . . . Nor can one forget that more than once this industrial might has served as the base for the arming of aggressive Germany.

Such are the premises from which we must draw our conclusions.

I proceed from the consideration that, in the interests of world economy and tranquility in Europe, it would be incorrect to adopt the line of annihilating Germany as a state, or of agrarianizing her, with the destruction of her main industrial centers.

* V. M. Molotov, *Problems of Foreign Policy: Speeches and Statements, April 1945–November 1948* (Moscow: Foreign Languages Publishing House, 1949), pp. 63–68, *excerpts.* This statement was made at the July 10, 1946, meeting of the Council of Foreign Ministers.

Such a line would undermine the economy of Europe, dislocate world economy, and lead to a chronic political crisis in Germany, which would spell a threat to peace and tranquility.

I think that, even if we were to adopt such a line, historical development would impel us subsequently to renounce it as abortive and groundless.

I think, therefore, that our purpose is not to destroy Germany, but to transform her into a democratic and peace-loving state which alongside of agriculture, would have its own industry and foreign trade, but which would be deprived of the economic and military potentiality to rise again as an aggressive force. . . .

It has of late become fashionable to talk about dismembering Germany into several "autonomous" states, federalizing her, and separating the Ruhr from her. All such proposals stem from this same line of destroying and agrarianizing Germany, for it is easy to understand that without the Ruhr Germany cannot exist as an independent and viable state. But I have already said that the destruction of Germany should not be our objective, if we cherish the interests of peace and tranquility. . . .

If the world is to be made safe against possible German aggression, Germany must be completely disarmed, militarily and economically; and as to the Ruhr, it must be placed under inter-Allied control exercised by our four countries, with the object of preventing the revival of war industries in Germany.

The program of complete military and economic disarmament of Germany is not something new. The decisions of the Berlin conference deal with it in detail. And it is natural that the Ruhr, as the main base of Germany's war industry, should be kept under the vigilant control of the principal Allied Powers. The aim of completely disarming Germany militarily and economically should also be served by the reparations plan. The fact that until now no such plan has been drawn up, in spite of the repeated demands of the Soviet Government that the relevant decision of the Berlin conference should be carried out, and the fact that the Ruhr has not been placed under inter-Allied control, on which the Soviet Government insisted a year ago, is a dangerous thing from the point of view of safeguarding future peace and the security of nations. We hold that it is impossible to put off the accomplishment of these tasks without running the risk of frustrating the decision to effect the complete military and economic disarmament of Germany. . . .

In order that the development of Germany's civilian industries may benefit other nations that need German coal, metal, and manufactured products, Germany should be granted the right to export and import and, if this right to engage in foreign trade is realized, we should not hinder Germany from increasing her output of steel, coal, and manufactured products for peaceful needs, naturally within certain bounds, and with the indispensable proviso that inter-Allied control is established over German industry, and over the Ruhr industries in particular.

As we know, the Control Council in Germany recently fixed the level which German industry should attain in the next few years. Germany is still a long way from this level. Nevertheless, it should be recognized now that her civilian industries must be given the opportunity to develop more widely, provided only that this industrial development is really used to satisfy the peaceful needs of the German people and for the promotion of trade with other countries. All this calls for the establishment of proper inter-Allied control over German industry and over the Ruhr industries in particular, responsibility for which cannot rest upon any one Allied country alone.

The adoption of an appropriate program for the development of Germany's peace industries, which will also provide for the development of her foreign trade, as well as the establishment of inter-Allied control over the whole of German industry, is essential for the implementation of those decisions of the Berlin conference which provide for treating Germany as an economic whole. . . .

The USSR, the UN, and the Veto

44. SOVIET DEFENSE OF THE VETO POWER*
September 14, 1946

V . M . M O L O T O V

An international organization, confronted with the serious tasks of struggling for the peace and security of nations, was for the first time founded at the San Francisco Conference. This organiza-

* Speech by V. M. Molotov, Minister for Foreign Affairs of the USSR, delivered September 14, 1946, at the session of the Committee on Political and Territorial Questions of the Peace Treaty with Italy of the Paris Peace Conference.

tion is built on the unity of all peace-loving Powers with the purpose of protecting universal peace.

It is precisely the right of the veto which was granted to the five Great Powers in the Security Council that is the chief element of the principle of this organization. According to the United Nations Organization's Charter, the veto means that in all important questions concerning the interest of peace, the United States of America, Great Britain, the Soviet Union, France, and China must act in accord, and the Security Council cannot adopt any decisions on those questions with which any of these powers may not be in accord. That means that the veto prevents a situation in which two or three or even four Powers could agree among themselves and act against one or another of the five chief states.

The veto stimulates the Great Powers to joint work, hampering intrigues of some against others, which undoubtedly conforms to the interests of all the United Nations and to the interests of universal peace.

It goes without saying that this does not eliminate the present disagreements and disputes; however, free and open discussion on disputed questions, when there is the right of veto, provides in the long run a better way for understanding and concessions, for cooperation and agreements. Thus the veto is aimed at benefiting all peace-loving states, large and small, by the actions of the Great Powers.

There was no right of veto vested in the Great Powers in the League of Nations. The League was formally built on the principles of equality of large and small states. Those who now advocate the abolition of the veto are dragging us back from the United Nations Organization to something of the sort of the League of Nations. But it is precisely this which determines the political meaning of those actions as well.

We must recall something concerning the developments of the prewar years. The League of Nations was created after the World War of 1914–1918. It was the first experiment in setting up an international organization, and it cannot be recognized as successful. In fact, the League of Nations failed to play a substantial part in defending the cause of peace. The League of Nations failed to become an efficient organization to protect the security of the peoples, and, moreover, it failed to defend even the security of the countries of the Anglo-French group, which enjoyed a dominating influence in that first international organization. How it ended—we know. . . .

In the course of the last war a bloc of Great Powers sprang up, and they took the lead of the democratic countries and routed the aggressor in the West and in the East. As a result of this, it was recognized as necessary to set up a new international organization to defend the peace and security of the peoples. The United Nations Organization appeared, as well as the Security Council and the right of veto. Thereby, an attempt was made to create at last an efficient organization to ensure universal security.

It is precisely the veto that plays the leading part in this. The principle of the veto demands that all the Great Powers display attention with regard to their common interests and the interests of universal peace, hindering the creation of narrow blocs and groups of some Powers against other Powers, and still more hampering opportunity for anyone's bargaining with an aggressor behind the backs and contrary to the interests of peace-loving countries.

What can refusal of the right of veto in the United Nations Organization mean? It is not difficult to guess that it can untie someone's hands for certain actions. Refusal of the right of veto would facilitate, of course, the setting up of narrow groups and blocs among the Great Powers, and in any case would untie the hands of those who oppose a united front of the United Nations in defending the cause of peace.

But we have already tried that path. Along that path we reached the Second World War. That path promises nothing but a disgraceful collapse of the United Nations Organization.

Such plans meet the desires of reactionary circles alone, and help the camp of unbridled imperialists only. They do not conceal that they feel uncomfortable about collaboration with the Soviet State. There are no few people in these circles, of course, who are inclined toward cooking up ever-new anti-Soviet projects. . . .

In our time it is dangerous to ignore the Soviet Union, to forget the importance of its support in matters of peace. This path could be taken only by those who, instead of collaboration with the Soviet Union, prefer to build their calculations on bargains and agreements with a future aggressor, which, of course, has nothing in common with the interests of peace and international security. . . .

A new organization to defend the peace has sprung up after the Second World War. The Security Council has now been authorized to ensure the collaboration of all the Great Powers and at the same time to display undeviating care for the interests of universal peace. No such organization existed in the nineteenth century, nor on the eve of the First or on the eve of the Second World Wars. An international organization has been created which is built on the principle of not allowing neglect, not only of the Soviet Union, but of other peace-loving states as well.

The right of veto is precisely intended for this purpose. Of course the veto is no panacea. Blocs and groups occur now, too, and yet the principle of the veto furnishes a certain basis for the development of collaboration among the Powers in defending the security of nations, no matter how great are the difficulties in this respect. If we really stand for peace and security, we must value this weapon, which is intended to serve such important aims. Among the Powers there are no few differences, of course, on these or other questions, and disputes are inevitable.

Yet we have already more than once found ways of solving disagreements. These ways are not barred to us in the future, either, and especially if we all understand that attempts to dictate the will of one Power or of one group of Powers to other Powers are inconsistent and out of place. We must look ahead and not permit ourselves to be dragged back to a broken trough—the League of Nations.

In this international organization created after the war, we must strive to set up a united front of peace-loving states which will not permit the ignoring of any Power, and which will be aimed against any attempts to resurrect aggressors. . . .

Soviet Views of American Foreign Policy

45. SOVIET COMMENTS ON THE TRUMAN DOCTRINE*

Izvestia, *March 13, 1947*

On March 12, President Truman addressed a message to the US Congress asking for 400 million dollars to be assigned for urgent aid to Greece and Turkey, and for authority to send to those countries American civil and military personnel, and to provide for the training by Americans of specially picked Greek and Turkish personnel.

Greece, said Truman, was in a desperate economic and political situation. Britain was no longer able to act as trustee for the Greeks. Turkey had requested speedy American aid. Turkey, unlike Greece, had not suffered from the Second World War, but

* Quoted from *Soviet News*, March 15, 1947, *excerpts.*

she needed financial aid from Britain and from the USA in order to carry out that modernization necessary for maintaining her national integrity. Since the British Government, on account of its own difficulties, was not capable of offering financial or other aid to the Turks, this aid must be furnished by the USA.

Thus Congress was asked to do two "good deeds" at once—to save Greece from internal disorders and to pay for the cost of "modernizing" Turkey. . . .

British troops have been on Greek territory since 1944. On Churchill's initiative, Britain took on herself the responsibility for "stabilizing" political conditions in Greece. The British authorities did not confine themselves to perpetuating the rule of the reactionary, anti-democratic forces in Greece, making no scruple in supporting ex-collaborators with the Germans. The entire political and economic activities under a number of short-lived Greek governments have been carried on under close British control and direction.

Today we can see the results of this policy—complete bankruptcy. British troops failed to bring peace and tranquillity to tormented Greece. The Greek people have been plunged into the abyss of new sufferings, of hunger and poverty. Civil war takes on ever fiercer forms.

Was not the presence of foreign troops on Greek territory instrumental in bringing about this state of affairs? Does not Britain, who proclaimed herself the guardian of Greece, bear responsibility for the bankruptcy of her charge?

The American President's message completely glosses over these questions. The USA does not wish to criticize Britain, since she herself intends to follow the British example. Truman's statement makes it clear that the USA does not intend to deviate from the course of British policy in Greece. So one cannot expect better results.

The US government has no intention of acting in the Greek question as one might have expected a member of UNO, concerned about the fate of another member, to act. It is obvious that in Washington they do not wish to take into account the obligations assumed by the US government regarding UNO. Truman did not even consider it necessary to wait for the findings of the Security Council Commission specially sent to Greece to investigate the situation on the spot.

Truman, indeed, failed to reckon either with the international organization or with the sovereignty of Greece. What will be left of Greek sovereignty when the "American military and civilian personnel" gets to work in Greece by means of the 250 million dollars brought into that country? The sovereignty and independence of Greece will be the first victims of such singular "defense."

The American arguments for assisting Turkey base themselves on the existence of a threat to the integrity of Turkish territory—though no one and nothing actually threatens Turkey's integrity. This "assistance" is evidently aimed at putting this country also under US control.

Some American commentators admit this quite openly. Walter Lippmann, for example, frankly points out in the *Herald Tribune* that an American alliance with Turkey would give the USA a strategic position, incomparably more advantageous than any other, from which power could be wielded over the Middle East.

Commenting on Truman's message to Congress, the *New York Times* proclaims the advent of "the age of American responsibility." Yet what is this responsibility but a smokescreen for expansion? The cry of saving Greece and Turkey from the expansion of the so-called "totalitarian states" is not new. Hitler used to refer to the Bolsheviks when he wanted to open the road for his own conquests. Now they want to take Greece and Turkey under their control, they raise a din about "totalitarian states" . . .

We are now witnessing a fresh intrusion of the USA into the affairs of other states. American claims to leadership in international affairs grow parallel with the growing appetite of the American quarters concerned. But the American leaders, in the new historical circumstances, fail to reckon with the fact that the old methods of the colonizers and die-hard politicians have outlived their time and are doomed to failure. In this lies the chief weakness of Truman's message.

46. INITIAL MOSCOW STATEMENT ON THE PROPOSED MARSHALL PLAN*

June 29, 1947

As is known, the Paris conference was called in connection with the speech delivered by the United States Secretary of State, Mr. Marshall, at Harvard University on June 5. In his speech Mr. Marshall expressed his apprehensions with regard to the economic conditions prevailing in the European countries following the Second World War.

* Quoted from *Soviet News*, July 1, 1947, *excerpts.*

He pointed to the grave consequences of the war, which caused immense losses in manpower and the destruction of towns, factories, mines, and railways, and he pointed also to postwar difficulties in the economic life of the European countries. He pointed out that the quantities of commodities now being produced are inadequate, that there are shortages of food, raw materials and fuel, and that machinery has become badly worn out, especially in the years of war.

Dealing with the possibility of America's rendering economic assistance to the European countries, Mr. Marshall said that the countries of Europe should themselves ascertain their needs and arrive at some kind of agreement among themselves, assuming the initiative in this matter. He said in this connection that the role of the USA should be to give friendly assistance in the working out of a European program and of giving subsequent support for such a program so far as was practicable for the USA.

Quite obviously, the rehabilitation and further development of the national economies of the European countries could be facilitated if the USA, whose production capacities—far from declining —considerably increased during the war, gave the economic assistance which those countries need. At the same time it is known that the USA is also interested in making use of its credit possibilities for expanding its external markets, especially in view of the approaching crisis.

When, in connection with Mr. Marshall's speech, the French and British Governments suggested a conference of the three ministers, the Soviet Government received this proposal favorably, despite the fact that the system of planning on which the Socialist national economy in the USSR is based precludes the possibility of the various crises and economic shake-ups mentioned in the above speech of the American Secretary of State.

Naturally, the present conference will achieve its object only if it correctly formulates its tasks and methods of work.

A definite plan of work prepared by the French Government and endorsed by the British Government has been presented at the conference. The Soviet delegation has expressed grave doubts with regard to this plan.

It is one thing to ascertain the economic needs of the European countries for American aid in the form of credits and deliveries of goods by means of estimates drawn up by the European countries themselves. This is acceptable and may prove useful to the European countries.

It will be an entirely different matter if the conference engages in drawing up an all-embracing economic program for the European countries as envisaged by the French project, and only in passing ascertains their needs of American economic aid. If the conference takes this path it will digress far from the task it has been set; and will fail to yield a positive result.

France has an economic plan of her own, and the French Government hopes for positive results from this plan. Great Britain also has an economic program of her own. It is widely known that in the Soviet Union the rehabilitation and development of the national economy is based on a State Socialist plan. . . .

It is also known that certain other European countries are now engaged in rehabilitating their national economies on the basis of two-year and three-year plans. Considerable successes have already been achieved in the implementation of these plans.

Hitherto it has been taken for granted that each nation should decide for itself how best to secure the rehabilitation and development of its economy. No European government intends to interfere and say whether Monnet's plan is good or bad for France. This is the affair of the French people themselves. But the same applies to Great Britain and the Soviet Union, Poland, Czechoslovakia, and every other European country.

That is how the matter is understood in the Soviet Union, which more than once has offered resistance to attempts at foreign intervention in its affairs. It was considered perfectly obvious that internal economic affairs are to be decided by the sovereign peoples themselves, and that other countries should not interfere in these internal affairs.

It is only on this basis that the normal development of relations among countries is possible. Attempts at outside interference in the economic life of various countries have not yielded favorable results, nor can they yield them.

If this is true, then attempts to compel the conference to engage in drawing up an all-embracing economic program for the European countries, which will inevitably entail intervention on the part of some states in the affairs of other states, cannot be accepted as a basis for cooperation among the European countries. Certain powers are at present making such attempts, which are doomed to failure and will only undermine their international prestige.

The conference is faced with the task of ascertaining the needs of the European countries for American economic aid, by receiving appropriate estimates from the countries concerned and subjecting them to a joint examination.

The task of the conference should be to establish cooperation among the European countries in drafting estimates of the needs of these countries for American economic aid, to ascertain the

possibility of obtaining such economic aid from the United States
and to assist the European countries in obtaining this aid. This
is no easy task and will require considerable effort. . . .

Which European countries should cooperate in this undertaking? There are differences in status among the various countries, and it would be wrong if the Allies did not differentiate
among Allied states, former enemy states and the neutral states.

47. SOVIET INTERPRETATION OF THE MARSHALL PLAN—SPEECH TO THE UN GENERAL ASSEMBLY*

September 18, 1947

ANDREI VYSHINSKY

The so-called Truman Doctrine and the Marshall Plan are particularly glaring examples of the manner in which the principles
of the United Nations are violated, of the way in which the
Organization is ignored.

As the experience of the past few months has shown, the proc-
lamation of this doctrine meant that the United States Government
has moved toward a direct renunciation of the principles of international collaboration and concerted action by the great Powers
and toward attempts to impose its will on other independent
states, while at the same time obviously using the economic
resources distributed as relief to individual needy nations as an
instrument of political pressure. This is clearly proved by the
measures taken by the United States Government with regard to
Greece and Turkey which ignore and by-pass the United Nations
as well as by the measures proposed under the so-called Marshall
Plan in Europe. This policy conflicts sharply with the principle
expressed by the General Assembly in its resolution of 11 December 1946, which declares that relief supplies to other countries
"should . . . at no time be used as a political weapon."

As is now clear, the Marshall Plan constitutes in essence merely
a variant of the Truman Doctrine adapted to the conditions of
postwar Europe. In bringing forward this plan, the United States
Government apparently counted on the cooperation of the Govern-

* UN General Assembly, *Official Records*, Plenary Meetings, Verbatim
Record, September 18, 1947, pp. 86–88, *excerpts*.

ments of the United Kingdom and France to confront the European countries in need of relief with the necessity of renouncing their inalienable right to dispose of their economic resources and to plan their national economy in their own way. The United States also counted on making all these countries directly dependent on the interests of American monopolies, which are striving to avert the approaching depression by an accelerated export of commodities and capital to Europe. . . .

It is becoming more and more evident to everyone that the implementation of the Marshall Plan will mean placing European countries under the economic and political control of the United States and direct interference by the latter in the internal affairs of those countries.

Moreover, this Plan is an attempt to split Europe into two camps and, with the help of the United Kingdom and France, to complete the formation of a *bloc* of several European countries hostile to the interests of the democratic countries of Eastern Europe and most particularly to the interests of the Soviet Union.

An important feature of this Plan is the attempt to confront the countries of Eastern Europe with a *bloc* of Western European States including Western Germany. The intention is to make use of Western Germany and German heavy industry (the Ruhr) as one of the most important economic bases for American expansion in Europe, in disregard of the national interests of the countries which suffered from German aggression.

I need only recall these facts to show the utter incompatibility of this policy of the United States, and of the British and French Governments which support it, with the fundamental principles of the United Nations.

Stalinism and Foreign Relations

48. SOVIET POLICY AND WORLD POLITICS*

A N D R E I   Z H D A N O V

The end of the Second World War brought with it big changes in the world situation. The military defeat of the bloc of fascist

* Andrei Zhdanov, *The International Situation* (Moscow: Foreign Languages Publishing House, 1947), *excerpts*.

states, the character of the war of liberation from fascism, and the decisive role played by the Soviet Union in the vanquishing of the fascist aggressors sharply altered the alignment of forces between the two systems—the socialist and the capitalist—in favor of socialism.

What is the essential nature of these changes?

The principal outcome of World War II was the military defeat of Germany and Japan—the two most militaristic and aggressive of the capitalist countries. . . .

[Second], the war immensely enhanced the international significance and prestige of the USSR. . . .

[Third], the capitalist world has also undergone a substantial change. Of the six so-called great imperialist powers (Germany, Japan, Great Britain, the USA, France, and Italy), three have been eliminated by military defeat. France has also been weakened and has lost its significance as a great power. As a result, only two great imperialist world powers remain—the United States and Great Britain. But the position of one of them, Great Britain, has been undermined. The war revealed that militarily and politically British imperialism was not so strong as it had been. . . .

[Fourth], World War II aggravated the crisis of the colonial system, as expressed in the rise of a powerful movement for national liberation in the colonies and dependencies. This has placed the rear of the capitalist system in jeopardy. The peoples of the colonies no longer wish to live in the old way. The ruling classes of the metropolitan countries can no longer govern the colonies on the old lines. . . .

Of all the capitalist powers, only one—the United States— emerged from the war not only unweakened, but even considerably stronger economically and militarily. The war greatly enriched the American capitalists. . . . But the end of the war confronted the United States with a number of new problems. The capitalist monopolies were anxious to maintain their profits at the former high level, and accordingly pressed hard to prevent a reduction of the wartime volume of deliveries. But this meant that the USA must retain the foreign markets which had absorbed American products during the war, and moreover, acquire new markets, inasmuch as the war had substantially lowered the purchasing power of most of the countries [to do this] . . . the United States proclaimed a new frankly predatory and expansionist course. The purpose of this new, frankly expansionist course is to establish the world supremacy of American imperialism. . . .

The fundamental changes caused by the war on the international scene and in the position of individual countries have

entirely changed the political landscape of the world. A new alignment of political forces has arisen. The more the war recedes into
the past, the more distinct become two major trends in postwar
international policy, corresponding to the division of the political
forces operating on the international arena into two major
camps; the imperialist and antidemocratic camp, on the one
hand, and the anti-imperialist and democratic camp, on the
other. The principal driving force of the imperialist camp is
the USA. Allied with it are Great Britain and France. . . . The
cardinal purpose of the imperialist camp is to strengthen imperialism, to hatch a new imperialist war, to combat socialism
and democracy, and to support reactionary and anti-democratic
pro-fascist regimes and movements everywhere.

The anti-fascist forces comprise the second camp. This camp is
based on the USSR and the new democracies. It also includes
countries that have broken with imperialism and have firmly set
foot on the path of democratic development, such as Rumania,
Hungary and Finland. . . .

Soviet foreign policy proceeds from the fact of the coexistence
for a long period of the two systems—capitalism and socialism.
From this it follows that cooperation between the USSR and
countries with other systems is possible, provided that the principle of reciprocity is observed and that obligations once assumed
are honored. Everyone knows that the USSR has always honored
the obligations it has assumed.

Britain and America are pursing the very opposite policy in
the United Nations. They are doing everything they can to renounce their commitments and to secure a free hand for the
prosecution of a new policy, a policy which envisages not cooperation among the nations, but the hounding of one against the
other, violation of the rights and interests of democratic nations,
and the isolation of the USSR. . . .

The strategical plans of the United States envisage the creation
in peacetime of numerous bases and vantage grounds situated at
great distances from the American continent and designed to be
used for aggressive purposes against the USSR and the countries
of the new democracy. . . .

Economic expansion is an important supplement to the realization of America's strategical plan. American imperialism is
endeavoring like a usurer to take advantage of the postwar difficulties of the European countries, in particular of the shortage
of raw materials, fuel, and food in the Allied countries that
suffered most from the war, to dictate to them extortionate terms
for any assistance rendered. With an eye to the impending
economic crisis, the United States is in a hurry to find new

monopoly spheres of capital investment and markets for its goods. American economic "assistance" pursues the broad aim of bringing Europe into bondage to American capital. The more drastic the economic situation of a country is, the harsher are the terms which the American monopolies endeavor to dictate to it. . . .

Lastly, the aspiration to world supremacy and the anti-democratic policy of the United States involve an ideological struggle. The principal purpose of the ideological part of the American strategical plan is to deceive public opinion by slanderously accusing the Soviet Union and the new democracies of aggressive intentions, and thus representing the Anglo-Saxon bloc in a defensive role, and absolving it of responsibility for preparing a new war. . . .

The unfavorable reception which the Truman doctrine was met with accounts for the necessity of the appearance of the Marshall Plan which is a more carefully veiled attempt to carry through the same expansionist policy. The vague and deliberately guarded formulations of the Marshall Plan amount in essence to a scheme to create a bloc of states bound by obligations to the United States, and to grant American credits to European countries as recompense for their renunciation of economic, and then of political, independence. . . .

The dissolution of the Comintern, which conformed to the demands of the development of the labor movement in the new historical situation, played a positive role. The dissolution of the Comintern once and for all disposed of the slanderous allegation of the enemies of Communism and the labor movement that Moscow was interfering in the internal affairs of other states, and that the Communist Parties in the various countries were acting not in the interests of their nations, but on orders from outside. . . .

In the course of the four years that have elapsed since the dissolution of the Comintern (1943), the Communist Parties have grown considerably in strength and influence in nearly all the countries of Europe and Asia. . . . But the present position of the Communist Parties has its shortcomings. Some comrades understood the dissolution of the Comintern to imply the elimination of all ties, of all contact, between the fraternal Communist Parties. But experience has shown that such mutual isolation of the Communist Parties is wrong, harmful and, in point of fact, unnatural. The Communist movement develops within national frameworks, but there are tasks and interests common to the parties of various countries. We get a rather curious state of affairs . . . the Communists even refrained from meeting one another, let alone consulting with one another on questions of mutual interest to them, from fear of the slanderous talk of their enemies regarding the "hand of Moscow." . . . There can be no doubt that if the situation were to continue it would be fraught with most serious consequences to the development of the work of the fraternal parties. The need for mutual consultation and voluntary coordination of action between individual parties has become particularly urgent at the present junction when continued isolation may lead to a slackening of mutual understanding, and at times, even to serious blunders. . . .

FOR FURTHER STUDY

Barghoorn, Frederick C., *The Soviet Image of the United States*. New York: Harcourt, Brace & World, 1950.

Betts, R. R. (ed.), *Central and South East Europe, 1945–1948*. London: Royal Institute of International Affairs, 1950.

Blackett, P. M. S., *Fear, War, and the Bomb*. New York: Whittlesey House, 1949.

Byrnes, James F., *Speaking Frankly*. New York: Harper & Row, Publishers, 1947.

Eagleton, William, *The Kurdish Republic of 1946*. New York: Oxford University Press, 1963.

Ebon, Martin, *World Communism Today*. New York: McGraw-Hill Book Company, 1948.

Fleming, D. F., *The Cold War and Its Origins, 1917–1960*, 2 vols. New York: Doubleday & Company, 1961.

Gluckstein, Yagael, *Stalin's Satellites in Europe*. London: George Allen & Unwin, 1952.

Ingram, Kenneth, *History of the Cold War*. New York: Philosophical Library, 1955.

Lane, Arthur B., *I Saw Poland Betrayed*. Indianapolis: Bobbs-Merrill Company, 1948.

Lenczowski, George, *Russia and the West in Iran, 1918–1948: A Study in Big Power Rivalry*. Ithaca: Cornell University Press, 1949.

Mikolajczyk, Stanislaw, *The Rape of Poland: Pattern of Soviet Aggression*. New York: McGraw-Hill Book Company, 1948.

Nagy, Ferenc, *The Struggle Behind the Iron Curtain*. New York: The Macmillan Company, 1948.

Rieber, Alfred J., *Stalin and the French Communist Party, 1941–1947*. New York: Columbia University Press, 1962.

Seton-Watson, Hugh, *The East European Revolution*. New York: Frederick A. Praeger, 1951.

Smith, Walter Bedell, *My Three Years in Moscow*. Philadelphia: J. B. Lippincott Company, 1950.

Truman, Harry S., *Memoirs*, 2 vols. New York: Doubleday & Company, 1955–1956.

CHAPTER VII

STALINIZATION AND EMPIRE, 1948–1953

The imperialist nature of Stalinist political and military objectives in Eastern Europe, and the renewed emphasis upon Marxist-Leninist orthodoxy at home and abroad, with its implication of uncompromising hostility, led inexorably to the institutionalization of the Cold War. Soviet intransigence sharpened in the United Nations, in Germany, and in Austria. By February 1948, when the Communist Party effected a *coup d'état* and Czechoslovakia disappeared behind the Curtain, the conquest of Eastern Europe was completed.[1] The fall of Prague had far-reaching consequences. More than any other single Soviet-inspired move, it dispelled remaining Western illusions concerning Soviet intentions, heightened anxiety over the Soviet threat, and hastened Western rearmament. In the early postwar period, democratic Czechoslovakia had represented a tenuous link between the Soviet Union and its former allies; it had symbolized the possibility of compromise and cooperation. The disappearance of Czechoslovakia as a middle ground ended such hopes. The lines of conflict were now clearly drawn.

Stalin next proceeded to end the last vestiges of coalition government in Eastern Europe—a process noticeably accelerated after the split with Tito—and to consolidate his empire. Through an intricate network of alliances, trade and economic agreements, joint-stock companies,* and Communist Party ties, Soviet hegemony was entrenched throughout the area. Cultural and political ties with the West were eliminated, and economic transactions reduced to an insignificant minimum. Previously negotiated political agreements were either ignored or so interpreted by the Kremlin as to accord with its expansionist aims (reading 49). By June 1948 the Soviet Union had seemingly succeeded in establishing a monolithic structure extending from the Baltic to the Black Sea. To the West it appeared that America's monopoly of atomic weapons constituted the only bar to Soviet domination of all Europe.

Two dramatic developments occurred in June 1948: the Berlin blockade and the expulsion of Tito from the Cominform. Each had an effect far beyond its immediate frame of reference. In retrospect, they constitute two of Stalin's major postwar miscalculations (the aggression in Korea might be considered a third), setting in motion a chain of events unfavorable to the consolidation and expansion of Soviet power.

On June 29, 1948, the Soviet Union imposed a blockade on the Western sectors of Berlin, deep inside the Soviet zone of Germany. During the previous months Soviet authorities had periodically interfered with Western access to Berlin, but had hesitated before imposing a full blockade. Several considerations motivated the Soviets. First, by forcing the Western Powers out of Berlin and bringing the entire city under their control, the Soviets expected to enhance their prospects of controlling Germany, the ultimate prize in the Cold War. Second, they hoped to undermine efforts then being made to establish West Germany as a united and independent country within the Western camp. Third, an Allied surrender in Berlin would have strengthened Communist Party prestige in the weakened countries of Western Europe, further softening them for future subversion by local

* According to the Soviets "the Joint Stock Company, half of whose capital belongs to the Soviet Union, and the other half to the Governments of the People's Democracies, is a new form of economic collaboration between the countries of the socialist camp based on the principle of equality and mutual economic advantage; all expenses and profits of the Joint Stock Company are shared equally." M. Paramov, "Forms and Methods of Economic Cooperation Between the U.S.S.R. and the People's Democracies," *Voprosy Ekonomiki*, Vol. III (December 1950), p. 46.

Through a convenient interpretation of the provision in the peace treaties dealing with "German assets," the Soviet Union acquired extensive holdings in Bulgaria, Hungary, Rumania, and Poland. These pre-empted assets gave the Soviets a position of economic importance without the actual outlay of any funds. Soviet managers controlled the enterprises.

Communist Parties. However, once the Berlin airlift started, the Soviets were committed to a lengthy test of strength. Western determination was on trial. The stakes were high, particularly for the West. Moscow mentioned none of these factors in its stated version of the reasons for imposing the blockade (reading 50). Moscow's specious reasoning stressed legalisms and split hairs, but bore little relation to the power realities then existing in Europe.

Allied willingness to pay the price of the airlift convinced Stalin of the futility of this tactic, and a settlement was finally reached in May 1949 after months of trying negotiation. The Kremlin had suffered its first postwar defeat in Europe. The abortive blockade failed not only to drive the Western Powers out of Berlin but also to prevent the establishment of the Western German Federal Republic on May 23, 1949. Moscow retaliated in kind by setting up a "German Democratic Republic" in October 1949. This formalized partition of Germany has endured to the present, exacerbating fear and insecurity and serving as an ever-present reminder of the deep-rooted incompatibility of East-West objectives in Europe.

The world first learned of the deep fissure within the supposedly solid edifice of international communism on June 28, 1948. The Cominform announced the expulsion of the Yugoslav Communist Party for "anti-Party and anti-Soviet views, incompatible with Marxism-Leninism." The Yugoslav leaders, the announcement stated:

. . . have placed themselves in opposition to the Communist Parties affiliated to the Information Bureau, have taken the path of seceding from the united socialist front against imperialism, have taken the path of betraying the cause of international solidarity of the working people, and have taken up a position of nationalism.[2]

The causes of the break were in great measure candidly revealed in the text of the correspondence between the Central Committees of the Soviet and Yugoslav Communist Parties, published by the Cominform. The Yugoslav reply to the Soviet charges of heresy affords a rare and remarkable view of intra-Communist relations (reading 51). Though the split was less one of principle than of power and personality, it had important ideological ramifications.

Stalin refused to accept Tito as an equal and grew dissatisfied with Yugoslav intransigence in commercial and political negotiations. He insisted upon the unchallenged and absolute economic and political control by the Kremlin over Eastern Europe. Irritated by failure either to dominate the Yugoslav Communist Party, to infiltrate it and the Yugoslav governmental apparatus with agents loyal to the Kremlin, or to reduce Yugoslavia to a subservient satrapy comparable to that of the other nations of Eastern Europe, Stalin invoked the "ultimate" weapon of excommunication against his former protégé. He expected to overthrow Tito by waging an intensive propaganda campaign through the Cominform and by utilizing Soviet prestige to alienate Yugoslav public opinion away from Tito. This Stalin assumed would bring to power a pro-Soviet, anti-Tito faction. However, in considering that the highest loyalty of all "good" Communists was to the Soviet Union, and not to any particular national Communist Party, Stalin underestimated the broad bases of Tito's strength, as well as the force of Yugoslav nationalism. Aided by the fortunate circumstance of geography, the loyalty of Party and military associates whose bonds had been forged in the crucible of a common struggle against the Germans, and the undoubted popularity of Tito as a national hero, the Yugoslav leadership withstood the Cominform assault.

"Titoism" signifies more than a reaction against Soviet domination; it represents a fusion of nationalism and communism into an ideology and a movement having a variety of forms and connoting a measure of independence not acceptable to Moscow.* No single formula can account for the phenomenon of Titoism. Rather, it must be viewed within a particular framework of historical circumstances, as in Yugoslavia and Poland. In the case of Yugoslavia, national support of Tito, coupled with generous infusions of Western economic and military aid, enabled it to withstand Stalin's attempt at subversion. Since then, the Yugoslavs have insisted that it is they who are the true interpreters of the Marxist-Leninist tradition and that Stalinism represented a perversion of this tradition.

Titoism poses a permanent dilemma for Soviet leaders: under what circumstances should the Kremlin use "diplomacy," as opposed to "compulsion," in order to eliminate threats to its estab-

---

* During the early postwar years a few leading East European Communists—notably Tito in Yugoslavia and Dimitrov in Bulgaria—entertained the age-old vision of a Balkan Federation. The two met at Bled, Yugoslavia, in the summer of 1947 and discussed the possibility of setting up a Yugoslav-Bulgarian customs union which would serve as the nucleus for such a federation. Independent, it was to be closely associated with the Soviet Union. However, Moscow had some second thoughts on the subject. It feared that a Balkan Federation might prove too difficult to control. Therefore, on January 28, 1948, *Pravda* declared that: "The countries of Eastern Europe do not need a problematic and invented federation or customs union but a strengthening of their independence and sovereignty through the organization of internal popular and democratic forces as had been stated in the Cominform declarations." To Moscow, Titoism and a "Third Force" in Eastern Europe are equally an anathema.

lished hegemony and unquestioned leadership? Events of the post-Stalinist period, e.g., in Poland and Hungary in 1956, have shown that any acceptance by Moscow of the "many roads to socialism" doctrine may well result in the release of those pent-up forces of frustration and opposition that the Kremlin tries to curb or channel through an easing of political and economic controls.

After 1948, Stalin initiated a series of purges of possible "Titos" and intensified the rate of sovietization. Thus, leading Communists were swept from power—Gomulka in Poland, Rajk in Hungary, Kostov in Bulgaria. Stalin moved to ensure the absolute obedience of the Party organizations to Moscow. Though the purges were rationalized in terms of faulty ideological attitudes on the part of the purged, the verbalisms merely camouflaged more primitive power considerations. The Stalinist pattern of organization was imposed upon Eastern Europe. Industry, foreign trade, and transportation were nationalized; centralized economic control and planning were introduced; and heavy industrialization was emphasized. Stalin sought to guarantee the permanence and stability of his empire by remaking the economic and social fabric of Eastern European society. He stopped short of military measures in his efforts to overthrow Tito, but the intensified sovietization of Eastern Europe heightened Western insecurity and led to the establishment of a more formalized system of military alliance. Military considerations thus increasingly dominated European affairs.

The North Atlantic Treaty was signed on April 4, 1949. It represented the West's military response to the sovietization of Eastern Europe, to Moscow's global effort to subvert Western governments, and to the enormous military disparity in conventional forces existing between the two camps. NATO was intended primarily as a defensive shield against any possible Soviet aggression; only secondarily was it concerned with promoting economic and political cooperation among its members. Its founders regarded NATO as a legitimate exercise of the "inherent right of individual or collective self-defense" granted under Articles 51 and 52 of the UN Charter, designed to cope with the inability of the fledgling United Nations to guarantee the peace. British Foreign Secretary Ernest Bevin, championing the NATO Treaty and emphasizing its defensive character, argued that Soviet duplicity, obstructionist tactics in the UN, and threatening posture had left the Western democracies with no choice. "The pact," he held, "does not seek to interfere, but equally it does resist the right of any Powers with aggressive intentions to upset our institutions, to bring us into bondage, or to create a situation which will enable them to introduce the police state, or carry out devices which have been applied in so many other countries."

The Soviets, on the other hand, regarded NATO in a completely different light (reading 52). Denying that their treaties with the Eastern European countries could be interpreted "as treaties which are in any degree aimed against the allies of the USSR in the late war," they declared that Western rearmament and establishment of NATO could "in no way be justified by the interests of self-defense." Rather, "the North Atlantic Pact is designed to intimidate the states which do not agree to obey the dictates of the Anglo-American grouping of Powers that lay claim to world domination"; indeed, continued the Soviet memorandum, it undermines the very foundations of the UN, and "far from corresponding to the aims and principles of the United Nations Organization, runs counter to the Charter of this organization."

The Soviet Government considered NATO the newest expression of aggressive capitalism, which, it held, could perpetuate itself only by embarking on imperialist ventures. Ideologically, its interpretation reflected the hostile tradition of Marxism-Leninism; politically, the Soviets saw their expansion in Europe halted, and watched with concern and surprise the unexpectedly rapid revival of Japan and Germany and their shift from passivity to active adherence to the Western bloc. To supplement its diplomatic activity, the Kremlin intensified its anti-Western propaganda campaign. Operating through a variety of organizations, the most important being the Partisans of Peace, it attempted to pre-empt the theme of peace and undermine Western influence in Asia and the Middle East. Militarily, the Soviets seemed to feel at a disadvantage with the West, despite their spectacularly improved postwar strategic position. However, by late 1949, two developments did much to affect advantageously the Soviet power position: the announcement that a Soviet atom bomb had been successfully produced and detonated; and the victory of the Chinese Communists on the mainland of China, which meant that domination of the Eurasian land mass had passed to the Communist world. As the lines of hostility stabilized in Europe, events in the Far East attracted increasing attention.

The Chinese People's Republic was proclaimed in Peking on October 1, 1949. An era of Far Eastern history had come to an end. For the first time in more than a century all of (mainland) China was controlled by one elite, a Chinese elite. China's destiny was no longer decided in Europe. The century of civil wars, unequal treaties, forced concessions to foreign powers, and progressively weakened central authority was now past. Out of

this crucible emerged a harsh, dedicated, disciplined leadership
—the Calvinists of Asia—ruthlessly intent on creating a powerful, industrialized, totalitarian China. This development inevitably affected great power relationships in Asia, relationships
already greatly altered as a consequence of World War II and
of the confused 1945–1949 interregnum.

There is no question that World War II was won in Europe.
But the postwar peace has experienced its severest stresses in
Asia, a trend apt to continue for the foreseeable future. On the
eve of victory over Nazi Germany, a spirit of optimism prevailed
in Washington concerning postwar Soviet objectives in the Far
East and particularly in China. But it was by no means universal.
A brilliant analysis of probable Soviet objectives in the Far East
was developed in a memorandum cabled by George F. Kennan,
then Chargé d'Affaires in Moscow, to Ambassador Harriman, in
Washington at the time for consultation:

Actually I am persuaded that in the future Soviet policy respecting
China will continue what it has been in the recent past: a fluid resili-
ent policy directed at the achievement of maximum power with minimum responsibility on portions of the Asiatic continent lying beyond
the Soviet border. This will involve the exertion of pressure in various
areas in direct proportion to their strategic importance and their
proximity to the Soviet frontier. I am sure that within the framework
of this policy Moscow will aim specifically at: (1) reacquiring in
substance, if not in form, all the diplomatic and territorial assets previously possessed on the mainland of Asia by Russia under the Czars;
(2) domination of the provinces of China in central Asia contiguous
to the Soviet frontier. Such action is dictated by the strategic necessity
of protecting in depth the industrial core of the USSR; (3) acquiring
sufficient control in all areas of North China now dominated by the
Japanese to prevent other foreign powers from repeating the Japanese
incursion. This means, to the Russian mind, the maximum possible
exclusion of penetration in that area by outside powers including
America and Britain. . . .

It would be tragic if our natural anxiety for the support of the Soviet
Union at this juncture, coupled with Stalin's use of words which mean
all things to all people and his cautious affability, were to lead us into
an undue reliance on Soviet aid or even Soviet acquiescence in the
achievement of our long term objectives in China.[3]

The postwar period has witnessed an alarming and progressive
shift in comparative military advantage to the Communist world.
This has been especially evident, with tragic results, in the Far
East. Strong American diplomatic pressure in June-July 1945,
the entry of the Soviet Union into the war against Japan, and
the rapidity of the Soviet advance in Manchuria—all served to
force China to sign a disadvantageous treaty with Moscow.

Acceptance by China of the concessions granted to the USSR at Yalta was the price of the treaty. Accordingly, China recognized the "independence" of Outer Mongolia, agreed to Soviet participation in the operation of the Chinese Changchun Railway* (thus affording Moscow an entering wedge into Manchuria), to joint Sino-Soviet use of the naval base of Port Arthur, and to the internationalization of the port of Dairen—all traditional Czarist objectives in the Far East. These Soviet gains were formally acknowledged in China in the Sino-Soviet Treaty of Friendship and Alliance, signed on August 14, 1945. In return, the Soviet Government recognized the government of Chiang Kai-shek as the legitimate government of China and pledged itself "to render to China moral support and aid in military supplies and other material resources, such support and aid to be entirely given to the National Government as the central government of China." The Soviet leaders never lived up to this pledge.

Our knowledge of the relations between the Soviet and Chinese Communist leaders during 1945–1949 is meager. Reliable data are lacking. As far as can be determined, Soviet contact with the Chinese Communists did not appear too extensive until early 1946, notwithstanding the common ideological heritage. However, we do know that the Soviets stripped Manchuria of virtually all usable industrial equipment shortly before the Chinese Communists took over. This raises the intriguing question of the extent to which Moscow expected Mao's sweeping conquest of all China. It is possible that Stalin was as surprised as the West at the dramatic deterioration of the Kuomintang forces and at the remarkable Communist advances in 1947–1948. The Kuomintang failure to cope effectively with China's myriad administrative and economic ills served to enhance the political appeal of the Communists. Mao adroitly exploited the spreading discontent with Kuomintang incompetence and corruption, the Communist legacy of resistance against the Japanese, the deep-rooted desire of the peasantry for fundamental agrarian reforms, and the appeal that a strong and united China had for students, intellectuals, and even middle-class elements.[4]

American efforts to mediate the Chinese civil war proved futile. Indeed, it is doubtful that they ever enjoyed the faintest prospect of success. Meanwhile, Moscow pursued a policy of ambiguity with the Kuomintang, though taking care to maintain outwardly "correct" diplomatic relations. But these rapidly deteriorated with the approaching victory of Mao. Throughout the 1945–1949

---

* The Japanese had combined the Chinese Eastern Railway with the South Manchurian Railway into one unified system—the Chinese Changchun Railway.

period Stalin concentrated mainly on recovery at home and the consolidation of the Soviet empire in Europe. Only after the rise to power of the Chinese Communists, and the sovietization of Eastern Europe, did Soviet interests shift markedly to the Far East. For the Communist victory in China raised Soviet hopes, as well as Western fears, that communism might sweep all Asia.

In December 1949 Mao went to Moscow and for two months negotiated the future of Sino-Soviet relations. On February 14, 1950, three agreements were signed (reading 53). They provided: (1) a military alliance clearly directed against the United States; (2) the renunciation by Moscow of all rights in Manchuria except in Dairen (Dalny), though the changes this involved were not to be implemented before "the conclusion of a peace treaty with Japan, but not later than the end of 1952"; (3) a five-year, 300-million-dollar Soviet credit to Peking. These agreements were modified in 1954 to the further advantage of China. Even in 1950, however, they reflected the Kremlin's awareness that Mao, like Tito, had come to power under circumstances completely unlike those leading to the establishment of Communist regimes in Eastern Europe. Traditional Russian policy had dealt with a weak China which had sought security in a pro-Western orientation. This situation, Stalin recognized, no longer existed. And, though he tried to get as much as possible from Mao, he did not overreach himself in trying to retain a privileged position for the Soviet Union. Mao, commanding his own army and controlling a vast land mass, was accorded a partnership in the Communist world, albeit a junior partnership. Stalin apparently had learned the lesson of Tito well. Besides, Mao's victory presented Stalin with the opportunity of improving his power position in Asia (with reference to Korea). From this, one expert has concluded that:

These and other considerations led us to pose the hypothesis that Stalin decided to pursue a "correct" if hardheaded policy toward Peking, to give minimum cause for Chinese suspicion that Soviet aims might include territorial aggrandizement and unmasked intervention in internal affairs, and to allow Peking a degree of freedom of expression and action in international Communism and in Asia hitherto unknown within the Soviet orbit.[5]

Within a few months the alliance was tested by conflict in Korea. American and Soviet troops had withdrawn from Korea by mid-1949, leaving that country divided at the 38th parallel "between two rival authorities, each bent on the elimination of the other and on the unification of Korea after its own pattern."[6] All prospects for a peaceful unification vanished on June 25,

1950, when North Korean Communist troops invaded South Korea in a calculated attempt to resolve the issue by force. Well-equipped, having the advantage of surprise, and encouraged by the signs of widespread discontent with the Syngman Rhee regime that appeared in the May election, they came perilously close to victory. As the conflict assumed global significance, it threatened to turn the Cold War into an all-encompassing conflagration.

In New York the Security Council convened in emergency session on the very day of invasion in response to a request by the United States Government. The Soviet Union was not represented at this or any of the subsequent meetings of the Council, having undertaken a boycott of the United Nations in January 1950 because of the exclusion of Chinese Communist representatives. Not until August 1 did the Soviet delegate return. With the Soviet delegate absent, the Security Council passed a resolution calling for the immediate cessation of hostilities and the withdrawal of the North Korean forces to their side of the border. It also requested all UN members to help in implementing this resolution. President Truman, noting the failure of the North Korean Government to heed the Security Council's injunction, announced the intention of the United States to provide air and naval support for the South Koreans in accordance with the Council's request, despite previous indications by Washington that it regarded Korea as indefensible and beyond the area strategically necessary for America's defense. On June 27, the Security Council called upon the United Nations to "furnish such assistance to the Republic of Korea as may be necessary to repel the armed attack and to restore international peace and security in the area." American (and UN) forces came to the support of South Korea.

In a note to the Soviet Government, the United States sought Soviet assistance in securing the withdrawal of North Korean forces. The Soviet reply placed the blame on South Korea and maintained that the Security Council was not competent to act in the absence of one of its permanent members (reading 54). Soon afterward, the Soviets set their vast propaganda apparatus in motion, attacking the United States for intervening in a civil war, for carrying on an aggression, and for practicing bacteriological warfare and assorted atrocities. Meanwhile, UN forces counterattacked and advanced toward the Yalu River—and the Manchurian border. Once across the 38th parallel, they were no longer merely repelling aggression; they were seeking to unify all Korea by force of arms. This decision was never explicitly sanctioned by the General Assembly, nor the Security Council.

Its wisdom and legality remain debatable. In early November the Chinese Communists, apprehensive over the approach of a hostile army and insecure enough to fear invasion of the mainland by Kuomintang troops, entered the struggle. A new dimension had been added to the conflict. General MacArthur stated that "we face an entirely new war."

After much bitter fighting, a stalemate developed roughly along the 38th parallel. Convinced that victory was impossible, anxious to localize the conflict, and disturbed by the acceleration of Western rearmament resulting from the Korean attack, Stalin pressured the North Koreans and Chinese to enter into truce negotiations in July 1951. These dragged on for almost two years, but an armistice agreement was finally signed in July 1953, and today an uneasy truce prevails in a divided Korea.

Why did Stalin order the invasion of South Korea? Indeed, did he? Though hypotheses abound, conclusive historical evidence is lacking for any objective assigning of responsibility. The North Korean invasion remains shrouded in uncertainty. The reasons usually advanced depend, in great measure, upon which set of assumptions one is disposed to accept. For example, most Western observers hold the Soviet Union solely responsible. They cite the elaborate preparations obviously required for the attack and the fact that the North Korean Communist Party was at the time unquestionably Kremlin-controlled and could not have launched such an effort without Moscow's prior knowledge and approval. Only after the Chinese intervention in Korea in November 1950 did Peking expand its influence and begin to compete with Moscow for a position of dominance in Pyongyang. Other observers suggest that the invasion was actually planned with Mao during his stay in Moscow. The experts all believe that the Soviets expected a quick victory and were surprised by the American decision to fight. Statements by Secretary of State Acheson in January and May (1950) encouraged the belief that the United States considered the defense of Korea as untenable. Also, all the experts interpret the continued Soviet absence from the Security Council as a grievous Soviet miscalculation. For, whereas Stalin may have expected the Security Council to pass some resolutions of admonition as the League of Nations had done in similar circumstances in the 1930s, he did not expect a vigorous American military response to a local aggression. A decidedly minority view goes so far as to hypothesize that Moscow was not directly to blame, that indeed the North Korean attack came as a total surprise. They concede that the Kremlin favored the elimination of South Korea as a separate state, but they maintain that there is evidence to indicate that the North Koreans acted on their own. Once the die was cast, however,

Moscow had no choice but to support its satellite and prevent any unfriendly forces from coming too close to Soviet industrial centers in Siberia.

Though thwarted militarily, the Soviets benefited politically in two important ways: first, the West was required to commit a large part of its limited strength-in-being to a remote, strategically peripheral area, thereby weakening Western Europe's defenses and forcing it to undertake a massive program of rearmament that it could economically ill afford. In a sense, the West fought "the wrong war, at the wrong time, in the wrong place." Second, the Korean war "confirmed the breach between Communist China and the Western World," thus emphasizing to the Chinese Communists their heavy dependence upon Soviet economic and military support.[7] The existence of a common enemy (the United States) further strengthened the bonds linking the colossi of the Communist world. Under such circumstances, Stalin could well be confident that China would not readily develop into a second Yugoslavia.

In Europe in 1951-1952, Stalin continued the sovietization of Eastern Europe and its economic and military integration into the Soviet empire, operating through such organizations as the Council for Mutual Economic Aid—the Soviet version of the Marshall Plan—and an elaborate network of interlocking military treaties. Indeed, Stalin went to far as to place a Soviet marshal, Rokossovsky, in command of the Polish army in order to ensure its reliability. The growing strength of the Soviet Union and its satellites, coupled with the overt aggression in Korea, spurred Western rearmament and intensified the Cold War. The threat of a Soviet attack in Europe still loomed large in Western thinking.

In retrospect, however, one can discern Stalin's innate conservatism in foreign policy. He did not seek to overwhelm the West by force; he probably never intended to do so. He sought rather to undermine Western power and prestige and to enhance correspondingly the strength and stability of his empire. In October 1952, at the Nineteenth Party Congress, Stalin outlined an approach to international tensions notable for its long-range perspective. In his view the revival of Germany and Japan would sharpen the contradictions *within* the capitalist world, and the ensuing struggle for markets would cause wars among the capitalists, rather than between the mutually irreconcilable camps of socialism and capitalism. Aware of the undercurrents of discontent in the satellites, as well as in the Soviet Union, Stalin moved with caution. But he took advantage of every opportunity to expand Soviet power. His strategy of protracted conflict with capitalism, however, halted short of war.

The year 1953 was a fateful one. Stalin had ruled the Soviet Union for a generation. One of history's most ruthless tyrants, he had transformed a backward, underdeveloped country into one of the world's great industrial-military powers and had created an empire dwarfing those of Genghis Khan and Tamerlane. He bequeathed an empire and an approach to power. Both continue to threaten world peace. Though Soviet expansion has been greatest in Europe, Stalin appreciated the importance of Asia. Undistinguished as a theorist, he insisted upon a confining orthodoxy in ideological and party affairs. He seldom deluded himself with fervent expectations of imminent world revolution, but he was quite willing to use revolutions abroad to spread Soviet power. He understood the nature of power and used it to advantage to expand the Soviet empire, fusing in the process the needs of national security with his imperialist ambitions. He ruled in the autocratic tradition of Peter the Great and westernized the economy of the Soviet Union; in the realm of foreign policy, he followed in the footsteps of the most expansionist of Czars. His successors have sought to maintain his tradition.

On March 5, 1953, Moscow announced the death of Stalin. An era had come to an end.

NOTES

1. For an excellent account of the Czech *coup* see Paul Zinner, "Marxism in Action: The Seizure of Power in Czechoslovakia," *Foreign Affairs*, Vol. XXVIII, No. 4 (July 1950), pp. 644–658; Dana Adams Schmidt, *The Anatomy of a Satellite* (Boston: Little, Brown and Company, 1952); and *The Coup d'Etat in Prague*, Supplement III(A) to Report of Subcommittee No. 5 of the Committee on Foreign Affairs, U. S. House of Representatives, on *The Strategy and Tactics of World Communism.*
2. *The Soviet-Yugoslav Dispute* (New York and London: Oxford University Press and the Royal Institute of International Affairs, 1948), pp. 68–69.
3. *United States Relations with China* (Washington, D.C.: Department of State, 1949), p. 97.
4. Though the literature on this subject is voluminous, several sources may be cited for those interested in pursuing the subject further: W. M. Ball, *Nationalism and Communism in East Asia* (Melbourne, 1952); M. Beloff, *Soviet Policy in the Far East, 1944–51* (New York: Oxford University Press, 1953); M. D. Kennedy, *A Short History of Communism in Asia* (London, 1957); Mao Tse-tung, *The Turning Point in China* (New York, 1948); R. C. North, *Moscow and the Chinese Communists* (Stanford: Stanford University Press, 1953); B. Schwartz, *Chinese Communism and the Rise of Mao* (Cambridge, Mass.: Harvard University Press, 1951); and E. Snow, *Red Star over China* (London: Gollancz, 1937).
5. Unpublished paper submitted by Emory C. Swank to the Foreign Service Institute. "The Moscow-Peking Axis: An Interpretation Based Primarily on Communist Source Materials, 1949-February 1953" (Department of State: External Research Staff), p. 15.
6. Peter Calvocoressi, *Survey of International Affairs, 1949–1950* (New York: Oxford University Press, 1953), p. 466.
7. Beloff, *op. cit.*, p. 255.

Background Data on Stalin's Imperialist Expansion

49. SOVIET VIOLATIONS OF TREATY OBLIGATIONS*

A. *Germany*

1. *Agreement:* The final delimitation of German-Polish frontier should await the peace settlement (Potsdam protocol, VIII, B).

Violations: USSR has repeatedly maintained that the Oder-Neisse line constitutes the definitive German-Polish frontier and has approved incorporation of territory east of this line into Poland.

2. *Agreement:* Payment of reparations to leave enough resources to enable the German people to subsist without external assistance. Reparation claims of USSR to be met by removals of capital goods and appropriation of external assets (Potsdam protocol, II, B, 15, 19).

Violations: USSR has taken large amounts of reparations from current production, has absorbed a substantial part of German industry in Soviet zone into Soviet state-owned concerns, and has otherwise exploited and drained German resources in a manner not authorized by Potsdam protocol or other agreements.

3. *Agreement:* Economic Directorate of Allied Control Authority agreed, May 24, 1946, that each member would submit report on reparations from its zone.

Violation: USSR has refused to submit report on any reparations removals from its zone.

4. *Agreement:* Germany to be treated as a single economic unit (Potsdam protocol, II, B, 14).

Violation: USSR has consistently obstructed all four-power attempts to implement this principle and has carried out a unilateral economic policy in its own zone.

5. *Agreement:* All democratic political parties to be allowed and encouraged throughout Germany (Potsdam protocol, II, A, 9).

Violations: Soviet authorities have restricted the freedom of action of non-Communist parties by depriving them of equal

* *U.S. Department of State Bulletin,* Vol. xviii (April 4, 1948), pp. 738–742, excerpts.

facilities with the SED (the Communist-dominated coalition), interfering in their internal affairs, coercing their leaders, dictating party actions, and in general denying them the autonomy essential to democratic political organizations. They have denied the Social Democratic Party the right to operate in the Soviet zone as an independent organization.

B. *Eastern and Southeastern Europe*

POLAND

1. *Agreement:* "This Polish Provisional Government of National Unity shall be pledged to the holding of free and unfettered elections as soon as possible on the basis of universal suffrage and secret ballot. In these elections all democratic and anti-Nazi parties shall have the right to take part and to put forward candidates" (Crimea Conference, February 12, 1945).

"The Three Powers (US, USSR, UK) note that the Polish Provisional Government in accordance with the decisions of the Crimea Conference has agreed to the holding of free and unfettered elections as soon as possible on the basis of universal suffrage and secret ballot in which all democratic and anti-Nazi parties have the right to take part and to put forward candidates" (Potsdam Agreement, August 2, 1945).

Violations: On several occasions prior to the elections and following persistent reports of reprehensible methods employed by the Government against the democratic opposition, this (US) Government reminded the Polish Provisional Government of its obligations under the Yalta and Potsdam agreements and was joined on these occasions by the British Government. On January 5, 1947, the British and Soviet Governments were asked to associate themselves with this Government in approaching the Poles on this subject, and the British Government made similar representations to the Soviet Government reiterating the request that the Soviet Government support the British and American Government in calling for a strict fulfillment of Poland's obligations. The Soviet Government refused to participate in the proposed approach to the Polish Government. The British and American representations were summarily rejected by the Polish Government as "undue interference" in the internal affairs of Poland.

Of the 444 deputies elected to the parliament in the elections of January 19, 1947, the Polish Peasant Party (reliably reported to represent a large majority of the population) obtained only 28 places, thus demonstrating the efficiency with which the Government had prepared the ground.

HUNGARY

1. *Agreement:* Under the armistice agreement an Allied Control Commission was established under the chairmanship of the USSR and with participation of the United States and United Kingdom (Armistice agreement, January 1945, art. 18 and annex F).

Violations: The USSR representative on the ACC for Hungary consistently acted unilaterally in the name of the ACC without consultation with or notice to his United States and United Kingdom colleagues, thus denying them any semblance of effective participation in the work of the ACC.

Contrary to the Yalta Agreement, the USSR, acting through the Hungarian Communist Party and its own agencies and armed forces in Hungary . . . unilaterally subverted the will of the Hungarian people to totalitarianism in negation of fundamental freedoms. For example:

(a) General Sviridov, Deputy Soviet Chairman of the ACC, without consulting the United States and United Kingdom ACC representatives, dissolved Catholic youth organizations, June 1946.

(b) General Sviridov precipitated a political crisis enabling the Communist minority to force the resignation of Prime Minister Nagy, May–June 1947.

(c) Discriminatory economic agreements were forced upon Hungary, including the establishment of joint Soviet-Hungarian companies, 1945–1947.

RUMANIA

1. *Agreement:* The three heads of Government of the USSR, the USA, and UK declared their mutual agreement to concert during the temporary period of instability in liberated Europe the policies of their three governments in assisting the peoples of the former Axis satellite states of Europe to solve by democratic means their pressing political and economic problems (Yalta agreement on liberated Europe, February 1945).

Violations: Contrary to its agreement at Yalta, the USSR, acting through the Rumanian Communist Party and its own agencies and armed forces in Rumania, systematically and unilaterally subverted the democratic will of the Rumanian people to totalitarianism in negation of their fundamental freedoms. For example:

(a) Unilateral intervention by Soviet occupation authorities and by Vyshinsky (February–March 1945) in effecting the overthrow of Premier Radescu's interim representative government and the installation of a Communist-controlled regime.

(b) Direct and indirect unilateral interference by the Soviet occupation authorities in the election campaign of 1946, extending to the use of Soviet troops to break up meetings of the opposition and the arbitrary exercise of censorship.

(c) Exploitation of the Rumanian economy . . . through the establishment of Soviet-controlled joint companies covering the principal economic activities of Rumania, and through commercial agreements the knowledge of whose terms was repeatedly refused to the other two Yalta powers.

C. *Korea*

1. *Agreements:* Reestablishment of movement of persons, motor, rail transport and coastwise shipping between the zones of North and South Korea (Agreement of Joint United States and Union of Soviet Socialist Republics Conference, January–February 1946).

Violations: The Soviet command in North Korea has since 1946 refused to discuss or implement the agreements reached on these matters, resisting efforts toward reestablishing the natural unity of the country.

2. *Agreements:* Consultation by the Joint US-USSR Commission with "Korean democratic parties and social organizations" in the preparation of proposals for the formation of a provisional Korean government (Moscow agreement, December 27, 1945, III, 2).

Violations: The USSR delegation on the Joint Commission consistently refused to allow such consultation except under unilateral interpretations of the phrase, "democratic parties and social organizations," which interpretation, in each case, would exclude all but pro-Soviet political groups.

D. *Manchuria*

1. *Agreements:* "The high contracting parties agree to render each other every possible economic assistance in the postwar period with a view to facilitating and accelerating reconstruction in both countries and to contributing to the cause of world prosperity" (*Sino-Soviet Treaty* of August 14, 1945, art. VI).

Violations: "Industry (in the three eastern provinces, also known as Manchuria) . . . was directly damaged to the extent of $858,000,000 during Soviet occupancy . . . the greatest part of the damage to the Manchurian industrial complex . . . was primarily due to Soviet removals of equipment" (Department of State press release No. 907 of December 13, 1947).

2. *Agreements:* ". . . in accordance with the spirit of the aforementioned treaty, and in order to put into effect its aims and purposes, the Government of the USSR agrees to render to China moral support and aid in military supplies and other material resources, such support and aid to be entirely given to the National Government as the central government of China."

Violations: The Chinese Government has failed to receive from the USSR since August 14, 1945, the promised military supplies and other material resources. But when Russian troops withdrew from Manchuria, "Chinese Communists in that area appeared with Japanese arms in very substantial quantities . . . the natural assumption is that they were taken with the acquiescence, at least, of the Russians."

3. *Agreement:* "The administration of Dairen shall belong to China" (Agreement concerning Dairen of August 14, 1945).

Violation: Chinese Government troops attempting to enter Manchuria subsequent to the Japanese surrender were denied the right to land at Dairen by the Soviet authorities there and were forced to utilize less advantageous landing points.

Due in large part to Soviet obstructionism, China has up to the present time been unable to establish a Chinese Government administration at Dairen.

The Berlin Crisis

50. REPLY OF THE SOVIET GOVERNMENT TO THE UNITED STATES NOTE OF JULY 6 WHICH PROTESTED AGAINST THE BLOCKADE OF BERLIN*

July 14, 1948

Firstly, the Soviet Government has acquainted itself with the note of the Government of the United States of America of July 6, this year, in which the situation that has at present arisen in Berlin is ascribed to measures taken by the Soviet side. The

* *The New York Times,* July 15, 1948.

Soviet Government cannot agree with this declaration of the Government of the United States and considers the situation that has arisen in Berlin has arisen as a result of the violation by the Governments of the United States of America, Great Britain, and France of an agreed decision adopted by the four powers in relation to Germany and Berlin, expressed in carrying out a separate currency reform, the introduction of special currency notes for the Western sectors of Berlin and a policy of dismembering Germany. . . .

The decisions adopted at the Yalta and Potsdam conferences, as well as the agreement of the four powers on the control machinery in Germany, set as their aim the demilitarization and democratization of Germany, undermining the very basis of German militarism, and prevention of the revival of Germany as an aggressive power, and hence, the conversion of Germany into a peace-loving and democratic state. These agreements stipulate Germany's obligation to pay reparations and thus, even if only partially, to compensate for the damage done to countries that suffered from German aggression.

In accordance with these agreements, the governments of the four powers accepted the responsibility for administering Germany and undertook to determine jointly the status of Germany or of any areas, including Berlin, that are part of the German territory, and conclude a peace treaty with Germany which should be signed by a democratic government of Germany adequate for the purpose.

The highly important agreements by the four powers in relation to Germany have been violated by the Governments of the United States of America, Great Britain, and France. Measures for the demilitarization of Germany have not been completed and such an important center of German war industry as the Ruhr region has been removed from the control of the four powers. Fulfillment of the decision on reparations from the Western zones of occupation of Germany has been disrupted by the Governments of the United States of America, Great Britain, and France. The quadripartite council has ceased to function.

Since the London conference of the three powers with the participation of the Benelux countries, measures are being carried out by the Governments of the United States of America, Great Britain, and France aimed at splitting and dismembering Germany, including the preparation now taking place for the appointment of a separate government for the Western zones of Germany and the separate currency reform carried out June 18 of this year for the Western zones of occupation. . . .

The Soviet Government must reject as altogether unfounded the declaration of the Government of the United States of America to the effect that measures for restricting transport and communications between Berlin and the Western zones of occupation of Germany, introduced by the Soviet command to protect the economy of the Soviet zone from disorganization, allegedly constitute a violation of existing agreements relating to the administration of Berlin.

The Government of the United States declares that it occupies its sector of Berlin by a right deriving from the defeat and surrender of Germany, referring in this connection to the agreement between the four powers in relation to Germany and Berlin. . . .

When the United States, Great Britain, and France, by their separate actions in the Western zones of Germany, destroyed the system of quadripartite administration in Germany and began to create in Frankfort-on-Main a capital for the Government of Western Germany, they thereby undermined also the legal basis on which rested the right to participate in the administration of Berlin.

The Government of the United States points out in its note that its right to stay in Berlin also is based on the fact that the United States withdrew troops from certain areas of the Soviet zone of occupation which they entered during the period of military operations in Germany and that had it foreseen the situation which has arisen in Berlin, it would not have withdrawn its troops from these areas.

However, the Government of the United States knows that by withdrawing its troops to the confines of the United States zone, as established by the four-power agreement on zones of occupation in Germany, it had merely fulfilled the obligations it had undertaken and the fulfillment whereof alone could give the United States the right to take its troops into Berlin. . . .

The Government of the United States declares that temporary measures introduced by the Soviet command for restricting transport and communications between Berlin and the Western zones created difficulties in the supply of the Berlin population in the Western sectors.

It cannot, however, be denied that these difficulties were caused by the actions of the Governments of the United States, Great Britain, and France and, above all, by their separate actions in introducing a new currency in the Western zones of Germany and a special currency in the Western sectors of Berlin.

Berlin is in the center of the Soviet zone and is part of that zone.

The interests of the Berlin population do not admit to a situation where there has been introduced into Berlin, or even only into the Western sectors of Berlin, a currency that is not in circulation in the Soviet zone. Moreover, the introduction of a separate currency reform in the Western zones of Germany placed Berlin, and with it the entire Soviet zone of occupation, in a position where the entire mass of currency notes invalidated by the Western zones threatened to pour into Berlin and into the Soviet occupation zone of Germany.

The Soviet command was compelled, therefore, to adopt urgent measures to safeguard the interest of the population as well as the economy of the Soviet zone of occupation and the area of "Greater Berlin" . . .

The Emergence of Titoism

51. STATEMENT OF THE CENTRAL COMMITTEE OF THE COMMUNIST PARTY OF YUGOSLAVIA ON THE RESOLUTION OF THE INFORMATION BUREAU OF COMMUNIST PARTIES ON THE SITUATION IN THE COMMUNIST PARTY OF YUGOSLAVIA*

June 29, 1948

The Resolution of the Information Bureau "On the Situation in the Communist Party of Yugoslavia" has a previous history, as is obvious from its contents. Its basis lies in a number of letters dispatched by the Central Committee of the Communist Party of the Soviet Union to the Central Committee of the Communist Party of Yugoslavia. The first of these letters, dated 27 March of this year, in which the CC of the CPSU sets forth its accusations against the CC of the CPY, was also simultaneously dispatched

* *The Soviet-Yugoslav Dispute* (London and New York: Oxford University Press for the Royal Institute of International Affairs, 1948), pp. 71–79, *excerpts.* Reprinted by permission of the publisher.

to all other members of the Information Bureau, a fact of which the CC of the CPY had not been informed. . . .

In these letters, the CC of the CPSU accuses the CC of the CPY and demands that it admit its mistakes, as: firstly, that the leading people of the CPY are paying lip service to the USSR while secretly slandering it and the CPSU; secondly, that leading personalities in Yugoslavia are slandering the Soviet army and that specialists from the Soviet Union are surrounded by enmity while Soviet citizens . . . are followed by state security agents; thirdly, that the Party cadres are under the surveillance of the Minister of Internal Affairs and that there is no democracy and criticism within the Party but that it is ruled by a system of military leadership; fourthly, that the Yugoslav Government wishes to get into the good graces of the imperialist countries through spies and to put itself under their control; fifth, that the Party submerges itself within the People's Front and cannot therefore be regarded as a Marxist-Leninist organization . . . ; sixth, that the ambassador of a certain imperialist power behaves as master of the house in Yugoslavia . . . ; seventh, that the Yugoslav leaders identify the foreign policy of the USSR with the foreign policy of the imperialist governments; eighth, that the leading members of the CPY have deviated from the Marxist-Leninist course in the question of the leading role of the working class; ninth, that German parachutists destroyed the "partisan" headquarters in Yugoslavia, that as a result of this a serious crisis ensued in the National Liberation Movement, and that thereafter the Soviet army came to assist, liberated Yugoslavia, and created the conditions which enabled the Communist Party to come to power; tenth, that the CPY has boasted excessively of its successes during the war although its services do not exceed those of the Communist Parties of Poland, Czechoslovakia, Rumania, Hungary, Albania, Bulgaria, etc. . . .

In connection with the publication of the Resolution of the Information Bureau, the Central Committee of the Communist Party of Yugoslavia makes the following statement:

1. The criticism contained in the Resolution is based on inaccurate and unfounded assertions and represents an attempt to destroy the prestige of the CPY both abroad and in the country, to arouse confusion amongst the masses in the country and in the international workers' movement, to weaken the unity within the CPY and its leading role. . . .

2. The Resolution maintains, without citing any proof, that the leadership of the CPY carried out a hostile policy towards the USSR. The statement that Soviet military specialists in Yugoslavia have been treated with scant respect, and that Soviet

civilian citizens have been under the surveillance of state
security agents does not in the least correspond to the truth.
Up to their withdrawal not one of the representatives of the
Soviet Union brought such matters to the attention of the
Yugoslav representatives. That any of the Soviet citizens . . .
were under observation in Yugoslavia, is altogether false. . . .

3. The Resolution criticized the policy of the CPY in regard
to the conduct of the class struggle and particularly the policy
of the CPY in the village. In connection with this, well-known
passages from Lenin are quoted. The CC of the CPY points out
that in its policy of restricting the capitalist elements in the
village, it is guided by the mentioned and similar passages from
Lenin, which the authors of the Resolution—had they taken the
trouble—might have read in the published Party documents and
articles, and might have convinced themselves concerning the
practical execution of this policy. For this reason, the charges
made in the Resolution and by the CC of the CPSU in fact only
knock on an open door; objectively, they inevitably tend to
encourage and support reactionary and capitalist elements in
town and village, and to provoke confusion among the population, as if the CC of the CPY and its policy were to blame for
objective difficulties especially in regard to supply, in the period
of transition from capitalism to socialism. The CC of the CPY
considers that as a method it is impermissible to evaluate its
activities on the basis of individual quotations taken from the
most varied periods of the struggle, or on the basis of individual,
isolated and distorted facts. The CC of the CPY considers that in
assessing the policy of the CPY, as of other Parties, it is the
practice of the Party that must be given primary consideration—
whether the Party scores or does not score successes in the
struggle for the socialist transformation of the country, whether
as a whole the capitalist elements are growing weaker or stronger,
whether the socialist sector of the national economy is growing
weaker or stronger.

4. The CC of the CPY cannot but reject with deep indignation
the assertions that the leading ranks in the CPY are deviating
to the course of a kulak party, to the path of the liquidation of
the Communist Party of Yugoslavia, that there is no democracy
in the Party, that methods of military leadership are fostered
within the Party, that the most basic rights of Party members
are trampled upon in the Party and that the mildest criticism
of irregularities in the Party is answered by sharp reprisals, etc.
Could the members of the Party who dauntlessly faced death in
thousands of battles, tolerate in the Party a state of affairs
unworthy of both men and Communists? . . . The CC of the CPY

emphasizes that because certain Party organizations have not yet held elections it cannot be maintained that there is no democracy within the Party. These are the remnants of the war period and the tempestuous postwar development through which the CPY passed and in their time they were to be found in other parties and in the CPSU as well. . . .

5. The CC of the CPY rejects as unworthy the accusation that a Turkish regime reigns in the CP and that the Yugoslav leaders concealed from the Party the "criticism of the Central Committee's incorrect policy" . . .

6. The CC of the CPY rejects as absurd the assertion that recently the Yugoslav leaders took measures for the nationalization of small-scale industry and small shops in a great hurry and for demagogical reasons. These measures as a matter of fact were prepared six months before the charges made by the CC of the CPSU against the CC of the CPY and are the result of the strengthening and development of the socialist sector . . .

7. The CC of the CPY asserts that none of its leaders considers that Yugoslavia, in the struggle for the building of socialism and the preservation of independence, does not need the help of the countries of people's democracy and the USSR. Only people who have lost all contact with reality could assert anything of the kind. . . . The assertion that the Yugoslav leaders are preparing to make concessions to imperialists and to bargain with them concerning the independence of Yugoslavia is completely invented and is among the most grievous slanders against the new Yugoslavia. . . .

8. The CC of the CPY does not consider that by refusing to discuss the mistakes of which it is not guilty, it has in any way injured the unity of the communist front. The unity of this front is not based on the admission of invented or fabricated errors and slanders, but on the fact of whether or not the policy of a Party is actually internationalist. One cannot, however, ignore the fact that the Information Bureau has committed a breach of the principles on which it was based and which provide for the voluntary adoption of conclusions by every Party. The Informbureau, however, not only forces the leaders of the CPY to admit errors which they did not commit but also calls members of the CPY to rebellion within the Party, to shatter the unity of the Party. The CC of the CPY can never agree to a discussion about its policy on the basis of inventions and uncomradely behavior without mutual confidence. Such a basis is not one of principle and in this and not only in this sense the CC of the CPY considered that it was not on an equal footing in the discussion and that it could not accept discussion on that basis.

Further, in connection with the above, the CC of the CPY resolutely rejects the accusation that the CPY has passed on to positions of nationalism. By its entire internal and foreign policy, and especially by its struggle during the national liberation war and the proper solution of the national question in Yugoslavia, the CPY has given proof of the exact opposite.

By the above-mentioned unjust charges, the greatest historical injustice has been done to our Party, our working class and working masses, the peoples in Yugoslavia in general and their unselfish and heroic struggle. . . .

> The Plenum of the Central Committee
> of the Communist Party of Yugoslavia

Soviet Opposition to NATO

52. MEMORANDUM OF THE SOVIET GOVERNMENT ON THE NORTH ATLANTIC TREATY*

March 31, 1949

On March 18 the State Department of the United States published the text of the North Atlantic Treaty which the Governments of the United States of America, Great Britain, France, Belgium, the Netherlands, Luxemburg, and Canada intend to sign within the next few days.

The text of the North Atlantic Treaty fully confirms what was said in the declaration of the USSR Ministry of Foreign Affairs of January 29 this year, which is being attached hereto, both as regards the aggressive aims of this Treaty and the fact that the North Atlantic Treaty contradicts the principles and aims of the United Nations Organization and the commitments which the Governments of the United States of America, Great Britain, and France have assumed under other Treaties and Agreements. The statements contained in the North Atlantic Treaty, that it is designated for defense and that it recognizes the principles of the United Nations Organization, serve aims which have nothing

* *The New York Times*, April 1, 1949.

in common either with the tasks of self-defense of the parties to the Treaty or with real recognition of the aims and principles of the United Nations Organization. Such great Powers as the United States, Great Britain, and France are parties to the North Atlantic Treaty. Thus the Treaty is not directed either against the United States of America, Great Britain, or France. Of the Great Powers only the Soviet Union is excluded from among the parties to this Treaty, which can be explained only by the fact that this Treaty is directed against the Soviet Union. The fact that the North Atlantic Treaty is directed against the USSR as well as against the countries of people's democracy was definitely pointed out also by official representatives of the United States of America, Great Britain, and France.

To justify the conclusion of the North Atlantic Treaty, references are being made to the fact that the Soviet Union has defensive treaties with the countries of people's democracy. These references, however, are utterly untenable.

All the treaties of the Soviet Union on friendship and mutual assistance with the countries of people's democracy are of a bilateral nature, and they are directed solely against a possible repetition of German aggression, the danger of which not a single peace-loving state can forget. The possibility of interpreting them as treaties which are in any degree aimed against the allies of the USSR in the late war, against the United States or Great Britain or France, is absolutely precluded.

Moreover, the USSR has similar treaties against a repetition of German aggression not only with the countries of people's democracy, but also with Great Britain and France.

In contradistinction to this, the North Atlantic Treaty is not a bilateral, but a multilateral Treaty, which creates a closed grouping of states and, what is particularly important, absolutely ignores the possibility of a repetition of German aggression, consequently not having as its aim the prevention of a new German aggression. And inasmuch as of the Great Powers which comprised the anti-Hitlerite coalition only the USSR is not a party to this Treaty, the North Atlantic Treaty must be regarded as a Treaty directed against one of the chief allies of the United States, Great Britain, and France in the late war, against the USSR. . . .

The preservation in Washington of the combined Anglo-American Staff organized during the Second World War, the recent establishment of the military staff of the so-called Western Union in Fontainebleu (France), as well as the intention immediately to set up the defense committee envisaged by the North Atlantic Treaty, are by no means an indication of the peace-loving or defensive aims of the participants of the Treaty, but, together with other numerous military preparations, contribute to intensifying anxiety and alarm and to the whipping up of war hysteria in which all sorts of instigators of a new war are so interested.

The North Atlantic Pact is designed to intimidate the states which do not agree to obey the dictate of the Anglo-American grouping of Powers that lay claim to world domination, though the bankruptcy of such claims was once again affirmed by the Second World War, which ended in the debacle of Fascist Germany which also had laid claim to world domination.

Among the participants in the North Atlantic Treaty are also countries whose governments expect to benefit at the expense of richer parties to the Treaty and make various plans with regard to obtaining new credits and other material advantages.

At the same time one cannot but see the groundlessness of the anti-Soviet motives of the North Atlantic Treaty, inasmuch as it is known to all that the Soviet Union does not intend to attack anyone and in no way threatens the United States of America, Great Britain, France, or the other parties to the Treaty.

The conclusion of the North Atlantic Treaty and the establishment of the new grouping of Powers is motivated by the weakness of the United Nations Organization. It is perfectly evident, however, that the North Atlantic Treaty does not serve the cause of strengthening the United Nations Organization, but on the contrary leads to undermining the very foundations of this international organization, because the establishment of the above grouping of Powers, far from corresponding to the aims and principles of the United Nations Organization, runs counter to the Charter of this organization.

The parties to the North Atlantic Treaty maintain that this Treaty allegedly represents a regional arrangement envisaged by Article 52 of the United Nations Charter. But such references are utterly groundless and untenable. There can be no question whatsoever of any regional character of this Treaty, inasmuch as the union provided for by this Treaty embraces settlement of any regional issues. This is also confirmed by the fact that, as has already been announced, states which are not members of the United Nations Organization (Italy, Portugal) are being drawn into participation in the North Atlantic Treaty, whereas Article 52 of the United Nations Charter has in view the conclusion of regional arrangements only among members of the United Nations Organization.

Nor can the establishment of the North Atlantic grouping of states be justified by the right of each member of the United

Nations to individual or collective self-defense in conformity with Article 51 of the Charter. Suffice it to say that such a right under the Charter of the United Nations can arise only in the case of armed attack against a member of the organization, whereas, as is known to all, neither the United States of America, Britain, France, nor the other parties to the Pact are threatened by any armed attack.

It is clear that the references to Articles 51 and 52 of the United Nations Charter are untenable and are designed merely to cover up the real aggressive aims of the military grouping of states which is being set up by the conclusion of the North Atlantic Treaty. . . .

On the basis of all the above, the Soviet Government arrives at the following conclusions:

1. The North Atlantic Treaty has nothing in common with the aims of the self-defense of the states who are parties to the Treaty, who are threatened by no one, whom no one intends to attack. On the contrary, this Treaty has an obviously aggressive character and is aimed against the USSR, which fact is not concealed even by official representatives of the states who are parties to the Treaty in their public pronouncements.

2. The North Atlantic Treaty not only does not contribute to the consolidation of peace and international security, which is the duty of all members of the United Nations Organization, but runs directly counter to the principles and aims of the United Nations Charter and leads to undermining the United Nations Organization.

3. The North Atlantic Treaty runs counter to the Treaty between Great Britain and the Soviet Union signed in 1942, under which both states assumed the obligation to cooperate in the maintenance of peace and international security and "not to conclude any alliances and not to participate in any coalitions directed against the other High Contracting Party."

4. The North Atlantic Treaty runs counter to the Treaty between France and the Soviet Union signed in 1944, under which both states assumed the obligation to cooperate in the maintenance of peace and international security and "not to conclude any alliance and not to take part in any coalition directed against one of the High Contracting Parties."

5. The North Atlantic Treaty runs counter to the agreements between the Soviet Union, the United States of America, and Great Britain concluded at the Yalta and Potsdam Conferences, as well as at other conferences of the representatives of these Powers held both during and after the Second World War, under which the United States of America and Great Britain, like the

Soviet Union, assumed the obligation to cooperate in the consolidation of general peace and international security and to contribute to the consolidation of the United Nations Organization.

The Moscow-Peking Axis

53. THE SINO-SOVIET TREATY

February 14, 1950

(A) *The Treaty*

The Presidium of the Supreme Soviet of the Union of Soviet Socialist Republics and the Central People's Government of the People's Republic of China;

Filled with determination jointly to prevent, by the consolidation of friendship and cooperation between the Union of Soviet Socialist Republics and the People's Republic of China, the rebirth of Japanese imperialism and a repetition of aggression on the part of Japan or any other State which should unite in any form with Japan in acts of aggression;

Imbued with the desire to consolidate lasting peace and universal security in the Far East and throughout the world in conformity with the aims and principles of the United Nations Organization;

Profoundly convinced that the consolidation of good neighborly relations and friendship between the Union of Soviet Socialist Republics and the People's Republic of China meets the fundamental interests of the peoples of the Soviet Union and China;

Resolved for this purpose to conclude the present Treaty and appointed as their plenipotentiary representatives:

The Presidium of the Supreme Soviet of the Union of Soviet Socialist Republics—Andrei Yanuaryevich Vyshinsky, Minister of Foreign Affairs of the Union of Soviet Socialist Republics;

The Central People's Government of the People's Republic of China—Chou En-lai, Prime Minister of the State Administrative Council and Minister of Foreign Affairs of China;

Who, after exchange of their credentials, found in due form and good order, agreed upon the following:

ARTICLE I

Both High Contracting Parties undertake jointly to take all the necessary measures at their disposal for the purpose of preventing a repetition of aggression and violation of peace on the part of Japan or any other State which should unite with Japan, directly or indirectly, in acts of aggression. In the event of one of the High Contracting Parties being attacked by Japan or States allied with it, and thus being involved in a state of war, the other High Contracting Party will immediately render military and other assistance with all the means at its disposal.

The High Contracting Parties also declare their readiness in the spirit of sincere cooperation, to participate in all international actions aimed at ensuring peace and security throughout the world, and will do all in their power to achieve the speediest implementation of these tasks.

ARTICLE II

Both the High Contracting Parties undertake by means of mutual agreement to strive for the earliest conclusion of a peace treaty with Japan, jointly with the other Powers which were allies during the Second World War.

ARTICLE III

Both High Contracting Parties undertake not to conclude any alliance directed against the other High Contracting Party, and not to take part in any coalition or in actions or measures directed against the other High Contracting Party.

ARTICLE IV

Both High Contracting Parties will consult each other in regard to all important international problems affecting the common interests of the Soviet Union and China, being guided by the interests of the consolidation of peace and universal security.

ARTICLE V

Both the High Contracting Parties undertake, in the spirit of friendship and cooperation and in conformity with the principles of equality, mutual interests, and also mutual respect for the State sovereignty and territorial integrity and noninterference in internal affairs of the other High Contracting Party—to develop and consolidate economic and cultural ties between the Soviet Union and China, to render each other every possible economic assistance, and to carry out the necessary economic cooperation.

ARTICLE VI

The present Treaty comes into force immediately upon its

ratification; the exchange of instruments of ratification will take place in Peking.

The present Treaty will be valid for 30 years. If neither of the High Contracting Parties gives notice one year before the expiration of this term of its desire to denounce the Treaty, it shall remain in force for another five years and will be extended in compliance with this rule.

Done in Moscow on February 14, 1950, in two copies, each in the Russian and Chinese languages, both texts having equal force.

Signed: *By Authorization of the Presidium of the Supreme Soviet of the Union of Soviet Socialist Republics—*
A. Y. Vyshinsky.

By Authorization of the Central People's Government of the People's Republic of China—Chou En-lai.

(B) An Agreement on the Chinese Changchun Railway, Port Arthur, and Dalny

The Presidium of the Supreme Soviet of the Union of Soviet Socialist Republics and the Central People's Government of the People's Republic of China state that since 1945 radical changes have occurred in the situation in the Far East, namely: Imperialist Japan suffered defeat; the reactionary Kuomintang Government was overthrown; China has become a People's Democratic Republic, and in China a new, People's Government was formed which has united the whole of China, carried out a policy of friendship and cooperation with the Soviet Union and proved its ability to defend the State independence and territorial integrity of China, the national honor and dignity of the Chinese people.

The Presidium of the Supreme Soviet of the Union of Soviet Socialist Republics and the Central People's Government of the People's Republic of China maintain that this new situation permits a new approach to the question of the Chinese Changchun Railway, Port Arthur, and Dalny.

In conformity with these new circumstances, the Presidium of the Supreme Soviet of the Union of Soviet Socialist Republics and the Central People's Government of the People's Republic of China have decided to conclude the present agreement on the Chinese Changchun Railway, Port Arthur, and Dalny.

ARTICLE I

Both High Contracting Parties have agreed that the Soviet

Government transfers gratis to the Government of the People's Republic of China all its rights in the joint administration of the Chinese Changchun Railway, with all the property belonging to the Railway. The transfer will be effected immediately upon the conclusion of a peace treaty with Japan, but not later than the end of 1952.

Pending the transfer, the now existing position of the Soviet-Chinese joint administration of the Chinese Changchun Railway remains unchanged; however, the order of filling posts by representatives of the Soviet and Chinese sides, upon the coming into force of the present Agreement, will be changed, and there will be established an alternating filling of posts for a definite period of time (Director of the Railway, Chairman of the Central Board, and others).

As regards concrete methods of effecting the transfer, they will be agreed upon and determined by the Governments of both High Contracting Parties.

ARTICLE II

Both High Contracting Parties have agreed that Soviet troops will be withdrawn from the jointly utilized naval base of Port Arthur and that the installations in this area will be handed over to the Government of the People's Republic of China immediately upon the conclusion of a peace treaty with Japan, but not later than the end of 1952, with the Government of the People's Republic of China compensating the Soviet Union for expenses incurred in the restoration and construction of installations affected by the Soviet Union since 1945.

For the period pending the withdrawal of Soviet troops and the transfer of the above installations, the Governments of the Soviet Union and China will appoint an equal number of military representatives for organizing a joint Chinese-Soviet Military Commission which will be in charge of military affairs in the area of Port Arthur; concrete measures in this sphere will be determined by the joint Chinese-Soviet Military Commission within three months upon the coming into force of the present Agreement and shall be implemented upon the approval of these measures by the Governments of both countries.

The civil administration in the aforementioned area shall be in direct charge of the Government of the People's Republic of China. Pending the withdrawal of Soviet troops, the zone of billetting of Soviet troops in the area of Port Arthur will remain unaltered in conformity with the now existing frontiers.

In the event of either of the High Contracting Parties being subjected to aggression on the part of Japan or any State which should unite with Japan and as a result of this being involved in military operations, China and the Soviet Union may, on the proposal of the Government of the People's Republic of China and with the agreement of the Soviet Government, jointly use the naval base of Port Arthur in the interests of conducting joint military operations against the aggressor.

ARTICLE III

Both High Contracting Parties have agreed that the question of Port Dalny must be further considered upon the conclusion of a peace treaty with Japan.

As regards the administration in Dalny, it fully belongs to the Government of the People's Republic of China.

All property now existing in Dalny provisionally in charge of or under lease to the Soviet side, is to be taken over by the Government of the People's Republic of China. For carrying out work involved in the receipt of the aforementioned property, the Governments of the Soviet Union and China appoint three representatives from each side for organizing a joint commission which in the course of three months after the coming into force of the present agreement shall determine the concrete methods of transfer of property, and after approval of the proposals of the Joint Commission by the Governments of both countries will complete their implementation in the course of 1950.

ARTICLE IV

The present agreement comes into force on the day of its ratification. The exchange of instruments of ratification will take place in Peking.

Done in Moscow on February 14, 1950, in two copies, each in the Russian and Chinese languages, both texts having equal force.

Signed: *By Authorization of the Presidium of the Supreme Soviet of the Union of Soviet Socialist Republics—*
A. Y. Vyshinsky.

By Authorization of the Central People's Government of the People's Republic of China—Chou En-lai.

(c)   An Agreement on the Granting of Credits by the USSR to China

In connection with the consent of the Government of the Union of Soviet Socialist Republics to grant the request of the Central People's Republic of China on giving China credits for paying for equipment and other materials which the Soviet Union has agreed to deliver to China, both Governments have agreed upon the following:

ARTICLE I

The Government of the Union of Soviet Socialist Republics grants the Central People's Government of the People's Republic of China credits, calculated in dollars, amounting to 300 million American dollars, taking 35 American dollars to one ounce of fine gold.

In view of the extreme devastation of China as a result of prolonged hostilities on its territory, the Soviet Government has agreed to grant credits on favorable terms of 1 per cent annual interest.

ARTICLE II

The credits mentioned in Article I will be granted in the course of five years, as from January 1, 1950, in equal portions of one-fifth of the credits in the course of each year, for payments for deliveries from the USSR of equipment and materials, including equipment for electric power stations, metallurgical and engineering plants, equipment for mines for the production of coal and ores, railway and other transport equipment, rails and other material for the restoration and development of the national economy of China.

The assortment, quantities, prices and dates of deliveries of equipment and materials will be determined under a special agreement of the Parties; prices will be determined on the basis of prices obtaining on the world markets.

Any credits which remain unused in the course of one annual period may be used in subsequent annual periods.

ARTICLE III

The Central People's Government of the People's Republic of China repays the credits mentioned in Article I, as well as interest on them, with deliveries of raw materials, tea, gold, American dollars. Prices for raw materials and tea, quantities and dates of deliveries will be determined on the basis of prices obtaining on the world markets.

Repayment of credits is effected in the course of ten years in equal annual parts—one-tenth yearly of the sum total of received credits not later than December 31 of every year. The first payment is effected not later than December 31, 1954, and the last on December 31, 1963.

Payment of interest on credits, calculated from the day of drawing the respective fraction of the credits, is effected every six months.

ARTICLE IV

For clearance with regard to the credits envisaged by the present agreement the State Bank of the USSR and National Bank of the People's Republic of China shall open special accounts and jointly establish the order of clearance and accounting under the present agreement.

ARTICLE V

The present agreement comes into force on the day of its signing and is subject to ratification. The exchange of instruments of ratification will take place in Peking.

Done in Moscow on February 14, 1950, in two copies, each in the Russian and Chinese languages, both texts having equal force.

Signed: *By Authorization of the Government of the Union of Soviet Socialist Republics—A. Y. Vyshinsky.*

By Authorization of the Central People's Government of the People's Republic of China—Chou En-lai.

Aggression in Korea

54. EXCHANGE OF VIEWS BETWEEN THE UNITED STATES AND THE SOVIET UNION REGARDING THE INVASION OF SOUTH KOREA*

(A) *Aide-Memoire from the United States Government Delivered to the Soviet Deputy Foreign Minister by the United States Ambassador, June 27, 1950:*

My Government has instructed me to call to your attention the fact that North Korean forces have crossed the 38th parallel and invaded the territory of the Republic of Korea in force at several points. The refusal of the Soviet Representative to attend the

* *United States Policy in the Korean Crisis* (Washington, D.C.: Department of State, 1950), pp. 63–64, *excerpts.*

United Nations Security Council meeting on June 25, despite the clear threat to peace and the obligations of a Security Council member under the Charter, requires the Government of the United States to bring this matter directly to the attention of the Union of Soviet Socialist Republics. In view of the universally known fact of the close relations between the Union of Soviet Socialist Republics and the North Korean regime, the United States Government asks assurance that the Union of Soviet Socialist Republics disavows responsibility for this unprovoked and unwarranted attack, and that it will use its influence with the North Korean authorities to withdraw their invading forces immediately.

(B) *The Soviet Reply, June 29, 1950:*

1. In accordance with facts verified by the Soviet Government, the events taking place in Korea were provoked by an attack by forces of the South Korean authorities on border regions of North Korea. Therefore, the responsibility for these events rests upon the South Korean authorities and upon those who stand behind their back.

2. As is known, the Soviet Government withdrew its troops from Korea earlier than the Government of the United States and thereby confirmed its traditional principle of noninterference in the internal affairs of other states. And now as well the Soviet Government adheres to the principle of the impermissibility of interference by foreign powers in the internal affairs of Korea.

3. It is not true that the Soviet Government refused to participate in meetings of the Security Council. In spite of its full willingness, the Soviet Government has not been able to take part in the meetings of the Security Council inasmuch as, because of the position of the Government of the United States, China, a permanent member of the Security Council, has not been admitted to the Council, which has made it impossible for the Security Council to take decisions having legal force.

FOR FURTHER STUDY

Beloff, Max, *Soviet Policy in the Far East, 1944–1951*. New York: Oxford University Press, 1953.

Davison, W. Phillips, *The Berlin Blockade: A Study in Cold War Politics*. Princeton, N.J.: Princeton University Press, 1958.

Kennedy, Sir Malcolm, *A History of Communism in East Asia*. New York: Frederick A. Praeger, 1957.

Kertesz, Stephen D., *The Fate of East Central Europe: Hopes and Failures of American Foreign Policy*. Notre Dame, Ind.: University of Notre Dame Press, 1956.

Korbel, Josef, *The Communist Subversion of Czechoslovakia*. Princeton, N.J.: Princeton University Press, 1959.

MacVicker, Charles P., *Titoism: Pattern for International Communism*. New York: St. Martin's Press, 1957.

Nettle, J. P., *Eastern Zone and Soviet Policy in Germany*. New York: Oxford University Press, 1951.

Seton-Watson, Hugh, *The East European Revolution*. New York: Frederick A. Praeger, 1951.

Shepherd, Gordon, *Russia's Danubian Empire*. London: William Heinemann, 1954.

Shulman, Marshall D., *Stalin's Foreign Policy Reappraised*. Cambridge, Mass.: Harvard University Press, 1963.

Ulam, Adam B., *Titoism and the Cominform*. Cambridge, Mass.: Harvard University Press, 1952.

Whiting, Allen S., *China Crosses the Yalu: The Decision to Enter the Korean War*. New York: The Macmillan Company, 1960.

Wolff, Robert Lee, *The Balkans in Our Time*. Cambridge, Mass.: Harvard University Press, 1956.

CHAPTER VIII

THE KHRUSHCHEV ERA AND AFTER

Since 1953, three major developments have strengthened Soviet power: the effective stabilization of empire in Eastern Europe; a steady economic and military growth; and the dramatic penetration into the politically vulnerable developing areas. The global balance of power has shifted perceptibly toward the Communist world and made "coexistence" more than ever the prerogative of the Kremlin. Though the extent of the Soviet empire has not increased since the death of Stalin, the international position of the Soviet Union has improved considerably.

First, during the 1953–1956 period, the Kremlin began to decentralize its Eastern European empire. This tentative easing of Moscow's iron grip reflected the struggle for power then being waged within the Soviet leadership. But the Polish and Hungarian revolutions of October-November 1956, confronting Soviet leaders with the prospective disintegration of their empire, forced them to reimpose their control. Soon thereafter, aware that further nationalist, anti-Communist, anti-Russian eruptions might jeopardize the entire Soviet military position in Eastern Europe, Moscow acceded to the demands of Communist "nationalists" and agreed to ever-larger measures of local autonomy. Additional concessions have been granted since 1961 in order to retain support in the sharpening rift with Peking. Thus, Moscow overcame the first serious threat of disintegration and separatism within Eastern Europe by relinquishing, albeit reluctantly, much of its former imperial control over the domestic affairs of the satellites and allowing them to settle their own intra-Party struggles and to evolve their road to socialism, in return for recognition of the primacy of Soviet military and strategic interests in the area.

Second, Soviet economic and military strength has expanded enormously. The increased nuclear and missile capabilities are particularly impressive; with Sputnik in 1957 and the Cosmonaut Gagarin in 1961, the USSR launched the space age. The diplomatic implications of these military achievements are evident: Moscow's confident approach to international problems reflects, in part, its growing sense of superiority in military technology.

Third, Soviet influence has mushroomed in the regions lying south of the Soviet Union—the developing areas of the Middle East, Southern Asia, and Africa. The death of Stalin hastened the injection of flexibility, imagination, and vigor into Soviet foreign relations. This new diplomacy, foreshadowed by Stalin's last public statement at the Nineteenth Party Congress in October 1952, has nowhere been more evident, or successful, than in the uncommitted areas of the world. Soviet interest in these areas—and, conversely, the significance of these regions for Soviet foreign policy—must now be regarded as a permanent feature of the continuing Cold War (a detailed treatment of this phase of Soviet policy is given in Chapter XI).

Stalin left no obvious successor. To effect an orderly transition of power, the Soviet leaders revived the principle of "collective leadership." Except in the Beria affair, shifts at the top have thus far been accomplished without recourse to the terror of the Stalinist period. Rather, the struggle for power remains bloodless, a reflection of the changing, more sophisticated nature of Soviet totalitarianism.

During the 1953–1956 period, the Soviet leaders, eager to establish the "legitimacy" of their rule, reassured the various privileged groups (such as the Party, the military, and the technocracy) whose support is essential for the stability of the regime, that their status and security would remain unimpaired —would indeed be enhanced. Further, a series of "involuntary" economic, demographic, social, and political pressures arising out of the nature of contemporary Soviet society itself impelled the leadership to disengage itself from the oppressive, inefficient aspects of the Stalinist legacy. In Eastern Europe this took the form of removing "Stalinists" from power, of granting limited autonomy within the framework of Soviet control, and of seeking a rapprochement with Tito.

Stalin's postwar objectives had been relatively clearcut: to eliminate Western influence from Eastern Europe and, concomitantly, to establish Moscow's dominion over the area; to undermine Western recovery through the manipulation of local Communist Parties; and finally, to weaken NATO, forestall West Germany's entrance into the Western coalition, and effect a withdrawal of American power from Europe. Except for the first, which admittedly was most important at the time, Stalin failed to achieve these objectives.

His successors, however, were faced with more subtle challenges: to preserve yet decentralize the Soviet empire, to obtain Western acceptance of the permanence of Soviet domination over Eastern Europe, and to expand Soviet power where possible without jeopardizing the security of the USSR. They were also confronted with the formidable task of coordinating strategy and maintaining the alliance with Communist China. They soon discovered that to preserve an empire is more difficult than to acquire one. Not only do the techniques of rule differ from those of revolution, but the price of empire may prove so exorbitant that it weakens the structure of power within the metropolitan country itself. To avoid this, Soviet leaders sought to perpetuate their Eastern European empire within a moderately decentralized framework designed to increase the economic productivity and political-military reliability of their satellites. They granted varying degrees of local autonomy, revised Soviet-satellite economic relations along less exploitative lines, and encouraged modest improvements in living standards.

The first satellite challenge to Soviet rule broke out in June 1953: a wave of riots swept East Berlin and parts of Soviet-occupied Germany. The West was unable or unwilling to hazard the consequences of intervention. Accordingly, the Soviets quickly and brutally suppressed the outbreaks. The danger of the situation, however, was not lost on Moscow. The Kremlin understood that in East Germany, as elsewhere in Eastern Europe, the problem was to chart a course between the Scylla of Stalinism on the one hand and the Charybdis of widespread convulsions stemming from a too rapid easing of controls on the other. In Moscow, Beria was purged, and Soviet leaders adopted a series of measures designed to mollify the undercurrents of discontent.

Through most of 1953 and 1954 intra-Communist-bloc problems preoccupied the Kremlin. To decrease the likelihood of effective pressure from the West and to sow discord among the NATO nations, Soviet leaders held out prospects of a respite from the Cold War. They also moved to make the Korean conflict less incendiary, thereby extricating themselves from an uncomfortable position and at the same time gaining favorable international response to the "new look" in Soviet policy. A truce agreement was concluded on July 27, 1953. Thus began an effort to liquidate the liabilities bequeathed by Stalin. It enabled the Soviet Government to reduce the economic-military drain on its economy, return the East-West conflict to the political arena, and provide the Chinese Communists with time to consolidate their power on the mainland. It also permitted the Kremlin to placate its people and strengthen the unity of the Communist world.

On August 9, 1953, Premier Malenkov announced the government's intention to allocate more resources to satisfy consumer needs. His foreign policy statement also hinted at a departure from the uncompromising hostility of Stalin. Changes were soon perceptible in the satellites. Though varying in degree and scope from country to country, the innovations followed a similar pattern: forced collectivization was halted; prices of staples were cut; the more oppressive features of the labor and criminal codes were changed; and most of the joint-stock companies were dissolved. Modest concessions to satellite discontent in the political sphere were also noticeable: Communist leaders too closely identified as "Stalinists" were removed; the omnipotence of the Party seemed to be subtly de-emphasized in favor of greater governmental authority and attention to "socialist legality"; and the attacks on Tito subsided.

In another important policy reversal, Moscow started to court Tito in earnest. A barter agreement was concluded in September 1954, ending the Cominform's economic blockade. The Khrushchev-Bulganin-Mikoyan visit to Belgrade in May 1955 highlighted the Soviet effort to "normalize" relations. Khrushchev appealed for a full resumption of relations between Yugoslavia and the Soviet Union, blithely blaming the rift on Beria and avoiding any allusion to continuing ideological-political differences. Upon the signing of a joint governmental declaration a few days later, a rapprochement appeared well under way—though significantly a comparable statement on Party accord was not agreed upon until Tito's visit to the USSR in June 1956. At that time Moscow formally subscribed to the concept that there were "many roads to socialism." Another trade agreement was negotiated in September 1955, and the Soviet Government also granted Yugoslavia a 54-million-dollar credit for the purchase of Soviet goods, as well as a 30-million-dollar credit.

The errant Tito's return to the fold was a necessary step for the Kremlin in the reconstitution of the formal unity of the Communist world. It hoped thereby to blunt the appeal of "Titoism" in Eastern Europe and to reduce that potentially disruptive

force to relative impotence. Moscow further sought to reconcile
loyalty to the Soviet Union with the desire of many Eastern
European Communists for greater national autonomy.

Short of this goal, the Soviet leaders hoped to weaken Yugoslav ties
with the West, eliminate the military usefulness of the Balkan Pact
(with Greece and Turkey), and gain more opportunities for increasing
Soviet influence over the regime. The rapprochement also harmonized
with the then current Soviet policy of attaining cooperation with the
respectable socialist parties of the West, demonstrating to the world
Moscow's reasonableness and flexibility, and of encouraging neutralist
tendencies in the free world by demonstrating that the USSR was not
a threat against which an unaligned country needed to seek protection
by joining the other bloc.[1]

The rapprochement was also consistent with the general pattern
developing in the Soviet Union during this period. But this
promising restoration of Yugoslav-Soviet unity lasted only until
late 1956, when the aftermaths of the Hungarian revolution, the
support by Communist China of Moscow's line in Eastern Europe,
and the introduction of neo-Stalinism in the USSR again alienated Belgrade from Moscow.

In the spring of 1955, Soviet leaders also reversed their
position on Austria. Their previous insistence that an Austrian
peace treaty be linked with settlement of the German question
had accounted, in part, for the failure of the 1954 Berlin Foreign
Ministers Conference. However the Soviet Government in March
1955 unexpectedly dropped its demand for a German treaty and
reinstituted negotiations to end the occupation of Austria. The
result, the Austrian treaty signed on May 15, 1955, committed
Austria to a policy of nonalignment with either bloc. In return,
Austria's "neutral" status was to be recognized and guaranteed
by the Great Powers.

The treaty was significant because it marked the first voluntary
postwar withdrawal by the Soviet leaders from an established
position in the center of Europe. Moscow's policy of amiability
extended to other areas. For example, the Soviet Union renounced
all claims against Turkey, attempted to promote closer relations
with Greece, moved to settle its differences with Iran, and began
to participate actively in the economic development and technical
assistance operations of the various United Nations specialized
agencies and economic commissions. The West's hopes for a
settlement of the major Cold War issues rose, as a meeting of
the heads of state of the Soviet Union, the United States, Great
Britain, and France was called in Geneva in July 1955.

Meanwhile, in Asia, the Kremlin was especially attentive to
Communist China. In October 1954, Khrushchev and Bulganin

visited Peking and negotiated a series of new economic and
political agreements that more accurately reflected China's growing stature within the Communist world (reading 55). These
agreements led to the withdrawal of Soviet forces from Port
Arthur in May 1955, the acknowledgment of Chinese hegemony
in Manchuria and Sinkiang and, with the dissolution of the
joint-stock companies, the end of visible Soviet economic control
in China. Trade and technical assistance arrangements were also
expanded. Though Moscow was still the senior partner of the
alliance, Peking's voice received an increasingly respectful hear-
ing in matters of international Communist strategy. China also
acquired added prestige as a result of the stalemate and subsequent armistice in Korea, the settlement of the war in French
Indo-China in 1954, and the brilliant diplomacy displayed by
Foreign Minister Chou En-lai at the Bandung Conference of
April 1955. The growing importance of China in Asian and
international affairs is a trend that the Soviets were quick to
notice, and for a time, seemingly to accept.

At the Geneva Summit Conference (July 1955) Khrushchev
offered to institutionalize the status quo in Europe and to enter
into "competitive coexistence" with the West in the developing
areas. He agreed to push the search for agreement on disarmament (see Chapter IX). To lessen international tension, the Soviet
Union offered minor compromises in marginal areas—the return
of the Porkkala naval base to Finland and the withdrawal from
eastern Austria. But it was not ready seriously to negotiate any
of the major questions of the Cold War; it was not prepared to
yield any of its Eastern European empire, nor to compromise
on German unification. In fact, it wanted mainly time in order
to expand its program of domestic development and to delay
Germany's rearmament and effective integration into the NATO
alliance. In another maneuver, Moscow sought to undermine the
Western alliance system by suggesting that NATO and the
nations of the Warsaw Pact—the Communist counterpart of
NATO established in May 1955—be fused into an over-all European security system. It is questionable whether Soviet leaders
ever expected the West seriously to entertain such a proposal.
But they did succeed in nurturing the image of Soviet "reasonableness" and in starting a series of diplomatic exchanges.
Thus, in September 1955, West German Chancellor Adenauer
visited Moscow and agreed to establish diplomatic relations
between Bonn and Moscow; in March 1956 Malenkov visited
Great Britain, followed the next month by Bulganin (who had
succeeded Malenkov as Premier in February 1955) and Khrushchev.

Soviet "manners" might have changed; however, Soviet objectives had not. The rapprochement with Tito and the conciliatory attitude toward the European and Asian Socialists paved the way for another diplomatic offensive, this time aimed southward and eastward. The Soviet sale of arms to Egypt in September 1955 dispelled much of the good will cultivated at Geneva and signaled an intensified Soviet effort to undermine the Western position in the Middle East. An unsettling variable had been introduced into an already delicate equation. This Soviet initiative, combined with the continued refusal to accept the principle of free German elections or the right of a unified Germany to order its own international relations and choose its own allies, doomed the October-November Foreign Ministers Conference to failure. The stalemate in Europe persisted. But in Southern Asia, the prestige of the USSR soared as Khrushchev and Bulganin toured the region. Their visits dramatized the increased post-Stalinist awareness of the important role these countries (Afghanistan, Burma, India) could play in improving the international position of the Soviet Union. An area once dominated by the West was now to be used to weaken it. As Soviet diplomacy acquired a more dynamic orientation, the dimensions of the Cold War increased.

Perhaps the most spectacular incident of the post-Stalin period occurred at the Twentieth Party Congress of the CPSU in February 1956: in a "secret" speech Khrushchev denounced Stalin for his "crimes" and self-deification. Yet even as the assault on the former demigod of international communism spread, and "de-Stalinization" gathered momentum, a chain of events was under way that threatened not only the Soviet empire, but the structure of power in the Soviet Union itself, and led to a partial return to Stalinism before the year was over.

In his discussion of foreign policy, Khrushchev introduced several significant doctrinal shifts affecting the Kremlin's approach to world affairs (reading 4). First, while affirming the Leninist dogma of the irreconcilability of capitalism and socialism, he stated that *war* between the two systems is not inevitable. According to Khrushchev, the changed balance of world power and the influence of the developing areas have made it possible for peace to be preserved and the "schemes of war-makers" thwarted. Second, Khrushchev accepted the Titoist contention that there are several roads to socialism, thereby creating a theoretical basis for closer cooperation not only with Yugoslavia but also with the socialist parties of Western Europe. Perhaps even more important, the Kremlin hoped to cultivate better relations between the Soviet Union and the nationalist movements of Asia, Africa, and the Middle East. Third, Communists were encouraged to seek power, where and when possible, through peaceful, parliamentary means in democratic countries. The stage was set for an attempted return to the "Popular Front" era. To substantiate these statements, reassure Tito, and further dissociate itself from the Stalinist foreign policy approach, the Kremlin dissolved the Cominform in April 1956. The Cominform attributed the action to:

(a) The modifications that have taken place in the international situation in the last few years;
(b) The emergence of socialism from the confines of a single country and its transformation into a world system;
(c) The formation of a vast "peace zone" that includes European and Asian states, socialist and non-socialist friends of peace;
(d) The development and strengthening of many Communist parties in the capitalist, dependent, and colonial countries; and, finally,
(e) The tasks of overcoming the splits in the working class movement and the reinforcement of working class unity to bring success in the struggle for peace and socialism.[2]

Soviet leaders also strengthened their alliance with Peking. China was not yet accorded full equality in formulating Communist-bloc policy, but its views received increasingly respectful consideration in Kremlin councils. During the Polish crisis and the early days of the Hungarian revolution, Peking apparently reacted sympathetically to these gropings for greater autonomy. Indeed, developments in Eastern Europe may have prompted Mao's attempt to mollify the restive Chinese intelligentsia with the ill-fated "Hundred Flowers" campaign. (Initiated in February 1957, this campaign was designed primarily to encourage self-criticism within the Chinese Communist Party. However, the flood of bitter denunciations forced a return to orthodoxy and unquestioning obedience to Party policy within six months.)

Eastern Europe

The period in 1956 between the Twentieth Party Congress in February and the revolutions in Poland and Hungary in the summer and fall marked the high point of the post-Stalinist "thaw" in Soviet domestic and foreign policy. An unwary Kremlin, intent on de-Stalinization, sanctioned a modest program of "liberalization" in the satellites and thus unwittingly released turbulent anti-Russian, nationalistic currents. The result was the most massive uprising against Soviet rule ever witnessed. Shaking the very foundations of the Soviet empire in Eastern Europe, it led to a neo-Stalinist revival and to some serious second thoughts by Soviet leaders on the permanence of their position in Eastern Europe.

Riots broke out in Poznan, Poland, in June 1956. Smoldering resentment against a decade of economic privation and Soviet domination, sparked by Khrushchev's "revelations," flared into widespread denunciations of the Moscow-controlled government and secret police. The Poles' traditional hatred of Russia erupted. The Kremlin realized the gravity of the situation and grudgingly made concessions. It permitted the ouster of many known Stalinists from the Central Committee of the Polish United Workers' (Communist) Party and in October 1956 accepted the Polish Communists' choice of Wladyslav Gomulka, a national Communist who had spent several years in prison for his opposition to Stalin, as Party Secretary. Moscow also publicly reaffirmed Poland's "sovereignty and independence," agreed not to interfere in Polish domestic affairs, and withdrew Soviet Marshal Rokossovsky as head of Poland's armed forces. Trade and financial relations were adjusted to Poland's advantage, and Soviet troops were "permitted" by special agreement to remain in Poland pending a settlement of the German question. Yet despite this greater independence in internal affairs, Poland remains inevitably influenced in important foreign policy decisions by its powerful Communist neighbor. The Soviet troops in East Germany (and in Poland itself), as well as Poland's deep-rooted fear of the claims of a revived, expansionist Germany to the territories east of the Oder-Neisse line, which are now incorporated into Poland, are levers to assure the continued adherence of Poland to the Soviet bloc. Indeed, the possibility of another Soviet-German "understanding" at the expense of Poland, as in 1939, is a pervasive, though rarely voiced, Polish phobia.

Meanwhile, events in Hungary took a tragic turn. Matyas Rakosi, a confirmed Stalinist and long-time ruler of Hungary, had been deposed in June 1956, but his successor, Ernö Gerö, refused to compromise sufficiently to lessen the mounting popular pressure for change. On October 23, revolution erupted in Budapest. Anti-Communist and anti-Soviet, it threatened the entire Soviet position in Central Europe. Moscow tried to maintain Communist rule, but it could not resolve this challenge as it had the one in Poland. The Hungarians wanted too much, too quickly. They sought to withdraw from the Warsaw Pact, end the political monopoly of the Communist Party, and liquidate all vestiges of Soviet rule. Confronted with the imminent loss of Hungary and disintegration elsewhere in Eastern Europe, Moscow hurled 250,000 troops and 5,000 tanks against the Hungarians on November 4, after a ruse had betrayed key Hungarian military leaders into Soviet hands. Though the Hungarians resisted valiantly, they were no match for Soviet power.

The United Nations General Assembly called upon the Soviet Government "to desist from its intervention in the internal affairs of Hungary, to withdraw its forces from Hungary, and to cease its repression of the Hungarian people." The Soviets ignored UN and Western protests. The coincidence of the Suez and Hungarian crises was unfortunate. Though the UN was able, through the temporary coalescence of Soviet-American policy on Suez, to end the Middle Eastern hostilities, no similar power and prestige could be marshaled on behalf of Hungary. As the Soviets ruthlessly overwhelmed the Hungarians, the West watched, helpless to intervene for fear of precipitating World War III. This "moment of truth" for the West tragically emphasized what Raymond Aron has described as "the unwritten law of the atomic age": that the Soviet Union can do as it pleases within its sphere of influence without fear of retaliation. And Hungary is part of that sphere.

But the Kremlin learned several bitter lessons. First, Soviet control in Eastern Europe can be preserved only if backed by the Red Army. Second, nationalism remains strong, even among avowed Communists. Third, authority once weakened cannot easily be reimposed. Fourth, a *sine qua non* for the continued political and military adherence of East European countries to the Warsaw Pact is acceptance of a substantial measure of economic and cultural diversity and autonomy. Moscow has refrained from reimposing forcibly its previously unquestioned rule and has settled for leadership in the realm of foreign policy. Eastern Europe can no longer be considered an unquestioned asset to the Soviets. Strategically, it remains important; and Moscow will undoubtedly resist any attempt, either by the West or by the satellites themselves, to dislodge Soviet influence and control. On the other hand, the area represents a material and military drain on Soviet resources; the reliability of Eastern European troops remains a continual question mark; and Eastern European nationalism, a force too often slighted, increases the strains of Moscow rule. Finally, Soviet prestige, especially among influential Western European intellectuals, suffered a sharp setback as a consequence of the Hungarian episode. The nations of the Afro-Asian bloc also expressed varying degrees of disappointment and alarm at Soviet policy, though generally they were far more sensitive and outraged over the British-French attack on Egypt, a country only recently emerged from colonial bondage, with which they felt close emotional ties. The "remoteness" of Hungary blunted their concern and indignation. Still, the 1956 crises in Eastern Europe showed that the Soviet Union continues to regard the area as vital to its security and is prepared to use force if necessary to preserve its dominance.

The Soviet Government took advantage of tensions in the Middle East and of disagreements within NATO over Suez (as well as over Cyprus and North Africa) to undertake an extensive diplomatic and propaganda campaign aimed at promoting Soviet prestige in the developing countries of the world and at undermining Western unity. While acting with a belligerency reminiscent of the Stalinist era, Moscow continued to play upon the theme of peaceful coexistence. During 1957–1958, and particularly after the launching of Sputnik in October 1957, it sent a series of notes to the various NATO nations warning them of the dangers of permitting American atomic and missile bases on their territory. In the UN Disarmament Commission, Soviet delegates raised the possibility of a military "disengagement" in Central Europe, proposing a demilitarized zone of 400 kilometers on either side of the Elbe, complete with aerial and other inspection procedures. Several variants of this proposal have been suggested: In October 1957 Polish Foreign Minister Rapacki called for the establishment of a nuclear-free area which would include Poland, East and West Germany, and Czechoslovakia. The West has thus far opposed such plans on the grounds that nuclear weapons constitute the first line of defense against Soviet attack, that inspection would be too uncertain in the present political situation, and that such an arrangement avoids a solution of the key European problem—the future of Germany.

In November 1957, the leaders of international communism met in Moscow to celebrate the fortieth anniversary of the Bolshevik revolution. A "Declaration of Unity" was issued which reaffirmed the solidarity of the socialist camp "headed by the Soviet Union," "the first and mightiest socialist power" in the Communist world. It implicitly acknowledged the disruptive effect of national communism, attacked "revisionism" (the sin of independent thinking by Communist leaders who disagree with the Moscow-promulgated party line), and emphasized the unity of the Communist world. Tito, however, refused to sign the declaration—an indication of the brittleness of Belgrade's accommodation with Moscow. He had supported Khrushchev's policy in Hungary partially out of fear that the "counter-revolutionary fever" might spread to Yugoslavia, but primarily out of a desire to bolster Khrushchev in curbing the influence of the "Stalinists" in the Kremlin. The November declaration undoubtedly disillusioned Tito, as did the abrupt dismissal of Marshal Zhukov from the CPSU Presidium in October immediately following his visit to Yugoslavia. In December 1957, the Soviet press initiated an intensive antirevisionist campaign designed to restore ideological conformity in the Communist world. Pressure against the Yugoslavs mounted, particularly after publication of their new program in April 1958.

During the 1958–1961 period, the Soviet-Yugoslav controversy centered on four main points: First, the Yugoslavs insisted that the Kremlin as well as NATO was responsible for the Cold War; second, they maintained that each Communist state should be free to determine its own course toward socialism; third, they asserted that the Soviet Union was continuing to evolve along Stalinist lines and had developed into a bureaucratic state which keeps "strengthening in all fields of social life" rather than withering away in accord with Marxist-Leninist theory; fourth, the 1958 Yugoslav Party Program, which was reaffirmed by the December 1964 Party Congress, claimed for Yugoslavia democratic developments which constituted a challenge to Moscow's ideological leadership of the Communist camp. The Kremlin issued a strong statement to counter the Yugoslav assertions (reading 56). It subsequently applied economic and political pressure but avoided any open split along 1948 lines. At the same time, Moscow moved to expand economic integration and planning through the Council for Mutual Economic Assistance (COMECON). However, after 1961, as relations between Moscow and Peking progressively worsened, the Soviet Union muted its quarrel with Yugoslavia, and relations between the two improved.

In general, Soviet policy toward Eastern Europe has undergone a number of important changes since the halcyon days of 1956. First, Moscow has accommodated to East European nationalism by granting substantial domestic autonomy to local Communist elites. Second, there has been a major readjustment of economic relationships. In particular, Moscow has attempted since 1960 to strengthen COMECON, to make it a viable instrument for closer integration of East European economies. However, there has been considerable opposition to Soviet proposals for coordinated planning, trade, and a "socialist international division of labor," in large part because the East European countries are sensitive to any possible infringements on their "national sovereignty." Though there are sound economic reasons for bloc integration, memories of the Stalin period linger and engender an opposition that Moscow has prudently not attempted to override. Third, Moscow seems reconciled to the expansion of East European economic and cultural links with the West, though it has cautioned bloc members against using "their relations with capitalist countries at the expense of other fraternal countries."

What are the limits of Soviet tolerance? By keeping alive fears of German "revanchism," particularly among the Poles, Czechs, and East Germans, Moscow ensures their military dependence upon the USSR. Should any of the East European regimes substitute Western for Soviet ties, or should their political posture assume an anti-Soviet coloration, Moscow may feel impelled to act, as it did in 1956, to safeguard its vital security and national interests.

The Sino-Soviet Rift

Of central importance to the USSR is its relationship with Communist China. As senior member of the alliance, Moscow's leadership was acknowledged during the Stalin period. Stalin's successors were diligent in maintaining close relations with Peking. In late 1956 China played, for the first time, a brief but not unimportant role in East European affairs. Originally a sympathetic supporter of increased autonomy for the Poles and Hungarians, it grew apprehensive over the unexpectedly sharp opposition not only in Eastern Europe but also in China as a consequence of "de-Stalinization." It quickly perceived the danger involved in even a limited "decompression" and came out uncompromisingly hostile toward all "revisionist" manifestations, a policy that made it bitterly critical of the Yugoslavs. Peking opposed any detente with the United States—against whom it has major political and territorial grievances—preferring to keep East-West tensions high in order to obtain more economic and military aid from the USSR and justify the perpetuation of ideological and political orthodoxy within the bloc. It also opposed summit conferences and any arms control or disarmament agreement that might retard its development as a great power.

There is convincing evidence to indicate that during the 1957–1960 period Moscow was frequently constrained by Chinese objections against moving too far in the direction of a detente with the West. For example, the Soviet Government appeared eager for a conference "at the summit" in late 1957 and early 1958. At the time of the Lebanese crisis (July 1958), a Khrushchev visit to the United Nations and a meeting with President Eisenhower seemed a certainty. However, Khrushchev made a sudden visit to Peking in August, and soon thereafter the Quemoy crisis broke out in the Taiwan Straits and the Soviets lost interest in top-level talks with Western leaders.

Moscow found itself increasingly pressured by Peking to act more militantly in furtherance of revolutionary wars in Asia, Africa, and Latin America, particularly after the USSR had launched its Sputnik in October 1957 and claimed missile superiority over the United States. Moscow's inability or unwillingness to extend China large-scale credits for imports of machinery, industrial plants, and metals, which were necessary for the success of China's ambitious 1958 "great leap forward" program of internal transformation and agricultural reorganization, constituted an additional irritant. Indeed, by late 1960 Soviet aid to China dropped sharply, leading the Chinese to charge subsequently that Moscow had deliberately sought to impede China's economic development.

Efforts were made throughout 1959 and 1960, and in particular at the November 1960 Moscow conference of eighty-one Communist Parties, to close the growing policy and ideological rift between Moscow and Peking and reach agreement on a unified strategy toward both the West and intra-Communist bloc developments. By 1961 the seriousness of the rift became a matter of public record, as Moscow and Peking exchanged charges and countercharges. At the Twenty-second Party Congress of the CPSU in October 1961, Khrushchev criticized the Albanian Communists for their espousal of "Stalinism" and reiterated his contention that war with the capitalist powers could and should be avoided. Peking promptly declared its friendship for Albania, condemned "revisionism," and averred its hostility toward the United States and all "lackeys of imperialism." At the Congress Chinese Premier Chou-en-lai implicitly castigated Khrushchev, observing that "If there are quarrels in the socialist camp, we consider that they should be settled through bilateral contacts and that a public denunciation does not contribute to the cohesion of the socialist camp."

The crescendo of condemnatory attacks rose throughout the remaining years of the Khrushchev era. Moscow assailed the "dogmatists" (Chinese Communists) "who have learned by heart the general formula about imperialism and stubbornly turn their eyes away from life." A high-level meeting of representatives of the CPSU and Communist Party of China (CPC) was held in Moscow from July 5 to 20, 1963, in an effort to mediate the dispute, but it failed abjectly. In a major statement on July 14, 1963, *Pravda* published an Open Letter from the Central Committee of the CPSU to all Party organizations and members in which were presented the main lines of the Soviet position (reading 57). During the following year, Moscow sought to gain support for an international Communist Congress, which many Western analysts believed was intended to bring about a final showdown with Peking. In July 1964, the CPSU sent invitations to twenty-five Communist Parties to attend a conference in

Moscow on December 15. Soviet-Chinese relations seemed on the brink of an open and formal rupture when Nikita S. Khrushchev was suddenly deposed on October 14, 1964.

The "collective leadership" headed by Leonid Brezhnev and Aleksei Kosygin quickly acted to halt the vituperative exchanges. To permit exploratory discussions with the Chinese, the conference scheduled for December 1964 was postponed until March 1, 1965. Though the new Soviet leadership made clear the "consultative" character of the meeting and disclaimed any intention of "excommunicating" any Communist Party from the international movement, the Chinese Communists and their adherents boycotted the sessions. The March meeting accomplished little more than to reaffirm the desirability of holding "a preliminary consultative conference of representatives of the 81 parties that gathered at the 1960 [Moscow] meeting in order to discuss the question of a new international meeting," and acrimonious exchanges were resumed.

There has been no significant improvement in Soviet-Chinese relations. The catalogue of grievances remains unchanged. Though the dispute is often cast within an ideological framework, it is fundamentally a rivalry over power and mirrors the divergent strategies, interests, and objectives of the two countries. Briefly, the main sources of discord center on the following issues: First, Moscow believes that as the senior and most powerful member of the international Communist community it should be accorded the authority to interpret Marxist-Leninist doctrine and establish basic strategy for the bloc and in particular to decide on the best way to deal with the capitalist world. It resents Chinese pretensions to leadership and feels that the Chinese are newcomers not familiar with global realities, that they seriously underestimate the strength of the United States, and that they do not appreciate the extent to which imperialism can be weakened by nonmilitary means. Second, there is disagreement over priorities: the areas and issues that are most important to Moscow are least important to Peking, and vice versa. For example, if for no other reason than that the main *military* threat to the USSR in the past and at present comes from the West, Moscow's primary political attention is drawn to European developments, e.g., centrifugal Communist tendencies in Eastern Europe, the resurgence of West Germany, the impact of the Common Market. A satisfied power territorially, the Soviet Union is not prepared to go to war against the United States over the Taiwan question, an issue that is paramount in Chinese thinking. Thus do geography, history, and economics shape the perception of political priorities. Third, Moscow and Peking differ in their approach to developing countries. While these differences are not as clearcut as is some-times imagined in the West, they do connote a greater readiness on the part of China to pursue militant policies that inevitably exacerbate relations with the United States. A major source of discord has been the Soviet courtship of India. Another is Moscow's program of extending extensive economic and military aid to neutralist countries, while aid to China was ended in 1961. By emphasizing the revolutionary path to power and opposing (in principle but not in practice) cooperation between local Communist Parties and bourgeois-nationalist parties, China is directly challenging the Soviet strategy for spreading Communist influence in the Third World. Fourth, Moscow's unwillingness after 1959 to assist China to develop a nuclear capability and its signing of the limited nuclear test-ban treaty in 1963 signified to China a Soviet desire to keep its Communist ally a second-rate military power. Once China acquires its own "credible" nuclear capability, it is likely to become even more independent-minded and truculent toward the USSR. Fifth, China has long-standing frontier grievances against the USSR. Under treaties imposed on Imperial China by Czarist Russia in 1858, 1860, and 1881, China was forced to cede almost one million square miles of territory in Central Asia and the Maritime Provinces of Siberia. Peking does not recognize the validity of these treaties and has called for the revision of existing borders, a demand that has been rejected by Moscow.

Officially, alliance with Peking remains the cornerstone of Soviet foreign policy. However, Moscow recognizes that the mushrooming disagreements of recent years, coupled with China's immense population, intensified program of industrialization, and ambitious aims, constitute a long-range threat to Soviet national interests in the Far East and Central Asia and a chal-lenge to Moscow's pre-eminent position within the Communist movement.

The Poles say with bitter humor: "Thank God for the Soviet Union. We are lucky to have a buffer state between us and the Chinese." The Soviets are not so fortunate; they must deal with the developing colossus of communism. The extent to which China and the Soviet Union cooperate or clash will greatly affect the future of world communism. Events of the past decade indicate that a formal split is a possibility, though for the present the alliance remains intact.

Germany and the Berlin Question

The foremost of European problems attracting Soviet attention is that of Germany. The remilitarization of West Germany is a cause of constant Soviet concern. In 1954 an article in *Kommunist,* the authoritative journal of the CPSU, contended that the United States, to realize its "aggressive plans," needed "a powerful, well-trained land army in Europe equipped with the latest weapons" and, accordingly, initiated German rearmament in order to make West Germany "into an obedient instrument of its aggressive policy, into a mailed fist that would be directed against the Soviet Union and the People's Democracies and at the same time be used to subject NATO to United States control." This Soviet interpretation has not changed.

Moscow bitterly attacked the Paris Agreements of 1954, which brought West Germany into NATO and sanctioned its rearmament. It has further insisted that the integration of West Germany into NATO further complicated the solution of the German problem. Since 1958, Soviet apprehensions have heightened as they see an increase in the possibility of West Germany's obtaining missiles and nuclear weapons. To Soviet leaders, the United States proposal for a multilateral nuclear force (MLF) was a step in this direction.

As the Chinese Communists eased their pressure on Quemoy and the offshore islands, the Soviet Union provoked a new crisis with the West over Berlin on November 27, 1958. In a belligerent note Khrushchev threatened to abrogate all existing agreements on Berlin and transfer Soviet rights as an occupying power to the East Germans. He insisted that West Berlin be set up as a "free city," guaranteed by the four former occupying powers and the two existing German states, and that the Western Powers withdraw from the city. Unless the West initiated negotiations within six months, Khrushchev indicated, the administration of East Berlin and the regulation of Western access routes to the city would be turned over to the East German Government.

The immediate aim of the Kremlin was probably to obtain Western diplomatic recognition of the East German regime, but the Berlin crisis reopened the entire question of Germany's future. By calling for a conference to draw up a German peace treaty, Moscow appeared also to seek anew attainment of its long-term objectives in Europe—the acceptance by the West of the status quo in Europe and the weakening of NATO.

The Khrushchev "ultimatum" was extended for almost three years, as the Soviet Government avoided any precipitous action. During a meeting with President Kennedy in Vienna on June 3–4, 1961, Premier Khrushchev declared that the Berlin problem must be settled before the end of the year or the Soviet Union would sign a separate peace treaty with East Germany. On August 13, 1961, without warning, the Berlin Wall was put up, physically sealing off the two sectors of the city. The precise reason for Khrushchev's intensifying the Berlin crisis was obscure. Perhaps it was pressure from the Chinese to adopt a more aggressive attitude toward the West, an effort to exploit Western preoccupation with Laos and the Congo and American embarrassment over Castro's Communist Cuba, a desire to bolster the East German regime by sealing off the major remaining escape route of East Germans to the West. Or perhaps Khrushchev felt that after almost three years he had to show something or face rising opposition among his Party colleagues.

On September 1, 1961, the USSR ominously resumed nuclear testing and the specter of Sarajevo loomed over an anxious Europe as the Berlin crisis deepened. Tensions eased in the ensuing months, only to erupt with dramatic intensity in October 1962 in Cuba. The removal of Soviet missiles and the signing of the test-ban treaty ten months later marked an upturn in Soviet-American relations, though the Berlin problem continued to fester. On June 12, 1964, the Soviet Union signed a twenty-year Treaty of Friendship, Mutual Assistance and Cooperation with East Germany which, to the great disappointment of the puppet Pankow regime, merely served to reaffirm the status quo character of the German and Berlin problems. This diplomatic gesture was a far cry from the dire threats inherent in Khrushchev's "ultimatum" of November 1958. East Germany was further jarred by the Soviet announcement in late July 1964 of Khrushchev's acceptance of an invitation to visit West Germany. This startling move indicated that Khrushchev was prepared to discuss the issue of German reunification with Bonn. Peking thereupon accused Khrushchev of preparing to "sell-out" the Ulbricht East German regime. The removal of Khrushchev in October shelved for the time being the prospect of a serious Soviet initiative to settle the issue of Germany.

There is little reason to believe that the Soviet Union is unhappy over the present division of Germany. However, Moscow might conceivably at some future date accept German reunification, if West Germany agreed to withdraw from NATO, a move that would materially impair NATO's effectiveness as a defensive shield for Western Europe and very probably disrupt Western Europe's promising moves toward economic and political integration. True, a second Rapallo involves grave risks for the Kremlin: A Soviet withdrawal from East Germany might dangerously weaken Moscow's domination of Eastern Europe, and there would be no way, short of war, to prevent a united Germany from subsequently initiating close ties with the West. On the other hand, substantial dividends could accrue to the USSR.

First, West German leaders might prove willing to accept a preliminary confederation of East and West Germany as the price for unification. This would preserve the East German regime and provide the Communists with an entering wedge for eventually subverting the parliamentary regime established to rule a united Germany. Second, as a condition for German reunification, the USSR would assuredly insist upon withdrawal of American troops from Germany. This, in turn, might occasion demands for American troop withdrawals elsewhere in Europe. Under such circumstances it is a short step from disengagement to disenchantment and United States neo-isolationism becomes a distinct possibility. Third, any substantial disengagement in Central Europe along the lines of the Rapacki proposals presumably would shift the military balance of power in Europe to the advantage of the Soviet Union, though this is contested by those who argue that a removal of Soviet troops from Eastern Europe would result in a strengthening of nationalism and national autonomy in the region and would mitigate against any increment of Soviet power. Fourth, and perhaps most important in the present period of uncertainty about the future of NATO, a willingness by the United States to negotiate German reunification along Soviet-suggested lines might be interpreted in Western Europe, and elsewhere, as a sign of weakness and lack of resolve to resist Soviet pressure. This, in turn, could sow grave doubts and distrust within NATO—a continuing objective of Soviet foreign policy.

The future of Berlin cannot be divorced from the broader question of the future of Germany, which remains the key to Europe. Soviet leaders continually profess uneasiness over German rearmament and nuclear ambitions. How much of this is genuine fear and how much is manipulation for political ends it is impossible to know.

Soviet Policy Since Khrushchev

During the time that has passed since Khrushchev's deposal, Soviet leaders have pursued a cautious and moderate course in foreign affairs. They have concentrated on the problems of the Soviet economy and avoided any major initiatives abroad for the time being. The acrimonious exchanges with China continue, but far less often and virulently than under Khrushchev. Moscow has shown little desire to become directly involved in the Vietnam war. The courtship of developing countries gives every indication of being continued, and even expanded. In an editorial in *Pravda* on August 8, 1965, the Soviet Government criticized both the

United States and Communist China, but expressed a willingness to consider "with deep sympathy every practical step and proposal directed to the preservation of peace and the organization of normal relations between all states and peoples" (reading 58).

There is little likelihood, however, that the Cold War will soon end. Minor adjustments may be carried out in Berlin, and there are sufficient variants on the disengagement and reunification themes to allow for extensive discussions. In Geneva, disarmament talks continue. However, none of this will in any way mitigate the intense struggle for the developing areas. Indeed, a relaxation of tensions in Europe and effective stabilization of its relationship with Eastern Europe might provide the Soviet Government with added opportunities and resources to penetrate the muddled critical areas of flux south of the USSR.

NOTES

1. *Soviet Affairs Notes*, No. 224 (Washington, D.C.: Department of State, July 28, 1958), p. 3.
2. *The New York Times* (April 18, 1956).

Strengthening the Moscow-Peking Alliance

55. SINO-SOVIET ACCORDS OF OCTOBER 11, 1954*

Taking into consideration the change in the international situation in the Far East in connection with the ending of the war in Korea and the establishment of peace in Indochina, as well as taking into account the strengthening of the defense potential of the Chinese People's Republic, the governments of the Soviet Union and the Chinese People's Republic . . . have agreed that Soviet military units are to be evacuated from the jointly used naval base of Port Arthur and the installations in that area are to be transferred without compensation to the government of the Chinese People's Republic . . . The evacuation of the Soviet

* *The New York Times*, October 12, 1954, *excerpts*.

troops and the transfer of the installations to the Government of the Chinese People's Republic in the Port Arthur Naval Base Area will be completed by May 31, 1955.

In 1950 and in 1951 . . . four mixed Soviet-Chinese companies were set up on a basis of parity; a company for the mining of nonferrous and rare metals in Sinkiang Province of the Chinese People's Republic; a company for the extraction and refining of oil in this province; a company for the building and repair of ships in the town of Dairen, and a company for the organization and exploitation of civil airlines. . . .

At present, when the Chinese People's Republic having reconstructed her economy is successfully fulfilling the first five year plan, Chinese economic organizations have accumulated the necessary experience and can themselves manage the activity of enterprises which are part of the mixed companies. The governments of the USSR and of the Chinese People's Republic have reached agreement that the Soviet share of participation in the mixed Soviet-Chinese companies will be transferred entirely to the Chinese People's Republic on January 1, 1955. The value of this share will be compensated over a number of years by supplying to the Soviet Union goods which are items of usual export from the Chinese People's Republic.

. . . Talks on Soviet-Chinese scientific-technical cooperation have been held in Moscow and Peiping. . . . The talks, which were conducted in a sincere and friendly atmosphere, ended in the signing on October 11 in Peiping of an agreement on scientific-technical cooperation between the USSR and the Chinese People's Republic. . . .

With the purpose of strengthening mutual economic and cultural relations, the Governments of the USSR and of the Chinese People's Republic have agreed that both sides, in the nearest future, should begin the building of a railway line from Lanchow through Urumchi (Sinkiang), on Chinese territory, to Alma Ata on Soviet territory.

New Strains Between Moscow and Belgrade

56. SOVIET CRITICISMS OF YUGOSLAV "REVISIONISM"*

The draft program of the Yugoslav League of Communists had the appearance of a document opposing the declaration (of November 16, 1957) of the conference of Communist and Workers' Parties of the socialist countries which was approved by all the fraternal Communist Parties. Because of this the [Yugoslav] draft program proved a document directed toward weakening rather than strengthening the unity of the Communist and Workers' Parties, toward weakening the unity of the socialist countries. . . .

The materials of the congress of the Yugoslav League of Communists showed that the incorrect theses of the draft program were developed in detail and defended by the congress speakers and certain of the others who took the floor. Such speeches require criticism and a decisive rebuff. It is impossible to ignore the appraisal of the international situation given at the congress, which was wrong in principle, and the distorted estimate of the reasons for the international tension.

The report by Tito . . . propounded the idea that the policy of [all] the Great Powers after the Second World War was based on the principle of strength and not on the principle of the right of all nations to decide their own destinies. According to Tito, an example of this foreign policy was the many years of Stalin's pressure on Yugoslavia. It emerges from that statement that the leaders of the Yugoslav Union of Communists placed the USSR on the same level as the imperialist powers. Crudely distorting the facts of history, they ascribed a policy of strength to the USSR. . . . To declare that Soviet policy in the first postwar years was characterized by a desire to win domination over other nations . . . means repeating the inventions of imperialist propaganda about a so-called Soviet empire surrounding itself with satellites. This attempt to whitewash the imperialist powers was most clearly evident in the allegation that the policy of the USSR was the main reason for the establishment of the Atlantic Pact.

* The New York Times, May 11, 1958, excerpts.

The distortion of the real reasons for the formation of the North Atlantic alliance is actually nothing more or less than a justification of US imperialism, which set up this aggressive war blow as its principal weapon in trying to achieve world domination. . . . The leaders of the Yugoslav League of Communists do not agree with the characterization generally recognized by the Communists of all countries of a world divided into two opposing camps—socialism and imperialism. They declare that Yugoslavia is outside these camps. But the division of the world into two camps did not occur at the whim of any persons or parties. The socialist and imperialist camps are a reflection of the indisputable fact that there are in the world today not one but two social and economic systems. . . . The problem of mutual relations between the socialist countries, and the Communist and Workers' Parties at their head, is of key significance for the development of socialism and communism. This is a new problem. It arose only after the Second World War with the appearance on the international arena alongside the USSR of other socialist countries of Europe and Asia . . .

The emergence of socialism beyond the bounds of a single country, its conversion into a world social and economic system, the formation and consolidation of the camp of socialist countries —this is the main thing which defines the international development characterizing the present epoch. Under present circumstances, when a new socialist society already unites more than one-third of humanity, the build-up of practical and theoretical cooperation between the socialist countries becomes a vital necessity. Yet the line followed in the speeches at the congress of the League of Communists is to substantiate the separate individuality of the socialist countries and to set them off in opposition to one another. . . .

The main speakers, and certain others, at the congress spoke with gratitude and appreciation of United States aid to Yugoslavia. When reading these speeches kowtowing to the US ruling circles, one is prompted to ask: Why is Yugoslavia in such favor with US monopolists? Every Communist is justified in wondering why the US imperialists, the worst enemies of socialism, consider it profitable to themselves to help Yugoslavia. For what services? Is it not because the Yugoslav leaders are trying to weaken the unity of the international Communist and working-class movement? Everyone knows that US aid to any country is not unselfish. It entails one or another form of economic and political dependence. . . .

. . . the framers of the draft program of the Yugoslav League of Communists flagrantly distorted the nature of the relations linking the socialist countries, accused them in an unfriendly and even slanderous way of a desire for hegemony. They claimed that in the initial phases of the development of socialism in individual nations or states there exists a possibility of utilizing economic exploitation of other countries in one form or another. . . .

The Yugoslav leaders think that existing ideological differences should not cause a worsening of state relations between Yugoslavia and the socialist countries. But a simple repetition of this platitude is insufficient, as experience shows. It is impossible not to see that ideological differences deepen if they are not eliminated. Naturally this leads to differences on political issues. The Soviet Union and its Communist Party have energetically advanced along the line of eliminating all injustices and mistakes made in the past with regard to Yugoslavia. But it must be bluntly stated that Yugoslavia, in 1948 and the following years, made mistakes of a nationalistic nature and departed from the principles of Marxism-Leninism on a number of major issues . . . the Yugoslav leaders continue to adhere to their positions, which contradict the principles of Marxism-Leninism and proletarian internationalism. The untenability of the positions held by the leadership of the Yugoslav League of Communists and their violation of the principles of inter-party relations, as well as the principles of proletarian internationalism were forcefully manifested in their incorrect attitude toward criticism on questions of principle. . . .

The Soviet Case Against China

57. OPEN LETTER FROM CPSU CENTRAL COMMITTEE TO PARTY ORGANIZATIONS AND ALL COMMUNISTS OF THE SOVIET UNION*

July 14, 1963

What is the gist of the differences between the Communist Party of China (C.P.C.) on the one hand and the C.P.S.U. and the international communist movement on the other? . . .

* *Soviet News*, July 16, 1963, *excerpts.*

Take, for instance, such cardinal problems as war and peace
. . . The C.P.S.U. central committee believes it to be its duty to
tell the party and the people with all frankness that in questions
of war and peace the C.P.C. leadership has cardinal differences,
based on principle, with us and with the world communist
movement. The essence of these differences lies in a diametrically opposite approach to such vital problems as the possibility
of averting thermonuclear world war, peaceful co-existence
between states with different social systems and the inter-
connection between the struggle for peace and the development
of the world revolutionary movement.

Our party, in the decisions of the 20th and 22nd Congresses,
and the world communist movement, in the Declaration and
Statement [of November 1960], set before communists as a task
of extreme importance the task of averting a thermonuclear
world catastrophe. We appraise the balance of forces in the
world realistically, and from this draw the conclusion that,
though the nature of imperialism has not changed, and the
danger of the outbreak of war has not been averted, in modern
conditions the forces of peace, of which the mighty community
of socialist states is the main bulwark, can, by their joint efforts,
avert a new world war.

We also soberly appraise the radical, qualitative change in the
means of waging war and, consequently, its possible aftermaths.
The nuclear rocket weapons which have been created in the
middle of our century change the old notions about war. These
weapons possess an unprecedented devastating force. Suffice
it to say that the explosion of only one powerful thermonuclear
bomb surpasses the explosive force of all the ammunition used
during all previous wars, including the First and Second
World Wars. And many thousand such bombs have been
accumulated!

Do communists have the right to ignore this danger? Do we
have to tell the people all the truth about the consequences of
thermonuclear war? We believe that, without question, we must.
This cannot have a "paralyzing" effect on the masses, as the
Chinese comrades assert. On the contrary, the truth about
modern war will mobilize the will and energy of the masses
in the struggle for peace and against imperialism—the source
of military danger . . .

To prevent a new world war is a real and quite feasible task.
The 20th Congress of our party came to the extremely important
conclusion that in our times there is no fatal inevitability of war
between states. This conclusion is not the fruit of good intentions, but the result of a realistic, strictly scientific analysis of

the balance of class forces on the world arena; it is based on the gigantic might of world socialism . . .

The Chinese comrades obviously underestimate the whole danger of thermonuclear war. "The atomic bomb is a paper tiger"; "it is not terrible at all," they contend . . . We would like to ask the Chinese comrades who suggest building a bright future on the ruins of the old world destroyed by a thermonuclear war whether they have consulted the working class of the countries where imperialism dominates? The working class of the capitalist countries would certainly tell them: are we asking you to trigger off a war and destroy our countries while annihilating the imperialists? Is it not a fact that the monopolists, the imperialists, are only a comparatively small group, while the bulk of the population of the capitalist countries consists of the working class, working peasantry, and working intelligentsia?

The nuclear bomb does not distinguish between the imperialists and working people: it hits great areas, and therefore millions of workers would be destroyed for one monopolist. The working class, the working people, will ask such "revolutionaries": what right have you to decide for us the questions of our existence and our class struggle? We also are in favor of socialism; but we want to gain it through the class struggle and not by unleashing a thermonuclear world war. . . .

The deep difference between the views of the C.P.S.U. and other Marxist-Leninist Parties on the one hand and the C.P.C. leaders on the other, on the questions of war, peace and peaceful co-existence was demonstrated with particular clarity during the 1962 crisis in the Caribbean Sea. It was a sharp international crisis: never before did mankind come so close to the brink of a thermonuclear war as it did in October [1962].

The Chinese comrades allege that in the period of the Caribbean crisis we made an "adventurist" mistake by introducing rockets into Cuba and then "capitulated" to American imperialism when we removed the rockets from Cuba. Such assertions utterly contradict the facts.

What was the actual state of affairs? The C.P.S.U. central committee and the Soviet government possessed trustworthy information that an armed aggression by United States imperialism against Cuba was about to take place. We realized with sufficient clarity that the most resolute steps were needed to rebuff the aggression and to defend the Cuban revolution effectively. Curses and warnings—even if they are called "serious warnings" and repeated two and a half hundred times over—have no effect on the imperialists.

Proceeding from the need to defend the Cuban revolution, the Soviet government and the government of Cuba reached agreement on the delivery of missiles to Cuba, because this was the only effective way of preventing aggression on the part of American imperialism. The delivery of missiles to Cuba meant that an attack on her would meet with a resolute rebuff and the use of rocket weapons against the organizers of the aggression. Such a resolute step on the part of the Soviet Union and Cuba was a shock to the American imperialists, who felt for the first time in their history that if they were to undertake an armed invasion of Cuba, a shattering retaliatory blow would be dealt against their own territory. Inasmuch as the point in question was not simply a conflict between the United States and Cuba, but a clash between the two major nuclear powers, the crisis in the Caribbean Sea area would have turned from a local into a world war. A real danger of thermonuclear world war arose.

There was one alternative in the prevailing situation: either to follow in the wake of the "madmen" (this is how the most aggressive and reactionary representatives of American imperialism are dubbed) and embark upon a course of unleashing a world thermonuclear war or, profiting from the opportunities offered by the delivery of missiles, to take all steps to reach an agreement on a peaceful solution of the crisis and to prevent aggression against the Republic of Cuba.

As is known, we chose the second path and are convinced that we did the right thing . . . Agreement to remove the missile weapons in return for the United States government's commitment not to invade Cuba and to keep its allies from doing so, the heroic struggle of the Cuban people and the support rendered to them by the peace-loving nations, made it possible to frustrate the plans of the extreme adventurist circles of American imperialism, which were ready to go the whole hog. As a result it was possible to defend revolutionary Cuba and to save peace.

The Chinese comrades regard our statement that the Kennedy government also displayed a certain reasonableness and a realistic approach in the course of the crisis around Cuba as "embellishing imperialism." Do they really think that all bourgeois governments lack all reason in everything they do? . . . The Chinese comrades argue that the imperialists cannot be trusted in anything, that they are bound to cheat; but this is not a case of faith, but rather a case of sober calculation. Eight months have passed since the elimination of the crisis in the Caribbean Sea area, and the United States government is keeping its word—there is no invasion of Cuba. We also assumed a commitment to remove our missiles from Cuba, and we have fulfilled it. . . .

The next important question on which we differ is that of the
ways and methods of the revolutionary struggle of the working
class in the capitalist countries, the struggle for national liberation, the paths of the transition of all mankind to socialism . . .
The Chinese comrades, in a haughty and abusive way, accuse the
Communist Parties of France, Italy, the United States, and other
countries of nothing less than opportunism and reformism, of
"parliamentary cretinism," and even of slipping down to "bourgeois socialism." On what grounds do they do this? On the
grounds that these Communist Parties do not put forward the
slogan of an immediate proletarian revolution, although even
the Chinese leaders must realize that this cannot be done without
the existence of a revolutionary situation.

Every knowledgeable Marxist-Leninist realizes that to put forward the slogan of an armed uprising, when there is no revolutionary situation in the country, means condemning the working
class to defeat. It is common knowledge how exceedingly serious
was Lenin's approach to this question, with what political perspi-
cacity and knowledge of the concrete situation he approached the
question of choosing the time for revolutionary action. On the
very eve of the October Revolution, Lenin pointed out that it
would be too early to start on October 24, too late on October 26—
everything might be lost—and, consequently, power had to be
taken, at whatever cost, on October 25. Who determines the intensity of class contradictions, the existence of a revolutionary
situation, and chooses the moment for the uprising? This can be
done only by the working class of each given country, by its
vanguard—the Marxist-Leninist party . . .

The Chinese leaders regard as a mortal sin of the Communist
Parties of the developed capitalist states the fact that they see
their direct tasks in the struggle for the economic and social
interests of the working people, for democratic reforms, feasible
even under capitalism and easing the living conditions of the
working class, the peasantry and the petty bourgeois sections of
the population, and contributing to the formation of a broad anti-
monopoly front, which will serve as a basis for further struggle
for the victory of the socialist revolution, that is to say, the fact
that they are doing precisely what is recorded in the Moscow
Statement of 1960 . . .

Yet another important question is that of *the relationship be-*
tween the struggle of the international working class and the
national liberation movement of the peoples of Asia, Africa, and
Latin America. The international revolutionary working-class
movement, represented today by the world system of socialism

and the Communist Parties of the capitalist countries and the national liberation movement of the peoples of Asia, Africa, and Latin America—these are the great forces of our epoch. Correct coordination between them constitutes one of the main prerequisites for victory over imperialism.

How do the Chinese comrades solve this problem? This is seen from their new "theory," according to which the main contradiction of our time is, you see, the contradiction, not between socialism and imperialism, but between the national liberation movement and imperialism. The decisive force in the struggle against imperialism, the Chinese comrades maintain, is not the world system of socialism, not the struggle of the international working class, but again the national liberation movement. In this way the Chinese comrades, apparently, want to win popularity among the peoples of Asia, Africa, and Latin America by the easiest possible means. But let no one be deceived by this "theory." Whether the Chinese theoreticians want it or not, this theory in essence means isolating the national liberation movement from the international working class and its creation—the world system of socialism. Yet this would constitute a tremendous danger to the national liberation movement itself.

Indeed, could the many peoples of Asia have been victorious, in spite of all their heroism and selflessness, if the October Revolution, and then the formation of the world system of socialism, had not shaken imperialism to its very foundations, if they had not undermined the forces of the colonialists? And now that the liberated peoples have entered a new stage in their struggle, concentrating their efforts on the consolidation of their political gains and economic independence, do they not see that it would be immeasurably more difficult, if not altogether impossible, to carry out these tasks without the assistance of the socialist states? . . .

The question arises: What is the explanation for the incorrect propositions of the C.P.C. leadership on the basic problems of our time? It is either the complete divorcement of the Chinese comrades from actual reality, a dogmatic, bookish approach to problems of war, peace, and the revolution, their lack of understanding of the concrete conditions of the present epoch, or the fact that behind the rumpus about the "world revolution," raised by the Chinese comrades, there are other goals, which have nothing in common with revolution. . . .

The erroneous views of the C.P.C. leaders on the paramount political and theoretical questions of our time are inseparably linked with their practical activities aimed at undermining the unity of the world socialist camp and the international Communist movement. In words Chinese comrades recognize that the unity of the U.S.S.R. and the People's Republic of China is a mainstay of the entire socialist community, but in actual fact they are undermining contacts with our party and with our country in all directions. The C.P.C. leadership often speaks of its loyalty to the commonwealth of socialist countries, but the attitude of the Chinese comrades to this commonwealth refutes their high-sounding declarations. The statistics show that in the course of the past three years the People's Republic of China cut the volume of its trade with the countries of the socialist community by more than 50 per cent. Some socialist countries felt the results of this line of the Chinese comrades particularly keenly . . .

Parallel with the line directed towards curtailing economic contacts, the leadership of the C.P.C. took a number of measures aimed at worsening relations with the Soviet Union. The Chinese leaders are undermining the unity, not only of the socialist camp, but also of the entire world communist movement, trampling underfoot the principles of proletarian internationalism and flagrantly violating the standards governing the relations between fraternal parties. The leadership of the C.P.C. is organizing and supporting various anti-party groups of renegades who are coming out against the Communist Parties in the United States, Brazil, Italy, Belgium, Australia and India . . . Comrades of the C.P.C. are making particular efforts to conduct subversive activities in the Communist and Workers' Parties in the countries of Asia, Africa, and Latin America . . .

And in its letter of June 14, 1963, the leadership of the C.P.C. sinks to insinuations that the C.P.S.U., too—so it alleges— "comes out in the role of a helper of imperialism." No one but Trotskyites has so far dared, in view of the obvious absurdity of this, to level such slanderous accusations against the great party of Lenin! . . .

One of the clear examples of the special line in the leadership of the C.P.C. in the socialist camp and the international communist movement is its position on the Albanian question. As is well known, in the second half of 1960 the Albanian leaders openly came out with a left opportunist platform on the main questions of our day and began to promote a hostile policy in relation to the C.P.S.U. and other fraternal parties. The Albanian leadership started an anti-Soviet campaign in the country, which led to a rupture of political, economic, and cultural ties with the Soviet Union . . . It is now known that the Chinese comrades openly pushed them on to the road of open struggle against the Soviet Union . . .

We see with regret how the leaders of the C.P.C. are under-mining the traditional Soviet-Chinese friendship and weakening the unity of the socialist countries.

Recent Kremlin Statement on International Affairs

58. AIMS OF SOVIET FOREIGN POLICY*

PRAVDA, August 8, 1965

The Soviet state has always put its strength and international prestige at the service of peace, of mankind's social progress, of the freedom and independence of the peoples, of the effort to guarantee peoples the opportunity of devoting themselves to peaceful constructive endeavor, and of deciding their problems for themselves—in short, at the service of those high aims which all peoples without exception set themselves. Imbued as it is with proletarian socialist internationalism, Soviet foreign policy is organically hostile to any kind of the great-power chauvinism which is characteristic of the big states of the capitalist world . . .

The Soviet Union has regarded the putting forward of the principles of the peaceful co-existence between states with different social systems and ridding mankind of the threat of a world war as one of the most important functions of its foreign policy. Peaceful co-existence is the Leninist foundation of the policy which the Soviet Union proposes and always defends in its dealings with the capitalist states. Peaceful co-existence today is the alternative to a thermonuclear war . . .

Attempts are still being made to represent the policy of peaceful co-existence with the capitalist countries as renunciation of the struggle against imperialism. Such attempts cannot in any way be justified.

"Peaceful co-existence," says the Programme of the Communist Party of the Soviet Union, "serves as a basis for the peaceful competition between socialism and capitalism on an international scale and is a specific form of the class struggle between them."

The policy of peaceful co-existence, directed against the most

* *Soviet News,* August 17, 1965, *excerpts.*

reactionary and bellicose forces of imperialism, is rooted in un-arguable respect for the right of every people to choose a suitable social and state system for itself. Conditions of peaceful co-existence make for successes in the liberation struggle and the fulfillment of the revolutionary tasks confronting the peoples . . .

Peaceful co-existence between the socialist and capitalist countries and the development of normal inter-state relations with them, presupposes rather than rules out a struggle against the aggressive plans and designs of imperialism in the international arena, it presupposes the exposure of the intrigues of militarist forces and the mobilization of the masses to struggle for peace . . .

Certain western circles cherish the hope that it will be possible to enter into some sort of "peaceful co-existence" with the Soviet Union while simultaneously conducting an aggressive policy towards other countries—socialist states or newly independent states of Asia and Africa. The Soviet Union will never agree to such an approach. True to its Leninist principles, the U.S.S.R. resolutely rejects this imperialist interpretation of peaceful co-existence. We abided and abide by Lenin's understanding of the policy of peaceful co-existence as one based on the crucial interests of peace and socialism . . .

Like other socialist countries, the Soviet Union is prepared to enter into many-sided peaceful co-operation and normal relations with all capitalist countries. It stands for the wide development of mutually advantageous trading, economic, scientific, technical, and cultural contacts with them, for co-operation for peace and international security. It regards with deep sympathy every practical step and proposal directed to the preservation of peace and the organization of normal relations between all states and peoples.

The Soviet Union, however, can neither be scared by imperialist blackmail nor deceived by imperialist phrase-mongering, no matter with what demagogic spices it is served. The Soviet Union will never swerve from the Leninist road in its foreign policy.

FOR FURTHER STUDY

Brzezinski, Zbigniew K., *The Soviet Bloc: Unity and Conflict*. Cambridge, Mass.: Harvard University Press, 1960.

Cheng, Chu-Yuan, *Economic Relations Between Peking and Moscow, 1949–1963*. New York: Frederick A. Praeger, 1964.

Crankshaw, Edward, *The New Cold War: Moscow and Peking*. Baltimore: Penguin Books, 1963.

Dallin, Alexander, *The Soviet Union at the United Nations*. New York: Frederick A. Praeger, 1962.

Floyd, David, *Mao Against Khrushchev*. New York: Frederick A. Praeger, 1963.

Freund, Gerald, *Germany Between Two Worlds*. New York: Harcourt, Brace & World, 1961.

Griffith, William E., *Albania and the Sino-Soviet Rift*. Cambridge, Mass.: The M. I. T. Press, 1963.

————, *The Sino-Soviet Rift*. Cambridge, Mass.: The M. I. T. Press, 1964.

———— (ed.), *Communism in Europe*, Vol. 1. Cambridge, Mass.: The M. I. T. Press, 1965.

Grzybowski, Kazimierz, *The Socialist Commonwealth of Nations*. New Haven, Conn.: Yale University Press, 1964.

Kennan, George F., *Russia, the Atom and the West*. New York: Harper & Row, Publishers, 1957.

Kertesz, Stephen D. (ed.), *East Central Europe and the World: Developments in the Post-Stalin Era*. Notre Dame, Ind.: University of Notre Dame Press, 1962.

Laqueur, Walter Z., *Russia and Germany*. Boston: Little, Brown & Company, 1965.

London, Kurt (ed.), *Unity and Contradiction: Major Aspects of Sino-Soviet Relations*. New York: Frederick A. Praeger, 1962.

Lukacs, John, *A History of the Cold War*. New York: Doubleday & Company, 1961.

Mehnert, Klaus, *Peking and Moscow*. New York: G. P. Putnam's Sons, 1963.

Neal, Fred Warner, *War and Peace and Germany*. New York: W. W. Norton & Company, 1962.

North, Robert C., *Moscow and Chinese Communists*, 2nd ed. Stanford: Stanford University Press, 1963.

Vali, F. A., *Rift and Revolt in Hungary*. Cambridge, Mass.: Harvard University Press, 1961.

Zagoria, Donald S., *The Sino-Soviet Conflict, 1956–1961*. Princeton, N.J.: Princeton University Press, 1962.

Zinner, Paul, *Revolution in Hungary*. New York: Columbia University Press, 1962.

CHAPTER IX

SOVIET POLICY AND THE DILEMMA OF DISARMAMENT

No problem has occupied the attention of the United Nations more than that of disarmament. Efforts to bring about Great Power disarmament and to establish a viable system of arms control and inspection continue to founder over the divisive realities of international politics. The military threat posed by the Sino-Soviet world, coupled with the persistent, expansionist drive of the Communist leaders into areas regarded by the West as vital to its security, have precluded any comprehensive disarmament agreement. As the impasse widens with the passage of time, the specter of civilization committing suicide looms more ominously on the horizon.

In recent years, during the periodic thaws in the Cold War, attempts have been made to negotiate at least a beginning to disarmament and/or nuclear inspection. These international deliberations represent a partial response to domestic pressures, to the growing realization by the present nuclear powers of the imperative need to limit their own membership, and to the rising demands of the politically important developing nations of Africa, the Middle East, and Southern Asia. But they have produced few tangible results. Indeed, they have often become the scene of acrimonious debate and been subjected to an obstructive, frustrating feature of twentieth-century diplomacy—propaganda and polemic.

The disarmament question, with its related issues of arms control, nuclear inspection, and test cessation, is a mosaic of intricately interwoven problems which cannot be discussed without appraisals of changing power relationships and foreign policy. The specifics of disarmament may be isolated and analyzed (for instance, the technical feasibility of a network of monitoring posts to detect underground nuclear explosions), but ultimate agreement must rest upon political accommodation, compromise, and trust—elements conspicuously absent from postwar discussions. There exist among national leaders legitimate differences of opinion over the emphasis to be given the various factors of power; such as, economic growth, military strength, scientific and educational development, etc., and over the extent to which national security might be adversely affected by political concessions. Too rigid an interpretation of the military needs of national security may in time prove to be as "unrealistic" as the visionary proposals for immediate and universal disarmament. On the other hand, recent history abounds with examples of dictators who equated the desire of the Western democracies for peace and disarmament with weakness and fear and who thereupon embarked on policies of aggression that could have been prevented by firm opposition at the appropriate moment.

In the present structure of international power, what kind of disarmament is feasible? Can disarmament be effectively policed? Is disarmament possible in a complex, technologically advanced world? How do you equate comparative military strengths? Indeed, what is meant by disarmament? Are the differing Soviet and Western plans capable of meaningful negotiation? What role does Communist China play in the Soviet position on disarmament? These questions cannot easily be answered, but it is important that they be reflected upon.

It is a truism to say that wars do not happen; they are made by men. Similarly, it is true that though any arms race tends to exacerbate existing tensions, thus adding to the probability of war, the *causes* of war must usually be sought elsewhere. They are rooted in economics, politics, and the *Weltanschauung* of the ruling elite. In this respect, the attitude of a potential aggressor toward its own people, its neighbors, and the international community is invariably more a determinant of war than is the level of armaments. The economic, military, and political condition of a country may be exploited to justify the ambitions of an expansionist-minded elite. To such rulers, disarmament negotiations are mere exercises in deception. Has not the diplomat been described as "one who is sent abroad to lie for his country"? However, we must proceed on the assumption, tenuous though it may seem, that national leaders will not resort to all-out nuclear war to attain political objectives as long as acceptable alternatives are available.

Throughout the postwar period, disarmament prospects have fluctuated with the rise and fall of East-West tensions. Each side has periodically made concessions, until new variables were introduced which acted to preserve the disarmament deadlock. The United Nations has been seriously concerned with the problem of disarmament since 1946. Its failure stems from circumstances beyond its control. It is the result of the persistence of unresolved fundamental political issues, such as the continued division of Germany and of Korea, the presence of Soviet power in Eastern Europe, the Great-Power struggle in the Middle East and Africa, and the uneasy peace in the Far East.

Underlying the 1946–1950 period was the American monopoly of atomic weapons and the Soviet preponderance in mobilized military manpower and conventional weapons. During these years Soviet leaders repeatedly called for prohibition of the production and use of nuclear weapons, though refusing to accept Western demands for a suitable system of international control and inspection. A stalemate also developed over establishing limitations on conventional armaments. All these discussions were carried on against a background of progressively deteriorating relations. As political conflicts sharpened, national positions hardened; considerations of national interest have thus far precluded any agreement on disarmament.

A comprehensive proposal for controlling the atom was offered by the United States in June 1946 at the first meeting of the UN Atomic Energy Commission. Commonly known as the Baruch Plan, it called for the establishment of an international agency to control, own, and operate all nuclear facilities "from the mine to the finished product." The agency's officials were to be international civil servants, standing above politics and having the power to conduct continuous inspection of all phases of the production of fissionable materials, carry on research in nuclear weapons, and promote the peaceful uses of atomic energy. The Baruch Plan provided for the eventual destruction of existing nuclear weapons, but *only after* an adequate international inspection system had been set up and an effective system of sanctions free from the veto of any power had been organized by the Security Council. Bernard Baruch emphasized that "there must be no veto to protect those who violate their solemn agree-

ments not to develop or use atomic energy for destructive purposes." Though this plan was endorsed in principle by the General Assembly, Soviet objections prevented any further action.

The Soviets responded along sharply different lines. At the
autumn 1946 session of the General Assembly, Soviet Foreign
Minister Molotov developed the general Soviet position in a series
of speeches (readings 59 and 60). Denouncing the Baruch Plan,
he reversed the American pattern of priorities and called first for
the abandonment by the United States of its pre-eminent nuclear
position, the destruction of all nuclear weapons, and the prohibition of their further manufacture or use. A system of inspection would be established only after these conditions had been
met. Also, under the Soviet plan, the proposed international
agency "would lack the authority to own, operate, and license
atomic facilities, would have only a vaguely defined and apparently quite limited competence to inspect national atomic establishments, and would function in definite subordination to the
Security Council, where the rule of great power unanimity would
prevail in respect to all decisions of substantive importance."[1]

It is impossible to analyze in detail here the statements of the
American and Soviet spokesmen at the United Nations or to trace
the nuances and shifts in national policy they reflected. However, intensive research tends to cast doubt upon the willingness
of the Great Powers to establish in 1946 a workable system of
disarmament. Two incidents are ignored by most studies on the
disarmament negotiations of this period. First, on November 20,
1946, Molotov, in proposing a comprehensive program of disarmament, did not specifically insist upon a prohibition of atomic
weapons, as he had several weeks earlier in his original arms-
limitation proposals. This seemed an important preliminary concession which should have invited further exploration. UN
delegates regarded this speech as one of the most constructive
made by any Soviet spokesman. Western representatives, however, did not comment on Molotov's revised resolution, nor did
the Soviets press the issue. Neither party chose to test the intentions of the other.

Second, and perhaps even more intriguing, Molotov stated, on
December 4, 1946, that the Soviet Union did not envisage
Security Council control (or veto) over the day-to-day operations
of inspection commissions that might be established to verify
compliance with an adopted program of arms limitation or nuclear
disarmament. In his speech before the UN Political and Security
Committee of the General Assembly, he held that:

. . . the question of the well-known principle of unanimity operating
in the Security Council has no relation at all to the work of the com-

missions themselves. Consequently, it is entirely wrong to consider the
matter in the light that any government possessing the "right of veto"
will be in a position to hinder the fulfillment of the control and
inspections.

The control commissions are not the Security Council, and, therefore, there are no grounds whatsoever for saying that any power
making use of the "right of veto" will be in a position to obstruct the
course of control. Every attempt to obstruct the control or inspection
carried out in accordance with the decisions taken by the Security
Council will be nothing other than a violation of the decisions of the
Security Council. That is why talk about a "veto" in connection with
control and inspection is devoid of foundation. Such talk cannot be
understood as anything other than an attempt to substitute one question for another, as an attempt to evade a straight answer to the
question raised regarding the general reduction of armaments.

This speech by Molotov was regarded as a major concession and
some agreement appeared possible. But nothing materialized.
Indeed, the proposal was ignored by *both* parties. A number of
questions remain unanswered. If the Soviets were sincere in their
proposal, why did they not elaborate upon it at subsequent UN
meetings? Or did Moscow have serious second thoughts about its
implications? Why did the Western Powers fail to investigate the
Soviet proposal more fully? Had international developments made
national policies on disarmament completely rigid by late 1946?

In general, Soviet arms proposals were designed to accord
military and psychological advantages to the Soviet Union. First,
they enabled the USSR to capitalize on the universal desire for
peace. Second, the proposals would have vastly improved the
Soviet military position. They demanded, in reality, unilateral
disarmament on the part of the United States, who would have
relinquished the most powerful weapon in her protective armor
without any corresponding decrease in Soviet conventional
weapons. Also, they failed to provide a way of checking Soviet
technological efforts in the nuclear field because the Soviets refused to submit to an international inspection authority. Indeed,
the trend within the Soviet Union was again toward isolation and
secrecy. The years 1946–1947 were characterized by an intensification of cultural conformity, labor discipline, and ideological
orthodoxy—a rapid return to the Stalinist excesses of the 1930s,
only temporarily eased under the pressure of war.

By early 1947 disarmament prospects faded. The nature of
Stalin's objectives in Eastern Europe became clearer and more
ominous. Intemperate Soviet attacks on Western proposals became a regular feature of UN sessions (reading 61). To obtain
support abroad for their policies, the Soviet Government launched
a global propaganda campaign, calling "for the unconditional

abolition of atomic weapons and the branding of any government which first used such weapons against another as guilty of war crimes against humanity."* The Soviet-instigated "Stockholm Peace Campaign" of 1950, for example, circulated petitions in virtually every nation in an attempt to exploit Western differences in approach to the disarmament problem. In June the North Korean Communists moved across the 38th parallel. Rearmament now overshadowed disarmament proposals.

In October 1950, speaking before the General Assembly, President Truman indicated a willingness to treat as a unit two issues the United States had previously considered as separate and distinct problems, and which the Soviet Union had held to be but phases of the same problem: the control of nuclear weapons and the regulation of conventional weapons. (To add to the confusion, the Soviets reversed their attitude in 1956 and stated there were no cogent reasons for linking the two problems.) However, the tense atmosphere engendered by the aggression in Korea precluded any follow-up until 1952 when, on the eve of armistice in Korea, the UN established a twelve-man Disarmament Commission, consisting of the eleven members of the Security Council and Canada, to replace the separate Commissions on Conventional Armaments and Atomic Energy. (*Note:* The Soviet Union boycotted the Disarmament Commission and its subcommittee in 1957, soon after launching Sputnik, on the ground that they contained a pro-Western majority. To meet Soviet objections and revitalize disarmament talks, the General Assembly expanded the Disarmament Commission in November 1958 to include all members of the United Nations. It was evident from the start that so unwieldy a commission could not negotiate the delicate and complex issues affecting the policies and alliances of the Great Powers. The full commission convened briefly in 1960 and again in 1965. However, the brunt of the negotiations has been handled, first, by a subordinate Ten-nation Disarmament Committee, which met from March to June 1960 and was disbanded after the Soviet Union abruptly walked out of the conference on June 27, 1960; and more recently, by a reconstituted Seventeen-nation Disarma-

---

* It is interesting to note the frequency with which Soviet leaders stress the theme, *in their propaganda abroad*, that a nuclear war would endanger the very existence of world civilization. *Internally*, however, they discount, de-emphasize, and avoid this theme of doom. Thus, an important article in *Pravda* (March 5, 1955) stated that "Assertions about the possibility of the destruction of world civilization if the imperialists unleash a third world war are theoretically erroneous and politically harmful. Such assertions suit only the warmongers, who hope to intimidate the people by atomic blackmail. . . . The camp of democracy and socialism is a formidable and indestructible force. If the imperialists unleash a third world war, the result will be the destruction not of world civilization but of the rotten capitalist system."

THE FOREIGN POLICY OF THE SOVIET UNION

ment Committee [membership was originally planned for eighteen but France has refused to participate] which was convened in March 1962 and has since met intermittently for prolonged periods.)

America's nuclear monopoly ended in September 1949, when the Soviets detonated their first atomic bomb. On November 1, 1952, the United States produced the first hydrogen bomb. The Soviets followed with a similar success in August 1953. With each passing year, the nuclear advantage of the United States has decreased. Today each camp possesses thermonuclear weapons of almost uncomprehendably destructive force. A "balance of terror" has been reached.*

After Stalin's death, the Soviet leadership, preoccupied with the struggle for succession, adopted a more conciliatory approach toward the West. This "thaw" in the Cold War encouraged expectations in the disarmament field. Soviet inspection proposals, however, continued to be too susceptible to evasion to meet Western demands. The Soviets insisted that the inspection authority would have only "the right to demand of states the necessary information concerning the execution of measures for the curtailing of armaments and armed forces." In other words, no UN inspection team was to be granted access to the Soviet empire. The West, on the other hand, insisted that an elaborate

---

* Some experts disagree with this assumption. For example, Geoffrey Hudson, of Oxford University, has expressed dissatisfaction with current disarmament discussions and the strategic approach of the Western Powers. He claims that, if carried much further, they will inevitably lead to a new era of appeasement.

He notes that: "It is clearly to the interest of the belligerent who is stronger on the ground to avoid the mutual carnage of hydrogen warfare, since he can be confident of winning without it; the losing side, on the other hand, may well shrink from invoking it—or may be prevented by popular panic from doing so—if the enemy declares that he will not use it first.

"The theory of the nuclear deterrent has never been adequately thought out, and this is in no way surprising. For it is essentially a piece of humbug designed to cover up the fact that the Western nations are unwilling to make the effort needed to provide themselves with adequate military defense. But there is no reason, as regards total manpower and resources, why the NATO nations should not be able to maintain military forces sufficient to engage the Russians on the Elbe on equal terms.

"They are unwilling to meet the sacrifices required to meet the Soviet challenge. Therefore they take refuge in the nuclear deterrent, and deceive themselves with the idea that it will be enough to avert the possibility of war.

"The present trend is morally and politically to the advantage of Russia. The more the Western powers rely on nuclear weapons, and particularly strategic nuclear weapons, for the defense which they shirk providing by proper means, the more they incur responsibility in the eyes of the neutrals, of the peoples behind the Iron Curtain, and of their own peoples, for putting their stake on the most frightful of all forms of warfare when Russia is constantly appealing for its abolition." *The New York Times*, June 26, 1957.

and carefully supervised inspection system be established *prior* to any actual limitation of nuclear or conventional weapons and that the prohibition of atomic weapons be part of a comprehensive plan of control and inspection.

At the fall 1954 session of the General Assembly, the Soviet delegate, Andrei Y. Vyshinsky, called for the reduction of conventional arms by 50 per cent, the establishment of a temporary commission under the Security Council to study methods of controlling atomic energy, and an end to the manufacture of atomic weapons. These proposals provided a basis for negotiation because they avoided an *a priori* demand for the immediate prohibition of nuclear weapons. Perennially hopeful, the General Assembly revived the activities of the Disarmament Subcommittee. Closed sessions were held in London in the spring of 1955, and the periodic communiques reflected a restrained optimism.

On May 10, 1955, the Soviet Government presented a new series of proposals (reading 62). Concrete and detailed, they encouraged hopes for the success of the forthcoming Big Four Conference. The proposals called for a gradual reduction of armed forces to fixed levels, the destruction of nuclear weapons after these levels had been reached, and the institution of measures designed to prevent surprise attack. Though recommending the establishment of "control posts at the big ports, railway junctions, motor roads, and in airfields . . . to see that no dangerous concentrations of land, air, or naval forces are effected," they failed to provide the mechanics of an actual inspection system. They also would have subjected to the veto power any decision to use atomic weapons defensively. The Soviet proposals were, nevertheless, important for two reasons: First, they recognized the need to account for nuclear stockpiles and guard against surprise attack; second, they afforded a basis for further negotiation. The stage was set for the Geneva "Summit" Conference of the heads of government in July.

President Eisenhower's "open skies" proposal was the highlight of the Geneva Conference. It was not intended as a substitute for disarmament. Rather, its main purpose was to enable the Great Powers to detect, and thereby to discourage, any concentration of military forces that might be used to launch a surprise attack. Under the proposal each country would carry out a systematic aerial photographing of the other. The Soviet leaders ignored the potentialities of the President's plan because they interpreted it as an entering wedge for United States intelligence-gathering activities and because they were more interested at the time in spreading Soviet influence in the Middle East through shipments of arms to Egypt. The Geneva Conference passed into history, with little to show for its efforts. The Disarmament Commission, however, continued its deliberations into 1956, and hope persisted that an accord could be reached.

During the Suez and Hungarian crises of October-November 1956, the Soviet Government expressed a willingness "to consider the question of using aerial photography in the area in Europe where basic military forces of the North Atlantic Pact are located and in countries participating in the Warsaw Pact to a depth of 800 kilometers to the East and West from the line of demarcation of the above-mentioned military forces, if there is agreement of the appropriate state." The offer of mutual aerial inspection narrowed national positions to a point where a preliminary accord seemed within grasp.

At the 1957 sessions of the Disarmament Subcommittee, the Soviet delegates dropped their demands for the elimination of nuclear weapons and the liquidation of American overseas bases and discussed means of setting up a limited, first-phase arms control plan. Their approach seemed serious and in good faith. Western observers, conditioned by more than a decade of futile negotiating with the Soviet Union, were surprised by the sudden shift in attitude. They speculated that Khrushchev needed a respite from the onerous armament burden, with its drain on manpower and resources, in order to consolidate his position at home, that the Soviet leaders genuinely feared an accidental nuclear conflagration, and that they desired to limit the number of powers possessing nuclear weapons, though they could not openly admit this for fear of antagonizing Communist China. On the other hand, there were many Western experts who regarded the Soviet stand as a tactical maneuver designed to sow political dissension among the NATO powers and bring about the realization of the main Soviet objective in Europe—the disintegration of the NATO defense structure. Whatever the reasons, agreement proved as elusive as ever.

After the failure of the 1957 negotiations, which were the longest and most intensive up to that time, prospects for any accord plummeted as national positions hardened. There were too many areas where considerations of national security conflicted with proposals for arms limitation, and there was no consensus among the major powers as to what would be feasible, politically acceptable, and militarily secure—all "must" prerequisites for a minimal agreement. Protracted discussions continued in UN disarmament meetings. In 1959, Premier Khrushchev, speaking before the General Assembly, issued his call for general and complete disarmament (GCD)—a theme the Soviet Government has propounded ever since. But GCD was a giant step no nation was prepared to take in the current international environment. With the persistence of political discord in crucial areas, the ability to reach agreement on some initial "confidence-building measures" seemed a precondition for any meaningful attack on the major aspects of arms control and disarmament. Accordingly, during the 1958–1963 period, the Great Powers concentrated upon the negotiation of a treaty ending nuclear tests— an aspect of the over-all disarmament problem that both superpowers had a stake in, if only to halt further pollution of the atmosphere by radioactive fallout.

In August 1958 an East-West conference of scientists agreed that it was technically possible to monitor most nuclear tests. It suggested establishment of a limited network of monitoring stations (100 to 200), including some located within the United States and the Soviet Union. At the same time, other scientists in the United States insisted that *without any monitoring stations* being set up in the USSR itself, nuclear testing could be detected through the use of microbarographs, airplanes which collect radioactive dust, etc., though they admitted small-scale explosions and devices tested underground could escape detection.

Diplomatic efforts have concentrated on four issues: (1) termination of nuclear testing, (2) protection against surprise attack, (3) limitation of the use of outer space to peaceful purposes, and (4) halting dissemination and proliferation of nuclear weapons. These efforts are closely related to the fundamentally different disarmament approaches of East and West. The Soviet Union insists upon an end to American overseas military bases; termination of the war in Vietnam; a ban on the use of nuclear weapons; and a halt to American military reconnaissance over its borders. These would be followed by actual disarmament and the introduction of inspection controls. The West, on the other hand, would reverse the order of priorities. It argues that in view of the tattered record of Soviet pledges an adequate inspection system, whether to detect underground nuclear explosions or to guard against surprise attack, must be established before any other step can be considered. A brief review of the above-mentioned issues may add to an appreciation of the intricacies of the entire disarmament question.

Termination of Nuclear Testing

The Soviet Government has been a vocal advocate of a nuclear test ban since it was first proposed by India in 1954. In March 1958, having completed a series of nuclear explosions, Moscow went so far as to announce its unilateral renunciation of further tests. (It was aware at the time of the West's intention to conduct tests during the summer.) By October the Soviets resumed testing, as military considerations apparently outweighed the propaganda advantage accruing from the ban. Prior to March 1958, the United States had rejected proposals calling for a cessation of nuclear tests unless they included a ban on the *production* of nuclear weapons. Moscow countered with the demand that the *use* of nuclear weapons be outlawed. It also stated that linking a test ban with an end to bomb production was not practical, for, while a cessation of tests could be policed, a production cut-off could not be verified. The United States subsequently modified its position and came out in favor of a nuclear test ban for one year, subject to renewal, "provided that the Soviet Union would do the same, that the agreed inspection system is installed and working effectively, and that satisfactory progress is being made in reaching agreement on and implementing major and substantive arms control measures." A one-year moratorium on nuclear testing was agreed upon, effective October 31, 1958, and lasted almost three years.

During the protracted discussions at the Geneva Conference on the Discontinuance of Nuclear Weapon Tests, which opened on that date, national positions differed, *inter alia*, on the voting procedures to be followed by the proposed control commission, the composition and functions of the international observation teams, and the threshold below which underground nuclear explosions could be accurately detected. Both sides made important concessions, and agreement often seemed close at hand. However with the downing of an American U-2 reconnaissance plane over Soviet territory on May 1, 1960, and the subsequent collapse of the Paris Summit Conference, the test-ban negotiations bogged down.

On August 31, 1961, amid mounting tensions over Berlin, Laos, and the Congo, the Soviet Government unilaterally abrogated the informal moratorium and resumed testing in the atmosphere the next day. It justified the resumption of testing on several grounds, e.g., the requirements of Soviet security, the testing by France during the time of the moratorium, and the inability to agree on the conditions of a treaty (reading 63).

In the negotiations following the Soviet resumption of nuclear testing, Moscow at first insisted that a nuclear test-ban treaty be made part of a comprehensive agreement on general and complete disarmament along the lines advanced by Premier Khrushchev in his 1959 address before the General Assembly. This condition was dropped once the USSR decided that a limited test ban was in its interest. At the last moment the negotiations foundered on the questions of the number of one-site inspections, the composition of the inspection teams, the area where there could be drilling, etc.

But finally, on August 5, 1963, the Treaty Banning Nuclear Weapon Tests in the Atmosphere, in Outer Space, and Under Water, was signed in Moscow. This was the *first* concrete result to emerge from post-World War II disarmament negotiations. The treaty does not cover underground nuclear testing because of the inability to agree on an acceptable system of international on-site inspections. The Soviet position is that such inspections are unnecessary because adequate seismographic equipment exists to permit detection and identification from a distance and that on-site inspections would be a front for espionage. The treaty is self-executory: its effectiveness rests on observance by each signatory. In the event of a violation, "each Party shall in exercising its national sovereignty have the right to withdraw from the treaty . . ."

Why did the Soviet Union sign the limited test-ban treaty? According to Khrushchev, the following considerations were controlling: to end the contamination of the atmosphere, to decrease international tension and pave the way for a settlement of the German problem, to slow down the arms race and permit a freezing or reduction of military budgets and a greater attention to domestic problems, and to facilitate the negotiation of an agreement on measures to prevent surprise attack. Four other factors may have been important: First, the urgency, dramatized by the Cuban missile crisis of October 1962, of reaching a detente before accelerating tensions deprived national leaders of control over their own policy actions; second, realization by Moscow (and Washington) that further atmospheric testing was not necessary for national security, that essential military requirements could be met with existing weapons; third, the intensifying deterioration of relations between Moscow and Peking; and fourth, the hope that the treaty might forestall the proliferation of nuclear weapons. Whether Moscow (or Washington) can, in the light of Communist China's nuclear aspirations, adhere to the test ban for an extended period, or indeed whether they can reach accord in related areas, is an open and controversial question which is no doubt being intensively debated in decision-making circles in each country.

Protection Against Surprise Attack

Measures to reduce the danger of surprise attack have been under study since 1955. Various conferences convened for this purpose since November 1958 have failed to reach any agreement. As the military capability of the Great Powers increases—both in terms of destructiveness and delivery systems—fear of a crippling "first strike" looms ever larger in national chancelleries.

Both the Soviet Union and the United States have accepted the principle that aerial and ground inspection, supervised by UN personnel, be set up in strategically comparable zones to guard against surprise attack. However, they have been unable to agree upon the areas or the inspection techniques to be adopted. Moscow also persists in tying prevention of nuclear attack to the dismantling of Western military bases situated on the periphery of the Soviet empire.

The noted military analyst, Hanson W. Baldwin, has described the existing dilemma as follows:

> Any inspection system that man can devise that is at once technically feasible and politically acceptable to both East and West is likely to be far less effective in safeguarding against surprise attack than the unilateral national defense measures of both the United States and Soviet Russia. Maintenance of the capability of massive nuclear retaliation is still the surest way of preventing a nuclear Pearl Harbor. This may be dubbed the "sword of Damocles," or the "strategy of terror." It is both. But this is the shape of the world of the nuclear age.[2]

A corollary of the concern over surprise attack is the attention being given to preventing misunderstandings and accidents in moments of grave peril. A pioneering agreement establishing a direct communications link between Moscow and Washington was signed in Geneva on June 20, 1963, and became operational on August 30, 1963. The "hot line" is intended for use only in situations requiring immediate and direct communications between the two governments. Other measures intended to minimize the risk of accidental war are under discussion, e.g., proposals for an exchange of military observation teams, mutual inspection of ports, railway centers, and airfields, and advance notification of military exercises.

Limitation of Outer Space to Peaceful Purposes

The Soviet Union has refused to separate the question of the use of outer space from the issue of American overseas bases, claiming that these bases constitute a threat to Soviet security and must be removed as a precondition for a permanent agreement on the restriction of outer space to peaceful purposes. The West's reply is that the Soviet Union seeks to eliminate American bases "so as to destroy the capacity of the non-Soviet world to defend itself." This disagreement is sharpened by the realization that mastery of outer space requires superiority in missiles; and missiles may be used for war as well as peace. Each nation, therefore, fears not the exploration of outer space, a seemingly "safe" area for competitive coexistence during the coming decade, but technological breakthroughs by the other that could upset the current balance of nuclear power. For example, a decided military advantage would accrue to the first nation developing an effective antiballistic missile defense or constructing missile-mounted space platforms which would reduce even further the number of minutes required to deliver a thermonuclear bomb thousands of miles.

Former UN Secretary-General Dag Hammarskjold expressed the hope that the General Assembly would "find the way to an agreement on a basic rule that outer space, and the celestial bodies therein, are not considered as capable of appropriation by any state, and that it would further affirm the overriding interest of the community of nations in the peaceful and beneficial use of outer space and initiate steps for an international machinery to further this end." Accordingly, an eighteen-nation Committee on the Peaceful Uses of Outer Space was established by the General Assembly in December 1958 and held its first meeting in May 1959. However, Soviet opposition, ostensibly on the ground that the committee was not sufficiently representative, prevented any discussion of substantive issues and led to a recasting of the committee in late 1961 and its expansion to twenty-eight members.

The legal aspects of outer space became particularly important after the first manned space flight in April 1961 by a Soviet cosmonaut and the succession of Soviet and American space probes. The United Nations passed a resolution in late 1961 which provided an answer to the crucial question: Where does space begin and national sovereignty end? The resolution stated that international law, including the UN Charter, applied to outer space and that outer space was free for exploration and use by all nations and not subject to appropriation by any nation.

The Soviet Union and the United States have since agreed not to orbit weapons of mass destruction in outer space, established a "cold line" in October 1963 to exchange weather data, and cooperated in the use of satellites to map the earth's magnetic field. In November 1963 they agreed on the general legal principles governing the exploration and use of space. But far-reaching accords are unlikely, especially as long as Moscow insists that space satellites be barred from gathering military information, a demand which assumes that it is possible to make a meaningful distinction between military and nonmilitary information and that a feasible inspection procedure can be developed. Moreover, since August 1965, both the USSR and the United States have proclaimed their intention of proceeding immediately with construction of Manned Orbiting Laboratories (MOL). The unmistakable military character of the MOL has added a new dimension and impetus to the budding arms race in space, notwithstanding the existing agreement against orbiting weapons of mass destruction in space. Restriction of outer space to peaceful purposes, like other disarmament issues, is contingent on a settlement of the major political and military problems of the Cold War.

Halting the Proliferation of Nuclear Weapons

The most recent issue, grown pressing ever since Communist China's first nuclear explosion in October 1964, relates to efforts to limit membership in the "nuclear club" to the present five—the United States, the USSR, the United Kingdom, France, and China. Any increase in the number of nuclear powers further complicates the negotiation of arms control and disarmament agreements and purportedly adds to international tension and instability. The Soviet Government has advocated a UN conference to draw up a convention to prevent the spread of nuclear weapons under which "countries not possessing nuclear weapons should enter into an undertaking not to manufacture such weapons, not to acquire them from powers which do possess them, and not to permit them in their territory." Moscow adamantly insists that West Germany be prohibited from directly or indirectly acquiring or manufacturing nuclear weapons and that any treaty "also include provisions which would guarantee that nuclear weapons would not be handed over, or access to them given, in some indirect way, through military blocs, for instance, through the so-called NATO multilateral nuclear force (MLF)." The U.S. position, rejected by Moscow, is that the establishment of MLF would not constitute proliferation because it would not result in an increase in the total number of nuclear powers.

Observations

What, then, are Soviet intentions in the field of disarmament? Given the present foreign policy of the Soviet Union, is there any possibility of reaching an inspection or disarmament agreement with Soviet leaders? To what extent does the Soviet Government feel impelled to end the threat of a nuclear war? The Disarmament Subcommittee of the Senate Foreign Relations Committee raised these and related questions with acknowledged experts on Soviet affairs.[3] Although their interpretations varied considerably, most authorities agreed on the following:

(a) That Soviet leaders recognize the threat of mutual annihilation created by the existence of nuclear weapons.

(b) That the implications of nuclear destruction have entered into the calculations of the Kremlin, but have not perceptibly altered its reluctance to accept a bona-fide arms control and inspection system.

(c) That any progress toward inspection "would have to be developed gradually, piece by piece, and not in one over-all agreement."

(d) That a change in Soviet leadership would not be likely to result in a more accommodating approach.

(e) That the present Soviet regime "would not be willing to submit to and abide by an enforcement agency established to deal with violations of a disarmament agreement" now or in the foreseeable future.

(f) That the Soviet Army would remain in Eastern Europe to ensure the reliability of the Communist regimes. (The experts regarded the Rapacki proposals for an "atom-free" zone in Central Europe as another effort to weaken Western power on the continent.)

(g) That although the Soviet Government would welcome relief from the present burden of armaments, it could maintain a high level of military expenditures and still effect a modest improvement in the standard of living of the average Soviet citizen.

(h) Finally, "that the legitimate security interests of the Soviet Union are the same as those of any other state, such as assurance against external attack and internal subversion, and that any disarmament agreement must be based on full and unmitigated reciprocity as to the rights, procedures, and operations of the mutual control establishments."

The Soviet concept of "legitimate interests," however, differs significantly from that of the Western Powers, including not only the perpetuation of the division of Germany, but continued control of Eastern Europe. Under present conditions, the security requirements of East and West represent an incompatible situation in which a broad political settlement is an impossibility.

When the Seventeen-nation Disarmament Committee convened in Geneva in late July 1965 after a ten-month recess, both Soviet and American delegates agreed that time was rapidly running out for ending the nuclear threat to world peace. But they could not agree on how to proceed. As seen by the Soviet Union, the West is not interested in disarmament (reading 64).

What remains of disarmament itself?

Nuclear weapons inspire universal fear. There is no defense against their destructiveness except the realization that total war means the end of civilization as we know it. The East-West struggle has come to a temporary military stalemate. Each coalition possesses the power to destroy the other. Paradoxically, these weapons currently play an important deterrent role. Knowledge of their existence militates against any precipitate all-out attack, for no aggressor could hope to emerge unscathed. The development of tactical nuclear weapons, however, adds a new dimension to the study and strategy of war.

Even if scientists can devise adequate inspection safeguards, statesmen, in their anxiety over national security, may hesitate indefinitely to adopt them. Thus, political measures for developing increased confidence must go hand in hand with, if not precede, any preliminary inspection agreement. An easing of political tensions could infuse vigor into the currently futile disarmament discussions. But there is little prospect of such developments. Furthermore, an increase in the number of nuclear powers will inevitably complicate the task of disarmament and add to international tension. Nuclear weapons in the hands of unstable or irresponsible governments may relegate all disarmament talks to the dung heap of history.

In an interview on May 22, 1963 over CBS television, the eminent Soviet physicist, Dr. Igor Tamm, deplored the "mutual distrust and suspicion" that exists on both sides. He implied that time was rapidly running out, and that it was vital to reach agreement on *any* aspect of the disarmament problem in order to take a first step toward agreement and toward a cultivation of mutual trust and understanding. Something must be done, he noted, to overcome the excessive caution that permeates the negotiating of disarmament accords. There is a danger, he said, in too much caution; it may bring on the destruction that we seek to avoid.

But the overcoming of deeply ingrained national anxieties will not soon or readily be managed. Most national leaders are reconciled to a continuation of the present "balance of terror." Yet, it is possible that negotiating out of fear may in the long run bring results as effective and enduring as negotiating out of a sense of trust. Toward the end of his active political life as Prime Minister, Sir Winston Churchill observed in the House of Commons that "it may well be that we shall, by a process of sublime irony, have reached a stage in this story where safety will be the sturdy child of terror, and survival the twin brother of annihilation."

A disarmament agreement between the Soviet Union and the United States on nuclear and conventional weaponry is unlikely not only because of misunderstandings and suspicions engendered by different outlooks and perceptions of reality—though these are major inhibitory elements—but also because in a changing world man does not behave according to any mechanistically predictable and rationalistic formulas. To change the attitudes of leaders and dispel their legitimate, as well as irrational, anxieties, and, indeed, to bring them to a stage where they will be prepared to introduce extensive policy changes, requires a fundamental restructuring of national and international institutions. Until such an evolution of attitudes and institutions occurs, the negotiation of peace and security will, of necessity, continue to be a piecemeal, untidy, and uncertain venture in the regulation of human behavior.

NOTES

1. Inis L. Claude, Jr., *Swords Into Plowshares*, 2nd ed. (New York: Random House, 1956), pp. 312–313.
2. *The New York Times* (November 16, 1958).
3. U.S. Senate Committee on Foreign Relations, Subcommittee on Disarmament, *Control and Reduction of Armaments: Attitudes of Soviet Leaders Toward Disarmament*, Staff Study No. 8, 85th Congress, 1st session (1957).

Early Postwar Attitudes

59. THE ATOMIC BOMB AND INTERNATIONAL COOPERATION—SPEECH BEFORE THE UN GENERAL ASSEMBLY*

October 29, 1946

V . M . M O L O T O V

. . . We must dwell on the question of the atomic bomb, which today plays such an important part in the political calculations of some circles.

* V. M. Molotov, *Problems of Foreign Policy: Speeches and Statements* (Moscow: Foreign Languages Publishing House, 1949), pp. 257–261, 264–267, *excerpts*.

Only recently J. V. Stalin, the head of the Soviet Government, cogently expounded the views of the Soviet Union on this question. He laid particular stress on the fact that atomic bombs "cannot decide the issue of a war, inasmuch as atomic bombs are altogether insufficient for that." Further, he said that, if we are to speak of menaces to peace, "of course, the monopoly possession of the secret of the atomic bomb creates a menace," against which "there exist at least two cures: (a) the monopoly possession of the atomic bomb cannot last long; (b) the use of the atomic bomb will be forbidden." . . .

As we know, there are two distinct plans with regard to the use of atomic energy. I refer to the plan of the United States of America, on the one hand, and the plan of the Soviet Union, on the other.

The American plan, known as the "Baruch plan," unfortunately suffers from a certain degree of egoism. It is based on the desire to guarantee the United States monopoly possession of the atomic bomb. At the same time, it demands the immediate establishment of control over the production of atomic energy in all countries—a control so shaped as, on the surface, to appear international, while in reality it is designed to secure a veiled monopoly for the United States in this field. Projects of this type are obviously unacceptable, for they are dictated entirely by the narrowly conceived interests of one country, by an impermissible negation of the equality of states and of their legitimate interests.

Moreover, this plan suffers from a number of illusions. Even in the sphere of atomic energy, no single country can count on retaining a complete monopoly. Science and its exponents cannot be shut up in a box and kept under lock and key. It is about time illusions on that score were discarded. Another illusion is the hope that the atomic bomb will have a decisive effect in war. . . . Excessive enthusiasm over the atomic bomb as a decisive factor in future war may lead to political consequences that will bring tremendous disappointment, first and foremost, to the authors of such plans. And finally, it must not be forgotten that atomic bombs on one side may draw a reply in atomic bombs, and perhaps something else to boot, from the other side. . . .

There is also another plan regarding the atomic bomb, a plan proposed by the Soviet Union. This plan is based on an entirely different standpoint.

We Soviet people do not connect our plans for the future with the use of the atomic bomb. You should remember, too, that the General Assembly has already expressed itself for the elimination of atomic weapons from national armaments. Hence, there are no grounds for postponing the adoption of the international convention the Soviet Union has proposed, prohibiting the production and use of atomic weapons. . . .

Back in the years that followed the First World War, the peoples reached agreement to prohibit the military use of asphyxiating gases, bacteriological means, and other inhuman means of warfare. All the more necessary is it today to prohibit the military use of atomic bombs, and of all other means of mass destruction of human beings, which in the present instance implies the mass destruction of city residents and of peaceful citizens generally, the ruthless blow falling chiefly on children and women, on the sick and the aged. Those who fought the aggressors yesterday, and those who are genuinely opposed to new aggression, must feel it their sacred duty to outlaw the use of atomic bombs and to direct the newly-discovered atomic energy exclusively to peaceful uses. . . .

It remains for me to draw certain conclusions and offer concrete proposals. The creation of the United Nations organization was a great and historic accomplishment. It is a task of even greater importance to secure the proper direction of its work. And that requires that the peoples be inspired with respect for the principles of this Organization. It requires also that attacks and assaults against these principles encounter the proper resistance. . . .

. . . In defining the functions and powers of the Security Council, the Charter makes it responsible for formulating plans for the regulation of armaments, in order to promote the establishment and maintenance of international peace and security with the least diversion for armaments of the world's human and economic resources (Article 26 of the Charter). Further, Article 47 of the Charter, which provides for the establishment of the Military Staff Committee and defines its functions and tasks, points out that the Security Council is to have in mind the regulation of armaments, and possible disarmament.

It must be recognized that the time is ripe for definite decisions in the way of accomplishing these tasks. Now that the chief aggressive countries have been disarmed, and measures have been taken for the stringent limitation of armaments in the remaining ex-enemy states, the time has come to adopt measures for the general reduction of armaments. The execution of such measures, moreover, will increase confidence in the genuine desire of the United Nations to achieve stable peace. Finally, the reduction of armaments will strike a well-deserved blow at the expansionist aspirations of groupings which have not yet sufficiently mastered the lessons taught by the ignominious rout of the aggressors in the last war. . . .

60. THE PROHIBITION OF ATOMIC WEAPONS— SPEECH BEFORE THE POLITICAL COMMITTEE OF THE UN GENERAL ASSEMBLY*

November 28, 1946

V. M. MOLOTOV

The Soviet Government has submitted a draft for an international convention prohibiting the manufacture and use of atomic weapons, and has proposed that by this convention atomic weapons be declared outlawed. The Soviet draft provides that the governments undertake to refrain from the use of atomic weapons under any circumstances, to prohibit their production, and to destroy all stocks of atomic bombs.

Further, the Soviet Government has submitted to the Atomic Energy Commission a plan for the work of the Commission in the initial period, which provides for the elaboration of this convention and, likewise, for the consideration of measures toward the prohibition of the manufacture and use of atomic weapons and of all other weapons adaptable to mass destruction. The plan also proposes that measures be worked out to secure control over the use of atomic energy and over the observance of the conditions of the international convention outlawing atomic weapons, and that a system of sanctions be worked out against the unlawful use of atomic energy. . . .

The problem of the general reduction of armaments confronts us with the need for instituting control over the fulfilment of whatever decisions may be adopted in this sphere. If we adopt a decision prohibiting the use of atomic energy for military purposes, this decision too will require serious control. When we speak of control over the reduction of armaments and over the prohibition of atomic weapons, we must keep always in mind the importance of this task. . . . Having recognized in principle the necessity of strict international control, we should also be able to reach agreement on the concrete points involved in control over

    * V. M. Molotov, *Problems of Foreign Policy: Speeches and Statements* (Moscow: Foreign Languages Publishing House, 1949), pp. 312–316, *excerpts.*

the prohibition of the use of atomic energy for military purposes and over the fulfilment of whatever decision may be adopted concerning the general reduction of armaments.

Soviet Criticisms and the Cold War

61. SOVIET ATTACKS ON AMERICAN DISARMAMENT POLICY*

September 16, 1949

. . . The United States . . . has taken a position in the matter of the prohibition of atomic weapons and the establishment of control of atomic energy that is known to all. The United States wants neither the one nor the other, and has resolutely opposed them for three years, resisting the simultaneous conclusion and enforcement of two conventions, a convention on the prohibition of atomic weapons and, in connection therewith, a convention on the control of atomic energy. This is not, of course, done openly and straightforwardly, but in disguised and devious ways.

The United States representatives on the Atomic Energy Commission declare that they, too, are in favor of the prohibition of atomic weapons. That is what they say; but what they do is to offer a plan according to which the prohibition of atomic weapons would represent only a remote and ultimate stage of control. The prohibition of atomic weapons would thus come into force, if at all, at some time in the distant future. The representatives of the United States say further that they are in favor of the establishment of atomic energy control, but in reality the plan they have submitted does not provide for the strict international control of atomic energy but for the transfer of all rights of ownership and management of all atomic facilities, and of the production of such facilities in all countries of the world, to an international organ, which would consequently not be an organ of control but a world supertrust or world monopoly, firmly controlled by the United States, and which would own the key branches of industry in other countries and use them as it wished . . .

* United Nations Security Council, *Official Records*, 446th meeting, September 16, 1949, *excerpts*.

In reality, this plan has nothing in common with the concept of control. It is a fantastic plan to place, through the instrumentality of an international organ, vast numbers of enterprises and whole branches of industry in other countries under United States control. It is unrealistic and politically indefensible. . . . The control plan proposed by the United States bears not the slightest resemblance to genuine control. This plan is not concerned at all with control, but with empowering an international body to take possession of, and to do as it wishes with, the production of nuclear fuel and atomic products throughout the world. Is that really control? It may be control in the eyes of Wall Street, but, in our opinion, it is an open attempt, on a worldwide scale, to place the most important branches of industry in other countries and on every continent under the control of the United States, such control to be exercised through the instrumentality of an international control agency. . . .

Developments Since 1955

62. PROPOSAL OF THE SOVIET GOVERNMENT ON INTERNATIONAL CONTROL OF ARMAMENTS REDUCTION AND PROHIBITION OF ATOMIC WEAPONS*

May 10, 1955

. . . Under existing conditions, when many states are legitimately concerned for their security, it is hard to expect that they would entrust to other states the inspection of industrial and other resources of vital importance to their security.

Inasmuch as the necessary confidence does not exist among the states at the present time, there may arise a situation in which the adoption of a decision on international control would

* *New Times*, No. 20 (May 14, 1955), *excerpts*. This proposal of the Soviet Government was submitted to the Subcommittee of the UN Disarmament Commission in London by USSR representative Y. A. Malik on May 10, 1955.

be reduced to a mere formality, and would not achieve its purpose. This would be all the more impermissible, since, in present conditions, the apprehensions of the peaceable nations are most aroused by the existence of atomic and hydrogen weapons, the establishment of international control of which is particularly difficult.

This danger stems from the very nature of atomic production. It is well known that production of atomic energy for peaceful purposes may be utilized for the stockpiling, in ever-increasing quantities, of atomic explosives. This means that states possessing atomic energy plants might, in violation of pertinent agreements, accumulate large quantities of weapon-grade atomic materials. . . .

There are thus possibilities, unamenable to international control, of evading supervision and organizing secret production of atomic and hydrogen weapons even when there is formal agreement on international control. This being so, there can be no guarantee of the security of the states which signed the international convention, since a potential aggressor would be in a position to accumulate stocks of atomic and hydrogen weapons for a sudden atomic attack on peaceable states.

So long as an atmosphere of confidence has not been created among the states, any agreement on international control may only lull the vigilance of the peoples. It may create a false sense of security, when actually there is a danger of atomic and hydrogen weapons being produced, and, hence, the danger of sudden attack and unleashing of atomic war, with all its drastic consequences for the peoples. . . .

The question of establishing international control and determining the rights and powers of the International Control Agency must therefore be examined in close connection with realization of the above-mentioned measures of lessening international tension and strengthening confidence among the states, and the carrying out of other measures in relation to reduction of armaments and prohibition of atomic weapons.

Accordingly,

The General Assembly institutes an International Control Agency with the following rights and powers:

1. *In the first period of implementation of the measures for reduction of armaments and prohibition of atomic weapons.*

(a) With a view to preventing surprise attack by one state on another, the International Control Agency shall establish, on a basis of reciprocity, control posts at the big ports, railway junctions, motor roads, and airfields in the territories of all the states concerned. It shall be the function of these posts to see that no dangerous concentrations of land, air, or naval forces are effected.

(b) The International Control Agency shall have the right to demand from the states all necessary information concerning the carrying out of the measures for reduction of armaments and armed forces.

(c) The Control Agency shall be allowed free access to materials relating to the military allocations of the states, including all pertinent decisions of their legislative and executive bodies. The states shall present to the Control Agency at definite intervals information concerning the carrying out of the measures envisaged in the convention (treaty).

2. *In the second period of implementation of the measures for reduction of armaments and prohibition of atomic weapons.*

Implementation of the measures envisaged in the above Declaration, and of the measures for reduction of armaments and armed forces and prohibition of atomic and hydrogen weapons provided for the first period, should create the necessary atmosphere of confidence among the states. This will ensure the proper conditions for extending the functions of the International Control Agency.

Given these conditions, the International Control Agency shall possess the following rights and powers:

(a) To exercise control, including inspection on a permanent basis, to the extent required to ensure the observance of the convention by all the states. The International Control Agency, shall in the exercise of these functions, also have the right to demand from the states all necessary information concerning the carrying out of the measures for reduction of armaments and armed forces.

The inspection personnel shall be selected on an international basis.

(b) To maintain permanently in all countries which signed the convention staffs of inspectors who, within the limits of their control functions, shall be allowed free access to all control installations at any time.

With a view to preventing surprise attack by one state on another, the International Control Agency shall, in particular, maintain on a basis of reciprocity control posts at the big ports, railway junctions, motor roads, and airfields in the territories of all the states concerned.

(c) The Control Agency shall be allowed free access to materials relating to the military allocations of the states, including all pertinent decisions of their legislative and executive bodies. The states shall present to the Control Agency at definite intervals information concerning the carrying out of the measures envisaged in the convention (treaty).

3. The Control Agency shall make recommendations to the Security Council concerning measures for preventing or stopping violations of the convention on reduction of armaments and prohibition of atomic weapons.

4. The functions and powers of the permanent International Control Agency shall be established in fuller detail, and corresponding instructions drawn up for this purpose, on the basis of the above-mentioned principles.

Breaking the Nuclear Test Ban

63. THE SOVIET JUSTIFICATION FOR THE RESUMPTION OF NUCLEAR TESTING IN THE ATMOSPHERE*

August 31, 1961

The peoples are witnessing the ever-increasing aggressiveness of the policy of the NATO military bloc. The United States and its allies are spinning the flywheel of their military machine ever faster, fanning up the arms race to unprecedented scope, increasing the strength of armies, making the tension of the international situation red-hot. Things have reached a point that the leading statesmen of the United States and its allies are resorting to threats to take to arms and to unleash war as a countermeasure to the conclusion of a peace treaty with the German Democratic Republic.

Being faced with these facts, which cannot but cause anxiety, the Soviet Government considers it its duty to take all measures so that the Soviet Union should be completely prepared to render harmless any aggressor if he tried to launch an attack. The tragedy of the first months of the great patriotic war when Hitler attacked the U.S.S.R., having ensured for himself superiority in military equipment, is too fresh in the memory of people to allow this to happen now.

This is the reason why the Soviet Government has already taken a number of serious measures for strengthening the security

* TASS statement, issued August 31, 1961, *excerpts*.

of the U.S.S.R. For the same reason, after a thoughtful and comprehensive consideration of this question, it has made a decision to carry out experimental explosions of nuclear weapons . . .

The question of control has for years been a stumbling block on the way to agreement on disarmament. This was so because control has been used by the Western powers as a pretext to turn down any proposal on disarmament . . . In order not to allow the essence of the matter—disarmament itself—to be ruined the Soviet Government has stated openly that it is ready to accept in advance any proposal of the Western powers on international control. Only one thing was expected from the Western powers and that was to accept our proposals on general disarmament and to submit their proposals on general control . . .

What can be the explanation for the fact that no specific proposals on that score have yet followed from the Western powers? This can be explained only by the fear that the Soviet Union will accept their proposals on control and then the Western powers would either have to agree to general and complete disarmament or would expose themselves to the last as opponents of disarmament and as opponents of control over disarmament.

The main thing in our days is disarmament, general and complete, and an agreement on such disarmament would cover the question of nuclear testing. Indeed, when the arms race is stopped and the stockpiled weapons are destroyed, there will be no stimulus for its perfection and consequently for the need to carry out our experimental nuclear tests but, on the contrary, merely an agreement to stop nuclear weapons tests cannot by itself put an end to the arms race.

The states that already possess atomic weapons will inevitably feel tempted to act violating such an agreement, to seek new ways and loopholes for perfecting weapons, to say nothing of the fact that the tests carried out by three-four powers are quite sufficient for unlimited stockpiling of the most dangerous thermonuclear weapons of the existing types.

The states which do not yet possess thermonuclear weapons will in their turn try to create them despite the agreement that prohibits atomic tests . . .

The Governments of the Western powers have persistently advanced and continue to advance the demand that a treaty on the discontinuance of nuclear tests should not provide for the prohibition of underground nuclear explosions. Meanwhile, it is obvious to every informed person that the carrying out of such explosions, even if it is claimed that they are conducted for peaceful purposes, is nothing else but a hidden form of perfecting the existing nuclear weapons or putting finishing touches to its new types. If a nuclear explosive device is effective, for example, for moving ground—and the Western powers want to secure for themselves the right of carrying out such explosions—the same explosive device will also be effective for military purposes . . .

The entire course of the negotiations in Geneva proves that the Western powers pursue the aim of actually legalizing those types of nuclear tests in which they are interested and of establishing an international control body which would be an obedient tool in their hands and in fact would be an appendage of the general staffs of Western powers . . .

The Soviet Government considers it its duty to draw special attention of the peoples of the world to the fact that now in the United States there is much ado about projects for developing a neutron bomb which would kill everything living but at the same time would not destroy material things. Only aggressors dreaming of plunder, of capturing foreign lands and foreign property can mobilize the efforts of scientists for the development of such weapons . . .

It is an open secret that the United States is standing at the threshold of carrying out underground nuclear explosions and only waits for the first suitable pretext to start them. However, it is clear to everybody that since the U. S. Government has the intention to resume nuclear weapons tests, it is only a matter of time.

The Soviet Government cannot ignore the fact that France, the ally of the United States in NATO, has been carrying out nuclear tests already for a long time. While the Soviet Union refrained from nuclear tests, trying to achieve agreement with the United States and Great Britain at the table of negotiations on their complete discontinuance, France conducted explosions of nuclear devices one after another. It continues to do so in spite of the appeal of the United Nations to all states to refrain from such tests, in spite of the protests of broad public circles in all countries of the world, in spite of the warnings of the Soviet Union that it will be forced to resume tests if France does not stop its experiments with nuclear weapons . . .

The View from Moscow

64. THE SOVIET EVALUATION OF THE WORK OF THE UN DISARMAMENT COMMISSION*

July 1965

Some may well ask whether it was worth convening the U.N. Disarmament Commission in the present aggravated international situation. The answer was given in the speeches of most of the neutralist members, who gave enthusiastic support to the Soviet Union's initiative in calling for a meeting of the Commission. Having disrupted the normal work of the 19th U.N. General Assembly, the United States had hoped to avoid a discussion on the problems of peace and disarmament in a broad and open international forum. Its hopes were not justified. American diplomacy had to give an explanation of its stand to the Commission, on which all 114 U.N. members are represented.

What is its stand? Even a brief analysis will show that it differs little from what the Americans have been proposing for the last three years. The U. S. Government's motto continues to be "control, and not disarmament."

In its April 18, 1962 plan, the United States does not in any way provide for the prohibition of nuclear weapons and destruction of their stockpiles. It is against the complete destruction of delivery vehicles at the start of disarmament and flatly opposes the liquidation of foreign military bases. But it has worked out the question of control in great detail, and is doing everything to transform control from a measure promoting the fulfillment of disarmament obligations into a means of legalised international espionage.

In these three years, the United States has actually in no way modified its initial plan. Nor has it done so this time, despite the numerous attempts of the Soviet side to find a way out of the impasse through compromise proposals. This U. S. posture continues to be an insuperable obstacle to progress in the discussions of general and complete disarmament.

Perhaps the American disarmament experts—and there are

* Commentator, "World Forum on Disarmament," *International Affairs*, Moscow (July 1965), pp. 53–56, *excerpts.*

more than 200 of them in the U. S. Arms Control and Disarmament Agency—have in some way modified or renewed their program of so-called partial measures for disarmament? No, they have not, as will be easily seen from the U. S. draft resolution tabled in the Commission. It insistently proposes that the 18-Nation Disarmament Committee should resume its sittings as soon as possible to examine questions of the prohibition of underground nuclear tests, non-proliferation of nuclear weapons, cessation of fissile materials production for military purposes, and freezing the production of strategic nuclear weapons delivery vehicles.

The explanations of the U. S. delegate make it clear that the United States, which has been carrying on its underground nuclear tests, is prepared to stop them only on the basis of the patently unacceptable demand for international control over such a cessation of tests. On non-proliferation, the United States is prepared to conclude an agreement that would not prevent NATO from getting on with its M.L.F. All these American proposals for ways of solving two key issues promoting disarmament are unacceptable and were rejected by the Soviet Union long ago.

Nor is there anything novel in the two other questions which the United States wants to put before the 18-Nation Committee. Without providing anything for the solution of the disarmament problem, these American proposals create the greatest possible convenience for military intelligence, one, through controls over the atomic industry of states, and the other, through controls over the manufacture of missiles and other strategic nuclear weapons delivery vehicles.

The fact that the United States has no new proposals is good evidence that it has at present no intention to search for a solution of disarmament questions. U. S. diplomats prefer to talk of maintaining the present equilibrium of forces, rather than of disarmament.

The hypocritical talk about disarmament and the empty proposals on the part of the U. S. delegation contrast with the Soviet Union's real measures which facilitate disarmament and bring it nearer.

In its complex of proposals, the Soviet delegation has brought two to the fore. They are, first, the liquidation of foreign military bases, and the withdrawal of foreign troops from the territories of other countries, and second, conclusion of a convention renouncing the use of nuclear weapons. On both these proposals, the Soviet delegation has laid corresponding draft resolutions before the Commission. . . .

The neutralist countries' idea of convening a world forum on disarmament is of great importance, for it is a reflection of the significant and undoubtedly positive phenomenon of our time, namely, that more and more nations want to take part in a businesslike and searching discussion of disarmament. The idea of disarmament is winning the minds of the vast majority of the world's population. It is becoming increasingly difficult to confine disarmament talks to restricted committee sessions or to subcommittees with a limited number of members.

The Soviet Union supports the proposals of the non-aligned countries for a world disarmament conference. The Soviet delegation emphasised that the holding of such a conference in the most immediate future is essential in the present circumstances and that such a conference—in which all the countries of the world must take part—would provide a very strong impetus for the attainment of concrete results both in the field of general and complete disarmament and also in respect of other disarmament measures. The idea of a world conference did not enthuse the United States and many other Western Powers, and their one concern was the earliest possible return to the 18-Nation Committee, where the negotiations drag on for years without any concrete results.

However, the Commission succeeded in overcoming the resistance of the United States and its allies, and came out in favor of a world disarmament conference by an overwhelming majority. That is a clear victory for the peace-loving forces. Eighty-nine countries voted for the resolution; sixteen (including the U.S.A., France, Portugal, the South African Republic and Spain) abstained, with the Chiang Kai-shek man making a show of refusing to vote; a number of countries (Chad, Dahomey, Dominican Republic, Gabon, etc.) were not present. . . .

An analysis of the work of the U.N. Disarmament Commission shows that the discussions at its sittings have played a positive part because, on the one hand, they helped to expose the aggressive policy of the Western Powers, who oppose any real measures for disarmament, and, on the other, they attracted attention to the timely and effective Soviet proposals on disarmament, which are winning the support of an ever wider circle of neutralist countries.

FOR FURTHER STUDY

Baldwin, Hanson W., *The Great Arms Race: A Comparison of United States and Soviet Power Today.* New York: Frederick A. Praeger, 1958.

Barnet, Richard, *Who Wants Disarmament?* Boston: Beacon Press, 1961.

Bechhoefer, Bernhard G., *Postwar Negotiations for Arms Control.* Washington, D.C.: Brookings Institution, 1961.

Clark, Grenville and Louis B. Sohn, *World Peace Through World Law.* Cambridge, Mass.: Harvard University Press, 1958.

Dallin, Alexander (ed.), *The Soviet Union and Disarmament: An Appraisal of Soviet Attitudes and Intentions.* New York: Frederick A. Praeger, 1965.

Deutsch, Morton (ed.), *Preventing World War III: Some Proposals.* New York: Simon and Schuster, 1962.

Dinerstein, Herbert S., *War and the Soviet Union.* New York: Frederick A. Praeger, 1959.

Garthoff, Raymond L., *Soviet Strategy in the Nuclear Age.* New York: Frederick A. Praeger, 1958.

Kissinger, Henry A., *Nuclear Weapons and Foreign Policy.* New York: Harper & Row, Publishers, 1957.

Levine, Robert A., *The Arms Debate.* Cambridge, Mass.: Harvard University Press, 1963.

Nogee, Joseph L., *Soviet Policy Toward International Control of Atomic Energy.* Notre Dame, Ind.: University of Notre Dame Press, 1961.

Schelling, Thomas C., *The Strategy of Conflict.* Cambridge, Mass.: Harvard University Press, 1960.

Sokolovskii, V. D. (ed.), *Soviet Military Doctrine.* Translated, analyzed and annotated by H. S. Dinerstein, L. Gouré, and T. W. Wolfe. Englewood Cliffs, N.J.: Prentice-Hall, 1963.

Spanier, John W. and Joseph L. Nogee, *The Politics of Disarmament: A Study in Soviet-American Gamesmanship.* New York: Frederick A. Praeger, 1962.

Voss, E. H., *Nuclear Ambush: The Test-Ban Trap.* Chicago: Henry Regnery Company, 1963.

Wadsworth, James J., *The Price of Peace.* New York: Frederick A. Praeger, 1962.

Wolfe, Thomas W., *Soviet Strategy at the Crossroads.* Cambridge, Mass.: Harvard University Press, 1964.

CHAPTER X

THE ROLE OF
DEVELOPING AREAS
IN SOVIET THOUGHT
AND POLICY

Since World War I, and especially since 1945, nationalism has been the principal force underlying the unrest and instability in the two-thirds of the world often referred to as the "developing areas." Soviet leaders have long appreciated the significance of these areas, though it is only in the post-World War II period that communism has succeeded in making significant political advances there. The victory of the Chinese Communists is the most dramatic example of this trend. A statement characterizing the role developing areas play in Soviet thought, often attributed to Lenin, holds that "the road to Paris lies through Calcutta and Bombay." This sentiment has certainly epitomized Soviet expectations and attitudes for almost half a century.

The essence of the Soviet approach to developing areas can be traced to the Leninist theory of imperialism—that capitalist countries, in their search for raw materials, cheap labor, and potential markets, have seized the less developed areas, thus forestalling their own eventual decay and disintegration. The struggle against imperialism must be waged on two fronts: first, the developing nations must break colonial rule, thereby weakening the global structure of capitalism; second, the proletariat of the imperialist countries must strive to defeat capitalism from within. This two-fold struggle will ensure the ultimate collapse of capitalism.

The ideological appeal of communism for colonial and dependent areas stems from its advocacy of national self-determination and from its promise of a better future. To nations long subject to foreign control and confronted with massive problems of poverty, economic backwardness, and burgeoning populations, communism offers a seemingly simple, direct, and effective path to economic development and political power. "Did not the Soviet Union transform itself from a backward nation to one of the world's most powerful industrial states in a generation?" ask the often myopic nationalists of the developing countries. The quest for simple solutions to complex problems has often led well-intentioned leaders astray, to their subsequent sorrow. But the evidence of Soviet industrial development is incontrovertible, and the formula *does* appear deceptively easy to apply elsewhere. Also, in many of these societies, the reformers, intellectuals and newly educated, covetous of position, prestige, and power, are too often denied these fruits by reactionary, venal, inbred aristocracies, who rule without regard for the needs of their peoples. It is among these frustrated, ambitious, idealistic, alienated groups, so insistent upon rapid change and intent upon discarding the past for an uncertain future, that communism makes its greatest inroads.

Lenin realized the political potential of the underdeveloped areas and made it an integral concern of Soviet ideology. Whereas Marx predicted the downfall of capitalism through the proletariats of the industrialized nations, Lenin understood that this defeat could be hastened by detaching the underdeveloped areas from the control of the colonial powers. He wove the twin themes of national self-determination and internationalism* into a common

---

* Lenin defined "internationalism" as follows: "There is one, only one kind of internationalism in deed: working wholeheartedly for the development of the revolutionary movement and the revolutionary struggle *in one's own country*, and supporting (by propaganda, sympathy and material aid) *such and only such a struggle* and such a line in *every* country without exception."

Ideally, internationalism united the workers of all nations in the struggle against imperialism; once independence was attained, it would act to diminish national differences and bring about a Communist world. As applied to developing areas, internationalism and national self-determination are closely interrelated. On the one hand, the proletariat of the advanced countries must work both for revolution in their own countries

policy fabric and tailored it to the situations existing in under-developed areas. Subsequent Soviet leaders have expanded and modified these concepts, varying the emphasis to accord with contemporary need. They are, in a sense, two aspects of the same problem: the national question (which is concerned with the relationships between the colonial powers and the subjugated peoples, and among national minorities within a particular nation). Lenin held that all nations were equal, a concept with enormous appeal, and that they had the right to determine their own future. He predicted that all nations would in time be united in a common bond of brotherhood—communism. However, since they first had to be free from the domination of "imperialist" powers, national self-determination for all nations had to be supported. To weaken imperialism, Lenin proposed an alliance between the proletarian forces in the advanced countries and the revolutionary forces in the colonial and semi-colonial areas. Internationalism aids both and constitutes the bond that links them in common cause.

The right of national self-determination was a principal contribution of the first Congress of the Russian Social Democratic-Labor Party which met in March 1898. (At its second Congress in 1903 this party split into the Menshevik and Bolshevik wings.) Lenin's views on national self-determination were not formulated in detail until the 1913–1914 period. Before that, there was nothing in his writings to indicate that "the right of nations to 'self-determination' meant their right of political secession, to set up their separate state," though he later insisted that such was his intention.[1] His approach to the problem had been more in terms of internationalism, of the unity of the proletariat of all nations. During the Czarist oppression preceding World War I, the problem of nationalities became increasingly aggravated. Lenin, aware of the growing disillusionment and discontent among the non-Russian nationalities, especially in the Caucasus, suggested to a young Georgian then visiting him that he undertake to write an essay setting forth the Bolshevik position on the entire problem of national minorities. The result was Stalin's essay, *Marxism and the National Question*.

Stalin's analysis became accepted Bolshevik doctrine and was incorporated in the Party platform at the seventh All-Russian Conference of the Russian Social Democratic Labor Party in May

---

and for the liberation and national independence of all colonial and semi-colonial areas. This alliance of the proletariat of the developed countries and the peoples of the developing areas transcends national allegiance. They have in common the goal of overthrowing capitalism, and eventually establishing a global system of Communist states.

1917 (readings 65 and 66). It encompassed national self-determination (if desired) for national minorities in the Russian empire, freedom for minority nationalities residing in a country controlled by a dominant nationality, and, after 1917, was expanded to include freedom for the colonial and semi-colonial countries ruled by a Great Power. In his report Stalin declared:

> . . . our views on the national question can be reduced to the following propositions: (a) recognition of the right of nations to secession; (b) regional autonomy for nations remaining within the given state; (c) special legislation guaranteeing freedom of development for national minorities; (d) a single, indivisible proletarian body, a single party for the proletarians of all the nationalities of the given state.

Bolshevik doctrine on the national question has undergone several changes, always in the interests of political expediency. For example, during the period of "War Communism," the Bolsheviks found it profitable to espouse the principle of national self-determination, including the right of secession. At that time, they encouraged national minorities to oppose the White armies, thus promoting Bolshevik prospects of survival. However, with victory assured, the Bolsheviks forcibly reincorporated these minority groups into the Russian state. In another situation, the policy of "national-cultural autonomy," long opposed by Lenin* and rejected as a solution to the national question by the Party resolution of May 1917, was in large measure the same solution subsequently adopted by Stalin, as Commissar of Nationalities, in the early 1920s.

National self-determination, in its usual implication of *political* freedom to establish and function as an independent nation, had but a brief, and almost exclusively tactical, significance in Russia. However, outside of the Soviet Union, the Leninist stress on *political* freedom is still used. As part of the Soviet ideological baggage abroad, it seeks to portray the Soviet Union as an advocate of liberation for all peoples from colonial rule, and as a firm opponent of imperialism. Soviet leaders today see national self-determination as an effective instrument for undermining Western political and economic power. The "myth" of Soviet support of national liberation movements has acquired a growing power

* In late 1913 Lenin declared that: "National-cultural autonomy implies the most refined and therefore the most pernicious kind of nationalism; it means that the workers are corrupted by the slogan 'national culture,' and by propaganda for a thoroughly harmful and even anti-democratic division of the educational system according to nationalities. In a word, this programme, which satisfies the ideals only of the nationalistic petty-bourgeois, is in absolute contradiction with the internationalism of the proletariat."

and appeal in developing areas. Thus a double standard is effectively used.

Earlier, Lenin had found it a useful expedient. Not only did national-liberation movements weaken imperialism, and strengthen the indigenous Communist Parties working with these bourgeois-nationalist elements, but they could also be used to establish a global system of Soviet republics. On the other hand, as interpreted *within* the Soviet Union, national self-determination "was to be the exclusive prerogative of the workers; and the national bourgeoisie was to have no voice in the matter." That is to say, national self-determination was to be granted only to the proletariat and its spokesman, the Communist Party, which, in the case of the USSR, had no "desire" to secede.

Such an approach would obviously have little appeal for the peoples of developing areas. Therefore, while *within* the USSR the right of national self-determination has been narrowly construed, in *non-Soviet* areas, a broader, more flexible interpretation has been developed.

During the period of "War Communism," 1917 to 1921, the Bolsheviks were occupied with their survival in European Russia. However, the political significance of the East was very much in Lenin's thoughts. Shortly after the Bolsheviks came to power, Lenin and Stalin made their famous appeal "To All the Toiling Moslems of Russia and the East" (reading 67). There was no mistaking their attempt to incite revolution in the Moslem-populated areas of Russia, the Middle East, and India. This active interest waned under the impact of more pressing concerns, but appreciation of the importance of these areas did not. Of the Bolshevik leaders only Stalin remained continually involved in Asian and non-European affairs. His interest in the potential of the East persisted during the post-armistice period, at a time "when every Soviet leader had his eyes fixed on Berlin and on the incipient German revolution."[2] In November 1918, Stalin wrote several articles, including "Don't Forget the East" (reading 68), in which he called attention to the revolutionary ferment spreading throughout the East. He feared that the Bolsheviks, in their intense focus on the expected revolution in Germany and Western Europe, would neglect vital interests in the East.

At the founding Congress of the Communist International in March 1919, the colonial question received relatively little attention. However, as the situation in Russia stabilized, Lenin shrewdly perceived that the East could be used to improve Russia's military-political position. Accordingly, he proceeded to assign colonial areas a more significant role in Communist strategy. In July 1920, at the second Comintern Congress, Lenin's "Prelimi-

nary Draft of Theses on the National and Colonial Questions"
(reading 69) was adopted and incorporated into Soviet ideology.*
These theses reflected the dominant theme of the Congress which
was "to apply the principles of world revolution to the Eastern
peoples, to develop the doctrine of a common struggle in which
all the workers of the world, West and East, had their part to
play, and, in particular, to strengthen the revolt under the leadership of the RSFSR against British imperialism."[3]

Lenin's double-edged program aimed at cutting off the West
from the resources and labor supply of the East and at expanding
the influence of the Communist Party in the developing areas.
Stressing the fundamental hostility between the capitalist and
socialist (Soviet) systems, and the division of the world into
oppressing and oppressed nations, Lenin called upon the Comintern to promote the alliance between the proletariat of the
advanced countries and the peoples of the developing areas. As
natural allies, the two would work toward the defeat of capitalism; the proletariat weakening imperialist power at its home
base, and the colonial peoples weakening imperialist power by
driving out the European rulers. According to Lenin, the cornerstone of Comintern policy in the national and colonial question
must be:

. . . to bring together the proletarians and the masses of the toilers of
all nations and countries for the joint revolutionary struggle for the
overthrow of the landlords and the bourgeoisie; for this alone guarantees victory over capitalism, without which the abolition of national
oppression and inequality is impossible.
. . . it is necessary to pursue a policy that will bring about the closest
alliance of all the national and colonial liberation movements with
Soviet Russia; the form of this alliance is to be determined by the
degree of development of the Communist movement among the proletariat of each country, or of the bourgeois-democratic liberation movement of the workers and peasants in backward countries or among
backward nationalities.[4]

Lenin acknowledged that nationalist movements in developing
areas would usually have a bourgeois character initially. Nevertheless, he enthusiastically endorsed temporary cooperation with
them, provided that the proletarian movement, however rudi-

* A set of theses was also introduced by Manabendra Nath Roy, the
Indian delegate, an able, well-educated, independent-minded individual who
split with Moscow in 1929. Roy recommended that the proletariat operate
independently of the bourgeois national-liberation groups in developing its
revolutionary movement. He also placed inordinate emphasis, the Congress
thought, upon the theme that the success of revolution in Europe depended
upon the *prior* success of revolution in Asia. Though adopted unanimously,
Roy's theses were rarely referred to afterwards by the Comintern, which
proceeded to regard Lenin's theses as its guide.

mentary, maintain its sense of identity and independence of action. Furthermore, the Comintern must not permit itself to be overshadowed by any of these bourgeois-national movements.

> . . . the Communist International must support bourgeois-democratic national movements in colonial and backward countries only on the conditions that the elements of future proletarian parties existing in all backward countries, which are not merely Communist in name, shall be grouped together and trained to appreciate their special tasks, *viz.*, the tasks of fighting the bourgeois-democratic movements within their own nations; the Communist International must enter into a temporary alliance with bourgeois democracy in colonial and backward countries, but must not merge with it, and must unconditionally preserve the independence of the proletarian movement even in its most rudimentary form.[5]

While the Comintern is aiding national-liberation movements, it must advance the interests of communism, defend the Soviet Union, strengthen the bonds between the Russian proletariat and the developing areas, and stimulate the revolutionary character of the agrarian movement, linking it with the revolutionary proletariat in Western Europe. Lenin emphasized the leading role of the Soviet Union. The relationship between the Soviet Union and the less developed countries "is to be determined by the degree of development" of the area involved; similarly, the relationship between the Soviet Union and the national-liberation movements will depend upon the strength of these movements, and particularly of their proletarian components. Lenin's theses became the accepted ideological and tactical basis of Soviet policy toward the developing areas. Though later Congresses expanded his views, the essentials of his program remained valid: to promote nationalist revolutions which in their advanced stage were to be captured by Communists and converted into socialist revolutions; to encourage cooperation between the proletariat of the advanced countries and the peoples of the colonial and semicolonial areas; to accept temporary alliances with bourgeois-nationalist groups, provided the proletariat could maintain its position as an "independent revolutionary factor in the anti-imperialist front as a whole."[6]

Soviet leaders did not wait long to link their foreign policy objectives with bourgeois efforts to foment nationalist revolutions. Under Comintern aegis, the first "Congress of the Peoples of the East" met in Baku on September 1, 1920. It openly and uncompromisingly espoused the doctrine of world revolution and tried to enlist Moslem support for an all-out crusade against the West. Soviet objectives were clear: to undermine British and French power in the Middle East, to associate Soviet Russia with the

aspirations of these areas, to penetrate, and eventually to dominate, the national-liberation movements.

The Baku Conference never fulfilled Comintern expectations.
But it did illustrate two things: Soviet awareness of the politically
important role the East could play in the struggle against the
West and the persistence of the Czarist tradition of an alternating
Western and Eastern foreign policy orientation. Finally, the propaganda invective of Baku dismayed the colonial powers. Britain,
for example, was clearly aware of the potentially disruptive
impact of Bolshevik appeals in its Middle Eastern and South
Asian possessions. Accordingly, one condition they insisted upon
in their trade agreement with the Soviets of March 16, 1921—
an agreement important to the Soviets in terms of ending their
diplomatic isolation and obtaining needed material from abroad
—stated the following:

> That each Party refrains from hostile action or undertakings against
> the other and from conducting outside of its own borders any official
> propaganda direct or indirect against the institutions of the British
> Empire or the Russian Soviet Republic respectively, and more particu-
> larly that the Russian Soviet Government refrains from any attempt
> by military or diplomatic or any other form of action or propaganda to
> encourage any of the peoples of Asia in any form of hostile action
> against British interests or the British Empire, especially in India and
> in the Independent State of Afghanistan.[7]

The Soviets never abided by these provisions, nor apparently
had they ever intended to do so. Subsequent Soviet agreements
with other nations usually contained a similar provision, just
as frequently violated. Throughout its history, the Soviet Government has persisted in the convenient fiction that the Comintern
(and between 1947–1956, the Cominform) operated independently of Kremlin control, and therefore its propaganda and subversive activities were not the responsibility of the Soviet
Government.

The colonial question continued to occupy an important position in Comintern deliberations. At the fourth Congress (November 1922) the Leninist position was reaffirmed by Zinoviev
in his "Theses on the Eastern Question," and the Comintern
agreed to support "every national revolutionary movement against
imperialism." The agrarian question and the nascent labor movements in the less developed areas received particular attention.
But, though propounding the theory that the revolutionary movement in these areas could not be successful without peasant
participation, the Comintern relied, in practice, principally upon
the urban proletariat. Not until the rise to power of Mao Tse-tung
and the Chinese Communists did Communist strategy *and prac-*

tice in the East accord the peasantry a significant role in the struggle for political power. The "united front from above" strategy—characterized by a friendly attitude toward bourgeois-democratic parties seeking liberation from imperialist rule—dominated Comintern policy until 1928. Zinoviev developed the outlines of this anti-imperialist strategy for the as-yet weak Party organizations in the developing areas, stating that "The Communist Parties of the colonial and semi-colonial countries of the East, which are still in a more or less embryonic stage *must take part in every movement which gives them access to the masses*" (italics are the author's); and that "the working class acknowledges that it is permissible and necessary to make partial and temporary compromises in order to win a breathing space in the revolutionary struggle for liberation against imperialism." In keeping with Leninist tradition, he maintained that Communists should become prominent in bourgeois-nationalist political parties but at the same time bind the peasants and the workers into a revolutionary force. Finally, the necessity for the international proletariat to remain allied with Soviet Russia was made unmistakably clear; indeed, a precondition for a genuine revolutionary movement was its acknowledged subordination to Soviet authority. This set the pattern for future Kremlin policy.

On January 21, 1924, after a prolonged illness, Lenin died. The struggle for succession, already well under way behind the scenes, assumed major proportions. All the aspiring heirs sought to associate themselves with the Leninist tradition and assume the mantle of legitimacy. In April 1924, at Sverdlov University, Stalin delivered a series of lectures on *The Foundations of Leninism*. In his speech on "The National Question" (reading 70) he embraced Lenin's position on the intimate connection between the vitality of national-liberation movements, the success of the proletarian revolution in Europe, and the preservation of socialism in the Soviet Union. Stalin lauded Lenin for expanding the national question to include all the oppressed peoples of Asia and Africa, and he expressed the view that, though it was but one aspect of the world proletarian revolution, "the road to the victory of the revolution in the West lies through the revolutionary alliance with the liberation movement of the colonies and dependent countries against imperialism."

Stalin also enunciated a series of principles on the national question, which he elaborated in his speech of May 18, 1925, on "The Political Tasks of the University of the Peoples of the East" (reading 71). Taken together, these two speeches constitute a comprehensive statement of Stalin's thinking on the tasks of the revolutionary movement in the colonies. They highlight the need:

1. To win over the best elements of the working class to the side of communism and to create independent Communist Parties.
2. To form a national-revolutionary bloc of workers, peasants, and the revolutionary intelligentsia against the bloc of the compromising national bourgeoisie and imperialism.
3. To ensure the hegemony of the proletariat in that bloc.
4. To fight to free the urban and rural petty bourgeoisie from the influence of the compromising national bourgeoisie.
5. To ensure that the liberation movement be linked with the proletarian movement in the advanced countries.

In his general appraisal, Stalin held that though capitalism was entering a period of stabilization, the national revolutionary movements in the colonies precluded the restoration of capitalism's former unity and strength. Accordingly, indigenous Communist Parties would support national-liberation movements, provided the *class* interest (of the proletariat) was not overshadowed in the process. The "revolutionary internationalism" of the proletariat acts to reduce the importance and the length of the period of national self-determination and accelerates the trend toward "the subsequent fusion of all nations." Above all, said Stalin, the Soviet Union represents the example of a country which is the "living prototype of the future amalgamation of nations in a single economic system" and exemplifies true internationalism. All developing nations were invited to emulate the Soviet experience. Stalin elaborated this theme in a piece commemorating the tenth anniversary of the Bolshevik Revolution. Three months earlier, in August 1927, he had also stated that internationalism required proletarians of all countries to support the Soviet Union, since an internationalist is one who "unhesitatingly, unconditionally, without vacillation, is ready to defend the USSR because the USSR is the basis of the world revolutionary movement, and it is impossible to defend and to advance (this movement) unless the USSR is defended."[8] These manifestations of growing Soviet egocentrism were further emphasized in the program adopted by the sixth Comintern Congress on September 1, 1928, which stated in part that:

In view of the fact that the USSR is the only fatherland of the international proletariat . . . [it] must on its part facilitate the success of the work of Socialist construction in the USSR and defend her against the attacks of the capitalist powers by all the means in its power.

Thus, Soviet national policy shaped proletarian internationalism in such a way that the two became increasingly synonymous.

The 1928 Comintern program constituted the clearest single statement on the general aims of communism made between the Communist Manifesto of 1848 and Andrei Zhdanov's speech to the first meeting of the Cominform in 1947. It became a guide for Communists throughout the world. The Comintern described its revolutionary objectives, the role of the proletariat, of bourgeois-national movements, and of the Soviet Union. It also revised one aspect of Leninist strategy operative in less developed areas since its second Congress in 1920, namely, the policy of Communist collaboration with bourgeois-nationalist groups.

The new line—the "united front from below" or anti-capitalist strategy—regarded these groups as "lackeys" of imperialism who had sold out and deserted the revolution. Therefore, the Comintern now held that only Communists could lead the liberation movements (reading 72). All cooperation with the non-Communist nationalists was abandoned, and the Communists sought to build up their following at the expense of the bourgeois-nationalist elements. Revolutionary agitation was encouraged, with the main stress placed on the urban proletariat; the peasantry was largely ignored. This left (anti-capitalist) strategy remained in effect until the Comintern's adoption of the Popular Front tactic in 1935, when there was not only a return to the Leninist accommodation and cooperation with bourgeois-nationalist parties, but even a collaboration with the colonial powers themselves. Confronted with the pressing threat of fascism, the Kremlin curbed its revolutionary activities and advanced the theme of coexistence with capitalism. The two basic strategies (right and left)—"united front from above" (anti-imperialist) and "united front from below" (anti-capitalist)—have since been incorporated into the broader framework of Soviet foreign policy, with emphasis on one or the other, according to the tactical dictates of the moment.

With the rise of Hitler in 1933 the Soviet Government took steps to improve relations with both the West and Japan. Mounting domestic and international tensions forced the Soviets to reappraise their relations with the capitalist world. Thus, in 1933 Molotov reported to the Central Committee that "in the Far East the Soviet Government consistently pursues a policy of non-intervention and strict neutrality in regard to other countries"; furthermore, Soviet foreign policy was "not only cautious but deliberate, since here too the Soviet Government proceeds, before all, in the interests of peace and of consolidating peaceful relations with other countries."[9] Soviet protests against Mussolini's invasion of Ethiopia in 1935 were designed primarily to foster collective security arrangements with Britain and France, though they also added to the image of the USSR as the leading opponent of imperialist ventures.

During the 1935–1945 period, with the exception of the brief Nazi-Soviet honeymoon, Stalin pursued a moderate policy in the developing areas. Because of the growing Hitlerian danger, he wanted to develop a security system with the colonial powers and was hence quite circumspect about Comintern activities in the colonial countries. Soviet national interest demanded accommodation and cooperation with the West. Generally speaking, the entire 1922–1945 period was one in which major Soviet efforts centered on European and Far Eastern (Japanese and Chinese) developments. Interest in the developing areas understandably remained secondary to the paramount problem of ensuring the security of the Soviet Union. The troubles within the Soviet Union itself (such as the intra-Party struggle for power after Lenin's death, the agricultural crisis occasioned by Stalin's decision to industrialize rapidly and collectivize agriculture, and the pervasive purges of the mid-1930s), further diluted Soviet interest in the developing areas. But with the end of World War II, and the emergence of the Soviet Union as one of the superpowers, a new era opened in Soviet policy toward developing areas.

Two policy principles emerge from the pre-1945 Soviet experience with developing areas. First, these areas have long played an important role in Soviet thinking, as a means of undermining Western power as well as of improving the international situation of the Soviet Union. Second, all nationalist movements are considered useful insofar as they weaken imperialism; yet they must not be permitted to monopolize popular sentiment nor overshadow for long the Communists themselves. Temporary alliances with bourgeois parties are permissible provided they serve the greater interests of communism. However, only Communist leadership of national-liberation movements can be deemed satisfactory in the long run.

In their adaptation to the changing international environment, Soviet leaders since Stalin have demonstrated a great readiness to revise matters of doctrine relating to developing nations. Three examples may be cited. First, Stalin's bipolar "two-camp" thesis was superseded by Khrushchev's "zone of peace" concept (reading 76). Second, Lenin's thesis that imperialist nations must go to war over the division of the spoils of colonialism is viewed as largely outdated by events since the 1950s. The pattern of evolving independence for developing countries has gone too far to be reversed. Moscow does maintain, however, that though *political* independence has been achieved, many of the new Afro-Asian countries are still the *economic* vassals of the Western

354 THE FOREIGN POLICY OF THE SOVIET UNION

Powers. The term "collective colonialism," which has become part of the Soviet lexicon since Khrushchev used it on February 26, 1960, during a visit to Indonesia, is now used to describe the cooperative efforts of the Western Powers to preserve their foothold in Asia, Africa, and Latin America (reading 73). Third, the term "national democracy," which was first enunciated by Khrushchev during a major foreign policy speech on January 6, 1961, refers to non-Communist, neutralist developing countries that pursue anti-Western, anti-imperialist foreign policies, that adopt domestic programs deemed socialistic rather than capitalistic in character, and that are considered likely to move gradually closer to the socialist camp and eventually to constitute themselves as People's Democracies. "National democracies" are thus used to describe a transitional stage of political development in neutralist countries whose leadership is regarded as showing a "progressive" or pro-Communist orientation. In recent years, Cuba, Ghana, Indonesia, and Mali have been so categorized by Soviet writers.

The capacity for revising outmoded doctrinal assumptions, and always within the broad framework of Marxism-Leninism, testifies to the continuing belief by Soviet leaders in the ability of ideology to guide them in understanding contemporary political phenomena.

NOTES

1. Samad Shaheen, *The Communist (Bolshevik) Theory of National Self-Determination* (Bandung, Indonesia: W. Van Hoeve-'S-Gravenhage, 1956), pp. 31, 79–89.
2. Edward Hallett Carr, *The Bolshevik Revolution* (New York: The Macmillan Company, 1953), Vol. III, p. 234.
3. *Ibid.*, p. 251.
4. V. I. Lenin, *Selected Works* (New York: International Publishers Co., 1938), Vol. x, p. 233.
5. *Ibid.*, p. 237.
6. Jane Degras, *The Communist International, 1919–1943* (New York: Oxford University Press, 1956), Vol. I, p. 390.
7. Leonard Shapiro, *Soviet Treaty Series* (Washington, D.C.: Georgetown University Press, 1950), Vol. I, p. 102.
8. Jane Degras, *Soviet Documents on Foreign Policy* (New York: Oxford University Press, 1952), Vol. II, p. 243.
9. Jane Degras, *Soviet Documents on Foreign Policy* (New York: Oxford University Press, 1953), Vol. III, pp. 4–5.

Bolshevik Policy and National Self-determination

65. RESOLUTION ON THE NATIONAL QUESTION*

*Adopted by the All-Russian Conference of the Russian
Social Democratic Labor Party on May 12, 1917*

To the extent that the elimination of national oppression is achievable at all in capitalist society, it is possible only under a consistently democratic republican structure and state administration that guarantee complete equality of status for all nations and languages.

The right of all the nations forming part of Russia freely to secede and form independent states must be recognized. To negate this right, or to fail to take measures guaranteeing its practical realization, is equivalent to supporting a policy of seizure and annexation. The recognition by the proletariat of the right of nations to secede can alone bring about complete solidarity among the workers of the various nations and help to bring the nations closer together on truly democratic lines . . .

The question of the right of nations freely to secede must not be confused with the question whether it would be expedient for any given nation to secede at any given moment. This latter question must be settled quite independently by the Party of the proletariat in each particular case, from the standpoint of the interests of the social development as a whole and of the class struggle of the proletariat for Socialism.

The Party demands wide regional autonomy, the abolition of tutelage from above, the abolition of a compulsory state language and the determination of the boundaries of the self-governing and autonomous regions by the local population itself, based on economic and social conditions, the national composition of the population, and so forth. The Party of the proletariat decisively rejects what is known as "national cultural autonomy," under which education, etc., is removed from the competence of the state and placed within the competence of something in the

---

* *Lenin-Stalin, 1917: Selected Writings and Speeches* (Moscow: Foreign Languages Publishing House, 1938), pp. 118–119, *excerpts.*

nature of National Diets. National cultural autonomy artificially divides the workers living in one locality, and even working in the same industrial enterprises, in accordance with their adherence to a particular "national culture"; in other words it strengthens the ties between the workers and the bourgeois culture of individual nations, whereas the aim of Social-Democracy is to strengthen the international culture of the proletariat of the world.

66. EXCERPTS FROM A REPORT ON THE NATIONAL QUESTION*

May 12, 1917

JOSEPH STALIN

The question of the *right* of nations freely to secede must not be confused with the question of whether a nation must *necessarily* secede at any given moment. This latter question must be settled by the party of the proletariat in each particular case independently, according to circumstances. When we recognize the right of oppressed peoples to secede, the *right* to determine their political destiny, we do not thereby settle the question of whether particular nations *should* secede from the Russian state at the given moment. I may recognize the right of a nation to secede, but that does not mean that I compel it to secede. A people has the right to secede, but it may or may not exercise that right, according to circumstances. Thus we are at liberty to agitate for or against secession, according to the interests of the proletariat, of the proletarian revolution. Hence, the question of secession must be determined in each particular case independently, in accordance with existing circumstances, and for this reason the question of recognizing the right to secede must not be confused with the expediency of secession in any given circumstances. For instance, I personally would be opposed to the secession of Transcaucasia, bearing in mind the general level of development in Transcaucasia and in Russia, certain conditions of the struggle of the proletariat, and so forth. But if, nevertheless, the peoples of Transcaucasia were to demand secession, they would, of course, secede, and would not encounter opposition from us.

* *Lenin-Stalin, 1917: Selected Writings and Speeches* (Moscow: Foreign Languages Publishing House, 1938), p. 108, *excerpts.*

67. TO ALL THE TOILING MOSLEMS OF RUSSIA AND THE EAST*

December 5, 1917

V. I. LENIN

JOSEPH STALIN

Comrades and Brothers,

Great events are taking place in Russia. The end of the bloody war started for the partitioning of foreign countries is approaching. The rule of the robbers who have enslaved the nations of the world is collapsing. The old edifice of bondage and slavery is tottering under the blows of the Russian revolution. The days of the world of despotism and oppression are numbered. A new world is being born, a world of those who toil and who are winning their emancipation. This revolution is headed by the Workers' and Peasants' Government of Russia, the Council of People's Commissars. . . .

In this sacred cause, Russia does not stand alone. The great call of liberation sounded by the Russian revolution is being echoed by the toilers of the West and the East . . . The rule of capitalist plunder and violence is collapsing. The ground is tottering under the feet of the imperialist marauders.

In face of these great events, we appeal to you, the toiling and disinherited Moslems of Russia and the East.

Moslems of Russia, Tatars of the Volga and the Crimea, Kirghiz and Sarts of Siberia and Turkestan, Turks and Tatars of Transcaucasia, Chechens and Gortsi of the Caucasus, all whose mosques and prayerhouses were destroyed and whose faith and customs were trampled underfoot by the tsars and oppressors of Russia:

Henceforth your faith and your customs, your national and cultural institutions are proclaimed to be free and inviolable. Order your national life freely and unrestrictedly. It is your right . . .

Support, then, this revolution and its authorized government. We announce that the secret treaties of the now overthrown

---

* *Lenin-Stalin, 1917: Selected Writings and Speeches* (Moscow: Foreign Languages Publishing House, 1938), pp. 664–666, *excerpts*.

tsar for the seizure of Constantinople, which were confirmed by the now overthrown Kerensky, have been torn up and destroyed. The Russian Republic and its government, the Council of People's Commissars, is opposed to the conquest of foreign territory. Constantinople must remain in the hands of the Moslems.

We announce that the treaty for the partition of Persia has been torn up and destroyed. As soon as hostilities cease, the troops will be evacuated from Persia and the Persians will be ensured the right freely to determine their own destiny.

We announce that the treaty for partitioning Turkey and "depriving" her of Armenia has been torn up and destroyed. As soon as hostilities cease, the Armenians will be ensured the right freely to determine their political destiny.

It is not from Russia and her revolutionary government that your enslavement is to be expected, but from the European imperialist robbers, from those who are waging the present war for the partitioning of your countries, from those who have transformed your fatherland into a plundered and despoiled "colony."

Overthrow the despoilers and enslavers of your countries. Now, when war and chaos are shaking the old world to its foundations, when the whole world is fired with resentment against the imperialist robbers, when every spark of indignation becomes transformed into a mighty flame of revolution, and when even the Indian Moslems, oppressed and tormented by a foreign yoke, are rising in revolt against their enslavers, it is impossible to remain silent. Lose no time and shake the ancient conquerors of your land from your backs! Do not allow them to despoil your hearths and homes any longer! You yourselves must be the masters in your country. You yourselves must arrange your lives in your own way. That is your right, for your destiny is in your own hands. . . .

68. DON'T FORGET THE EAST*

November 24, 1918

JOSEPH   STALIN

At a time when the revolutionary movement is rising in Europe, when old thrones and crowns are tumbling and giving place to

* Joseph Stalin, *Works* (Moscow: Foreign Languages Publishing House, 1953), Vol. IV, pp. 174-176, *excerpts*.

revolutionary Soviets of Workers and Soldiers, and the occupied regions are ejecting the creatures of imperialism from their territories, the eyes of all are naturally turned to the West. It is there, in the West, that the chains of imperialism, which were forged in Europe and which are strangling the whole world, must first of all be smashed. It is there, first of all in the West, that the new, socialist life must vigorously develop. At such a moment one "involuntarily" tends to lose sight of, to forget the far-off East, with its hundreds of millions of inhabitants enslaved by imperialism.

Yet the East should not be forgotten for a single moment, if only because it represents the "inexhaustible" reserve and "most reliable" rear of world imperialism.

The imperialists have always looked upon the East as the bases of their prosperity. Have not the inestimable natural resources (cotton, oil, gold, coal, ores) of the East been an "apple of discord" between the imperialists of all countries? That, in fact, explains why, while fighting in Europe and *prating* about the West, the imperialists have never ceased to *think* of China, India, Persia, Egypt, and Morocco, because the East was always the real point at issue. It is this that chiefly explains why they so zealously maintain "law and order" in the countries of the East—without this, imperialism's far rear would not be secure.

But it is not only the wealth of the East that the imperialists need. They also need the "obedient" manpower which abounds in the colonies and semi-colonies of the East. They need the "compliant" and cheap "labor power" of the Eastern peoples. They need, furthermore, the "obedient" "young lads" of the countries of the East from whom they recruit the so-called "colored" troops which they will not hesitate to hurl against "their own" revolutionary workers. That is why they call the Eastern countries their "inexhaustible" reserve.

It is the task of communism to break the agelong sleep of the oppressed peoples of the East, to infect the workers and peasants of these countries with the emancipatory spirit of revolution, to rouse them to fight imperialism, and thus deprive world imperialism of its "most reliable" rear and "inexhaustible" reserve.

Without this, the definite triumph of socialism, complete victory over imperialism, is unthinkable.

The revolution in Russia was the first to rouse the oppressed peoples of the East to fight imperialism. The Soviets in Persia, India, and China are a clear symptom that the agelong sleep of the workers and peasants of the East is becoming a thing of the past.

Revolution in the West will undoubtedly give a new spur to

the revolutionary movement in the East, will infuse it with courage and faith in victory.

And no little help in revolutionizing the East will be rendered by the imperialists themselves, with their new annexations, which are drawing new countries into the fight against imperialism and extending the base of world revolution.

It is the duty of the Communists to intervene in the growing spontaneous movement in the East and to develop it further, into a conscious struggle against imperialism.

From that standpoint, the resolution of the recent Conference of Moslem Communists (held in Moscow in November 1918), calling for more intense propaganda in the East—in Persia, India, and China—is undoubtedly of profound revolutionary significance.

Let us hope that our Moslem comrades will carry out their highly important decision.

For the truth must be grasped once and for all that whoever desires the triumph of socialism must not forget the East.

> *Joseph Stalin*
> *November 24, 1918*

International Communism and the Colonial Areas

69. PRELIMINARY DRAFT OF THESES ON THE NATIONAL AND COLONIAL QUESTIONS*

June 5, 1920

V. I. LENIN

1. Bourgeois democracy, due to its very nature, usually raises the question of equality, including the question of national equality, in an abstract or formal way. In the guise of equality for all persons generally, bourgeois democracy proclaims the formal or

* V. I. Lenin, *Sochinenia*, 4th ed. (Moscow: Institute of Marx-Engels-Lenin, 1950), Vol. xxxi, pp. 122–128, *excerpts*. Editor's translation.

juridical equality of the propertyowner and the proletarian, of the exploiter and the exploited, and in this way greatly deceives the oppressed classes . . .

2. The Communist Party, as the conscious expression of the struggle of the proletariat for the overthrow of the yoke of the bourgeoisie, must put as the bases of the national question not abstract and not formal principles, but, first, an exact calculation of the historical-concrete, and above all economic, situation; second, it must distinctly set forth the interests of the oppressed classes of the toilers, of the exploited, out of the general concept of national interests as a whole; third, it must make a similar distinction between oppressed, dependent, and subject nations and oppressing, exploiting, and sovereign nations, in order to counterbalance the bourgeois-democratic lie which obscures the colonial and financial enslavement of the overwhelming majority of the world's population by an insignificant minority of the richest advanced capitalist countries, a condition characterizing the epoch of finance capital and imperialism.

3. The imperialist war of 1914–1918 revealed, with particular clarity to all nations and to all the oppressed classes of the world, the falseness of bourgeois-democratic statements, and showed that the Versailles Treaty of the notorious "Western democracies" is a more brutal and despicable type of coercion against weak nations than was the Brest-Litovsk Treaty of the German Junkers and the Kaiser.

4. The cornerstone of the whole policy of the Comintern on the national and colonial question must be to link the proletarians and the toiling masses of all nations and countries for the joint revolutionary struggle for the overthrow of the landlords and the bourgeoisie. Only such a fusion guarantees victory over capitalism.

5. All events in world politics are inevitably concentrating around one central point, namely, the struggle of the world bourgeoisie against the Soviet Russian Republic, which is gathering around itself, on the one hand, the Soviet movement of the advanced workers of all countries, and on the other, all the national-liberation movements and oppressed nationalities in the colonies, which have become convinced through bitter experience that there can be no salvation for them except in the victory of Soviet power over world imperialism.

6. Consequently . . . it is necessary to conduct a policy that will bring about the closest union of all the national and colonial liberation movements with Soviet Russia. . . .

7. Federation is a transitional form to the complete unity of the workers of the various nations. . . .

8. Recognizing federation as the transitional form to complete unity, it is necessary to strive for a closer federal union, keeping in mind, first, the impossibility of preserving the existence of the Soviet Republics, which are surrounded by the incomparably more militarily powerful imperialist nations of the world, without the closest alliance of the Soviet Republics; second, the necessity of a close economic union of the Soviet Republics; and third, [the need for] the creation of a single world economy regulated by the proletariat of all nations according to a common plan.

9. Not only must the continual violations of the equality of nations and of the guaranteed rights of the national minorities that take place in all capitalist countries, notwithstanding their "democratic" constitutions, be steadily exposed by the propaganda and agitation of the Communist Parties—in and out of parliament—but it is necessary also, first, to explain continually that only the Soviet system can grant real equality of nations by uniting first the proletariat and then the whole mass of the toilers in the struggle against the bourgeoisie; second, it is necessary for all Communist Parties to provide direct support to the revolutionary movements in the dependent and subject nations (for example, in Ireland, the Negroes in America, etc.) and in the colonies.

10. Proletarian internationalism demands, first, the subordination of the interests of the proletarian struggle in one country to the interests of this struggle on a world-wide scale; and second, it demands the ability and willingness on the part of nations, which are realizing victory over the bourgeoisie, to make the greatest national sacrifices for the sake of overthrowing international capitalism.

11. In regard to the more backward governments and nations . . . it is particularly important to bear in mind:

First, the need for all Communist Parties to aid the bourgeois-democratic liberation movement in these countries; the primary duty of rendering the most active assistance rests upon the workers in those countries upon which the backward nation is dependent as a colony or in its financial relations;

Second, the necessity to fight against the clergy and other influential reactionary and medieval elements in backward countries;

Third, the necessity to fight Pan-Islamism and similar tendencies which strive to combine the liberation movement against European and American imperialism with the strengthening of the positions of the Khans, the landlords, the mullahs, etc.;

Fourth, the need to support especially the peasant movement in the backward countries against the landlords . . . and to give it the most revolutionary character and establish the closest possible alliance between the West European Communist proletariat and the revolutionary peasant movement in the East, in the colonies and in the backward countries, generally;

Fifth . . . the Communist International must enter into a temporary alliance with bourgeois democracy in colonial and backward countries, but must not merge with it, and must unconditionally preserve the independence of the proletarian movement even in its most elementary form;

Sixth, the need continually to explain to and expose among the toiling masses of all countries, and particularly of backward countries, the deception which the imperialist powers systematically practice under the guise of creating politically independent states, states which are completely dependent upon them economically, financially, and militarily; in the present international situation there is no salvation for dependent and weak nations except in a union of Soviet republics.

12. It is the duty of the class-conscious Communist proletariat of all countries to treat with particular caution and with special attention the vestiges of national sentiments among the countries and nationalities which have been oppressed for long periods, and it is also necessary to make certain concessions to them in order to remove quickly the distrust and prejudices mentioned earlier.

Stalin and the Colonial Question

70. THE NATIONAL QUESTION*

April 1924

JOSEPH STALIN

During the last two decades the national question has undergone a number of very important changes . . . Formerly, the national question was usually confined to a narrow circle of questions,

* Joseph Stalin, *Works* (Moscow: Foreign Languages Publishing House, 1953), Vol. VI, pp. 143–152, *excerpts*.

concerning, primarily, "civilized" nationalities. The Irish, the Hungarians, the Poles, the Finns, the Serbs, and several other European nationalities—that was the circle of unequal peoples in whose destinies the leaders of the (Socialist) Second International were interested. The scores and hundreds of millions of Asiatic and African peoples who are suffering national oppression in its most savage and cruel form usually remained outside their field of vision. . . . Now we can say that this duplicity and half-heartedness in dealing with the national question has been brought to an end. Leninism laid bare this crying incongruity, broke down the wall between whites and blacks, between Europeans and Asiatics, between the "civilized" and "uncivilized" slaves of imperialism, and thus linked the national question with the question of the colonies. The national question was thereby transformed from a particular and internal state problem into a general and international problem, into a world problem of emancipating the oppressed peoples in the dependent countries and colonies from the yoke of imperialism.

Formerly, the principle of self-determination of nations was usually misinterpreted, and not infrequently it was narrowed down to the idea of the right of nations to autonomy. . . . As a consequence, the idea of self-determination stood in danger of being transformed from an instrument for combating annexations into an instrument for justifying them. Now we can say that this confusion has been cleared up. Leninism broadened the conception of self-determination, interpreting it as the right of the oppressed peoples of the dependent countries and colonies to complete secession, as the right of nations to independent existence as states. This precluded the possibility of justifying annexations by interpreting the right to self-determination as the right to autonomy . . .

Formerly, the national question was regarded from a reformist point of view, as an independent question having no connection with the general question of the power of capital, of the overthrow of imperialism, of the proletarian revolution. It was tacitly assumed that the victory of the proletariat in Europe was possible without a direct alliance with the liberation movement in the colonies, that the national-colonial question could be solved on the quiet, "of its own accord," off the highway of the proletarian revolution, without a revolutionary struggle against imperialism. Now we can say that this anti-revolutionary point of view has been exposed. Leninism has proved, and the imperialist war and the revolution in Russia have confirmed, that the national question can be solved only in connection with and on the basis of the proletarian revolution, and that the road to victory of the revolution in the West lies through the revolutionary alliance with the liberation movement of the colonies and dependent countries against imperialism.

. . . Are the revolutionary potentialities latent in the revolutionary liberation movement of the oppressed countries *already exhausted,* or not; and if not, is there any hope, any basis, for utilizing these potentialities for the proletarian revolution, for transforming the dependent and colonial countries from a reserve of the imperialist bourgeoisie into a reserve of the revolutionary proletariat, into an ally of the latter?

Leninism replies to this question in the affirmative, i.e., it recognizes the existence of revolutionary capacities in the national liberation movement of the oppressed countries, and the possibility of using these for overthrowing the common enemy, for overthrowing imperialism. . . . Hence the necessity for the proletariat of the "dominant" nations to support—resolutely and actively to support—the national liberation movement of the oppressed and dependent peoples.

This does not mean, of course, that the proletariat must support *every* national movement, everywhere and always, in every individual concrete case. It means that support must be given to such national movements as tend to weaken, to overthrow imperialism, and not to strengthen and preserve it. Cases occur when the national movements in certain oppressed countries come into conflict with the interests of the development of the proletarian movement. In such cases support is, of course, entirely out of the question. . . .

The same must be said of the revolutionary character of national movements in general. The unquestionably revolutionary character of the vast majority of national movements is as relative and peculiar as is the possible reactionary character of certain particular national movements. The revolutionary character of a national movement under the conditions of imperialist oppression does not necessarily presuppose the existence of proletarian elements in the movement, the existence of a revolutionary or a republican program of the movement, the existence of a democratic basis of the movement. The struggle the Emir of Afghanistan is waging for the independence of Afghanistan is objectively a *revolutionary* struggle, despite the monarchist views of the Emir and his associates, for it weakens, disintegrates and undermines imperialism; whereas the struggle waged by . . . democrats and "Socialists" . . . during the imperialist war was a *reactionary* struggle, for its result was the embellishment, the strengthening, the victory of imperialism. . . . There is no need to mention the national movement in other, larger, colonial and dependent countries, such as India and China, every step of which along the road to liberation, even if it runs counter to the demands of formal democracy, is a steam-hammer blow at imperialism, i.e., is undoubtedly a *revolutionary* step.

The Liberation Movement of the Oppressed Peoples and the Proletarian Revolution

In solving the national question Leninism proceeds from the following theses:

(a) The world is divided into two camps: the camp of a handful of civilized nations, which possess finance capital and exploit the vast majority of the population of the globe; and the camp of the oppressed and exploited peoples in the colonies and dependent countries, which constitute that majority;

(b) The colonies and the dependent countries, oppressed and exploited by finance capital, constitute a vast reserve and a very important source of strength for imperialism;

(c) The revolutionary struggle of the oppressed peoples in the dependent and colonial countries against imperialism is the only road that leads to their emancipation from oppression and exploitation;

(d) The most important colonial and dependent countries have already taken the path of the national-liberation movement, which cannot but lead to the crisis of world capitalism;

(e) The interests of the proletarian movement in the developed countries and of the national-liberation movement in the colonies call for the union of these two forms of the revolutionary movement into a common front against the common enemy, against imperialism;

(f) The victory of the working class in the developed countries and the liberation of the oppressed peoples from the yoke of imperialism are impossible without the formation and the consolidation of a common revolutionary front;

(g) The formation of a common revolutionary front is impossible unless the proletariat of the oppressor nations renders direct and determined support to the liberation movement of the oppressed peoples against the imperialism of its "own country";

(h) This support implies the upholding, defense, and implementation of the slogan of the right of nations to secession, to independent existence as states. . . .

71. THE POLITICAL TASKS OF THE UNIVERSITY OF THE PEOPLES OF THE EAST*

May 18, 1925

JOSEPH STALIN

Let us pass to . . . the question of the tasks of the Communist University of the Toilers of the East in relation to the colonial and dependent countries of the East. What are the characteristic features of the life and development of these countries, which distinguish them from the Soviet republics of the East?

Firstly, these countries are living and developing under the oppression of imperialism.

Secondly, the existence of a double oppression, internal oppression (by the native bourgeoisie) and external oppression (by the foreign imperialist bourgeoisie), is intensifying and deepening the revolutionary crisis in these countries.

Thirdly, in some of these countries, India for example, capitalism is growing at a rapid rate, giving rise to and molding a more or less numerous class of local proletarians.

Fourthly, with the growth of the revolutionary movement, the national bourgeoisie in such countries is splitting up into two parts, a revolutionary part (the petty bourgeoisie) and a compromising part (the big bourgeoisie), of which the first is continuing the revolutionary struggle, whereas the second is entering into a bloc with imperialism.

Fifthly, parallel with the imperialist bloc, another bloc is taking shape in such countries, a bloc between the workers and the revolutionary petty bourgeoisie, an anti-imperialist bloc, the aim of which is complete liberation from imperialism.

Sixthly, the question of the hegemony of the proletariat in such countries, and of freeing the masses of the people from the influence of the compromising national bourgeoisie, is becoming more and more urgent.

Seventhly, this circumstance makes it much easier to link

* Joseph Stalin, *Works* (Moscow: Foreign Languages Publishing House, 1954), Vol. VII, pp. 146–154, *excerpts*.

the national-liberation movement in such countries with the proletarian movement in the advanced countries of the West.

From this at least three conclusions follow:

(1) The liberation of the colonial and dependent countries
from imperialism cannot be achieved without a victorious revolution: you will not get independence gratis.

(2) The revolution cannot be advanced and the complete
independence of the capitalistically developed colonies and dependent countries cannot be won unless the compromising
national bourgeoisie is isolated, unless the petty-bourgeois revolutionary masses are freed from the influence of that bourgeoisie,
unless the policy of the hegemony of the proletariat is put into
effect, unless the advanced elements of the working class are
organized in an independent Communist Party.

(3) Lasting victory cannot be achieved in the colonial and
dependent countries without a real link between the liberation
movement in those countries and the proletarian movement in
the advanced countries of the West.

The main task of the Communists in the colonial and dependent countries is to base their revolutionary activities upon these
conclusions. What are the immediate tasks of the revolutionary
movement in the colonies and dependent countries in view of
these circumstances?

The distinctive feature of the colonies and dependent countries
at the present time is that there no longer exists a single and all-
embracing colonial East. Formerly the colonial East was pictured
as a homogeneous whole. Today, that picture no longer corresponds to the truth. We have now at least three categories of
colonial and dependent countries. Firstly, countries like Morocco,
which have little or no proletariat, and are industrially quite
undeveloped. Secondly, countries like China and Egypt, which
are underdeveloped industrially, and have a relatively small
proletariat. Thirdly, countries like India, which are capitalistically more or less developed and have a more or less numerous
national proletariat.

Clearly, all these countries cannot possibly be put on a par
with one another.

In countries like Morocco, where the national bourgeoisie has,
as yet, no grounds for splitting up into a revolutionary party and
a compromising party, the task of the Communist elements is
to take all measures to create a united national front against
imperialism. . . .

In countries like Egypt and China, where the national bourgeoisie has already split up into a revolutionary party and a
compromising party, but where the compromising section of the

bourgeoisie is not yet able to join up with imperialism, the Communists can no longer set themselves the aim of forming a united national front against imperialism. In such countries the Communists must pass from the policy of a united national front to the policy of a revolutionary bloc of the workers and the petty bourgeoisie. . . . The tasks of this bloc are to expose the half-heartedness and inconsistency of the national bourgeoisie and to wage a determined struggle against imperialism. Such a dual party is necessary and expedient, provided it does not bind the Communist Party hand and foot, provided it does not restrict the freedom of the Communist Party to conduct agitation and propaganda work, provided it does not hinder the rallying of the proletarians around the Communist Party, and provided it facilitates the actual leadership of the revolutionary movement by the Communist Party. . . .

The situation is somewhat different in countries like India. The fundamental and new feature of the conditions of life of colonies like India is not only that the national bourgeoisie has split up into a revolutionary party and a compromising party, but primarily that the compromising section of this bourgeoisie has already managed, in the main, to strike a deal with imperialism. Fearing revolution more than it fears imperialism, and concerned more about its money bags than about the interests of its own country, this section of the bourgeoisie, the richest and most influential section, is going over entirely to the camp of the irreconcilable enemies of the revolution, it is forming a bloc with imperialism against the workers and peasants of its own country. The victory of the revolution cannot be achieved unless this bloc is smashed. But in order to smash this bloc, fire must be concentrated on the compromising national bourgeoisie, its treachery exposed, the toiling masses freed from its influence, and the conditions necessary for the hegemony of the proletariat systematically prepared . . .

Hence, the immediate tasks of the revolutionary movement in the capitalistically developed colonies and dependent countries are:

(1) To win the best elements of the working class to the side of communism and to create independent Communist Parties.

(2) To form a national-revolutionary bloc of the workers, peasants, and revolutionary intelligentsia against the bloc of the compromising national bourgeoisie and imperialism.

(3) To ensure the hegemony of the proletariat in that bloc.

(4) To fight to free the urban and rural petty bourgeoisie from the influence of the compromising national bourgeoisie.

(5) To ensure that the liberation movement is linked with the proletarian movement in the advanced countries. . . .

In this connection it is necessary to bear in mind two deviations in the practice of the leading cadres in the colonial East, two deviations which must be combated if real revolutionary cadres are to be trained.

The first deviation lies in an underestimation of the revolutionary potentialities of the liberation movement and in an overestimation of the idea of a united, all-embracing national front in the colonies and dependent countries, irrespective of the state and degree of development of those countries. That is a deviation to the Right, and it is fraught with the danger of the revolutionary movement being debased and of the voices of the Communist elements becoming drowned in the general chorus of the bourgeois nationalists. It is the direct duty of the University of the Peoples of the East to wage a determined struggle against that deviation.

The second deviation lies in an overestimation of the revolutionary potentialities of the liberation movement and in an underestimation of the role of an alliance between the working class and the revolutionary bourgeoisie against imperialism. . . . That is a deviation to the Left, and it is fraught with the danger of the Communist Party becoming divorced from the masses and converted into a sect.

72. THE PROGRAM OF THE COMMUNIST INTERNATIONAL*

September 1, 1928

The tasks of the Communist International connected with the revolutionary struggle in colonies, semi-colonies, and dependencies are extremely important strategical tasks in the world proletarian struggle. The colonial struggle presupposes that the broad masses of the working class and of the peasantry in the colonies be rallied round the banner of the revolution; but this cannot be achieved unless the closest cooperation is maintained between the proletariat in the oppressing countries and the toiling masses in the oppressed countries. . . .

* U.S. House of Representatives, Committee on Foreign Affairs, *The Strategy and Tactics of World Communism*, House Document No. 619, 80th Congress, 2nd session (1948), pp. 120–140, *excerpts*.

While organizing, under the banner of the proletarian dictatorship, the revolution against imperialism in the so-called civilized States, the Communist International supports every movement against imperialist violence in the colonies, semi-colonies, and dependencies themselves (for example Latin America); it carries on propaganda against all forms of chauvinism and against the imperialist maltreatment of enslaved peoples and races, big and small . . . and supports their struggle against the bourgeoisie of the oppressing nations. . . .

The Communist Parties in the imperialist countries must render systematic aid to the colonial revolutionary liberation movement and to the movement of oppressed nationalities generally. The duty of rendering active support to these movements rests primarily upon the workers in the countries upon which the oppressed nations are economically, financially, or politically dependent. The Communist Parties must openly recognize the right of the colonies to separation and their right to carry on propaganda for this separation, i.e. propaganda in favor of the independence of the colonies from the imperialist State; they must recognize their right of armed defense against imperialism (i.e. the right of rebellion and revolutionary war) and advocate and give active support to this defense by all the means in their power. The Communist Parties must adopt this line of policy in regard to all oppressed nations.

The Communist Parties in the colonial and semi-colonial countries must carry on a bold and consistent struggle against foreign imperialism and unfailingly conduct propaganda in favor of friendship and unity with the proletariat in the imperialist countries. They must openly advance, conduct propaganda for and carry out the slogan of agrarian revolution, rouse the broad masses of the peasantry for the overthrow of the landlords, and combat the reactionary and medieval influence of the clergy, of the missionaries, and other similar elements.

In these countries, the principal task is to organize the workers and the peasantry independently . . . and to free them from the influence of the national bourgeoisie, with whom temporary agreements may be made only on the condition that they, the bourgeoisie, do not hamper the revolutionary organization of the workers and peasants, and that they carry on a genuine struggle against imperialism. In determining its line of tactics, each Communist Party must take into account the concrete internal and external situation, the correlation of class forces, the degree of stability and strength of the bourgeoisie, the degree of preparedness of the proletariat, the position taken up by the various intermediary strata in its country, etc. The Party determines its slogans and methods of struggle in accordance with these circumstances, with the view to organizing and mobilizing the masses on the broadest possible scale and on the highest possible level of this struggle. . . .

When the revolutionary tide is rising, when the ruling classes are disorganized, the masses are in a state of revolutionary ferment, the intermediary strata are inclining towards the proletariat and the masses are ready for action and for sacrifice, the Party of the proletariat is confronted with the task of leading the masses to a direct attack upon the bourgeois State. This it does by carrying on propaganda in favor of increasingly radical transitional slogans . . . and by organizing mass action, upon which all branches of Party agitation and propaganda, including parliamentary activity, must be concentrated. This mass action includes: a combination of strikes and demonstrations; a combination of strikes and armed demonstrations; and finally, the general strike conjointly with armed insurrection against the state power of the bourgeoisie. The latter form of struggle, which is the supreme form, must be conducted according to the rules of war; it presupposes a plan of campaign offensive fighting operations and unbounded devotion and heroism on the part of the proletariat . . .

When the revolutionary tide is not rising, the Communist Parties must advance partial slogans and demands that correspond to the everyday needs of the toilers, and combine them with the fundamental tasks of the Communist International. . . . United front tactics also occupy an important place in the tactics of the Communist Parties throughout the whole pre-revolutionary period as a means towards achieving success in the struggle against capital, towards the class mobilization of the masses and the exposure and isolation of the reformist leaders.

The correct application of united front tactics and the fulfillment of the general task of winning over the masses presuppose in their turn systematic and persistent work in the trade unions and other mass proletarian organizations. It is the bounden duty of every Communist to belong to a trade union, even a most reactionary one, provided it is a mass organization. Only by constant and persistent work in the trade unions and in the factories for the steadfast and energetic defense of the interest of the workers, together with ruthless struggle against the reformist bureaucracy, will it be possible to win the leadership in the workers' struggle and to win the industrially organized workers over to the side of the Party. . . .

In the struggle against colonial oppression, the Communist Parties in the colonies must advance partial demands that correspond to the special circumstances prevailing in each country such as: complete equality for all nations and races; abolition of all privileges for foreigners; the right of association for workers and peasants; reduction of the working day; prohibition of child labor; prohibition of usury and of all transactions entailing bondage; reduction and abolition of rent; reduction of taxation; refusal to pay taxes, etc. All these partial slogans must be subordinate to the fundamental demands of the Communist Parties such as: Complete political national independence and the expulsion of the imperialists; workers' and peasants' government; the land to the people; eight-hour day, etc. The Communist Parties in imperialist countries, while supporting the struggle proceeding in the colonies, must carry on a campaign in their own respective countries for the withdrawal of imperialist troops, conduct propaganda in the army and navy in defense of the oppressed countries fighting for their liberation, mobilize the masses to refuse to transport troops and munitions and, in connection with this, to organize strikes and other forms of mass protest, etc.

The "New Imperialism"

73. THE ESSENCE OF COLLECTIVE COLONIALISM*

V. BOGOSLOVSKY

The Suez crisis, the war in Algeria, and the intervention of the Belgian colonialists in the Congo have proved that *separate colonial powers are now unable to suppress, as they did before, the national-liberation movement of the peoples single-handed.*

The new alignment of forces in the world in favour of the anti-imperialist front has made the imperialists change their political and economic approach to the exploitation of the Asian, African, and Latin American countries. Aware that the imperialist Powers are today no longer able to cope singly with the

* V. Bogoslovsky, "The Essence of Collective Colonialism," *International Affairs*, No. 12 (December 1960), pp. 20–24, *excerpts*.

national-liberation movement, the colonialists have started to apply the policy of collective colonialism. This policy signifies *joint* participation of the imperialist countries in suppressing the liberation movement (Algeria, the Congo, etc.), *joint* exploitation of the natural wealth of the Asian and African countries (activities of international companies), *joint* action of the colonialists in the United Nations and other international organizations against the legitimate demands of the Asian, African, and Latin American peoples.

Today, as never before, the imperialists are giving priority to the active defence of their common class interests because the abolition of colonialism means the collapse of the hinterland of imperialism, the loss of their reserves, and far-reaching economic consequences which they are most unwilling to see . . .

Today there is hardly any underdeveloped but formally independent country which is under the exclusive influence of one "metropolitan country" or in which only one group of monopoly capital operates. The exception is some Latin American countries which to this day remain the predominant sphere of American companies. But in Latin America, too, the imperialist monopolies of various countries are frequently entering into all kinds of combinations. Thus, U. S. capital, together with the British, fully controls the mining of nitrates in Chile, which accounts for nearly 95 per cent of the total output in the capitalist world.

Collective colonialism stands out most vividly in the form of various monopoly and state alliances of the Eurafrica type. In March 1958, for example, the so-called Middle East Industrial Development Corporation was set up with the participation of companies of the United States, Britain, France, Canada, the German Federal Republic, Italy, Sweden, Denmark, Norway, Switzerland, the Netherlands, and Belgium . . .

A Government which concludes an agreement with monopoly associations deals not with one metropolitan country, as was the case in the past, but with a number of imperialist Powers. On the other hand, the United States, Britain, France, and the other capitalist countries are doing everything to bring collective pressure to bear on any underdeveloped country to direct its economy and policies into the channel they want . . .

What new factors are compelling the colonialists frenziedly to form alliances to exploit the peoples of Asia, Africa, and Latin America? The main thing is growing fear for the future of their raw material markets and cheap labour. The winning of state sovereignty by Asian and African countries first of all deprived the metropolitan countries of the means of non-economic exploitation, that is, all the forms of colonial enslavement directly associated with the control of the state machine by the imperialists . . .

The recovery by the Asian, African, and Latin American countries of their raw material resources through nationalization threatens to reduce the fabulous profits which still flow into the coffers of the imperialist companies operating in these countries, both in the sphere of production (mining companies, industrial enterprises, plantations, transport facilities) and in the sphere of circulation (banks, insurance, and trading companies).

As a result of the widespread movement for nationalization of the natural resources in Asia, Africa, and Latin America, the imperialists are no longer confident that their investments are "safe." They see a guarantee of such "safety" in collective colonialism.

Uniting in monopolistic alliances, sometimes enlisting in these alliances local capital and placing it in a subordinate position, American, French, West German, and British monopolies expect to preserve and perpetuate the exploitation of the Afro-Asian countries, to deprive them of the chance of independent industrial development.

On the one hand, the system of collective colonialism serves as a sort of "shield," raised by the colonialists in face of the Asian, African, and Latin American peoples who demand the nationalization of their wealth; on the other hand, the imperialists have utilized it as a weapon for reinforcing the colonialist positions in Asia and Africa and attacking the rights of the peoples . . .

As we see, on the economic plane collective colonialism is a system of colonial exploitation which is being introduced and consists of joint actions by the colonialists, whose aim is to suppress the national-liberation movement of the Asian and African peoples and at the same time secure large dividends for the monopolists.

The collective colonialism of the imperialist Powers is strikingly manifested in international organizations, the United Nations in particular. Ever since the United Nations was established the colonial Powers belonging to it have been using the flag of this international organization for their expansionist policy. The imperfect structure of the leading UN bodies enables the Western monopoly forces in a number of cases to dictate their will to, and direct the activities of, the United Nations for the promotion of their selfish interests. The actions of the UN Secretary-General in the Congo provide a concrete example of the United Nations being used as a tool of neo-colonialism . . .

In an attempt to undermine the national-liberation movement,

Western monopoly capital is employing against the Asian, African, and Latin American countries not only international organizations but its economic strength as well. Above all, it seeks to unite the capitalist camp on a military basis . . .

It is not for "defence" against the non-existent "Communist danger" that the system of military blocs in the Middle East and Asia has been whipped together. By building up this system and inveigling some Asian countries into it, the imperialists are trying to save the remnants of the colonial system, to block the road to social progress for the Asian peoples, and, on the pretext of fighting Communism, to stem the mighty drive of the Asian peoples for national liberation.

FOR FURTHER STUDY

Boersner, Demetrio, *The Bolsheviks and the National and Colonial Questions, 1917–1928.* New York: Lounz, 1957.

Caroe, Sir Olaf, *Soviet Empire.* London: Macmillan & Co., 1953.

Cobban, Alfred, *National Self-Determination.* New York: Oxford University Press, 1945.

Low, Alfred D., *Lenin on the Question of Nationality.* New York: Twayne Publishers, 1958.

Meyer, Alfred G., *Leninism.* Cambridge, Mass.: Harvard University Press, 1957.

Pipes, Richard, *The Formation of the Soviet Union, 1917–1923,* 2nd ed. Cambridge, Mass.: Harvard University Press, 1964.

Thornton, Thomas P., *The Third World in Soviet Perspective.* Princeton, N.J.: Princeton University Press, 1964.

Ulam, Adam, *The Unfinished Revolution.* New York: Random House, 1960.

CHAPTER XI

SOVIET EXPANSION INTO DEVELOPING AREAS

The end of World War II ushered in an era of revolutions in the developing world. Former colonial empires crumbled under an explosive, widespread nationalism, the defeat of Japan, and the weakening of British, French, and Dutch power. The new international balance of power produced new tensions as these areas were caught, directly and indirectly, in the developing global struggle between the Western Powers and the Communist world.

Underdeveloped countries had long occupied an important place in Soviet ideological pronouncements and long-range political calculations. With the emergence of the Soviet Union as one of the two great powers, and the corresponding decline of Western prestige and strength, these countries acquired an operational significance as well. Communism has made notable advances in them as both a creed and a political movement. It promises to make even greater inroads in coming years. The appeal communism holds for these undeveloped, pre-industrial, tradition-bound, weak societies is stronger, paradoxically, in *non-Communist* areas than in those living under Communist rule. The Soviet Union has succeeded alarmingly in fostering the belief

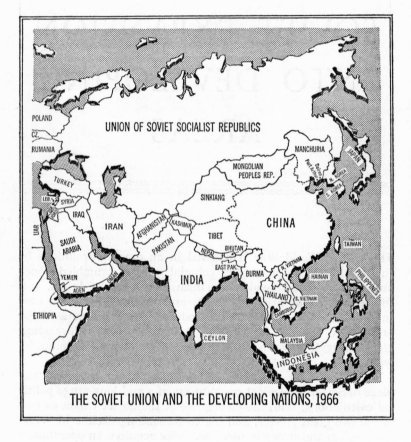

THE SOVIET UNION AND THE DEVELOPING NATIONS, 1966

that only communism represents change and in encouraging the uncritical acceptance of this image among influential segments of the educated elites of the developing countries. Communism offers a facile explanation for past poverty and present weakness, as well as a formula for future growth and strength. Though not always responsible for the ferment and turmoil pervading these areas, the Communists have exploited it; and Soviet policy has increasingly maneuvered to influence the economic and political development of the "gray" areas between the Western and Communist worlds.

To the peoples living to the south of the Soviet Union—from the Dardanelles to the China Sea, in Southern Asia, in Africa, and throughout the Arab world—the Soviet Union stands for a break with a dormant, dreary past. Though neither the West nor the USSR can hope to control the revolutions of these once subjugated peoples, the Soviet Union is in a far more advantageous position to exploit the "revolutions of rising expectations" now sweeping this part of the world. Ironically, the ideas of freedom and revolution which influenced the nationalist movements came initially from the West. But it is the Soviet Union which may reap the harvest. It alone is equipped with a revolutionary ideology, is free from any imperial heritage (though not from imperial aspirations) in these areas, and is served by Moscow-oriented, indigenous Communist Parties. Nor is the USSR hampered by the legacy of inequality, exploitation, and imperialism besetting Western leaders.

Despite such a politically promising environment the Kremlin was slow to use its opportunities, for several reasons. Stalin was engrossed during the initial postwar years with the imperatives of economic reconstruction and recovery, the consolidation of the Soviet empire in Eastern Europe, and the need to formulate intra-Communist-bloc power relationships as a consequence of the rapid rise to power of Communist China. Stalin also tended to underestimate the role the developing areas might play in promoting the international position of the Soviet Union. For example, Communist revolutions in Southern Asia after 1948 were the result of an unquestioning application by local Communist Parties of the Cominform "hard" line which had been formulated primarily with Europe in mind. This brought about the alienation of Communists from the mass-supported nationalist movements and severely damaged the prestige of the USSR.

Between 1945 and 1953, Moscow's approach was tailored to Stalin's rigid, antagonistic attitude toward the non-Communist world. Regarding the emerging Cold War as a global phenomenon, he lumped all non-Communist countries together, regard-

less of their political orientation, and classified them as "hostile."
As a result, Communist influence waned in the developing areas.
At a time when struggles for national independence were on the
threshold of success, Communist Parties in such countries as
India, Burma, and Indonesia were ordered to adopt policies that
tended to isolate them from political reality and to alienate them
from the national struggle for freedom. In general, this period
may be subdivided into two phases: from 1945 through 1947,
and from 1948 through 1953.

During the first phase, when Soviet-Western hostility had
not yet hardened completely, local Communist Parties were
instructed to infiltrate national-liberation movements, to support
anti-colonial, anti-imperialist themes and to exploit agrarian discontent and agitation for land reform. Soviet propaganda blamed
the West for the backwardness and poverty of the developing
areas, while lauding the "progressive" role of the Soviet Union
in championing national-liberation movements and economic
developments. These themes, reaffirming Marxist-Leninist orthodoxy, were widely proclaimed by the Soviet press. An article in
Pravda by E. Zhukov, a leading Soviet authority on underdeveloped areas, typified the official Soviet line (reading 74).

Moscow permitted, though it did not explicitly encourage, local
Communist Parties to cooperate with bourgeois-nationalist elements during these early, uncertain postwar years. It did direct
them to acquire strategic positions in the new governments, labor
movements, political parties, and student organizations in order
to be advantageously situated to channel the anti-Western struggle
along lines favored by Moscow. But no detailed, uniformly
applicable, Moscow-drawn plan seemed to exist. Communist
tactics varied from area to area and from country to country.
Thus, in Southern Asia, Communist Parties openly supported
nationalist movements for independence, whereas, in the Middle
East, their activity was secretive, conditions there being unsuitable
for overt political operations.

The second phase was initiated by the establishment of the
Cominform in September 1947 and the adoption of the Zhdanov
"two-camp" thesis. The Kremlin adopted a revolutionary strategy
which dictated the rupture of Communist cooperation with
bourgeois-nationalist elements in favor of a program of armed
insurrection. Accordingly, revolts were attempted in India, Indonesia, Burma, Malaya, and the Philippines. But in most cases
they bore little relevance to existing political conditions in these
countries and were quickly suppressed. Having thus placed themselves in open opposition to mass-supported nationalist revolutions and movements, the Soviet Union and the local Communist

Parties declined disastrously in prestige and influence. Moscow's callous disregard for foreign Communists showed once again that its paramount concern was the security and power of the Soviet Union. For Stalin's principal objective in fomenting revolutions in colonial and former colonial areas was to divert Western attention while he consolidated the Soviet empire in Eastern Europe and restored the economic strength of the USSR. To achieve these ends, he was prepared to sacrifice foreign Communist Parties and their prospects for attaining political power.

In the Middle East, Moscow followed a "hands-off" policy after efforts to pressure Turkey and Iran in 1945–1946 failed dismally. Thereafter, until 1955, the Kremlin remained relatively aloof from developments in the area. It did recognize Israel in 1948 in the hope of sharpening Middle Eastern tensions arising out of the partition of Palestine. But aside from this, Moscow played no important role in Middle Eastern affairs during the Stalinist period, though Soviet propaganda continued to exploit Arab-Western discord and antagonism. Stalin's "withdrawal" was, however, as subsequent events showed, temporary and motivated by more pressing concerns elsewhere. Ironically enough, it is clear in retrospect that the marked absence of direct Soviet involvement in the political controversies plaguing the Middle East during the 1947–1953 period accrued to Moscow's benefit. According to Walter Z. Laqueur, a noted analyst of Middle Eastern affairs:

Soviet and Communist propagandists could point to the stark contrast between Moscow's policy of "hands-off" and Western imperialist attempts to "organize" the area, to draw the various countries into all kinds of suspect "defence" blocs. These Western activities tended to fan smouldering anti-Western resentment and to antagonize most of the Arabs, who were psychologically quite unprepared; the Soviet danger was in their eyes some mythical invention, or perhaps a clever stratagem of American and European "imperialists" desirous of perpetuating their rule in the Middle East. As a result, Soviet prestige grew.[1]

In Southern Asia, on the other hand, the aggressive implementation of the "hard" Cominform line led Moscow and local Communists to pursue policies which proved detrimental to the continued expansion of their influence. Moscow was out of step with popular sentiment. Nowhere was this more startlingly apparent than in the Soviet attitude toward Gandhi and his role in India's struggle for independence.

Gandhi's hold upon the Indian masses transcended party, caste, and class. He was the bridge between the essentially middle-class, educated Congress Party leadership and the poverty-bound, illiterate millions. Gandhi's policy for attaining India's independence, *satyagraha* (nonviolent direct action), contrasted with Moscow's inflexible insistence upon class struggle and violence. Stalin's bipolar view of international and national politics forced all Communists to condemn Gandhism as a reactionary movement. Soviet interpretation of Gandhi and of his activities blinded Moscow to the realities of the Indian scene and weakened the Indian Communist Party, which had reluctantly accepted the distorted Soviet image and the political liabilities resulting from it. A leading Soviet Indologist, writing in 1949, interpreted Gandhism as "the most important ideological weapon in the hands of the Indian bourgeoisie for keeping the masses under its influence." He criticized Gandhi for preaching class peace and the inviolability of existing private property and social relationships, and thereby representing the interests of the Indian bourgeoisie and landlords (reading 75).

Furthermore, Stalin maintained that countries such as India, Burma, Ceylon, and Indonesia, which had obtained their independence under non-Communist leaderships, were not really free —they were puppets, exercising the formal prerogatives of sovereignty, but in reality controlled by a combination of Western capitalists and indigenous wealthy elements. Stalin regarded these governments as agents of "Anglo-American imperialism in Southeast Asia," and acted accordingly. For example, the Soviet Government did not contribute "one red ruble," either in the United Nations or on a bilateral basis, toward the economic development of these countries. Soviet statements in the United Nations frequently advocated aid for developing areas, particularly for Asian countries recently freed from colonial rule, but the Soviet *record* contradicted these professions so starkly as to cast doubt upon their sincerity. As a result, Soviet prestige among these nations plummeted to a new low by the end of the Stalinist era.

Brief mention must be made of the related policy of Communist China. With Mao Tse-tung's victory in China, Communist strategy in Southern Asia shifted. Recognizing Mao's "National Front" strategy as the proper road for Asian communism, Moscow accepted cooperation with bourgeois parties in broadly based nationalist, anti-imperialist coalitions as a tactical necessity. Though this line of approach was openly acknowledged as "correct" during the last three years of the Stalinist era, it was not actively implemented until the post-Stalinist period. Stalinist doctrine, which insisted upon a *leading* role for the Communist Party in the struggle against foreign imperialism and indigenous capitalism, has since given way to the more flexible Maoist view which encourages cooperation with bourgeois-nationalist groups against foreign domination and with the "progressive" elements of the national bourgeoisie against the "big" bourgeoisie and the native capitalist class. Once independence has been achieved, Maoist strategy calls for an all-out Communist effort to seize the leadership of the nationalist movement from the bourgeois parties and assume control of the entire revolutionary struggle, with heavy reliance upon the peasantry as the base upon which to build the revolutionary movement. However, neither the Soviet Union nor Communist China has uniformly applied the Maoist line. Each has adapted its strategy in the interest of maximizing its own prospects for influence-building among bourgeois-nationalist elites in developing countries. Both have repeatedly cooperated with and supported the national bourgeoisie in countries where the Communist Party is weak, where the regime is neutralist or anti-Western, and where friendly diplomatic ties are deemed more in the national interest than the promotion of internal revolutions. Formulation of the "correct" strategy involves identification of the main enemy and the ranking of political priorities. In recent years, the differences between Moscow and Peking over the question of "wars of national-liberation"—the Communist term for armed efforts to overthrow pro-Western regimes by force and establish Communist control—reflect the inability of the two to agree upon a common strategy.

Since 1954 the Soviet Union has vigorously pressed its great-power ambitions in the developing world. Its success has been impressive, and important inroads have been made in South Asia, the Middle East, and Africa. One aspect of the Soviet "new look" involves expanded trade relations, cultural exchanges, and substantial financial and technical commitments. Of comparable significance has been the USSR's effective creation of an image of itself as *the* benevolent, disinterested champion of developing nations against the imagined threat of a return of "Western imperialism." This image has been strengthened by supple and imaginative diplomacy, shrewd propaganda, and high-powered salesmanship.

By skillfully blending the economic, the political, and the cultural, by stressing trade not aid, and by supporting the developing nations whenever possible in the United Nations (especially when they oppose Western policy), the Soviet Union is assuring itself of a warm, often uncritical, reception. There are also other factors operating in the Soviet favor.

First, the newly independent nations, though not unaware of the danger of Communist subversion, are often compelled by domestic political considerations to avoid military alliances with the West. Independence has yet to produce elites sufficiently stable or responsible to deal effectively with extremist groups bent on exploiting nationalist, anti-imperialist passions. Democratic forces are frail, and in the struggle to survive they must follow a policy of noninvolvement in what is often regarded as merely a great-power conflict. Thus does the past weigh heavily upon the present.

Second, Soviet imperialism is not apparent in Southern Asia, the Middle East, or Africa, as it is in Europe and the Far East. These areas have never known Soviet rule, and the postwar experience of Eastern Europe has meant little to them. Even the brutal suppression in Hungary did not materially injure Soviet prestige in most developing countries.

Third, the memory of Western domination endures as a vivid reminder of a not too distant past. Reason and reasonableness do not usually guide the injured and the weak. Most of these nations are far more sensitive to imagined efforts at restoring Western power than to the expansionist and subversive potential of communism. But these attitudes are slowly changing. Soviet interference in the internal affairs of several African and Middle Eastern states has alerted nationalist elites to the danger of Great-Power domination from the East. In addition, Communist China's attack on India in October 1962 and its aggressive activity in Laos and along Thailand's frontier have occasioned reappraisals of Chinese intentions by several South Asian governments.

Finally, an intense preoccupation with domestic problems has been a natural by-product of independence. Wary of any foreign entanglements, these nations are primarily concerned with the critical need to accelerate internal development and improve the economic and social well-being of their rapidly expanding— already overburdening—populations. Economic development is necessary for political stability. In their search for an appropriate formula the developing nations are impressed by the Soviet success in industrializing rapidly. The Soviet emphasis on nationalization of key industries, heavy public-sector investment, and central economic planning finds a receptive audience in developing countries. They tend to see in the Soviet experience a pattern for their own development, a view carefully nurtured by Soviet spokesmen in international affairs.

By July 1953 it had become apparent that Soviet policy toward Southern Asia was undergoing a fundamental change. In the United Nations the Soviet Government made its first offer of a contribution to the UN Expanded Program of Technical Assistance. More significantly, it inaugurated an ambitious "Point Four" program of its own and negotiated a number of bilateral trade agreements with developing nations. Since much publicity has been accorded Soviet foreign economic activities, a distinction should be made between "gifts" and "loans" in order to place Soviet "generosity" within the proper framework of "national interest." Thus, except for a small number of tractors and commercial airliners, the Soviet Union has not extended any outright economic grants—in contrast to the substantial gifts of food and material presented by the United States. Rather, Soviet economic assistance is extended in the form of long-term, low-interest-bearing loans. A new innovation in Soviet economic activity with the non-Communist world, these loans are usually small, allotted for a dramatic, easily recognizable project, and adroitly publicized. Their impact has nevertheless been great, economically and politically.

At the Twentieth Congress of the CPSU in February 1956, Nikita Khrushchev emphasized the importance of the uncommitted, developing countries. He devoted much attention to their role in international politics and to the political significance of the fact that "a vast 'peace zone,' including both socialist [Communist] and non-socialist peace-loving states in Europe and Asia has emerged in the world arena. This zone embraces tremendous expanses of the globe, inhabited by nearly 1,500,000,000 people, that is, the majority of the population of our planet" (reading 76). Khrushchev did not propound any new doctrine, but he did reintroduce an interest in the developing areas of the world which had been absent from the previous Congress (1952). This interest has since been reaffirmed by his successors.

The present Soviet leadership has discarded the dogmatism of the Stalinist era and revitalized the Leninist injunction to defeat the West through promoting the disaffection of developing areas. Exploitation of tensions between the "have" and "have-not" nations, between the industrial West and the underdeveloped East—long a convenient propaganda tool—now plays an active role in Soviet diplomacy. Two objectives loom large in the Kremlin's calculations. First, it seeks to convince the developing nations of the peaceful character of Soviet aims, thereby encouraging their present adherence to a policy of nonalignment. Second, Moscow hopes to enhance its status, and that of local Communist Parties, by discrediting the military emphasis of the United States in its agreements with nations of the Middle East (CENTO), Southeast Asia (SEATO), and Latin America, in contrast to the economic and cultural approach of the Soviet Union. However, the Soviet Union is quite prepared to provide arms and munitions, if they can be used to aggravate tensions and create a more receptive political climate for the expansion of Soviet influence. Thus, it has sold military equipment to the United Arab Republic, Afghanistan, Indonesia, Cuba, Somalia, and a dozen other countries. By mid-1965, the Soviet bloc had extended approximately 2 billion dollars in military credits to non-Communist countries, the bulk of it to the United Arab Republic, India, and Afghanistan. Cuba is also a major recipient.

Paradoxically, it is as businessmen and "capitalists" that the Soviets find their warmest welcome and achieve their most dramatic success. By emphasizing mutual expansion of trade, largely through barter agreements, they avoid any semblance of the rich-relation largesse that so often stigmatizes and stymies Western efforts. Soviet trade, state-controlled and politically motivated, has effectively competed with the fragmented, disorganized commercial approach of the capitalist world. Soviet negotiators are noted for their businesslike bargaining; price quotations usually approximate those found in world markets; attempts are rarely made to influence the direction or pace of economic development; and trade is pushed along bilateral, barter lines. The financially hard-pressed countries need not spend scarce hard currencies and can dispose of their main export commodities at prices they consider satisfactory. Thus, the Soviet Union has, at various times, taken advantage of Burma's temporary rice surplus, Egypt's cotton disposal difficulties, and Afghanistan's wool surplus to increase its economic relations with these strategically important countries. Though barter agreements may limit the choice of imports available to developing countries when they accumulate substantial export balances with the Soviet bloc, this shortcoming is not readily apparent. The over-all impact of the Soviet approach is favorable. To highly sensitive countries, so recently removed from colonial status, Soviet trade policy implies a sense of equality which further enhances its appeal.

Khrushchev once remarked to a group of visiting Congressmen that "We value trade least for economic reasons and most for political reasons." With such an attitude, Soviet trade policy can be manipulated with a convenient disregard for cost considerations and market needs. As an instrument of national policy, and an important one presently with respect to countries such as Afghanistan, India, and the United Arab Republic, it is designed primarily to enmesh the vulnerable economies of these one or two cash-crop countries with those of the Soviet-bloc nations —an invariable precursor of closer political ties. There are dissonances in the progression of Soviet successes, but the tune thus far must be heard by Moscow with great satisfaction.

Not only has Moscow shown a willingness to expand trade and extend economic and technical assistance to the "neutralist" nations, but its ability to do so on a large scale can no longer be doubted. Indeed, its foreign aid achievements are beginning to overshadow those of the West in certain countries. For example, Soviet credits, loans, and grants to the United Arab Republic exceed one billion dollars. Among the many projects being built with Soviet assistance is the Aswan High Dam, a hydroelectric and irrigation complex that dwarfs the pyramids in magnitude and that will, when completed in 1968, constitute a vivid testimonial to Soviet ability and aid. In general, Soviet-bloc (excluding China) loans, both promised and delivered, to non-Communist countries are close to the 7-billion-dollar mark, a sum comparing favorably with Western efforts toward the same target countries. Soviet credits provide for the shipment and construction of entire industrial plants, for machinery, and for technical advisers. These loans have also been negotiated without any visible political strings attached. If the Soviet bloc continues to accept repayment in the agricultural and raw material surpluses of developing countries, it will find ready markets for its industrial goods and reap a rich political harvest. Thousands of Soviet-bloc technicians have already been utilized by the developing countries, and other thousands from these areas have received training in the Soviet Union. Such exchanges are inexpensive ways of cultivating favorable impressions. Among the developing countries, dissatisfaction and disillusionment have cropped up in recent years, both with the "ugly Russian" serving abroad and with the racial discrimination and societal drabness experienced in the Soviet Union. However, the over-all effect of the foreign aid and exchange programs has been to the benefit of the USSR.

A look at the Soviet record in four key areas—Southern Asia, the Middle East, Africa, and Latin America—may help illumine the reasons for present Soviet influence among the neutralist countries and the possible future sources of discord between Moscow and the neutralist leaders.

Southern Asia

The Soviet campaign to cultivate developing nations began in Southern Asia. The prime target is India, the most populous, strategically situated, and by virtue of its leading role among other neutralists, politically important. Interesting case studies could also be made of Afghanistan, Burma, Indonesia, and Ceylon, but the importance of India in Southern Asia and of the

United Arab Republic in the Middle East warrants giving them closer attention.

Nowhere else in non-Communist Asia has Soviet foreign policy achieved so much so rapidly as in India. Stalin's successors were quick to appreciate the role a friendly India could play in enhancing the international position and prestige of the Soviet Union. The shift in Soviet policy toward India may be dated from September 1953, with the appointment as ambassador of Mikhail A. Menshikov (later to serve as envoy to the United States), who immediately initiated discussions aimed at cultivating closer economic relations with India. The most dramatic success was the signing of an agreement on February 2, 1955, under which the Soviet Government obligated itself to construct and finance a one-million-ton steel mill in the Bhilai region of Central India. This agreement marked the debut of the USSR as a lender of investment capital to non-Communist countries. (Similar agreements with other nations have become familiar features of post-1955 Soviet diplomacy.) And Soviet amiability was soon supplemented by increased trade, cultural exchanges, and a steady flow of technical missions.

Soviet credits to India have exceeded one billion dollars, placing the Soviet Union second only to the United States in helping India implement its program of economic development and industrialization. Psychologically, Soviet aid may be reaping disproportionate rewards because of the manner in which it is expended. Whereas American aid has concentrated on helping India meet its pressing food requirements and pushing the vital Community Development program, Soviet credits are used to build easily identifiable, strategically necessary, and much publicized plants and industries. In addition to the Bhilai steel plant, the Soviet Government has financed a 300-million-dollar program to expand the manufacture of heavy machinery, which included the construction of a major machine-building plant at Ranchi (Bihar), cooperated in the financing and construction of India's pharmaceutical industry, and conducted an extensive geological survey of India's oil resources. The discovery of oil in the Punjab and on the west coast by Soviet and Rumanian geologists in 1958 and the construction of a refinery in Assam in 1961 received much publicity in oil-poor India. Of particular importance to India is the second steel plant to be built by the Soviet Union in the public sector: the agreement to construct the plant at Bokaro was signed on January 23, 1965, and the USSR will extend initial credits of 211 million dollars for the project.

To carry out these projects, increasing numbers of Soviet engineers and technicians are being employed in India. There has also been an increase in Soviet-Indian trade, though the Soviet bloc as a whole still accounts for little more than 4 per cent of India's total foreign trade. A five-year trade agreement was signed on December 2, 1953, a supplementary exchange agreement on December 13, 1955, another five-year pact on November 16, 1958, and a third five-year pact in June 1963. In return for Soviet machinery, steel, rolling stock, oil products, and cereals, India exports tea, spices, hides and wool, jute products, and assorted handicraft goods. Soviet willingness to accept payment in rupees and in Indian goods is of special significance to a country harassed by a chronic shortage of hard currency. At the present time there is nothing to indicate any basic Indian dissatisfaction with Soviet goods, business practices, or technicians. Indeed, Indian officials have been lavish in their praise of Soviet contributions to India's industrial development. Though minor irritants exist, a steady expansion of trade and Soviet aid can be expected.

Soviet support of India in the United Nations, and their apparent similarity of approach toward the questions of Chinese Communist membership in the UN and of nuclear disarmament, have strengthened Moscow's diplomatic standing in New Delhi. Soviet leaders stress their anti-colonialism and support India's claims to Kashmir (though in the undeclared war that erupted between India and Pakistan in September 1965, Moscow was instrumental in persuading the two disputants to end hostilities and sign the Tashkent Declaration of January 1966). They have repeatedly endorsed the Indian-approved concepts contained in the *panch shila* ("The Five Principles" of peace: mutual respect for territorial integrity and sovereignty, nonaggression, noninterference in internal affairs, equality and mutual benefit, peaceful coexistence).

Leaving no stone unturned in the courtship of India, the Soviets "reinterpreted" Gandhi's role in India's independence struggle in a more flattering vein; he is now considered to have played a "progressive" role in the national-liberation movement. Finally, India is no longer viewed as a lackey of Western imperialists, a nation without status or sovereignty. Nor is India's integrity in foreign relations any longer disparaged. Soviet commentators, in revising their interpretations of Indian foreign policy to accord with political reality, have intentionally and expediently catered to Indian political sensibilities by their laudatory statements on India's constructive and peaceful foreign policy (reading 77).

At a time when India is experiencing intense difficulties in its foreign relations, the support of the Soviet Union is most welcome. Friendship with Moscow rests upon a community of mutually reinforcing interests. Moscow supports New Delhi's opposition to the American-sponsored Southeast Asia Treaty Organization (SEATO), to the vestiges of Western colonialism in Africa, and to the deepening American involvement in South Vietnam and Laos. During the Goa affair of December 1961, the Soviet Union alone among the Great Powers fully upheld India's action against the Portuguese enclave. Moscow's benevolent neutrality on the Sino-Indian border dispute has been especially appreciated. The Chinese attack on India in October 1962, coming as it did during the height of the Cuban missile crisis, faced Moscow with a serious dilemma: to stand by its Communist ally or to support India and safeguard its expensively cultivated stake in Asia's leading neutralist nation. Moscow's neutrality and calls for a settlement of the border dispute, which were bitterly denounced in Peking, were warmly welcomed in New Delhi, as were subsequent Soviet offers of guided missiles for air defense and other military equipment. Khrushchev's successors have reaffirmed Moscow's major commitment to India. But Moscow must also be somewhat unhappy with India's greater willingness since October 1962 to take military aid from the United States (reading 78).

Friendship with India serves the Kremlin well in its drive for influence among neutralist countries. It demonstrates to the Afro-Asians that closer relations with the Soviet bloc can bring them tangible economic, military, and political dividends; it encourages India to pursue its policy of nonalignment, thus forestalling the formation of a united anti-Communist coalition in Asia; it serves as a convenient, long-term hedge against an ambitious Chinese expansionism which may, in time, precipitate an open split within the Communist world; and it provides the Communist Party of India with a measure of respectability which could make the CPI an important force in Indian political life in the decades ahead.

The Middle East

Since 1955, with the resurgence of Soviet interest in the Middle East, Egypt has been a major target of Soviet foreign policy. As we have noted, Moscow had previously maintained a relatively detached attitude toward this area, being preoccupied elsewhere with the consolidation of the Eastern European empire, the establishment of the Sino-Soviet alliance after 1949, and the threat of direct military involvement in Korea. Its recognition of Israel had also temporarily barred closer relations with the Arab nations.

At the Afro-Asian Bandung Conference (April–May 1955), Soviet leaders laid the groundwork for a reversal of this Stalinist legacy, a reversal that took definite shape with the Soviet-Egyptian arms deal of September 1955. By agreeing to accept cotton in repayment and by providing the additional military strength desired by Egypt, the USSR set the stage for closer economic and political ties. Soviet efforts were aided by President Nasser's anti-Westernism and opposition to the Western-sponsored Baghdad Pact (established in 1955 and reorganized as CENTO in 1959, following the revolution in Iraq which brought in a neutralist regime). Nasser's "positive neutralism" increasingly conflicted with Western moves to establish a viable alliance system against the threat of Soviet expansion in the Middle East. Meanwhile, Moscow offered substantial credits to Egypt for modernization of its army as well as for economic development. The withdrawal of a tentative Western offer to assist Egypt in building the Aswan Dam provoked Nasser to nationalize the Suez Canal in July 1956. The Soviet Government supported the Egyptian action.

The Israeli invasion of Egypt in October 1956, followed closely by the Anglo-French military attempt to overthrow Nasser, afforded the Soviet Union a unique opportunity to ingratiate itself with the Arab world. Moscow called for immediate action against the aggressors and offered to send "volunteers" to aid the Egyptians. Confronted with the prospect of an imminent Soviet military intervention and the open opposition of the United States, the invading countries acceded to UN demands, effected a cease fire, and removed their troops from Egypt. As a result, Moscow's prestige rose spectacularly in the Arab world. In addition to replacing Egyptian arms lost to the Israelis in Sinai, Moscow agreed to lend Egypt and Syria several hundred million dollars for economic development, technical assistance, and industrial equipment. It also agreed to participate in the construction of the Aswan Dam, a project essential to Egypt's agricultural and industrial development. Soviet-Egyptian trade has multiplied manyfold since 1954. Indeed, the USSR has now become one of Egypt's most important export markets.

This pattern of closer relations has been periodically strained since July 1958. At that time a military coup overthrew the pro-Western Government of Iraq and brought to power General Abdel Karim Kassem. Nasser's jubilation turned to bitter opposition as it became apparent that Kassem had no intention of uniting Iraq with the United Arab Republic. Meanwhile, Communist influence in Iraq increased and led to Soviet support. Nasser's enmity toward Kassem was accompanied by a crackdown on Communists within the United Arab Republic (as Egypt was renamed after the merger with Syria on February 1, 1958) that led Khrushchev to criticize Nasser at the Twenty-first Congress of the CPSU (reading 79). Soviet resentment over Cairo's harsh policy toward Arab Communists did not jeopardize diplomatic ties nor decrease the flow of economic and military aid to the UAR. Once again we see that as long as the international position of the Soviet Union is strengthened, Moscow often disregards the interests of local Communist Parties. A similar situation developed in Iraq. On February 8, 1963, a *coup d'etat* overthrew Kassem. The new regime, which was pro-Nasser, arrested and executed hundreds of local Communists. Soviet relations with Baghdad deteriorated for a short time, but Moscow, no doubt reluctant to jeopardize the 400-million-dollar economic and military investment that it had made during the 1959–1962 period, soon improved relations with the new regime. During Khrushchev's May 1964 visit to Cairo, Nasser effected a further reconciliation between the Soviet Union and Iraq. In March 1965, Moscow promised to provide aid for a dam on the Euphrates River, although the situation of the local Communists remains precarious.

Soviet-UAR relations improved during 1964–1965. Cairo released several hundred local Communists, and the Soviet bloc promised more than 500 million dollars in economic credits for the UAR's second five-year plan, which began in July 1965. This pledge of aid clearly established the Soviet Union as the major foreign aid contributor to the Nasser regime. Moscow is also Cairo's chief supplier of military equipment—two very important reasons for expecting continued close ties between the two countries, notwithstanding the persisting ideological and political irritants.

Soviet objectives in the Middle East are easily catalogued. They are primarily political and strategic, not economic. Moscow seeks: (1) the elimination of Western military and economic influence from the area, specifically the abandonment of Western bases in Turkey, Iran, and Pakistan; (2) the expansion of Communist influence in the Middle East through Moscow's alignment with, and exploitation of, Arab nationalism (Moscow's espousal of the Arab position against Israel, support of Egypt during the Suez crisis, and subsequent outlays of economic and military assistance are all designed to place it atop the crest of the pan-Arabic tide); (3) the denial of Middle Eastern oil to Western European industry; (4) the acquisition of warm-water ports on the Mediterranean Sea and the Persian Gulf, an objective dating from Czarist times; (5) the communization, or at least domination, of the Middle East, which is the strategic land bridge between Europe and Asia.

Africa South of the Sahara

The struggle for Africa is in its initial phase, and Moscow is playing a cautious hand. Soviet strategy is attempting to adapt to the conditions of Africa, to develop an organizational weapon which can vie for political power. There are no African proletariat (except perhaps in South Africa), no well-organized Communist Parties, and no divisive class antagonisms. African societies are largely agrarian and rural, rent by tribal feuds, economically undeveloped, and politically fragile. In such a setting, traditional Communist tactics and formulations demand revision.

An immediate Soviet objective is to exploit African resentment against the remaining European possessions and the deep-rooted fears of Western interference. Soviet leaders expect a deterioration in African-Western relations and hope to turn the ensuing crises to their advantage. Meanwhile, they are striving to convince the neutralist African nations that they can depend on unstinting Soviet diplomatic support and economic and military aid. They have embarked on an extensive foreign aid program and negotiated bilateral agreements with Ghana, Guinea, Mali, Somali, Sudan, Senegal, etc.

For a while, Moscow had hoped to make Ghana and Guinea Communist showcases in Africa. Millions of dollars in credits were extended, trade and cultural missions exchanged, and Ghana's Kwame Nkrumah and Guinea's Sekou Touré visited Moscow. Despite the anti-Western, neutralist bent of Ghana and Guinea, they have not shown themselves to be easy targets for Communist penetration. Their leaders, though professing adherence to Marxism, have shown no inclination to replace their former Western rulers with Soviet commissars.

Soviet diplomacy has blundered on a number of occasions. An attempt in late 1961 by the Soviet ambassador to Guinea to interfere in local politics and force President Touré to accept Communists in his government led to the ambassador's unceremonious expulsion and occasioned a hasty visit by Anastas Mikoyan to repair the damage. As a result of this incident, Soviet prestige in Africa suffered a sharp setback, and Guinea embarked on a policy of reconciliation with France and the West. In the Congo, where in mid-September 1960 it had appeared that the Soviet Union was on the verge of a major diplomatic triumph, Moscow was effectively thwarted and is resigned to waiting for another opportunity for infiltration. There, as in Guinea, Moscow is learning through trial and error to appreciate the complexities and pitfalls of African politics. It may also be acquiring a grudging respect for the tenacity and toughness of the leaders of these new African nations and their determination to resist any foreign encroachment in their domestic affairs. Economic underdevelopment does not signify any lack of political astuteness.

The Soviet aid record so far has been marred by experts who do not speak the local language, frequent breakdowns of equipment which is not suited to tropical conditions, and an inability to offer much constructive assistance in the fields of agriculture and light industry, the main areas of African need. Particularly embarrassing to Moscow was Kenya's rejection in early 1965 of a shipment of Soviet arms and military equipment as "old and second-hand," and her abrupt curtailment of the Soviet-organized Patrice Lumumba Ideological Institute.

Moscow places great reliance upon propaganda and education as avenues for influencing African intellectuals. It finds that "socialism" exerts wide appeal among these groups, many of whom were schooled in Western institutions. But available evidence indicates that Moscow does not completely understand the dynamic forces of nationalism and a race-conscious Africanism that are sweeping Africa and conflict with orthodox Soviet prescriptions for political rule and modernization. Moscow may find that conditions in Africa, far from being ripe for Communist pickings, are antithetical and resistant to Soviet penetration.

Latin America

Of all the regions of the "third world" none seemed to Moscow a less promising target for influence-building than Latin America. Prior to 1959, Soviet writings reflected an assumption of American overlordship in the Western Hemisphere. The success of Fidel Castro's guerrilla-generated revolution in 1959 and his early conversion to communism opened new vistas to Soviet diplomacy (reading 80). As one writer noted, "The ease with which Castro defeated military dictatorship in one of the most prosperous countries of Latin America and subsequently defied the United States dramatized the revolutionary potential of Latin America."[2]

Realizing that closer diplomatic relations were a necessary preliminary to the ambitious design of encouraging Latin American neutralism, and thereby of undermining United States influence in the hemisphere, the USSR quickly acted to improve its relations with the few Latin American states with which it had formal diplomatic ties and sought to obtain diplomatic recognition from, and exchange ambassadors with, the countries of the hemisphere—many of which have thus far refused to deal with it. Some success was achieved, notably the re-establishment of diplomatic relations with Brazil in 1962 and with Chile in 1964.

The establishment of a Communist state in Cuba gave Moscow a foothold in the Western Hemisphere. Through the Castro revolution, the USSR hopes to promote strong Communist movements in other Latin American countries. The abortive American-engineered effort to overthrow Castro in April 1961 provided Moscow with a convenient cudgel with which to flail the United States and denounce the Monroe Doctrine; it also led Moscow to expand its economic and military commitments to Cuba. Early in 1962, the Soviet Government decided to introduce missiles into Cuba and develop it as a military base. On September 2, 1962, Moscow announced an expansion of arms deliveries and the sending of unspecified "technical specialists" to help Cuba meet "the threats" from "aggressive imperialist quarters." On September 11 the Soviet Government, in a major policy statement, asserted that "the armaments and military equipment sent to Cuba are designed exclusively for defensive purposes" and warned that "if war is unleashed," the Soviet Union will render assistance to Cuba "just as it was ready in 1956 to render military assistance to Egypt at the time of the Anglo-French-Israeli aggression in the Suez Canal region"; it deliberately played down the extent of its military commitment to Cuba and maintained that Soviet rocket power made it unnecessary "to search for sites . . . beyond the boundaries of the Soviet Union."

On October 22, 1962, President Kennedy startled the world with the information that Soviet missile installations were being constructed in Cuba. The dramatic account of the "eyeball-to-eyeball" Soviet-American confrontation in the Caribbean is well-known. At no time in the Khrushchev period was there a greater danger of nuclear war. Behind Moscow's gamble there were a number of bold calculations. First, by this "adventurist" course Soviet leaders sought to upset the power balance of the Cold War. They no doubt reasoned that the establishment of a nuclear weapons capability in Cuba would provide a profound military advantage which could be used to exact major concessions in Berlin. Second, Soviet leaders gambled that, once the missiles were introduced into Cuba under the guise of "defensive weapons," the United States would not respond resolutely, particularly in light of the Soviet warning of September 11. Third, the success of the Soviet maneuver would force the Chinese to recognize the superiority of Soviet strategy and re-establish Moscow's pre-eminent authority in the bloc.

Though forced to back down, Khrushchev subsequently defended the Soviet action by asserting that he had removed the missiles only in return for a United States pledge not to invade Cuba, and since Cuba had not been invaded his policy had been vindicated (reading 57). Since 1963, Cuba's dependence on the Soviet Union has kept Castro tied to Moscow, though Peking's militant calls for expansion of "wars of national-liberation" find a sympathetic audience in Havana. For its part, Moscow is heavily committed to assist Cuba's economic development and national security. This commitment costs the Soviet Union more than 300 million dollars a year. It is a price Moscow is prepared to pay for a Communist Cuba, which remains an ever-present irritant to the United States, a source of supply to revolutionary groups in the Western Hemisphere, and a base for propaganda.

Notwithstanding Moscow's deep involvement in Cuba, Latin America is at present low on the list of Soviet priorities. Heavily committed elsewhere in the developing world, and faced with growing demands upon its resources at home and within the bloc, the Soviet Union does not seem capable of undertaking a massive aid program to many Latin American countries. It has extended small credits to Argentina and Brazil, but the main recipient of its aid has been Cuba.

Expanded trade offers the most promising avenue of approach to Latin American countries, e.g., Argentina, Brazil, Bolivia, and Uruguay, which have burdensome surpluses of primary commodities and might, if Soviet offers were attractive, be prepared to enter into barter agreements. Aware of their precarious economic condition, Moscow has used UN forums to advertise the benefits of trade with the USSR. At meetings of the Economic and Social Council, Soviet delegates have deplored "the absence of normal trade relations between the socialist countries and Latin America." They note that each year the USSR purchases more raw materials from developing countries and suggest that these purchases "could be further increased to the benefit of the less industrialized countries if they would restore normal economic relations with the USSR and the People's Democracies." They also stress the harm which the Common Market might do to vulnerable Latin American export economies and imply that Latin American countries could find dependable markets in the Soviet bloc. Holding out the olive branch and the checkbook, one Soviet delegate asserted that "if they decided to change their policy, the socialist countries would certainly be willing to grant them credits and loans on worthwhile terms."

Observations

Continued Soviet penetration of developing areas is one of the realities of contemporary world politics. The effort to cultivate closer relations with the new nations of the third world is a permanent feature of Soviet foreign policy. Since 1954, Moscow has concentrated its diplomatic efforts on Afghanistan, Algeria, Cuba, Ghana, India, Indonesia, Mali, and the United Arab Republic. Careful not to offend needlessly, the Soviet Government has developed an approach generally marked by shrewd planning and timing.

During the Khrushchev period, the Soviet Union entered into diplomatic relations with most of the new nations, aligned itself with anti-Western and anti-colonial movements, launched an ambitious foreign aid program, expanded trade, promoted cultural exchanges, and courted intellectuals and opinion-molders. The Soviet Union came to Afro-Asia with "clean hands," without the taint of a colonial legacy. It experienced an intoxicating initial accumulation of diplomatic influence and goodwill.

Yet in coming decades Soviet diplomacy will be forced to adapt to an environment quite different from the one into which it adroitly moved in the mid-1950s. Moscow is no longer unknown or unblemished. The next stage—the preservation and extension of diplomatic influence and the transference of economic and military aid into political advantage—is a more trying, expensive, capricious affair, as other Great Powers have already learned. In its relations with developing countries, the Soviet Union is becoming more pragmatic, less doctrinaire, and less abrasive. As a Great Power, its interests have become global, and paradoxically, it may be less preoccupied with the instigation of revolutions and more interested in the extension of its influence along the traditional paths of diplomacy.

NOTES

1. Walter Z. Laqueur, *Communism and Nationalism in the Middle East* (New York: Frederick A. Praeger, 1956), p. 261.
2. David T. Cattell, "Soviet Policies in Latin America," *Current History*, Vol. XLVII, No. 279 (November 1964), p. 287.

The Stalinist Period, 1945–1953

74. THE COLONIAL QUESTION AFTER THE SECOND WORLD WAR*

E . ZHUKOV

Thirty years ago, overthrowing the landowners and capitalists, the Great October Socialist Revolution smashed the means of national oppression, freed without exception all the oppressed peoples of Russia and opened in front of them the broad possibility of free national development. The Soviet multinational government showed to all the world, and confirmed in practice, that it is possible to effect a voluntary union of equal peoples into one socialist family. Mutual trust and national equality, peaceful existence and fraternal cooperation of peoples are characteristics of the triumph of Leninist-Stalinist national policy in the USSR.

The nations in the capitalist world are found in a completely different situation. Imperialism, teaches Comrade Stalin, can bring nations together only forcibly, by means of predatory war and by the forcible retention of colonies in the framework of "one system." The imperialists, in essence, did not solve the national question, they did not establish relations of mutual trust and friendship among peoples. Capitalism cannot and does not want to eliminate the division between nations which are, on the one hand, suppressed, dependent, and unequal, and, on the other those [nations] who oppress, exploit, and possess all the rights. Such a division exists and deepens "in the contradictions of the bourgeois-democratic lies, which hide what is characteristic in the epoch of finance capitalism and imperialism, the colonial and financial enslavement of the great majority of the population of the earth by the insignificant minority of wealthy advanced capitalist countries."

Only Leninism offers a solution of the national-colonial problem. In spite of the apologists of the bourgeoisie, which attempts by different means to excuse and to institutionalize the inequality

* *Pravda*, August 7, 1947, *excerpts*. Editor's translation.

of peoples, in spite of reformers, who carry on, in essence, the same bourgeois policy on the national question, Marxism-Leninism calls all the oppressed peoples to the struggle for their complete liberation, binding the national-liberation movement of the oppressed peoples of the colonies and dependent countries with the revolutionary struggle of the proletariat. The great teachers—Lenin and Stalin—revealed profoundly and exhaustively in their works the existence of the national-colonial question, and worked out the theoretical methods of its solution. Leninist-Stalinist nationality policy found complete fulfillment in the USSR, where the problem of cooperation of nations, and the national question were solved better than in any other state. The brotherhood of peoples seems to be the wellspring of power of the Soviet state.

The colonial question belongs to the group of the most crucial problems of world politics. During the course of many decades the domination of some countries over others, the rivalry of the colonial powers and their struggle for the partition of the dependent and colonial countries were among the main sources of international conflict and military clashes.

The colonial question continues to disturb world public opinion even after the Second World War, when it was further intensified. . . .

The Second World War could not help influencing profoundly the situation in the colonial countries. In the struggle against the Fascist slaveholders, all the democratic forces of the world combined with the Soviet Union as the leader. The victory over Hitlerite Germany and militaristic Japan marked the ruin of the plans of the German and Japanese imperialists, who attempted to expand the sphere of national-colonial slavery. . . .

Even in the course of the Second World War a significant rise of the national-liberation movement appeared in several colonial and dependent countries. The anti-imperialist struggle in the Arab East, in Syria, Lebanon, and Egypt, intensified remarkably. The forms of struggle against English control in India and Burma also intensified. The masses of Indochina rose, cast off the yoke of Japanese and French imperialists, and declared their independence. The wide anti-imperialist movement which spread in British Malaya, in Indonesia, in the Philippines, assumed in these countries the form of armed partisan struggle against the Japanese seizure. The peoples of the colonial countries could not help declaring themselves against fascism which was the most blatant form of racial and national oppression. . . .

The war caused serious economic dislocations throughout the world. It affected the economic situation of the colonial countries.

. . . The development of industry in the colonies brought certain changes in the forms of economic dependence of the colony on the metropolitan power. [The article then develops the economic changes wrought in the pattern of colonial-metropolitan relations.]

The Maneuvers and Methods of Disguising Imperialism in the Colonies

The postwar period is characterized by the serious maneuvers of the imperialist states in the colonies. These maneuvers have for their task the strengthening of the shaken position of imperialism by means of the establishment of more flexible and experienced disguised forms of domination in the colonies. This is done by granting partial concessions to the national needs of the colonial countries. Among the ruling circles of the colonial empires a theory has received great popularity which says that the backward peoples in their development, undoubtedly, have to go through successive stages of dependence on or trusteeships by the more developed, advanced states. This theory is extremely suitable for the imperialists, and helps them preserve old colonial regimes under the supposedly benevolent suggestion that the peoples of this or that colonial country are not yet ready for independent existence. No wonder this theory received particular popularity in the classical colonial empire—in England. It is necessary to remark that the colonial policy of the British Labor Government, as well as its foreign policy, in essence is no different from the policy of the Conservatives. . . .

It was not in vain that Churchill could not hide his delight at the adroitness with which the Labor Government "solved" the sensitive problem of India. The partition of India into two dominions, which was effected on the religious-communal basis, along with the preservation of the principalities as an important supplementary factor of English pressure, was satisfactory from the point of view of English imperialism for the national liberation movement in India. The significance of this measure for English imperialism consisted in the fact that, viewed from the outside, it seemed an important concession, but at the same time it affords the possibility of using, in the future, the traditional English tactic of artificially inflaming and utilizing national, religious, and other internal antagonisms in India in the interests of preserving British domination. Parallel with this is the development of one of the characteristic features of postwar policy of the imperialistic countries in relation to the colonies, namely, the creation of new forms of "unity" of the colonies and metropolis (mother country) under the guise of the establishment of "federation" or "union." Those "unions" consist in principle of nominally equal colonial and metropolitan states, which, with the latter's other colonies are granted larger or smaller degrees of internal autonomy.

[*Pravda* then proceeds to condemn French policy in Indochina and Dutch policy in Indonesia.]

The grant of formal independence to the colonies by no means guarantees their actual independence. Many instances exist of strong capitalist states clearly and unceremoniously pressing their will on the weak, but formally "independent" countries. The grant in 1946 of "independence" to the Philippines did not free them from the domination of American imperialism. . . .

The Imperialism of the USA and the Colonial Question

One of the peculiarities of the postwar period is the increased number of governments which find themselves dependent on American imperialism in greater or lesser degree. As a result of the increased American expansion, the lines between independence and a semi-colonial state for many of the formerly independent countries became largely indeterminate and difficult to discern. . . . Earlier the main policing of the colonial system was carried out by England, which, as the most important colonial power, invariably took upon itself the initiative for suppressing the national liberation struggles of the peoples of the colonial and dependent countries. Now this role of England's is disputed by the United States of America. This is manifested both by the straightforward support by the USA of the reactionary, feudal elements in many of the semi-colonial, dependent countries, and by the immediate willingness of the USA to lead the intervention for the suppression of the peoples of Southeast Asia—of Indonesia and Indochina, who are throwing off by themselves the yoke of foreign imperialism. . . .

The Soviet Union and the Colonial Question

The position of the Soviet Union on the colonial question differs radically from that of the capitalist countries. The Soviet Union was always the implacable enemy of all forms and appearances of colonial suppression. Soviet democracy, as the most advanced form, does not accept any kind of racial or national suppression. . . .

Appearing before a press conference on May 7, 1945, in San Francisco, V. M. Molotov emphasized that "from the point of view of the interests of international security we must take care first of all that the dependent countries develop as soon as possible their own road to national independence." But the Soviet point of view did not receive any support from other great powers.

[The writer then proceeds to criticize the West for hindering the effective establishment of the Trusteeship Council in 1946, and for attempting to maintain its control over the former mandates in Africa.] . . . *The colonial question demands a solution.* Imperialist expansion, aimed against the sovereign rights of peoples, always had as its goal the prevention of the anti-imperialist, liberation struggle. The Second World War clearly showed to all the world the adventurism and determination of all the imperialistic plans to enslave the freedom-loving peoples, under such false guises that these plans could not be detected. In the course of the Second World War, the decay of the colonial system was evident in all its ramifications, the instability of the colonial empires and the awakening of all the peoples of the colonies who did not wish to live any longer under foreign yoke. The international reactionary cliques and the capitalist monopolies, seeing the hopelessness of the present situation, nevertheless, tried to spread the borders of colonial exploitation with impunity, and to chain the new countries and peoples to dollar servitude.

75. A STALINIST INTERPRETATION OF GANDHI AND GANDHISM*

A . M . D I A K O V

The utilization by Gandhi of the religious prejudices of the peasant masses, his exploitation of their oppressed state and backwardness, of their tradition of blind obedience to the Congress Party and its leadership and, in particular, to the person of Gandhi, whom the backward masses consider a saint, fettered the activity of the masses, demoralized and made them once again

* A. M. Diakov, "The Crisis of British Domination in India and the New Stage of the Liberation Struggle of Her Peoples," one of a series of studies in *Krizis Kolonial'noi Sistemy: Natsional'no-Osvoboditel'naia Bor'ba Narodov Vostochnoi Asii* [*The Crisis of the Colonial System: The National-Liberation Struggle of the Peoples of Eastern Asia*] (Moscow, 1949), pp. 109–111, excerpts. Editor's translation.

victims of treachery by the bourgeoisie and the landlords. The demagoguery of Nehru also helped the Congress Party dupe the vigilance of even the more politically sophisticated members of the Indian working class. . . .

The Governments of India and Pakistan not only do not want to struggle for complete independence, but they try in every way to strengthen their ties with England. Though the Congress Party proclaimed the struggle for full independence as its basic objective, in 1949 it nonetheless stated that India would remain within the British Empire; only for the deception of the masses was an "independent" republic proclaimed with the English crown as the symbol "of the united cooperation of nations." . . .

The Indian Government has become the principal agent of Anglo-American imperialism in Southeast Asia. Thus, the Governments of India and Pakistan have continued the old line of British policy directed toward the support and preservation of feudalism and, in their foreign policy, have completely entered the Anglo-American camp of warmongers.

The Congress Party has openly become the party of the reactionary bloc of the big Indian bourgeoisie and landowners. In spite of the murder of Gandhi . . . Gandhism remains the most important ideological weapon in the hands of the Indian bourgeoisie for keeping the masses under its influence. Moreover, after the partition of India, the reactionary nature of Gandhism was further strengthened. . . .

The attempts to utilize the authority of Gandhi for "defense of democracy" in India are extremely harmful and dangerous. Gandhi has never headed the armed struggle against imperialism and has never come out against traitors from among the Indians. On the contrary, he has always been the principal traitor of the mass national-liberation movement. The struggle against Gandhism—the ideology of the counter-revolutionary bourgeoisie of India—is impossible without a struggle against the authority of Gandhi, against the cult of Gandhi, without an exposure of all the activities of Gandhi who has constantly betrayed the national movement and by this rendered enormous services to the British enslavers of India.

Khrushchev and the Third World

76. THE DISINTEGRATION OF THE IMPERIAL-ISTIC COLONIAL SYSTEM—REPORT OF THE CENTRAL COMMITTEE OF THE CPSU TO THE TWENTIETH PARTY CONGRESS*

February 14, 1956

N . S . K H R U S H C H E V

The organizers of the military blocs claim that they are uniting for defense, for protection against the "Communist menace." But that is sheer hypocrisy. We know from history that, when planning a redivision of the world, the imperialist powers have always lined up military blocs. Today the "anti-Communism" slogan is again being used as a smoke screen to cover up one power's claims for world domination. The new thing here is that the United States wants, by means of all kinds of blocs and pacts, to secure the dominating position in the capitalist world and to reduce its partners in the blocs to the status of obedient executors of its will . . .

The arms race, the "positions of strength" policy, setting up aggressive blocs, and the "cold war"—all this cannot but aggravate the international situation, as indeed it has. This has been one trend of world events . . .

But other processes have also taken place in the international arena during these years, processes showing that in the world today by no means everything is under the thumb of the monopolist circles. The steady strengthening of the forces of socialism, democracy, and peace and of the forces of the national liberation movement is of decisive importance . . .

The forces of peace have been considerably augmented by the emergence in the world arena of a group of peace-loving European and Asian states which have proclaimed nonparticipation

* Moscow: Foreign Languages Publishing House, 1956, *excerpts.*

in blocs as a principle of their foreign policy. The leading political circles of these states rightly hold that to participate in closed military imperialist alignments would merely increase the danger to their countries of becoming involved in the aggressive forces' military gambles and being drawn into the ruinous maelstrom of the arms race.

As a result, a vast "peace zone," including both socialist and nonsocialist peace-loving states in Europe and Asia, has emerged in the world arena. This zone embraces tremendous expanses of the globe, inhabited by nearly 1.5 billion people—that is, the majority of the population of our planet.

The vigorous work for peace by the broadest masses has greatly influenced international events. In scope and organization of the masses' struggle against the war danger, the present period has no comparison in history.

The Communist Parties have shown themselves to be the most active and consistent fighters against the war danger and reaction . . . At the same time many other social circles are also opposing war. The effectiveness of their activity would naturally be greater should the various forces upholding peace overcome a certain disunity. Unity of the working class, of its trade unions, unity of action of its political parties, the Communists, the Socialists and other workers' parties, is acquiring exceptional importance . . .

Life has placed on the order of the day many questions which not only demand rapprochement and cooperation among all workers' parties, but also create real possibilities for this cooperation. The most important of these problems is that of preventing a new war. If the working class comes out as a united, organized force and acts with firm resolution, there will be no war . . . Cooperation is possible and essential with those circles of the socialist movement which have different views from ours on the forms of transition to socialism. Among them are many who are honestly mistaken on this question, but this is no obstacle to cooperation . . .

The position of the imperialist forces is growing weaker, not only because the peoples of their countries reject their aggressive policy but also because in the past ten years imperialism has been defeated in the East, where the centuries-old mainstays of colonialism are crumbling and the peoples themselves are, with increasing boldness, beginning to decide their own destinies . . .

The defeat of fascist Germany and imperialist Japan in the Second World War was an important factor stimulating the liberation struggle in the colonies and dependent countries. The democratic forces' victory over fascism instilled faith in the possibility of liberation in the hearts of the oppressed peoples. The victorious revolution in China struck the next staggering blow at the colonial system; it marked a grave defeat for imperialism. India, the country with the world's second biggest population, has won political independence. Independence has been gained by Burma, Indonesia, Egypt, Syria, Lebanon, the Sudan, and a number of other former colonial countries. More than 1.2 billion people, or nearly half of the world's population, have freed themselves from colonial or semi-colonial dependence during the last ten years.

The disintegration of the imperialist colonial system now taking place is a postwar development of history-making significance. Peoples who for centuries were kept away by the colonialists from the high road of progress followed by human society are now going through a great process of regeneration . . . The new period in world history which Lenin predicted has arrived, and the peoples of the East are playing an active part in deciding the destinies of the whole world, are becoming a new mighty factor in international relations. In contrast to the pre-war period, most Asian countries now act in the world arena as sovereign states or states which are resolutely upholding their right to an independent foreign policy. International relations have spread beyond the bounds of relations between the countries inhabited chiefly by peoples of the white race and are beginning to acquire the character of genuinely world-wide relations.

The winning of political freedom by the peoples of the former colonies and semi-colonies is the first and most important prerequisite of their full independence, that is, of the achievement of economic independence . . . These countries, although they do not belong to the socialist world system, can draw on its achievements to build up an independent national economy and to raise the living standards of their peoples. Today they need not go begging for up-to-date equipment to their former oppressors. They can get it in the socialist countries, without assuming any political or military commitments.

The very fact that the Soviet Union and the other countries of the socialist camp exist, their readiness to help the underdeveloped countries in advancing their industries on terms of equality and mutual benefit, are a major stumbling block to colonial policy. The imperialists can no longer regard the underdeveloped countries solely as potential sources for making maximum profits. They are compelled to make concessions to them . . .

77. THE SOVIET "DISCOVERY" OF INDIA*

E . VARGA

After the liberation from the English colonizers India, though still formally remaining a dominion and a member of the sterling bloc, quickly achieved full independence for itself in the sphere of foreign policy. In contradiction to Pakistan which entered the Baghdad Pact and generally coordinates its foreign policy with England and the USA, India conducts an independent, peaceful policy differing sharply from the policy of the USA and England, maintains friendly relations with the USSR and the Chinese People's Republic, and supports the peoples of the colonies and semi-colonial territories in their struggle against imperialism. . . .

The position of a dominion does not prevent this. There is no longer an English army of occupation in India, no Viceroy, no English administration. Soon after liberation India also abolished the role, however unimportant, of the English king as a "symbol" of the English empire. India in fact, in spite of its dominion status, has become a completely sovereign state, with its own independent foreign policy, which England is obliged to consider as it does the policy of any world power . . . The peace-loving foreign policy of India is a great defeat for the Western powers who hoped to use India against the other nations of Asia. According to the calculations of the imperialists of England and the USA, India was to have played an important role in the struggle against the national liberation movement in Asia. . . . But the hopes of the imperialists that India could perhaps be used successfully in a war against the peace-loving countries and peoples are unfounded. For, in general, the peoples of India do not want war, and, in particular, they do not want war against the Asiatic peoples, having liberated themselves or conducted a struggle for their liberation from imperialist oppression. . . .

The peaceful policy of India aroused great dissatisfaction in imperialist circles of the USA. They are indignant because of

* E. Varga, *Osnovnye Voprosy Ekonomiki i Politiki Imperializma: Posle Vtoroi Mirovoi Voiny* [*The Fundamental Questions of the Economics and Politics of Imperialism: After the Second World War*], 2nd ed. (Moscow: Institute of World Economics and International Relations, 1957), pp. 431–436, *excerpts.* Editor's translation with assistance of Dr. Norma Noonan.

the fact that India accepts loans from the USA but refuses any demand of the USA to accommodate its foreign policy to American interests. . . . American reactionary circles in no way wish to understand that it is impossible to bribe the great India with dollars. . . .

The firm stand of India against the military plans of the USA in Asia, its demand that China occupy its lawful place in the UN instead of the American mercenary, Chiang Kai-shek, the speeches of the Indian Government supporting a truce in Indochina and the prohibition of atomic weapons—all taken together constitute an important service by the peoples of India for the peace and independence of Asia. The peaceful policy of the Government of Nehru receives the support of all working toilers including the Communist Party of India. . . .

Friendship between India and the Soviet Union was strengthened by the visit to India of the leaders of the USSR, by the visit to the USSR of Prime Minister Nehru and other Indian statesmen, and by the exchange of delegations. The speeches of N. A. Bulganin and N. S. Khrushchev, condemning colonialism and emphasizing the great historical significance of friendship between the Soviet and Indian peoples, made a great impression on the masses of India. The Soviet Union supported the peoples of India in such important problems for them as Goa, Kashmir. The Indian republic, second in the world in terms of population, plays a prominent role on the international scene as a powerful factor in the struggle for peace, and against the organizing of military blocs.

The Suez conflict distinctly showed that dominion status does not prevent India from conducting an independent and, if necessary, anti-English foreign policy. In spite of the cry of the English imperialists that the Suez Canal in the hands of Egypt represents a mortal threat to the vital interests of England and to the entire "Commonwealth," India consistently defended the legal rights of Egypt to the Suez Canal. India, together with the USSR, Indonesia, and Ceylon, declined the "Dulles Plan," firmly condemned any use of force against Egypt, and made every effort to effect a peaceful settlement of the Suez conflict without prejudice to the legitimate interests of Egypt. She resolutely condemned the military assault of the Anglo-French aggressors on Egypt.

Thus, India is a most valuable member of the zone of peace and closely cooperates with the Soviet Union and the Chinese People's Republic for the preservation of peace throughout the world.

78. THE STRATAGEMS OF AMERICAN IMPERIALISM IN SOUTHEAST ASIA*

S. NESTEROV

India occupies a special place in the expansionist plans of American imperialism. In her footsteps and following her example, a large group of countries, who had just attained independence, began to follow a neutralist policy, refusing military and political agreements with the imperialists. To knock India off the path of neutralism, to dynamite the "Zone of Peace," precisely there where the most important and influential states have joined it—such is the cherished aim of the imperialists.

The Sino-Indian border conflict appeared as a real godsend to American imperialism. The reactionary imperialist forces in the U. S. decided that in no case would they let slip by this "golden chance" which comes up "once in a century," and would use it to undermine the international prestige of the countries of the socialist system, in particular, their influence on the neutralist governments of Southeast Asia.

The fact that the leaders of the Chinese People's Republic bear a certain responsibility for worsening this conflict gives hope to the imperialists in their attempts to use it to discredit the foreign policy of socialist countries. On the other hand, at this particular juncture, the reactionary elements recognize wide possibilities for the suppression of revolutionary, democratic forces in India and for dealing a blow to the policy of nonalignment to military blocs, followed by India and other neutralist governments.

The USA and England have used the situation thus created to force on India military "aid." With lightening speed, they have dispatched there large shipments of armaments and groups of military advisers.

The USA, whose "aid" to India in the form of loans and "gifts" has surpassed 4 billion dollars, has significantly increased "economic" aid to India, calculating to use it to support the reactionary forces. On February 25, 1963, the USA signed an

* S. Nesterov, "The Stratagems of American Imperialism in Southeast Asia," *Mirovaia ekonomika i mezhdunarodnye otnosheniia*, No. 10 (October 1963), pp. 71–74, *excerpts*.

agreement with India for a loan of 240 million dollars. This is the biggest loan ever granted by the USA to an underdeveloped country. Moreover, the USA offered India still another series of large credits. The curtain over the real reasons for such generosity was lifted on the occasion of the discussion of the problem involving the building in India of a big government steel mill at Bokaro. The Committee on Foreign Aid, headed by Clay, declared itself against allocations for the building of the mill, criticizing in principle "building projects of state enterprises which could compete with private enterprise." Partisans of a more flexible approach, such as the former Ambassador to India Galbraith, came out in favor of the allocation of the above mentioned funds, but with the provision that the USA should be assured of "a lengthy period of control."

Analyzing the motives of those who support the financing of the state sector of the Indian economy, the weekly *Link* noticed that this development is of a temporary nature and tied in with efforts to strengthen India for the purpose of fighting international communism. "But," *Link* went on to say, "as soon as the border conflict is settled and it is impossible any longer to use India, even indirectly, in the struggle against international communism, she will have to pass a test to find out whether she is entitled to receive American assistance."

These explanations obviously cannot be considered as the whole story. Everyone knows that the main reason which forces the imperialists now to grant even partial limited assistance for the purpose of industrializing newly liberated countries is the fact that the Soviet Union and the socialist countries have liquidated the imperialist monopoly in the delivery of industrial equipment to underdeveloped countries. As reported in the American press, outspoken fears were expressed, in reference to the construction of a steel mill at Bokaro, that, "If the Americans do not complete the project, the Russians will do it." The later refusal by the Indians themselves of the above-mentioned credits is explained precisely by the fact that the liberated countries saw new openings for the building of an independent economy.

At the same time, the Western Powers hoped to use the grant of military "assistance" to India for the purpose of inducing the government of India to grant concessions to Pakistan in the Kashmir dispute . . . "Pressure tactics" in the Kashmir problem did not produce any concrete results. Imperialist circles and internal reactionary forces pursued with increased stubbornness their attempts to make India abandon her neutralist course and to drag her into military blocs—as witnessed by the agreement made by the All-India Radio with the "Voice of America," permitting this loudspeaker of the "Cold War" to use the Calcutta radio station to transmit to Southeast Asia. *The Times of India,* criticizing the agreement [which was shelved by Nehru], noticed that "not even all the members of SEATO agreed to the location of 'Voice of America' transmitters on their territories."

The joint military maneuvers of the air force, imposed on India by American and other imperialists, potentially threaten India with still more serious consequences. A resolution of the Central Secretariat of the Communist Party of India stresses that these maneuvers are actually part of a plan of "joint defense," by which the imperialists aim to "drag us into a real military alliance, impose their will on our country and on the air space along our borders, and threaten by all this our sovereignty and our independence."

Such concessions to imperialist pressure could happen only under conditions where reactionary forces within the country were activated. With the cooperation of the U. S. intelligence services, chiefly the CIA, in India extreme rightist parties—"Swatantra," "Jan Sangh," and others—indulged in drastic activities. Creating an atmosphere of war psychosis, the rightist chauvinistic circles attempted to consolidate their positions . . .

Finally, the imperialist adventures were facilitated by the fact that precisely at the time of the Sino-Indian conflict, which by the way did not accidentally coincide with the Caribbean crisis, the Chinese leaders openly began to undermine the solidarity of the socialist camp and of the world-wide communist movement . . . The position taken by the Chinese leaders of maintaining tension and of delaying the settlement of the territorial dispute with India is quite characteristic of their attitude towards the principles of peaceful coexistence. . . . Apparently the Chinese leaders decided to use this conflict also for the purpose of proving the accuracy of their thesis on the necessity of pushing revolutionary development from the outside. But the course of developments confirmed the fallacy of the thinking of the Chinese leaders . . .

79. ON THE MIDDLE EAST—SPEECH TO THE TWENTY-FIRST CONGRESS OF THE CPSU *

January 27, 1959

N. S. KHRUSHCHEV

All progressive mankind can be satisfied with the development of events in countries of the Near and Middle East. We welcome the national-liberation movement of the Arab peoples and other peoples of Asia and Africa who have escaped from colonialist oppression. The expulsion of the forces of the imperialist colonialists from several countries of that area was a major victory of the Arab peoples and all peace-loving forces. However, it should not be assumed that an exacerbation of the situation is precluded there, since the colonialists expelled from the colonies will not take their defeat lying down.

The Western powers, and above all the United States and Britain, are trying to set the Arab states against one another; they spin webs of intrigue in Iraq and other Arab countries; they are looking for weak spots for the purpose of disuniting the liberated peoples and primarily, the peoples of the Arab East. When peoples fight for their national independence against the colonialists, all patriotic forces are merged in a single national front. That was the case, for instance, during the struggle waged by the people of Egypt and other Arab peoples for liberation from the yoke of imperialist colonialists. . . . Since the expulsion of the colonialists, now that the national tasks have been basically completed, the peoples look for an answer to the social problems brought forth by reality. These are, primarily, the solution of the agrarian-peasantry question and the problem of the struggle between labor and capital. Social processes which inevitably lead to different views as to the further steps in the development of their states, arise in the ranks of the national liberation movement. As have other socialist countries, our country has supported and will continue to support the national liberation movement. The Soviet Union has not interfered and does not intend to interfere in the domestic affairs of other countries.

* Foreign Broadcast Information Service, *Daily Report* (Washington, D.C., January 29, 1959), *excerpts.*

We cannot, however, fail to make clear our attitude toward the fact that a campaign against progressive forces is being waged in some countries under the false slogan of anti-communism.

Since pronouncements against the ideas of communism have been recently made in the United Arab Republic and accusations have been brought forward against communists, I as a communist deem it necessary to state at the Congress of our Communist Party that the communists are wrongly accused of contributing to the weakening or splitting of the national effort in the struggle against imperialism. The reverse is true. There are no people more steadfast and devoted to the cause of the struggle against colonialists than communists. More steadfast forces in the struggle against imperialism do not exist than those of communism. It is due to no mere accident that the imperialists are directing the spearhead of their attack against the communist movement.

The struggle against the communist and other progressive parties is a reactionary affair. One does not rally the national forces through conducting an anti-communist line of policy; on the contrary, this splits them. Hence, it weakens the efforts of the whole nation in the defense of its interests against imperialism. It is wrong to accuse the communists of acting counter to the national interests of the Arab peoples. It is likewise naive to place on the same footing communism and Zionism. It is a matter of general knowledge that the communists, including those in Israel, are waging a struggle against Zionism. . . .

We do not conceal the fact that we and some leaders of the UAR have different views in the ideological field, but in questions of struggle against imperialism, in the matter of strengthening the political and economic independence of the countries which have freed themselves from colonialism, in the struggle against the danger of war, our positions coincide with the positions of those same leaders. Differences in ideological views must not hinder the development of friendly relations between our countries and the cause of the common struggle against imperialism. . . .

The countries which have attained their national emancipation need, and will go on needing, the support of the socialist countries, the support of all progressive people. The Soviet Union and the other socialist countries are strengthening friendly relations with the countries which have freed themselves of the colonial yoke; they are now, and will go on, rendering them assistance. . . .

80. THE SOVIET IMAGE OF LATIN AMERICA*

The fundamental instrument of expansion of the U.S.A. into the countries of the Western Hemisphere after World War II was the so-called Inter-American system, which was intended to mask the imperialistic policy of the U.S.A. and to paralyze the struggle of the peoples of the Latin American countries for national independence and economic liberation. The reactionary, cosmopolitan doctrine of Pan-Americanism is based on the ideology of American imperialism which alleges an existent community of interests of the countries of the Western Hemisphere, one based on their geographical closeness and on an affinity of political ideals and systems. In essence, however, Pan-Americanism is a new edition of the renowned Monroe Doctrine, certifying the domination of the U.S.A. in the Western Hemisphere . . .

With the help of and under the cover of the Inter-American organs, the U.S.A. unfolded a wide expansion into Latin America in the postwar period. Taking advantage of the enfeeblement of her imperialistic competitors, the U.S.A. from 1946 to 1953 increased the general capital investment in Latin America from 4.3 billion to 8 billion dollars, and the private investment, from 3 to 6 billion dollars. The monopolies of the U.S.A. have wide recourse to the creation of so-called joint companies with local capital. This form ensures the control of the American companies, allows them to operate under the brand of national firms, and masks the imperialistic character of their activities . . . Controlling the economy of the Latin American countries, the monopolies of the U.S.A. stimulate the development only of those branches of industry and agriculture which do not compete with the American ones.

After the beginning of the Korean War, the U.S.A. called for further expansion of military strategic ties of the Latin American countries with the United States. The American monopolies received new concessions for the exploiting and prospecting of serviceable minerals having military significance, in particular those going into the production of atomic weapons. The number

* F. G. Zuev, I. F. Ivashin, V. P. Nikhamin (eds.), *Mezhdunarodnye otnosheniia i vneshniaia politika SSSR, 1917–1960* [*International Relations and Foreign Policy of the USSR, 1917–1960*] (Moscow: State Publishing House of the Higher Party School of the Central Committee of the CPSU, 1961), pp. 506–518, *excerpts.* Editor's translation with the assistance of Miss Xenia Sochor.

of U. S. military delegations going to Latin America increased noticeably . . .

American imperialism used its economic and political influence to obtain support for the external political course of the U.S.A. and active participation of the Latin American countries in the "cold war." . . .

The ruling circles of the U.S.A. considered as one of the main tasks of its policy in Latin American countries the struggle against national-liberation movements, which in the first postwar years were found on the increase. Under the pressure of the U.S.A. in Chile, Brazil, Venezuela, Colombia, Paraguay, Peru, and a row of other countries, Communist parties were declared illegal, thousands of Communists and other progressive agents were thrown into prisons. American imperialism, nevertheless, could not frighten, nor buy off the freedom-loving peoples of Latin America. In spite of repressions and defamation, they continued their struggle for independence, peace, and democracy . . .

Nevertheless, national-liberation movements of the peoples of Latin American countries spread; the idea of a united national front in the struggle against imperialism, which the Communists consistently upheld, received wider support among the masses. In 1954–1960, a massive protest movement swelled in Latin America . . . peasant agitations grew, and democratic organizations strengthened themselves . . .

The overthrow of reactionary regimes in countries which were considered patrimonial estates of American capital, e.g., Colombia and Venezuela, was met with exultation by the national masses of Latin America and evoked among them a new upsurge of national-liberation movements, particularly in Cuba.

For seven years the Cuban nation fought against the reactionary dictator Batista, who, having come to power in 1952 as a result of a government upheaval which had been organized through the active cooperation of the U.S.A., expansively opened the doors of the country to American monopolies and soldiery.

In December 1956, a group of Cuban patriots, headed by the lawyer Fidel Castro, landed in Cuba and carried on an armed fight for the overthrow of the Batista regime. Castro's appearance marked the beginning of the creation of guerrilla detachments, which consequently formed the revolutionary insurrectionary army. Through the active support of the masses, this army destroyed the government army which had been equipped and trained by the U.S.A. On January 1, 1959, Batista fled from Cuba and hid in the Dominican Republic . . .

Command passed into the hands of the revolutionary government headed by Fidel Castro, who initiated a radical program of democratic reform. The old government apparatus, which had been serving the interests of the monopolies and Cuban landed magnates and the large bourgeoisie connected with them, was destroyed; revolutionary armed forces were created; and the military mission of the U.S.A. was sent out of the country. The new government presented the nation with extended democratic rights and set upon a program of agrarian reform, leading to a liquidation of *latifundia* American sugar monopolies and Cuban landlords.

The triumph of the revolution in Cuba dispelled the myth of the omnipotent power of American imperialism in Latin America. It showed that the U.S.A. in the present international situation cannot undertake armed intervention in the countries of Latin America with her former ease. The Cuban revolution demonstrated that even a small country has the possibility of overthrowing a dictatorial regime, which relies on U. S. support, and of following an independent policy.

The Cuban revolution evoked enthusiasm and warm support among the peoples of Latin American countries and became the model of national-liberation movements in the Western Hemisphere. Experiencing a sudden scare in the face of the revolutionary impact of the Cuban revolution on the other countries of Latin America, the U.S.A. is trying with all her strength to crush or transform it [the Cuban revolution] internally. To achieve this goal she will not refrain from using any means . . .

The overthrow of reactionary pro-American dictatorships in Colombia, Venezuela, and Cuba dealt a strong blow to American imperialism in the Western Hemisphere, and constituted a serious defeat for the American policy of "positions of strength." These facts indicate the beginning of a new stage in the national-liberation struggle of the peoples of Latin America, the characteristic feature of which is the decisive and organized struggle against American imperialism and its allies in Latin American countries.

FOR FURTHER STUDY

Allen, Robert Loring, *Soviet Economic Warfare*, Washington, D.C.: Public Affairs Press, 1960.

Barghoorn, Frederick C., *The Soviet Cultural Offensive*, Princeton, N.J.: Princeton University Press, 1960.

Berliner, Joseph S., *Soviet Economic Aid: The New Aid and Trade Policy.* New York: Frederick A. Praeger, 1958.

Kautsky, John H., *Moscow and the Communist Party of India.* New York: John Wiley & Sons, 1956.

Laqueur, Walter Z., *Nationalism and Communism in the Middle East.* New York: Frederick A. Praeger, 1956.

————, *The Soviet Union and the Middle East.* New York: Frederick A. Praeger, 1959.

London, Kurt (ed.), *New Nations in a Divided World.* New York: Frederick A. Praeger, 1963.

Nollau, Gunther and Hans Jurgen Wiehe, *Russia's South Flank: Soviet Operations in Iran, Turkey and Afghanistan.* New York: Frederick A. Praeger, 1963.

Overstreet, Gene and Marshall Windmiller, *Communism in India.* Berkeley: University of California Press, 1959.

Poppino, Rollie E., *International Communism in Latin America, 1917–1963.* New York: Free Press of Glencoe, 1964.

Rubinstein, Alvin Z., *The Soviets in International Organizations: Changing Policy Toward Developing Countries, 1953–1963.* Princeton, N.J.: Princeton University Press, 1964.

Spector, Ivar, *The Soviet Union and the Muslim World: 1917–1958.* Seattle: University of Washington Press, 1959.

Thornton, Thomas P. and Cyril E. Black (eds.), *Communism and Nationalism: The Strategic Uses of Political Violence.* Princeton, N.J.: Princeton University Press, 1964.

CHAPTER XII

PROBLEMS AND PROSPECTS

We are moving toward an uncertain tomorrow. No other single factor will so shape the character of the next decade as will the foreign policy of the Soviet Union. The issues of war or peace and, more specifically, the scope and intensity of the Cold War, will be decided largely in Moscow, the principal beneficiary of international disequilibrium. With alarming effectiveness, the Soviet Union has exploited Western indecision and penetrated the developing areas of the world. It has maneuvered skillfully and now threatens to attain by a combination of political blackmail and economic expansion objectives that it has hitherto been reluctant to attempt by military means. In effect, Moscow aspires to dominate the world through *peace*—not war. Its policies are constantly adjusted, the better to exploit changing world conditions. Hence, there is a continuing and urgent need to re-evaluate soberly the Kremlin's seemingly bewildering profusion of ultimatums, threats, offers to negotiate, and bland assurances of international goodwill.

Attempts to interpret Soviet behavior become more important as Soviet power grows. Though beset with pitfalls and subject to widespread disagreement, they must be made. For, in great measure, any effective foreign policy depends upon an accurate appraisal of the strengths and weaknesses, the ambitions and fears, of one's opponent. One must be wary of the emotional, the superfluous, and the fanciful, for the stakes are peace and survival. John S. Reshetar, Jr., discusses a few of the problems encountered in analyzing and predicting Soviet behavior (reading 81). It is also essential to appreciate the manifold difficulties involved in the actual process of negotiating with the Soviets on specific issues. According to Philip E. Mosely, a leading specialist on Soviet affairs, the negotiator must be patient, resourceful, and tough-minded (reading 82). He must thoroughly understand the peculiarities of the Soviet system, its highly centralized, conspiratorial tradition, the distorted image of the outside world held by its leaders, and their inflated confidence in the "inevitability" of communism. Above all, he must be prepared for long, drawn-out sessions and seemingly futile discussions. There are no easy roads to negotiating with the Kremlin, as experience has vividly, often tragically, shown.

Summit conferences have a value, but only if held after lengthy preliminary discussions have narrowed some areas of discord to well-defined, manageable proportions. Even then, too much must not be expected. They will not result in any sudden end to the Cold War. However, such top-level meetings can play a positive role in reducing international tension and decreasing the likelihood of miscalculated ventures. In dealing with the Soviet Government, principle must at all times be supported by power. Moscow may dismiss the former, but it will respect the latter. In general, the present struggle between the West and the Soviet Union must be regarded as transcending the tensions of particular areas. What are involved are incompatible concepts of national security and of the future shape of the international community. Time and changing historical conditions may mellow the intensity of the antagonism, but they cannot negotiate it out of existence.

The unremitting hostility of the Soviet Union toward the Western world need not be further documented here. It is enough to note that since 1917 the USSR has systematically sought to undermine non-Communist governments and intrude Communist influence wherever possible. During the post-World War II period, Soviet leaders extended their control over Central and Eastern Europe. To ensure the stability of their empire, they have attempted to disrupt the NATO alliance system, promote Western disunity, and diminish American military and political influence in Europe, Africa, Asia, and the Middle East. They have resorted to subterfuge and subversion, as well as to overt aggression. No immediate departure from this pattern of behavior can be expected. Soviet leaders have repeatedly reaffirmed their intention to wage an unceasing struggle to destroy capitalism. Indeed, Khrushchev warned the Western countries that "We will bury you." Robert Strausz-Hupé has termed this the strategy of "protracted conflict" and emphasized its all-embracing, continuing character. It is a strategy "for annihilating the opponent over a period of time by limited operations, by feints and maneuvers, psychological manipulations and diverse forms of violence."[1] It involves a total conflict of cultures and precludes any meaningful, enduring settlement between the Soviet and non-Soviet worlds.

On the other hand, the image of intractable and unrelieved Soviet hostility is an oversimplification. Concurrent with its growing strength and influence, Moscow finds itself confronted with an unsettling array of problems within the Communist world, the consequence of the de-Stalinization of Soviet society, the recrudescence of nationalism in Eastern Europe, and the Chinese challenge to Soviet leadership of the international Communist movement. Set against this complex of problems is the competition from the United States and an economically resurgent Western Europe. The achievements of the Khrushchev era which made the Soviet Union a global power have also given it a vital and growing stake in a regularized and stable international environment. Writing of Moscow's interest in such a world in the twilight of the Khrushchev period, one Western analyst observed that: "Khrushchev's Russia emerges as a conservative state fending off the pressures for a policy of uncompromising hostility to the West, uncompromising support of Communist against capitalist, and uncompromising support of so-called national-liberation movements. What primarily motivates the Soviet Union are the material and technical demands of its own society, which in international terms requires peace not revolution, accommodation not adventurism."[2] This evaluation remains equally persuasive for the post-Khrushchev period.

Even if we acknowledge the institutionalization of Soviet hostility, the question of the motivations behind Soviet foreign policy, and of its principal objectives during the coming decade, must be considered. Is "peaceful coexistence" possible for any prolonged period? Can the West cope for an indefinite period with the relentless pressures from the Sino-Soviet world without sacrificing its strength and vitality and the very structure of its society? What are the Kremlin's specific objectives in Europe, in Asia, in Africa, in the Middle East, in Latin America?

The West and the Soviet Union often use the same phrases, but with different meaning. For example, to the Western Powers, peaceful coexistence implies a willingness to accept an essentially status quo situation. To the Soviet leaders, it has only a transitory and tactical relevance, to be discarded at their convenience as the "revolutionary tide" rises; it affords them time to increase their power, expand the struggle to new areas, and undermine Western unity and resolve. In such matters totalitarian regimes enjoy distinct short-term advantages. They can conduct their foreign policy with a freedom from political opposition and a disregard for public opinion alien to a democratic society. Soviet enmity toward the West and determination to improve the international power position of the USSR remain constants of Kremlin behavior. Soviet space achievements have inflated the Kremlin's confidence in its military strength, thus encouraging its more belligerent political maneuvers along the brink of possible war— witness the Quemoy crisis of August-September 1958, the challenge to the Western position in Berlin, and the Cuban crisis of 1962. The impressive advances in missile and nuclear development may have emboldened those Soviet leaders who seek to employ more active pressure against the West and are perhaps more impatient (and overconfident) than their predecessors to communize the world. Such rocket rattling and calculated provocation increase the possibility that war may occur through accident rather than through design. This uncertainty, and the deep-rooted insecurity it engenders, is a tragic by-product of the nuclear age in which we live.

Before hazarding a few speculative remarks about the probable pattern of Soviet foreign policy during the coming decade, we must consider the question of whether there are forces operating within Soviet society "that by themselves, and independent of the balance of power" seem to impel the Soviet Union along an expansionist course. According to Barrington Moore, Jr., there are a number of factors to be considered—the nature of Soviet totalitarianism, the power drive of the Soviet leaders, the lines of continuity linking Czarist and Soviet foreign policies, and the messianism implicit in Marxism-Leninism (reading 83). As the social structure of the Soviet Union undergoes important transformations, the relative significance of these factors may be expected to change. But there is little evidence to justify the hope that changes in the structure of Soviet society (for example, the increase in the number of educated people) will materially affect the character of Soviet foreign policy in the foreseeable future. Indeed, the increasingly formidable Soviet challenge stems precisely from the fact that Soviet leaders have shown an amazing capacity to make the necessary economic and social adjustments without in any way sacrificing the monopolistic power of the Communist Party or their own unquestioned and absolute control of foreign policy. Soviet society, despite its many economic, educational, and social changes, is as autocratic as ever. The autocracy has merely grown more subtle and, correspondingly, more effective. In addition, Soviet leaders appear to have developed a broad base of support for their foreign policy. Certainly, they have effectively muted any open or fragmented opposition that may exist.

Soviet-Western relations face a difficult future. This writer is sensitive to the pitfalls involved in attempting to forecast the intentions and actions of the Soviet leaders, or the innumerable events which may advance, retard, or upset the best-laid plans of the Kremlin. But this venture should be made, if only to prove anew to the student the enduring validity of a statement made by Paul Winterton, a shrewd observer of Soviet affairs, to the effect that "There are no experts on the Soviet Union, merely varying degrees of ignorance."

What, then, of the coming decade?

First, of paramount importance to Soviet leaders is the concern for the integrity and security of the Soviet state. An awesome thermonuclear capability goes a long way toward assuring the *military* security of the USSR, toward insulating it from possible attack. But as long as the Cold War exists, accelerating arms expenditures—especially for research and development of new weapons and new defenses—will be mandatory, and these limit the ability of Soviet leaders not only to achieve greater security, but also to improve the standard of living of their people. A detente with the United States, however, throws into question Soviet leadership of the non-European wings of the international Communist movement where the call of the Chinese to revolution and "wars of national-liberation" offers to foreign Communists the possibility of acquiring political power. It opens Moscow to Peking's charges that the Soviet Union is indifferent to the cause of world revolution and is prepared to discard it in the interest of an accommodation with the United States.

Second, Soviet leaders still believe that "All roads lead to Communism." In their view the transition period will be a long and difficult one. And though the process may be advanced by national revolutions, diplomatic maneuver, and economic crises, the Soviet home base must not be jeopardized by any act likely to provoke an all-out war. Accordingly, no major war involving nuclear weapons will be attempted by Moscow during the next decade. Rather, the Cold War will continue to dominate the international scene, with alternate periods of crisis and relaxation. The "balance of terror" will forestall any precipitate Soviet military action in Europe or in any area the West has clearly committed itself to defend. A mutually destructive nuclear war is a totally unacceptable alternative for attaining coveted political objectives. Besides, there is little warrant for the belief that the Soviet leaders intend to overwhelm Western capitalism by primarily military means. This may afford some solace. But Soviet strength, and its imperialist expansion since 1945, caution against excessive optimism concerning the ultimate intentions of the Kremlin and against a too heavy reliance solely on the nuclear deterrent. The West must be prepared to cope with limited wars; it must be strong enough to meet any eventuality.

Third, the principal Soviet objectives in Europe are, and will continue to be, the preservation of its Eastern European empire, the weakening of NATO, and the retardation of West German rearmament, particularly with respect to nuclear and missile weapons. The division of Germany will remain the critical, unresolved problem of Europe. Though West Germany will grow more powerful economically and militarily, exerting greater influence within the NATO alliance, reunification will not be realized. Moscow's price—the withdrawal of American power from the continent—will be too high.

The Kremlin is confronted with a serious dilemma: It holds the key to German reunification. On the one hand, it might be willing to agree to preliminary steps toward reunification in the hope of weakening NATO's unity and thwarting German rearmament. On the other hand, the specter of a unified, powerful Germany, dominating Western and possibly Central Europe, must evoke painful memories. Accordingly, Moscow will most likely retain its firm grip on East Germany. To do otherwise might encourage opposition to its authority in Eastern Europe. Control of East Germany assures Moscow of a compliant and Communist Poland and Czechoslovakia. Although a severe succession crisis within the Kremlin could reverse this policy and precipitate a further withdrawal of Soviet power from the heart of Europe, this is not likely in the near future. Moscow will not readily surrender its empire, even though the Eastern European countries are now an economic, military, and political liability and the military strategy of a missile age increasingly makes possession of Eastern European real estate a defensive anachronism. Consequently, it will continue to press for Western acceptance of the status quo in Europe and recognition of Soviet hegemony in Eastern Europe.

Fourth, Moscow will not permit any anti-Communist or non-Communist regime to come to power in Eastern Europe. The transformation of Soviet-East European relationships has progressed to a stage where only force could reimpose the pattern of rule of the Stalin era. For political reasons, and because political attitudes and perceptions always lag far behind technological advances, Moscow will insist upon at least nominal adherence to the Warsaw Pact. The more critical question for Moscow is how far it can permit the nationalist and independent manifestations to proceed without endangering its military dominance and ambiguous political authority. Moscow has accepted, and will continue to accept, decentralization as a formula for preserving its imperium, but too much decentralization might encourage centripetal tendencies which would render Soviet control an anachronism and disrupt the Soviet economic stake in the region. This is a dilemma Moscow is well aware of, but which it is not now prepared to tackle.

Fifth, the deterioration of relations between Moscow and Peking since 1961 has reached the threshold of an open rupture that few expected. The short-term retention of the alliance seems likely, if only because of the presence of a common enemy—the United States—and because the main territorial and strategic objectives of China and the Soviet Union are different: Moscow is vitally concerned with developments in Eastern and Western Europe, especially in Germany, and in the general area south of the USSR in the direction of the Mediterranean, the Persian Gulf, and the Indian Ocean; while Peking's concern is with the Formosa Strait and Southeast Asia, particularly with Vietnam, Cambodia, Laos, Thailand, and Burma. But tensions precipitating a rupture may develop in the future over incompatible and competing Soviet and Chinese objectives toward Japan, the Mongolian People's Republic, and India.

Sixth, at a time when the military capacity of the Soviet Union is rapidly expanding, the main Soviet challenge to the West is unfolding in the developing world. The weapons are economic and political—not military. Soviet agents are exploiting anti-Western sentiment and social discontent, spreading their influence, and threatening to subvert several of the newly independent Afro-Asian states. Soviet agitation in these countries will continue to mount. Political penetration is being facilitated by expanded economic and cultural exchanges. Not only does Moscow align itself with the national aspirations of former colonial peoples, but it also buttresses political encouragement with concrete and extensive economic and technical aid. It seeks, first, to undermine still further a fast-fading Western influence and, second, to set the stage for future subversion by Communist and pro-Communist elites.

Seventh, disarmament, about which so much has been written and so little done, will prove impossible to achieve during the coming decade. Nuclear arsenals will grow. The number of nuclear powers will increase. This will further complicate the apparently insurmountable political problems any prospective agreement entails concerning an inspection system, a prerequisite for disarmament. Frequent negotiations will be carried on, but nothing meaningful seems likely to emerge.

Finally, the concept of "disengagement," a subtle and circumscribed variation on the disarmament theme, has attracted considerable attention as a possible formula for easing tensions in Central Europe. Calling for a gradual and supervised withdrawal of Soviet and American military power from the area, "disengagement" would initially seek to establish a nuclear-free zone in East and West Germany, Czechoslovakia, and Poland (the Rapacki Plan). This would serve as the first step toward the implementation of a more comprehensive arms-reduction program in these countries. There are, however, many modifications of "disengagement" and perhaps even more widespread disagreements over its military and political implications for the balance of power in Europe. Soviet leaders state that they are prepared "to participate in the examination of such a question as that of disengaging the armed forces of NATO and the Warsaw Pact countries for the creation of a zone where the troops and armaments of the two sides would be limited, and of an inspection system." But recent discussions have not resulted in any visible progress toward accord. Nor, with the present precariousness of East-West relations, is any extensive compromise of existing concepts of national security likely in the near future. Moscow gives no indication of moving to terminate the Cold War, but changes in Soviet policy may develop as a result of involuntary pressures not now readily apparent. In this respect, Alex Inkeles, an eminent sociologist and specialist on Soviet affairs, pointed out in testimony before the Senate Foreign Relations Committee "three main sources from whence a fundamental change in the pattern of Soviet development may spring, especially as it affects the Soviet impact on the rest of the world" (reading 84). These speculations afford some measure of comfort. The future must be faced with courage and patience and with particular care to nurturing Western strength and unity.

Beyond that, we must accept the fact that we live in a time of troubles from which there is no promise of a respite. In this we are not unique. Each generation has tended to regard its own challenges and dangers as particularly difficult and has wistfully envied previous generations their comparative security and tranquility. The dilemmas of yesterday invariably seem uncomplicated and manageable when viewed from the perspective of today. Time passes and the seemingly insurmountable ills of man somehow find solutions which, in turn, give rise to new problems and new challenges. We may draw hope from this recurring pattern and reassure ourselves that it will continue in the future.

To recall the opening lines of Charles Dickens' immortal *A Tale of Two Cities:*

> It was the best of times, it was the worst of times, it was the age of wisdom, it was the age of foolishness, it was the epoch of belief, it was the epoch of incredulity, it was the season of Light, it was the season of Darkness, it was the spring of hope, it was the winter of despair, we had everything before us, we had nothing before us, we were all going direct to Heaven, we were all going direct the other way—in short, the period was so far like the present period, that some of its noisiest authorities insisted on its being received, for good or for evil, in the superlative degrees of comparison only.

NOTES

1. Robert Strausz-Hupé, "Protracted Conflict: A New Look at Communist Strategy," *Orbis,* Vol. ii, (Spring 1958), p. 25.
2. Bernard S. Morris, "Ideology and American Policy," *The Virginia Quarterly Review,* Vol. xl, No. 4 (Autumn 1964), p. 539.

Negotiating with the Soviet Union: Considerations and Limitations

81. PREDICTING SOVIET BEHAVIOR*

JOHN S. RESHETAR, JR.

One problem encountered in citing every consistent factor which may have influenced or determined a particular decision is that we sometimes tend to endow the Soviet leadership with a degree of sophistication, omniscience, and foresight which it does not actually possess. The Soviet rulers almost always interpret the actions of others as deliberate, purposeful, and calculated, and refuse to recognize that chance or accident can play a role in determining such actions. Yet it would probably be incorrect to assume that the Soviet leaders, since they attribute such cold

* John S. Reshetar, Jr., *Problems of Analyzing and Predicting Soviet Behavior* (New York: Random House, 1955), pp. 42–45, *excerpts.* Reprinted with permission of the publisher.

calculation and inner logic to the acts of others, always act in this way themselves and apply in practice their belief that nothing is accidental. Thus when one observes a certain degree of vacillation in Soviet policy, as in Sino-Soviet relations in 1945, it is cause to question whether the Kremlin operates with a fully elaborated master plan. . . .

Soviet policy must be regarded as having certain basic strategic goals which are probably not tied to any timetable. The tactical goals and weapons of Soviet policy also possess a certain fluidity with respect to both technique and timing. This invariably involves selection, and once this is admitted it is necessary to recognize a degree of flexibility in Soviet policy which may invalidate rigid monistic interpretations of Soviet behavior. While we know the general framework within which the Soviet leaders operate as well as their general attitudes and values, we cannot predict with very much accuracy what they may do in a given situation except to say that they will attempt to maximize their gains with a minimum of risk. We can say that they usually calculate the balance of power or "relation of forces" and decide on the basis of this analysis whether they can advance or can only hold their position or must retreat, and whether "capitalism" is approaching a "crisis" which might lead to war or has stabilized itself, and if so, for how long. However, the difficulty is that they can miscalculate the balance of forces or the intentions of other states at almost any time within a particular area or in the total international scene. . . .

The ultimate question is not so much what the [Soviet] regime is capable of doing as what it can be expected to do and how it will arrive at the decision. It is here that key assumptions determine the results of any attempt to predict Soviet behavior. If, for example, it is assumed that fear plays a determining role in Soviet policy, then the possibility of actions committed out of desperation is correspondingly increased and looms larger in any estimate of what the Kremlin might do in a given situation. If it is assumed that the Soviet leadership always means what it says in its policy pronouncements and does not bluff, then such statements must be taken at face value. If it is assumed that what is said is not always meant to be taken literally—as, for example, the Soviet diplomatic note of October 19, 1950, in which the Kremlin stated that it "will not tolerate" West German rearmament—then it is necessary to distinguish between what might be an actual ultimatum and what might be a calculated attempt to dissuade without entailing sanctions. If it is assumed that the principal Soviet technique is military rather than economic or propaganda-oriented, then the tendency will be to overlook the degree of flexibility which the Soviet leadership can be said to permit itself, even though it is limited and possibly only tactical in nature. Thus the problem may be less one of anticipating an armed Soviet or satellite attack against a particular country than one of forestalling Soviet anti-colonial propaganda campaigns and appeals to neutralist elements or attempts to break up coalitions designed to "contain" Soviet power.

82. PROBLEMS OF NEGOTIATING WITH THE SOVIETS[*]

PHILIP E. MOSELY

The Soviet negotiator is tight as a spring, deeply suspicious, always trying to exert the Soviet will power outward and to avoid reflecting non-Soviet facts and aspirations inward, a rigid agent knowing only the segment of policy which he must carry out with mechanical precision. Does this mean that "negotiation" in any real sense of the term is impossible? Admitting that negotiation under these conditions is a very limited affair and very difficult and unrewarding, it may still be both possible and essential. But it requires a special approach. Naturally, a knowledge of Russian in its Soviet nuances is important. It is equally important to understand the role of the Soviet negotiator in relation to his own government and to its ideology. . . .

In the absence of informal channels of communication with Soviet representatives it is important for an American delegation to be able to determine whether the Soviet negotiators have no instructions, have definite instructions, or merely have instructions to build up a propaganda position. A well equipped negotiator can go much more thoroughly into the range of Soviet intentions if he follows the discussion in the original, without being handicapped by the opaque veil of translation. In addition he should review each document exchanged or each statement made in the light of its clear rendering into Russian. It is unfortunate, for example, that many American public figures con-

[*] From "Some Soviet Techniques of Negotiation" by Philip E. Mosely, one of several essays edited by Raymond Dennett and Joseph E. Johnson, *Negotiating with the Russians* (Boston: World Peace Foundation, 1951), pp. 297–303, *excerpts.* Reprinted with permission.

tinually speak of the need for an "aggressive policy" to counteract Soviet pressures, when they mean an "energetic" or "vigorous" policy. In Russian "aggressive" means only "intending to commit or engaged in committing aggression," and the colloquial American use of "aggressive" inevitably receives a sinister meaning in Russian translation, which is the form in which documents must be utilized by all but a handful of Soviet negotiators and policymakers.

In conducting negotiations with Soviet representatives it is important to adopt in the beginning a single clear position, one which can be upheld logically and politically during long discussions. The Soviet delegation will not report this position as the final and strongly held one until they have had a chance to attack it from all sides. Indefinite repetition of arguments must be accepted as an inevitable preparation to negotiate. The American negotiator is inclined to make a single presentation and then to become impatient when the Soviet response makes it plain that the Soviet representative either has not understood it or does not believe it. The Soviet negotiator, of course, does not believe what he hears, but he listens for undertones of firmness or uncertainty which tell him whether or not he is shaking the determination of his adversary. Strong but controlled feeling, rather than impatience or anger, is an effective way of giving him his answer to this question. When a position is firmly established, it is often advantageous to prepare a special memorandum, accompanied by a clear and idiomatic translation into Russian, in order to be sure that one's own position is adequately reported to Moscow, the only spot at which new instructions are likely to be initiated. . . .

Once a position has been worked out, the non-Soviet negotiator must be prepared to uphold it in detail, and for a long time. The technique of constantly trying out variant versions, which works well in the western style of negotiation, only confuses the Soviet representative, who suspects some new trick in each new variant and must subject each in turn to exhaustive interpretation. Constantly modifying one's position or the way in which it is expressed means also that the Soviet negotiator is at a loss to know what version is based on bedrock and should therefore be reported to Moscow. Even slight shifts in position or wording increase his belief that the adversary's position is a shaky one and thus encourage him to hold out that much longer for the full Soviet position. Western negotiators are usually in a position to accept slight adaptations, but even the slightest variation must be reported back to Moscow for decision there. . . .

Even the "program statements" of Soviet negotiators must be

reviewed or written in Moscow before they can be delivered, and therefore Soviet statements at conferences often seem to have little relation to the immediately preceding statements of other delegations.

When a negotiation is actually under way, it is useful to avoid pressing the Soviet delegation to commit itself on a new proposal or draft. . . .

When stating a position, it is well to be sparing in the use of general or broadly stated principles, and when such principles are an essential part of the position, it is necessary to remember that they are not shared by the Soviet negotiator. Broad statements of principle can, however, be effectively anchored in the historic experience of one's own people and, explained in that setting, they can have a certain impact on Soviet thinking. Soviet policymakers may then accept them as a fact which must be taken into account, even though they do not believe in them or share them.

Wherever possible it is more useful to state one's position in terms of a definite material interest . . . Soviet trained negotiators pride themselves on identifying material interests and can therefore more readily visualize them as facts to which a certain adjustment can be made. . . .

Is it worthwhile to dwell on these experiences or to talk about negotiating at all? Even during the wartime alliance against the common menaces of Germany and Japan negotiations with the Soviet Government were extremely difficult and frustrating, and, aside from the advantage of having established the United Nations, even before the end of the war, as a "forum for the opinions of mankind," none of the wartime agreements on postwar cooperation has worked out as was hoped, even against hope. Since the war the Soviet Government has striven by all the means in its extensive arsenal to gain and retain every advantage for its side, regardless of the fact that thereby it quickly dissipated a very large reservoir of good will and aroused the deep alarm of all nations which lay beyond its direct control. In a period of Soviet expansion and of hope for further expansion, negotiation could have only the purpose of confusing and dividing the nations which opposed its pressure, and since the war the Soviet purpose in negotiating has not been to reach agreements with strong opponents but to intimidate weaker and adjacent countries and to undermine the stamina of its principal potential adversaries.

Protected by two oceans and remote from the direct origins of previous world wars, Americans have been accustomed to ignore the rising storm and then, once it had burst upon them, to work solely for victory over the immediate menace. Thus, they tend to feel a sharp dichotomy between "war" and "peace." When at peace they are reluctant to think of the possibility of war. When at war they concentrate solely on winning the war, as if it were a grim football match, and refuse to worry about the peace which is the goal of war. Through Lenin and Stalin Soviet thinking has fully absorbed the Clausewitz maxims that national strength and strong alliances determine the effectiveness of national policy in peace, and that in war one must never lose sight of the aims of policy for which it is waged. To the Soviet way of thinking, conflict is inherent in the development of "capitalist" society, and cannot be wished out of existence by "subjective good will."

Within this ongoing history of conflict, however, Soviet tactics and techniques are not inflexible. . . .

For the time being negotiation of those issues which are negotiable between the Soviet Union and the West is, generally speaking, in abeyance. But the art of policy will be to recognize, from a position of strength, future potentialities of negotiation, not with an expectation of bringing about a lasting or world-wide relaxation of Soviet ambitions, but as a means of alleviating individual sources of tension and thus of strengthening the free world. And if negotiation must go in harness with consistent and purposeful building of strength, the art and technique of international dealings must also be broadened to take full account of the peculiar character of the Soviet approach to negotiation.

Continuity and Change in Soviet Policy

83. THE PRESSURES BEHIND SOVIET EXPANSIONISM*

BARRINGTON MOORE, JR.

. . . Has Soviet expansion during the past decade been primarily defensive, and would it come to rest if external threats were removed? Or is the world now witnessing a special variety of

* Barrington Moore, Jr., *Soviet Politics—The Dilemma of Power* (Cambridge, Mass.: Harvard University Press, 1950), pp. 394–401, *excerpts*. Reprinted with permission of the author and publisher.

expansionism: Communist imperialism? The same general questions would have to be answered about the United States, but the analysis in this study must necessarily be confined to the Russian side of the equation.

Four considerations enter into the conclusion advanced by many that the Soviet system contains a number of internal expansionist forces impelling it to seek one conquest after another. It is often said that, because the USSR is an authoritarian state, its rulers need a continuous series of triumphs in order to maintain their power. The rulers of a dictatorship, it is claimed, cannot afford to rest on their laurels. Occasionally this type of argument is supported by a neo-Freudian chain of reasoning. It is asserted that the frustrations imposed upon the individual in modern society, especially under a dictatorship, tend to produce socially destructive impulses that have to be channeled outward against an external enemy if the society is not to destroy itself. The second line of argument, at a different level of analysis, emphasizes the indications of a strong power drive in Stalin's personality. Parallels can be drawn on this basis between his urge for new worlds to conquer and the political aspirations of Napoleon, Hitler, and others. A third line of reasoning points to various indications in Soviet statements and actions of an old-fashioned interest in territorial expansion that shows strong resemblances to traditional Tsarist policy. The latter argument draws its reasoning from the facts of geography and history, emphasizing traditional Russian interest in warm water ports, the long drive to the South and East, and similar matters. Under the fourth type of argument, Marxist-Leninist ideology is selected as a separate expansionist force. Persons who hold this view point out the Messianic qualities of Marxist doctrine and the continuous need for struggle and victory that it generates.

Each of these arguments and hypotheses represents some portion of the truth. . . .

Concerning the first point, that authoritarian states tend to be expansionist ones, it is necessary to express reservations and doubts on both general and specific grounds. The connection between the internal organization of a society and its foreign policy is a complex question that cannot yet be answered on the basis of simple formulas. Athens engaged in foreign conquest perhaps more than did warlike Sparta, and the Japanese, despite the militaristic emphasis of their society, lived in isolation for centuries until the time of their forced contacts with the West. To show that the authoritarian structure of any state is a source of expansionist tendencies, one would have to show the way in which these pressures make themselves felt upon those responsible for foreign policy. At this point the argument often breaks down, though there are cases where it can be shown that the rulers have embarked on an adventurous policy to allay internal discontent. But those at the apex of the political pyramid in an authoritarian regime are frequently freer from the pressures of mass discontent than are the responsible policymakers of a Western democracy. They can therefore afford to neglect much longer the dangers of internal hostilities. Furthermore, modern events reveal the weakness of the argument that a warlike policy is the result of hostilities toward outsiders among the individuals who make up the society. In the days of total war it is necessary to use all sorts of force and persuasion, from propaganda to conscription, to make men and women fight. To regard war as primarily the expression of the hostilities of rank-and-file citizens of various states toward one another is to fly in the face of these facts.

In the case of the Soviet Union, the Nazi-Soviet Pact of 1939 shows that the rulers of modern Russia had no difficulty in disregarding the hostilities to Nazism that had been built up during preceding years, and that in this respect they enjoyed greater freedom for prompt adjustment of disputes than did other countries. Both totalitarian partners were able to keep mass hostility under control as long as it suited purposes and plans based on the configuration of international power relationships. . . .

An acceptable modification of the argument that the authoritarian nature of the present Soviet regime is a source of an aggressive and expansionist foreign policy may be found along the following lines. It is probable that a certain amount of hostility toward the outside world is an essential ingredient in the power of the present rulers of Russia. Without the real or imagined threat of potential attack, it would be much more difficult to drive the Russian masses through one set of Five Year Plans after another. Yet it does not seem likely that this hostility is in turn a force that reacts back on the makers of Russian foreign policy. Their power can be more easily maximized by the threat of war than by war itself—a precarious enough situation. Nor is there evidence that mass hostility is in any way cumulative or sufficient to force the Soviet leaders into an aggressive policy. There are a number of devices for draining off internally generated hostility into channels other than those of external expansion. Military and combative sentiments, aroused for specific purposes, can be and have been directed into the socially productive channels of promoting a conquest of the physical environment.

There are good grounds for concurring in the conclusion that a drive for power in Stalin's personal make-up has been and will remain a very significant element in Soviet policy as long as his leadership is maintained. [*Note:* Professor Moore wrote this in 1950.] Although biographical data on Stalin are scanty, it is probable that conclusions concerning this trait will stand the test of further impartial investigation. The way, however, in which this trait displays itself has important implications. It is difficult to accuse Stalin of being rash or foolhardy. One has but to contrast the bombastic speeches and writings of Hitler with the cold pedantic logic of Stalin, illuminated by rare flashes of heavy sarcasm, to get important clues to the differences in their personalities. Stalin has nearly always managed to keep his aggressive impulses and his drive for power under rigid control, for which he has been well rewarded in the defeat of his domestic and foreign enemies. He has arrived at his most important decisions cautiously and empirically, testing the political ground at each step of the way. The major decisions of collectivization and industrialization were reached only after numerous tentative trials. Once decisions have been reached by Stalin, he has not failed to display sufficient energy to carry them through. And like Lenin, though in a lesser degree, he has shown the ability to back out of an impossible situation without serious damage to his forces. Thus it is unlikely that Stalin would plunge the Soviet Union into war when the chances of victory were highly problematical.

Those who emphasize the continuity of the Russian historical tradition and the importance of Russia's geographical position in the determination of Soviet foreign policy are correct insofar as Russia's place on the globe and her past relations with her neighbors set certain limitations and provide certain readily definable opportunities for Russian foreign policy. In other words, an expansionist Soviet foreign policy can follow only certain well-defined lines of attack. It may have Persia, China, or Germany as its major object of infiltration, but Latin America and the Antarctic are much more remote objectives.

The reappearance of old-fashioned Russian territorial interests in various parts of the globe has been associated with the revival of Russian strength from the low ebb of revolution, intervention, and civil war. It may be suspected that the early idealist statements of the Bolshevik leaders about the abandonment of Tsarist imperialism were inspired not only by Marxist doctrine but were also made on the grounds that they were the only possible tactics to follow in Russia's weak condition. Now that the proletarian revolution has a territorial base, it is understandable that attempts should be made to combine the interests of the two, and that some of the results should show marked similarities to Tsarist policy. Furthermore, the possibility may readily be granted that the present rulers of Russia are somewhat influenced by the model of Tsarist diplomacy. But the driving forces behind any contemporary Soviet expansionism must be found in a contemporary social situation. Historical and geographical factors may limit the expression of an expansionist drive. They cannot be expansionist forces in their own right.

Turning to the ideological factor, it has already been noted that the Messianic energies of Communism can be, and at times in the past have been, very largely directed toward tasks of internal construction. The "creative myth of Leninism," to use Sorel's suggestive term, involves the building of factories in desert wastes and the creation of a more abundant life for the inhabitants of the Soviet Union. One must agree, however, that a creative myth, if it is effective, is usually an article for export as well as for domestic consumption. Those who really believe in socialism usually believe it is necessary for the world as a whole, just as do the more emotional believers in the virtues of democracy and the four freedoms. There remains, however, another important aspect of Soviet doctrine, which sets at least temporary limits to its expansionist qualities. It is a cardinal point in the Leninist-Stalinist doctrine that a retreat made in good order is not a disgrace. The Soviet myth does not have a "victory or death" quality—there is no urge to seek a final dramatic showdown and a *Götterdämmerung* finale. When faced with superior strength, the Soviets have on numerous occasions shown the ability to withdraw with their forces intact. Although the withdrawal may be followed by a renewal of pressures elsewhere, it may be repeated once more if superior forces are again brought to bear.

The foregoing considerations are enough to suggest the complexity of the problem of interpreting the expansionist forces contained in the Soviet system. They should make us wary of dramatically pessimistic conclusions to the effect that the Soviet leaders, propelled by forces beyond their control, are marching to a world holocaust. But they give many more grounds for pessimism than for optimism concerning the probability of preventing a further increase in tension in the power relationships of Moscow and Washington. Even though Soviet expansionism of the past decade may be explained as primarily an adaptation to the changing balance of power, such an explanation by no means precludes the possibility, perhaps even the probability, that the series of adaptations and "defensive" measures taken by the United States and the USSR may culminate in war.

The situation in which the two major powers stand at uneasy guard, carefully watching each other's activities and countering one another's strengthenings in all portions of the globe, contains internal forces of its own that could lead to a violent explosion. That it has not done so already is an indication that both sides are still making their political calculations largely in defensive terms, inasmuch as neither antagonist is committed by its own system of values to war for war's sake. . . .

If the prospects of fundamental improvement in American-Russian relations are dim indeed, they are not necessarily hopeless. One of the few warrants for hope is the Communist tradition that retreat from a situation that threatens the power of the leaders is no defeat. If, as seems most likely, neither side is yet actively seeking war, there is still room for the reduction of tension through the familiar devices of highly skilled diplomacy. To succeed, this diplomacy would have to part company with the parochial moralism that has characterized much American negotiation and free itself from the miasma of dogmatic suspicion likely to become chronic on the Russian side. Whether modern diplomats can escape from the pressures engendered by their own societies remains to be seen.

84. SOURCES OF POSSIBLE CHANGE IN THE PATTERN OF SOVIET DEVELOPMENT*

ALEX INKELES

There are three main sources from whence a fundamental change in the pattern of Soviet development may spring, especially as it affects the Soviet impact on the rest of the world. One possibility is that the problem of the succession crisis will never be solved, eventually one of the struggles for power at the top will break out in the open, and in the process of resultant conflict the old order will be destroyed. Although I regard such an event as being of a rather low order of probability, it certainly cannot be discounted. But I believe it an error to assume that the inevitable outcome of such a struggle would necessarily be a demo-

---

* From a prepared statement by Professor Alex Inkeles, Russian Research Center, Harvard University, before the Senate Foreign Relations Committee (February 19, 1958), excerpts.

cratic Russia. On the contrary, I believe it highly likely that whoever was the victor in such a struggle would in his turn impose
the standard pattern of totalitarian rule, and probably with renewed vigor.

A second possibility is that a future breakup of the Soviet
satellite empire will come about, as exemplified by the revolt in
Hungary, and the relative defection of Poland and this might have
sufficiently serious repercussions within the Soviet Union to
change materially the path of Soviet development. Although there
are major sources of instability in the Soviet empire, or coalition,
I do not believe that it is markedly unstable. But even if there
were serious defections from Soviet control, there is no absolute
reason to assume the response within the Soviet Union would be
in the direction of democracy. On the contrary, there is greater
likelihood that, under the circumstances, there would be increased
totalitarianism in an effort to recapture lost or ebbing control
over the satellites. I think what is happening in Hungary today
points in that direction, although what is happening in Poland
perhaps points in another direction.

A third prospect is that the industrial maturation of Soviet
Russia, the mellowing of its social structure will "erode" the dictatorship and set in motion important processes of social change
which will lead to a democratization of Soviet society, and perhaps
also a transformation of its foreign policy. While such a transformation is to be hoped for it seems hardly to be counted on.
The Soviet system has changed. But in my opinion the formidable
challenge which faces the world rises not from the unchanging
character of the Soviet Union, but precisely from the fact that
its present leaders have been able to make adjustments in the
structure which have adapted it to take account of the earlier
development of the society. The crucial point is that they have
done so without sacrificing the basic features of the system—
the monopoly power in the elite of the one-party system, the absolute dominance of the state in the control and direction of
economic life, the limitation of freedom of opinion and expression
to those few cases and to that degree which the regime regards
as politically harmless, and the use of force or extra-legal measures, however selective, to impose the will of the leaders in such
a way as to make an ultimate mockery of the law and constitution. It is no less autocratic and certainly not more democratic,
in the sense of the supremacy of law and individual rights. But
such a society—that is, the new and transformed Soviet leadership and what it has developed—is more, not less, a challenge
to the free world.

The leadership may have lost some of its freedom of maneuver, in the sense that it can no longer so readily commit the whole nation to an assault on objectives the people do not support, which I think was characteristic of it earlier. But the regime is far compensated by the vastly increased popular support for the objectives to which it has committed the nation. And it presents an immeasurably improved facade to the world.

In the balance hangs the decision as to what the dominant cultural and political forms of human endeavor will be for the remainder of this century and perhaps beyond. It is, perhaps, only a little thing that separates the Soviet world from the West —freedom. Inside the Soviet Union there are some who ultimately are on our side. But there they are a minority, perhaps a small one. Their ranks were first decimated by Stalin and later thinned by the refugee exodus. We had, therefore, in my opinion, better turn our face elsewhere, rest our hopes on other foundations than on the hope that the Soviet system will mellow and abandon its long-range goals of world domination. We must look for our defense to the capacity of our own social order to yield fuller, richer, more dignified life under freedom not only for ourselves, but for the uncommitted, the half committed, the neutralists, and even those who have already cast their lot with the Soviet Union. If we are not equal to the task, we will leave it to the Soviet Union to set the pattern of human existence for the next half century.

FOR FURTHER STUDY

Barnet, Richard J. and Marcus G. Raskin, *After 20 Years: Alternatives to the Cold War in Europe.* New York: Random House, 1965.

Brzezinski, Zbigniew K., *Alternative to Partition.* New York: McGraw-Hill Book Company, 1965.

Goodman, Elliot R., *The Soviet Design for a World State.* New York: Columbia University Press, 1960.

Harriman, Averell, *Peace with Russia?* New York: Simon and Schuster, 1959.

Kennan, George F., *On Dealing with the Communist World.* New York: Harper & Row, Publishers, 1964.

Lindsay, Michael, *Is Peaceful Coexistence Possible?* East Lansing: Michigan State University Press, 1960.

Lippmann, Walter, *The Communist World and Ours.* Boston: Beacon Press, 1959.

Rock, Vincent P., *A Strategy of Interdependence: A Program for Control of Conflict Between the U. S. and the Soviet Union.* New York: Charles Scribner's Sons, 1964.

Shulman, Marshall D., *Beyond the Cold War.* New Haven, Conn.: Yale University Press, 1966.

Chronology
of Key Events for
Soviet Foreign Policy

1917   *November 7.* Bolsheviks come to power. (1917–1921: Period of War Communism.)

        December 15. Preliminary armistice negotiated on the Eastern front.

1918   *March 15.* Bolsheviks sign the Treaty of Brest-Litovsk with Germany.

        November 11. Germany surrenders. World War I is over.

        November 13. Bolsheviks abrogate Brest treaty.

1919   *March 2–6.* Communist International established. Allied intervention and civil war continue through the year.

1920   *April 25–October 12.* War with Poland.

        July 19–August 7. Second Congress of the Comintern.

1921   *March 16.* Trade agreement signed with Great Britain.

        March 18. Treaty of Riga ends war with Poland.

1922   *April 16.* Russia and Germany sign the Treaty of Rapallo.

1923   *January 26.* Sun Yat-sen and A. A. Joffe issue a joint manifesto in Shanghai on Sino-Soviet relations.

1924   *January 21.* Death of Lenin.

1925   *March 12.* Death of Sun Yat-sen in Peking.

1926   *April 26.* Treaty of Friendship and Neutrality signed with Germany.

1927   *November.* Mao Tse-tung establishes a Soviet regime in Hunan.

        December. Soviet relations with Kuomintang severed.

1929   *February 9.* East Pact concluded with nations of Eastern Europe.

        November 17. Stalin emerges from intra-Party struggle as undisputed ruler.

1931   *September 19.* Mukden incident. Japan occupies Manchuria.

        November 7. Chinese Soviet Republic set up, with Mao Tse-tung as Chairman.

1932   *July 25.* Nonaggression pacts concluded with Poland, Estonia, Latvia, and Finland.

        November 29. Treaties of Nonaggression and Conciliation negotiated with France.

1933 *May 27.* Japan withdraws from the League.
      October 14. Germany withdraws from the League.
      November 17. Diplomatic recognition extended by the United
      States.
1934 *September 18.* USSR joins the League of Nations.
1935 *March 23.* Soviets sell their interest in Chinese Eastern Rail-
      way to Japan. Border incidents continue, however.
      May 2. Franco-Soviet Treaty of Mutual Assistance signed in
      Paris.
      May 16. Treaty of Mutual Assistance signed with Czecho-
      slovakia.
      July–August. Seventh Comintern Congress announces shift to
      "Popular Front" policy of cooperation with West against
      fascism.
      October 3. Italy invades Ethiopia.
1936 *March 7.* Germany reoccupies the Rhineland.
      July 18. Civil war in Spain begins.
      November 25. Japan and Germany sign the Anti-Comintern
      Pact in Berlin.
1937 *July 7.* Sino-Japanese war begins.
      August 21. Sino-Soviet Nonaggression Pact signed.
1938 *March 12.* Germany annexes Austria.
      July 11–August 10. Soviet-Japanese clashes along Siberian-
      Manchurian border.
      September. Munich crisis.
1939 *March.* Germany occupies all of Czechoslovakia.
      May 3. Litvinov replaced by Molotov as Foreign Minister.
      August 23. Nazi-Soviet Treaty of Nonaggression signed.
      September 1. Germany invades Poland.
      September 3. Britain and France declare war on Germany.
      September 15. Japanese-Soviet armistice ends the fighting along
      the northern Manchurian border.
      September 16. Soviet forces invade eastern Poland in accord-
      ance with the secret protocol added to the Nazi-Soviet Treaty
      of August 23.
      September 28. Poland partitioned.
      November 3. USSR incorporates its Polish acquisitions into the
      Belo-Russian and Ukrainian Soviet Republics.
      November 28. Moscow denounces its nonaggression treaty with
      Finland.
      November 30. Soviet armies invade Finland.
      December 14. Soviet Union withdraws from the League after
      being denounced for its aggression in Finland.
1940 *March 12.* Finland signs Treaty of Peace in Moscow.
      April 9. German forces occupy Denmark and invade Norway.
      May 10. Belgium, Luxemburg, and the Netherlands invaded by
      Germany.
      June 15. Soviet troops enter Lithuania. France falls.
      June 27. Bessarabia and northern Bukovina ceded by Rumania.

August 26. Estonia, Latvia, and Lithuania formally incorporated into the Soviet Union.

1941 *January 10.* Soviet-German trade pact signed in Moscow.

April 13. Five-year neutrality pact signed with Japan.

June 22. Germany invades the USSR.

July 12. Mutual Assistance Agreement signed with Great Britain.

August 25. Soviet and British troops occupy Iran.

November 7. Lend-lease aid extended by the United States.

December 7. Japanese bomb Pearl Harbor.

1942 *January 29.* Great Britain and USSR agree to respect territorial integrity of Iran.

May 26. Treaty of Alliance signed with Great Britain.

November 8. American forces land in French North Africa.

1943 *February 2.* Germans capitulate at Stalingrad. End of German military advance.

April 27. Soviet Government severs relations with Polish Government-in-exile.

May 22. Dissolution of the Communist International announced by Moscow.

September 9. Italy surrenders.

November 28–December 1. Teheran Conference.

1944 *January 26.* Moscow rejects American offer to mediate the Polish issue.

June 6. Second front opens in Europe as Allies land in France.

July 27. Moscow recognizes pro-Communist Polish Committee of National Liberation.

September 19. Soviet-Finnish armistice signed.

1945 *January 11.* Soviet troops enter Warsaw.

February 4–11. Big Three meet at Yalta (Crimea).

April 5. Neutrality pact with Japan denounced.

May 8. Germany surrenders.

August 6. Atomic bomb dropped on Hiroshima.

August 8. USSR declares war on Japan.

August 14. Japan surrenders. Sino-Soviet Treaty of Alliance signed.

September–October; December. Council of Foreign Ministers meets.

1946 *February 9.* Stalin delivers a speech heralding a return to open Soviet hostility toward the West.

March 5. Churchill's speech at Fulton, Missouri, calls attention to the Iron Curtain and cites the need for closer Anglo-American cooperation.

July 24. Soviet delegate rejects Baruch Plan for international control of atomic energy.

1947 *March 12.* Truman Doctrine announced. U. S. agrees to help Turkey and Greece oppose Communist pressure.

June 5. Marshall Plan for European recovery announced at Harvard University.

June 16. Moscow states its opposition to Marshall Plan.

October 5. Moscow announces establishment of a "Communist Information Bureau" (Cominform).

1948 *February 25.* Communist coup overthrows Czechoslovak Government.

June 28. Cominform expels Yugoslavia.

June 29. Berlin blockade started.

1949 *April 4.* North Atlantic Treaty Organization (NATO) established.

May 11. Berlin blockade lifted.

May 12. Establishment of West German Republic.

September 23. President Truman announces Soviet detonation of an atomic bomb.

October 1. Central People's Government of China established, with Mao Tse-tung as Chairman. Soviet Union recognizes People's Republic of China.

1950 *January 10.* Soviet delegate walks out of Security Council over failure of United Nations to seat Communist China.

February 14. Sino-Soviet Treaty of Friendship, Alliance, and Mutual Assistance signed in Moscow.

June 25. North Korean forces cross 38th parallel.

August 1. Soviet Union ends its boycott of Security Council.

1951 *July 10.* Armistice negotiations started in Kaesong (Korea).

September 8. Japanese Peace Treaty signed in San Francisco. The Soviet Union refuses to sign.

1952 *May 25.* West Germany granted its sovereignty.

September 25. Moscow strengthens its ties with Peking and makes concessions over Manchuria and Korea.

1953 *March 5.* Stalin dies.

June 17. East Berlin riots suppressed.

July 27. Korean armistice signed at Panmunjom.

August 20. Pravda announces explosion of a hydrogen bomb.

1954 *January 25–February 18.* Big Four Foreign Ministers meet in Berlin to discuss German and Austrian questions.

April. USSR rejoins International Labor Organization.

1955 *May 11–14.* Warsaw Pact signed. Eastern European armies placed under Soviet general.

May 15. Austrian Peace Treaty signed in Vienna by Big Four Foreign Ministers.

July 18–23. Heads of State meet in Geneva.

September 19. Soviet Union returns Porkkala military base to Finland.

September 20. USSR restores East German sovereignty.

September 27. Arms and munitions sold to Egypt.

October 27–November 16. Big Four Foreign Ministers meet in Geneva.

November 18–December 19. Khrushchev and Bulganin visit India, Burma, and Afghanistan.

1956 *February 14–25.* Twentieth Congress of the CPSU. Stalin denounced for his "crimes."

April 18. Cominform dissolved.

June 20. Inter-Party ties normalized between the USSR and Yugoslavia.

June 28. Riots in Poznan, Poland.

October 20. Gomulka returned to power in Polish Communist Party.

October 20–November 4. Revolution and repression in Hungary. Soviet troops overthrow Nagy Government.

October 29–November 5. Israeli, British, and French forces invade Egypt. Crisis over Suez.

1957 *January.* Chou En-lai visits Moscow, Warsaw, and Budapest.

March 25. Treaty of Rome establishing the Common Market signed.

October 5. Moscow announces launching of Sputnik.

November 22. Moscow declaration calls for intra-Communist bloc unity.

1958 *January 27.* Soviet-American Cultural Pact signed in Moscow. Renewed every two years since.

October 31. Geneva Conference on the cessation of nuclear weapon tests convenes.

November 27. Soviet Government precipitates a new Berlin crisis.

1959 *January 28–February 5.* Twenty-first Congress of the CPSU held in Moscow.

May–July. Foreign Ministers meet in Geneva to discuss Berlin problem.

September 16–27. Khrushchev visits the United States.

September 29–30. Khrushchev visits Peking.

1960 *February.* Khrushchev visits India, Burma, and Indonesia.

March. Khrushchev visits France.

April. Chinese attack Soviet policy of peaceful coexistence.

May 1. U. S. U-2 reconnaissance plane shot down over Soviet territory.

May 17. Summit Conference in Paris breaks up.

June 27. Soviet delegates walk out of disarmament talks in Geneva.

July–August. Congo crisis erupts.

September 19. Khrushchev arrives in New York to address UN General Assembly and demands establishment of troika arrangement in UN Secretariat.

November. Moscow Conference of "81" Communist Parties convenes to resolve Sino-Soviet differences and restore unity to the bloc.

1961 *January 6.* Khrushchev outlines basic strategy for Soviet diplomacy in speech in East Berlin.

August 31. USSR unilaterally ends moratorium on nuclear testing.

October. New Party Program adopted at the Twenty-second Congress of CPSU. Stalin's body removed from the mausoleum in Red Square.

December 9. USSR breaks off diplomatic relations with Albania. Rift between Moscow and Peking widens.

1962 *October 22–29.* Cuban missile crisis results in Soviet-American confrontation in the Caribbean.

October 20–November 20. China attacks India.

November 21. China orders a cease fire.

December 5. USSR and U. S. reach agreement on cooperation in peaceful uses of outer space.

1963 *February 9.* Kassem executed in Iraq. Local Communists repressed.

February 19. Soviet Union agrees to remove all troops from Cuba.

June 20. Agreement on "hot line" between Moscow and Washington signed in Geneva.

August 5. Limited Nuclear Test-ban Treaty signed in Moscow.

November. USSR and U. S. agree in UN not to orbit nuclear weapons.

1964 *May.* Khrushchev visits UAR.

July. Khrushchev proposes to convene meeting of all Communist Parties to discuss intrabloc problems. Peking denounces proposal. Conference scheduled for December 15.

October 14. Khrushchev deposed. Brezhnev becomes First Secretary and Kosygin made Premier.

October–November. December 15 Conference of Communist Parties, originally convened by Khrushchev, postponed until March 1965, as Soviet leaders try to improve relations with Peking.

1965 *February.* Premier Kosygin visits North Vietnam, North Korea, and Communist China.

March. Low-level conference of Communist Parties held in Moscow. Chinese refuse to attend.

August 16. UN financial crisis ended when U. S. agrees not to push for application of Article 19.

Index

Communist revolt in, 380
Soviet relations with,
379–380, 387–390, 402–403, 407–408
Tashkent Declaration (1966), 389
trade agreement with Russia, 389
Indonesia, 380, 386, 387
Initial Moscow Statement on the Proposed Marshall Plan, 231–234
Inkeles, Alex, 425
Sources of Possible Change in the Pattern of Soviet Development, 425, 436–438
Inner Mongolia, 125
Inter-Allied Conference (London, 1941), 169
International Red Cross, 171 fn.
Internationalism, as defined by Lenin, 343 fn.
Iran
British and Soviet occupation of, 168, 183–185, 208
Communist Party in, 208
crisis in, 204, 207, 208
Soviet relations with, 168, 183–185, 209–210, 281, 381
Treaty of Alliance with, 168
Iraq, 412
Israel, 413
Soviet recognition of, 381, 390, 392
Italy
Communist Party in, 216
Greece invaded by, 135
invasion of Ethiopia, 122
peace treaty, 207, 210
Soviet relations with, 95
treaty of friendship with, 95
Iwo Jima, 175
Izvestia, 216, 229

Japan
Allied Control Council for, 207
American occupation of, 207
invasion of Manchuria, 94, 124, 125
invasions of China, 126–127
Pearl Harbor attack, 168
postwar plans for, 207
Secret Agreement Regarding Entry of Soviet Union into War Against, 202–203

Soviet relations with, 115, 124–126, 135, 178
surrender of (1945), 179
World War II and, 168, 178
Joffe, A. A., 88–89
Joint Manifesto, 89, 100–101
Joint Stock Company, 241, 282

Kamenev, Leo, 85
Kashmir, 389, 408, 410
Kassem, Abdel Karim, 391, 392
Katyn Forest controversy, 171–172
Kellogg-Briand Pact, 86, 128
Kemp, P. K., 130 fn.
Kennan, George F., 43, 46, 49, 246
Kennedy, John F., 293, 395
Kenya, 394
Khrushchev, Nikita S., 419, 420
Belgrade visited by, 280
Berlin crisis, 293
Cuban crisis, 395–396
deposed, 291
disarmament, 318–319, 320–321
Disintegration of the Imperialistic Colonial System, The, 404–406
doctrine of "peaceful coexistence," 12–13, 282
foreign policy, 33–38, 283–284
Great Britain visited by, 282
international affairs, statements on, 33–38
Nasser criticized by, 391–392
nuclear testing, 319–321
On the Middle East, 412–413
Peking visited by, 281–282
Some Fundamental Questions of Present-day International Development, 33–38
Stalin denounced by, 283
Stalin's concepts modified by, 14
Stalin's shortcomings revealed by, 166
Summit Conference (Geneva, 1955), 282
tour of Southern Asia, 283
trade policy, 386
underdeveloped areas, 385, 396–397, 404–406
Yugoslavia and, 280